Exclusionary Abuse after the *Post Danmark I* Case

International Competition Law Series

VOLUME 69

Editor

In its series editor, Alastair Sutton, Kluwer is fortunate to engage and benefit from the experience and expertise of one of the world's outstanding authorities on European Union and international economic law.

Introduction

In their efforts to regulate competition in an increasingly complex business environment, competition authorities face a daunting task. The European Commission and Courts, as well as national courts and legislatures, policymakers, and regulators, are constantly proposing, enacting, reviewing, and enforcing new legal measures, often addressing novel situations. Every industry and service is affected.

Contents/Subjects

With many titles currently available and new ones appearing regularly, the series' coverage includes detailed analyses of relevant legislation and case law in major global trading jurisdictions, defences used in cases involving the digital network economy, state aid cases, enforcement methodologies and a great deal more.

Objective & Readership

The purpose of Kluwer's International Competition Law Series is to follow the ever-changing contours of this dynamic area of the law, keeping the practice in sharp focus so that practising lawyers (including in-house counsel) and academics can be assured of the most up-to-date guidance and sources, in the widest possible range of applications.

The titles published in this series are listed at the end of this volume.

Exclusionary Abuse after the
Post Danmark I Case

The Role of the Effects-Based Approach under Article 102 TFEU

Anders Jessen

Published by:
Kluwer Law International B.V.
PO Box 316
2400 AH Alphen aan den Rijn
The Netherlands
Website: www.wolterskluwerlr.com

Sold and distributed in North, Central and South America by:
Wolters Kluwer Legal & Regulatory U.S.
7201 McKinney Circle
Frederick, MD 21704
United States of America
Email: customer.service@wolterskluwer.com

Sold and distributed in all other countries by:
Quadrant
Rockwood House
Haywards Heath
West Sussex
RH16 3DH
United Kingdom
Email: international-customerservice@wolterskluwer.com

Printed on acid-free paper.

ISBN 978-90-411-8996-7

e-Book: ISBN 978-90-411-9016-1
web-PDF: ISBN 978-90-411-9017-8

Printed in the United Kingdom.

FSC

MIX

FSC® C103993

Table of Contents

Table of Contents

Acknowledgements

This book is the outcome of a three-year industrial PhD project, submitted on 31 August 2016 and defended on 17 November 2016. The thesis was written during my time as a research fellow at the Department of Law, Aarhus University, and as a legal and economic consultant at the law firm Bech-Bruun.

Many people should be acknowledged for their contribution to the completion of this book. It is not possible to thank everyone who, in different ways, has contributed. I will only mention a few.

Special thanks go to my supervisors Professor Pernille Wegener Jessen and Partner and Chief Economist Jørgen Dryer Hemmsen for their professional discussions, expert feedback, great interest in the project and overall support during the course of the project. Their guidance, advice and critical observations have been crucial for this project. Thank you very much.

I also want to thank everyone at Aarhus University and Bech-Bruun as well as all of those I have met through the last three years for their immense support; none mentioned, none forgotten.

Special appreciations also go out to BECCLE (Bergen Center for Competition Law and Economics) for allowing me to stay with them for four months providing me with a valuable experience. Without these four months, this project would not have been completed on time. And thanks to Ignacio Herrera Anchustegui for taking the time to discuss our projects.

I am ever grateful to Simon Bellamy and Kluwer Law International for publishing this book.

Last, but not least, I will like to thank my family and friends for their support and accepting my absentmindedness.

The law is stated as of 1 of February 2017. Any errors and omissions are mine alone, and the opinions I express are strictly personal; they do not represent the views of Bech-Bruun, Aarhus University or any other institution, entity, person, etc.

Anders Fløjstrup Jessen
February 2017

CHAPTER 1

Introduction

1 INTRODUCTION TO THE TOPIC

A central objective of the Treaty on the Functioning of the European Union (the "TFEU") is to ensure a system of free competition within the Internal Market.[1] Accordingly, the TFEU features provisions which, among other things, regulate firms' conduct to ensure competition is not distorted; thereby, protecting consumers. One of these provisions is Article 102 of the TFEU ("Article 102 TFEU"). It follows from that provision that a firm holding a dominant position in the relevant market is not allowed to abuse this power through unilateral conduct. It must be stressed that, in both theory and practice, it is well established that merely holding a dominant position does not infringe Article 102 TFEU in itself.[2] A dominant firms' conduct is only contrary to Article 102 TFEU when it constitutes abuse of that dominant position. In other words, unilateral conduct only infringes Article 102 TFEU when it is deemed anti-competitive.[3]

---

1. *See* Protocol No. 27, annexed to the TEU and TFEU. Before the Lisbon Treaty came into force, the objective was found in Article 3(1)(g) EC. However, it was removed with the introduction of the Lisbon Treaty and substituted with Protocol 27. With the objective transferred to a Protocol uncertainty emerged in regards of whether the objective is still applicable. The conclusion is that it is still as important as before the introduction of the Lisbon Treaty. *See also* Chapter 3, section 3.1.
2. *See* Judgment of 9 November 1983 in Case 322/81, *NV Nederlandsche Banden-Industrie Michelin v Commission of the European Communities* ("*Michelin I*"), at 53. Instead, a firm that holds a dominant position has a special responsibility not to allow its conduct to impair genuine undistorted competition on the common market.
3. *See* for that effect Communication of the Commission of 24 February 2009 OJ 2009/C 45/02, *Guidance on the Commission's enforcement priorities in applying Article 82 of the EC Treaty to abusive exclusionary conduct by dominant undertakings* ("the Article 102 Guidance Paper"), at 19–20; Bishop, Simon & Walker, Mike, *The Economics of EC Competition Law: Concepts, Application and Measurement*, 2010.

The aim of Article 102 TFEU is, therefore, to safeguard and maintain effective competition within the Internal Market,[4] thereby kerbing the adverse effects of market power. It is well established in legal and economic literature that a firm[5] possessing a dominant position (i.e., market power) may be able to increase prices and restrict output, with the effect of harming consumer welfare.[6] Competition policy targeted at dominant firms is, therefore, appropriate compared to having only Article 101 of the TFEU ("Article 101 TFEU") which targets collusive behaviour between firms.

One difference between Article 101 TFEU and Article 102 TFEU is worth noticing. In legal literature, Article 102 TFEU is treated as the second of the twin pillars of the competition policy established under the EU Treaty.[7] While Article 102 TFEU primarily aims to control conduct of a single firm, Article 101 TFEU primarily concerns anti-competitive agreements between undertakings, decisions of the associations of undertakings and concerted practices. Therefore, for the types of conduct subject to an assessment under Article 101 TFEU, the market power is created through the establishment of a type of coordination by a number of firms, and through such coordination, anti-competitive effects are achieved. In other words, the "abused" market power exists only due to the type of coordination, and it is, thereby, the product of such coordination. As opposed to this, a [single] firm's conduct is subject to an assessment under Article 102 TFEU when market power already exists due to its dominant position. Accordingly, it is not the product of the specific type of conduct. As a result, the types of exclusionary conduct that may be abusive are relying on existing market power rather than created market power to achieve anti-competitive foreclosure.[8] Accordingly, [unilateral] conduct that relies on existing market power to harm competition is the focus of Article 102 TFEU, whereas united conduct that creates market power to harm competition is the focus of Article 101 TFEU. Anti-competitive foreclosure found under both provisions may then either strengthen or preserve the (dominant) firm's market power. Both provisions complement thereby each other.

In consequence, Article 102 TFEU is worded as:

> Any abuse by one or more undertakings of a dominant position within the internal market or in a substantial part of it shall be prohibited as incompatible with the internal market in so far as it may affect trade between Member States.
> Such abuse may, in particular, consist in:
> (a) directly or indirectly imposing unfair purchase or selling prices or other unfair trading conditions;
> (b) limiting production, markets or technical development to the prejudice of consumers;

---

4. *See* Judgment of 21 February 1973 in Case 6/72, *Europemballage and Continental Can v Commission of the European Communities* ("*Continental Can*"), at 25. *See also* Chapter 2.
5. Not only are the concern attached to a single firm, but also the event where a group of firms hold a dominant position (i.e., collective dominance).
6. *See* e.g., Carlton, Dennis & Perloff, Jeffrey, *Modern Industrial Organization*, 2004; Tirole, Jean, *The Theory of Industrial Organization*, 1988.
7. *See* Goyder, Joanna & Albors-Llorens, Albertina, *Goyders's EC Competition Law*, 2009.
8. Conduct may also directly exploit consumers by, for example, charging excessive prices. However, due to the topic of this book, such conduct will not be addressed.

(c) applying dissimilar conditions to equivalent transactions with other trading parties, thereby placing them at a competitive disadvantage;

(d) making the conclusion of contracts subject to acceptance by the other parties of supplementary obligations which, by their nature or according to commercial usage, have no connection with the subject of such contracts.

1.1 The Background to the Topic

Concern for abuse of market power is nothing new. The concern is that abuse of a dominant position will lead to increased prices, lower output and/or reduced innovation/quality. This is shown in the classic industrial economic models. They illustrate how a monopoly can exercise its market power by setting prices above the competitive level while simultaneously reducing quantities.[9] In other words, prices are increased through a reduction of output, and vice versa. According to this monopoly theory, the issue relating to exercised market power is excessive pricing or other exploitive conduct.

Nonetheless, only few Article 102 TFEU cases involve exploitive conduct.[10] Instead, cases tend to concern exclusionary abuse. These types of abuse involve the exclusion or marginalisation of actual or potential competitors through, for example, pricing below the competitive level. The conspicuous concern is, therefore, not the excessive pricing [and lower outputs], but the harm to competition. By harming competition, the concern is that the dominant firm's market power will be strengthened or preserved, enabling it to raise its prices [and lower its output]. The concern is still exploitive conduct; however, at a later stage. While such exploitive conduct is seen in the short term with, for instance, excessive pricing, it is seen in the long run when dealing with an exclusionary abuse. In consequence, even if exclusionary conduct may appear as welfare increasing – for example, setting prices below rather than above the competitive level – it may still constitute abuse within the meaning of Article 102 TFEU.

Therefore, the issues relating to exploitive abuse and exclusionary abuse differ significantly. Concerning exploitive abuses, the effect is directly visible, while it is more inconspicuous in regards to exclusionary abuse. As a result, spotting an exploitive abuse may be easier than spotting an exclusionary abuse. That being the case, it is far from clear when dominant firms are abusing their position through exclusionary abuse, and consequently unclear how to assess such within Article 102 TFEU. This aspect is clearly seen in regards to conduct which benefits consumers in the short term, but at the same time may harm them in the long run; for example, pricing below the competitive level.[11] This is, among other things, because the line between legitimate

---

9. *See*, among others, Tirole (1988); Carlton & Perloff (2004).

10. For a general discussion of exploitative and exclusionary abuse *see* e.g., Geradin, Damien, et al., *EC Competition Law and Economics*, 2012, at Chapter 4.

11. The fear is that such conduct will exclude competitors from the market and/or deter their entrance to market with the result of excessive pricing, limiting production/innovation or the like. This is made possible since the dominant firm does not face any (significant) competitive pressure and is, therefore, able to profit optimize to the detrimental of consumers.

conduct and exclusionary conduct has not been fully delimited due to their similarities, and thus, a very fine line exists between infringing and complying with Article 102 TFEU.[12] The motivation for this book lies, among other things, in this uncertainty.

1.2 Developments and Legal Issues

Until recently, academic interest in Article 102 TFEU was limited.[13] Likewise, the Commission of the European Communities (the "Commission") has cared less for cases concerning abuse of dominance compared to, for example, the types of cases concerning coordination between firms (i.e., Article 101 TFEU) or mergers (i.e., the EU Merger Regulation[14]). That being the case, the Commission has only been engaged in a limited number of Article 102 TFEU cases over the years. This has provided the EU Courts[15] little opportunity to deliver rulings on exclusionary abuse, and thereby, to assist in the understanding and development of Article 102 TFEU in the same way as it has done in Article 101 TFEU and the EU Merger Regulation.[16] This causes uncertainties for dominant firms and its competitors.

However, there has been a growing interest from both academics and practitioners in the provision over the last decades, and the provision may even be held as the object of attention in recent years. This has caused the emergence of different controversies that had been hidden due to the previously limited interest.[17] The reasons for this new attention are various and many, but some important ones are worth mentioning. They include, first, the increased development in and involvement of economic theory in relation to competition law, second, an increased collaboration between competition authorities, and finally, the fact that Article 101 TFEU and the EU Merger Controls have been subject to a reform suggesting that Article 102 TFEU was likely to receive a similar treatment.[18]

This "rediscovery" of Article 102 TFEU gave rise to an attempt to modernize the provision.[19] The result was, among other things, that the Commission, in late 2008, published a communication[20] indicating how it intends to assess exclusionary conduct by dominant firms (the *Article 102 Guidance Paper*). In brief, the *Article 102 Guidance Paper* reveals that the Commission will shift its approach to the enforcement of Article 102 TFEU by, to some extent, increasing the application of economic analyses

---

12. *See* e.g., Padilla, Jorge & O'Donoghue, Robert, *Law and Economics of Article 102 TFEU*, 2013, at 217.
13. *See* e.g., Rousseva, Ekaterina, *Rethinking Exclusionary Abuses in EU Competition Law*, 2010, at 1.
14. *See* Council Regulation of 20 January 2004, *on the control of concentrations between undertaking* ("*the EU Merger Regulation*").
15. The European Court of Justice and the General Court.
16. Additionally, it was not before the early 1970s that the ECJ was given the opportunity to deliver its first ruling concerning Article 102 TFEU, see Case 6/72, *Continental Can*.
17. *See* e.g., Rousseva (2010), at 1.
18. *See id.*
19. The first serious consideration of a shift from a more form-based approach to a more economic approach was a rapport by the Economic Advisory Group on Competition Policy, see Gual, Jordi, et al., *An Economic Approach to Article 82*, 2005, EAGCP Report.
20. *See* footnote 3.

and applying the so-called effect-based approach. This communication was broadly welcomed by the literature – although criticism did exist.[21] This included, for example, that the concept of anti-competitive foreclosure effects is too over inclusive,[22] that the rigid and relatively precise language of EU case law was to be abandoned in favour of a more fluid set of principles in the *Article 102 Guidance Paper*,[23] and the practical guidance from the communication is limited.[24]

Similar discussions have also taken place in relation to the approach to Article 101 TFEU[25] and the EU Merger Regulation, in which the form-based approach (to a large extent) has been deserted in favour of a more effect-based analysis that has been implemented.[26] In contrast to these policy rules, it is unclear which role the effect-based (and the form-based) approach has within Article 102 TFEU (see below) as it has yet to be clarified by the EU Courts; thus, making it the last major component of competition law to be reformed.[27] In addition, case law, which will be addressed below, seems only to have contributed to this uncertainty instead of bringing clarity to the issue. For those reasons, uncertainty regarding the assessment of exclusionary abuse by dominant firms has emerged. This includes: (i) the approach that should be applied, and (ii) when exclusionary conduct is anti-competitive.

1.2.1 The Relevance of the Form-Based and Effect-Based Approach

One issue with the proposed reform arose around the uncertainty of whether the EU Courts would share the same vision for Article 102 TFEU; an issue which did not follow from the *Article 102 Guidance Paper*.[28] The *Article 102 Guidance Paper* explicitly stated that it merely sets out the enforcement priorities and "is not intended to constitute a statement of the law and is without prejudice to the interpretation of Article [102 TFEU] by the [EU Courts]."[29] Case law has only further enhanced this uncertainty, as the *Article 102 Guidance Paper* has been rejected as a binding on national competition authorities and courts' assessment of exclusionary conduct,[30] while it has applied both

---

21. For an overview see Padilla & O'Donoghue (2013), at 80.
22. *See* Lang, John Temple, *Article 82 EC – The Problems and the Solution*, 2009, FEEM Working Paper No. 65, available at SSRN: http://ssrn.com/abstract=1467747.
23. *See* Padilla & O'Donoghue (2013), at 80.
24. *See* Blanco, Luis Ortiz & Colomo, Pablo Ibáñez, *Evolving Priorities and Rising Standards: Spanish Law on Abuses of Market Power in the Light of the 2008 Guidance Paper on Article 82 EC*, in European Competition Law: The Impact of the Commission's Guidance on Article 102 (Lorenzo Federico Pace ed., 2011.
25. It worth mentioning that the "by object" test within Article 101 TFEU may still be regarded as a form-based approach since the assessment is based on the characteristics of the agreement. *See* further Chapter 4.
26. *See* Gual, et al. (2005), at 5; Padilla & O'Donoghue (2013).
27. *See* Akman, Pinar, *The Reform of the Application of Article 102 TFEU: Mission Accomplished?*, Forthcoming Antitrust Law Journal (2016), at 1.
28. *See* Monti, Giorgio, *Article 82 EC: What Future for the Effects-Based Approach?*, 1 Journal of European Competition Law & Practice (2010) 2.
29. *See the Article 102 Guidance Paper*, at 3.
30. *See* Judgment of 6 October 2015 in Case C-23/14, *Post Danmark A/S v. Konkurrencerådet* ("*Post Danmark II*"), at 52.

the form-based and the effect-based approach when assessing exclusionary conduct.[31] Therefore, while both academics and practitioners had high expectations for future assessments of exclusionary conduct to follow the effect-based approach, as advocated in the *Article 102 Guidance Paper*, it is unclear whether the EU Courts is prepared to change its approach, and hence, whether such reform should be expected.

Contrary to what happened in other areas of EU competition law,[32] the change of enforcement priorities has not put an end to the controversies surrounding Article 102 TFEU. Debates concerning the approach that ought to be applied to the assessment of exclusionary abuse are still very much alive which will be seen throughout the following chapters. This may be explained, at least in part, by case law prior and subsequent to the *Article 102 Guidance Paper* and the discussions devoted to these judgments.[33]

One of the most noticeable examples has been the [missing] link between *Post Danmark I* (delivered on March 2012) and *Tomra* (delivered on April 2012); two cases that have been, for some part of the academics, difficult to reconcile. The issues raised in *Post Danmark I* strongly suggested that Article 102 TFEU is only concerned with conduct having an actually or likely effect on effective competition while *Tomra*, in turn, reiterated the traditional approach towards exclusive dealing and rebates, which is not informed by such considerations.[34] In other words, *Post Danmark I* indicated approval of implementing the effect-based approach advocated by the Commission while *Tomra* indicated the opposite. As a result, *Tomra* has afterwards been criticized

---

31. *See* Chapter 4.
32. The approach towards Article 101 TFEU and the EU Merger Regulation saw a change in enforcement priorities and thereby the approach taken due to criticism by academics and practitioners. For example, the approach to vertical restraints was subject to criticism during the 1980s and 1990s – *see* e.g., Hawk, Barry, *System Failure: Vertical Restraints and EC Competition Law*, 32 Common Market Law Review (1995) 973; Korah, Valentine, *EEC Competition Policy – Legal Form or Economic Efficiency*, 39 Current Legal Problems (1986) 85 – which led to new vertical guidelines, see Commission Regulation of 22 December 1999, *on the application of Article 81(3) of the Treaty to categories of vertical agreements and concerted practices ("the Former Vertical Guidelines")* – now Commission Regulation of 20 April 2010, *on the application of Article 101(3) of the Treaty on the Functioning of the European Union to categories of vertical agreements and concerted practices ("the Vertical Guidelines")*. The approach seems to gather a wide consensus among commentators and stakeholders, see *Colomo, Pablo Ibáñez, Beyond the "More Economics-Based Approach": A Legal Perspective on Article 102 TFEU Case Law*, 53 Common Market Law Review (2016) 709, at page 2.
33. This includes, in particular, Judgment of 17 February 2011 in Case C-52/09, *Konkurrensverket v. TeliaSonera Sverige AB ("TeliaSonera")*; Judgment of 27 March 2012 in Case C-209/10, *Post Danmark A/S v. Konkurrencerådet ("Post Danmark I")*; Judgment of 19 April 2012 in Case C-549/10 P, *Tomra Systems ASA and others v. Commission of the European Communities ("Tomra")*; Judgment of 10 July 2014 in Case C-295/12 P, *Telefonica SA v. Commission of the European Communities ("Telefónica")*; Judgment of 12 June 2014 in Case T-286/09, *Intel Corp. v. European Commission ("Intel")*; Case C-23/14, *Post Danmark II*.
34. *See* e.g., Allan, Bill, *Rule-Making in the Context of Article 102 TFEU*, 13 Competition Law Journal (2014); Rousseva, Ekaterina & Marquis, Mel, *Hell Freezes Over: A Climate Change for Assessing Exclusionary Conduct under Article 102 TFEU*, 4 Journal of European Competition Law & Practice (2013) 32; Lundqvist, Björn & Ølykke, Grith Skovgaard, *Post Danmark, now Concluded by the Danish Supreme Court: Clarification of the Selective Low Pricing Abuse and Perhaps the Embryo of a New Test under Article 102 TFEU?*, 34 European Competition Law Review (2013) 484.

for contradicting *Post Danmark I*, and the European Court of Justice (ECJ) has been criticized for returning to its old ways by applying a form-based approach.[35]

More striking is *Intel* and the great interest from academics and practitioners.[36] The debate caused by *Intel* concerns, in particular, the fact that the General Court ("GC") explicitly rejected the need to show any actual or likely anti-competitive foreclosure effects to establish abuse.[37] This debate reveals that case law is unclear on the approach to exclusionary conduct. This is seen in, for instance, the fact that the endorsement of mainstream economic principles as a guide for law and policy-making is far from gathering a consensus.[38] This is not only true for the academic world, but it also goes for the Commission.[39]

It is obvious that uncertainty relates to the approach to the assessment of exclusionary conduct. As will be covered later in the book, this may be explained by a misunderstanding of case law. In brief, the thrust of legal and economic literature has been devoted, first, to explain the ways in which case law is allegedly at odds with mainstream economic positions and, second, to propose administrable and sound principles on the basis of that economic position.[40] However, this does not clarify the case law or the principles behind it. In other words, without a clear understanding of which approach, or approaches, to apply to the assessment of exclusionary conduct within the meaning of Article 102 TFEU, one is apt to misunderstand case law and thereby not capture the essence of the provision. As a result, it is of utmost importance that this uncertainty/misunderstanding regarding the assessment of exclusionary conduct is clarified. This includes the principles underpinning the interpretation of Article 102 TFEU by the EU courts, the effects that the provision prohibits, and finally, whether different strands of case law can and should be reconciled.

1.2.2 Anti-competitive Foreclosure Effects under the Effect-Based Approach

Besides the uncertainty embracing the approach to exclusionary conduct, it is unsettled how to demonstrate exclusionary abuse when the effect-based approach is chosen or

---

35. *See* e.g., Allan (2014); Federico, Giulio, *Tomra v. Commission Communities: Reversing Progress for Rebates?*, 32 European Competition Law Review (2011) 139.
36. As a few examples of the vast literature see Whish, Richard, *Intel v. Commission: Keep Calm and Carry on*, 6 Journal of European Competition Law & Practice (2015) 1; Venit, James, *Case T-286/09 Intel v. Commission – The Judgment of the General Court: All Steps Backward and No Steps Forward*, 10 European Competition Journal (2014) 203; Rey, Patrick & Venit, James, *An Effect-Based Approach to Article 102: A Response to Wouter Wils*, 38 World Competition (2015) 3; Wils, Wouter, *The Judgment of the EU General Court in Intel and the So-Called "More Economic Approach" to Abuse of Dominance*, 37 World Competition (2014) 405; Nihoul, Paul, *The Ruling of the General Court in Intel: Towards the End of an Effect-based Approach in European Competition Law?*, 5 (2014) 521; Peeperkorn, Luc, *Conditional Pricing: Why the General Court is Wrong in Intel and What the Court of Justice Can Do to Rebalance the Assessment of Rebates*, 12 Concurrences (2015) 43; Petit, Nicolas, *Intel, Leveraging Rebates and the Goals of Article 102 TFEU*, 11 European Competition Journal (2015) 26.
37. *See* Case T-286/09, *Intel*, at 77, 81, 85, 103, and 203.
38. *See* Colomo (2016), at 3.
39. Wouter Wils and Luc Peeperkorn have different views on *Intel* and the approach to Article 102 TFEU, see Peeperkorn (2015); Wils (2014).
40. *See* Colomo (2016), at 3.

even required (it emerges from the one above). As indicated above, the effect-based approach represents a novelty within Article 102 TFEU meaning that it has not been fully developed. For example, in *Post Danmark I* the ECJ held that demonstrating anti-competitive [foreclosure] effects were needed but did not, at the same time, provide any clear guidance on how to assess such effects. The ECJ only stated that an actual or likely exclusionary effect to the detriment of competition (and thereby consumers) had to be established.[41]

In contrast, the Commission's decisional practice has had a tendency of applying a (more) effect-based approach in recent time,[42] which can provide indications regarding how to assess exclusionary conduct under the effect-based approach. In its *Article 102 Guidance Paper*, the Commission has further provided indications of which elements that are to be included in an assessment. However, in the light of its decision in *Intel*, it is unsure whether the Commission will truly follow its *Article 102 Guidance Paper*.[43] The value of these indications is, therefore, subject to uncertainties. According to the ECJ, the *Article 102 Guidance Paper* is not binding on national competition authorities and courts.[44] In addition, the ECJ has yet to confirm if it agrees with the approach laid out in the *Article 102 Guidance Paper*.

To a certain extent, the same applies in situations where the form-based approach is chosen for the assessment of exclusionary conduct. It does not represent a novelty for Article 102 TFEU in the same sense as the effect-based approach, but the underlying structure of that approach has not been clearly articulated by the EU Courts. While the primary focus of the book is that of the assessment under the effect-based approach, the assessment under the form-based approach will be addressed when addressing the issue of when the effect-based approach is to be applied (see above).

2   RESEARCH QUESTION

Based on these developments and issues within Article 102 TFEU, this book seeks to analyse and discuss exclusionary abuse within the meaning of Article 102 subsequent *Post Danmark I* and other recent case law. The aim of the book is two folded as it seeks to analyse: (i) when the effect-based approach applies to exclusionary conduct, and (ii) how anti-competitive foreclosure effects contrary to Article 102 TFEU can be demonstrated according to the effect-based approach.

The research question consists of two separate and at the same time-related questions; the second is a consequence of the first. The assessment of anti-competitive foreclosure effects under the effect-based approach is likely to be more comprehensive

---

41. *See* Chapter 4, in which the anti-competitive effect is addressed.
42. *See* e.g., Commission Decision of 20 December 2012 in Case AT.39230, *Rio Tinto Alcan*; Commission Decision of 11 October 2007 in Case Case COMP/B-1/37966, *Distrigaz*. The Commission's decision in Intel can to some extent also been seen as applying a more effect-based approach, see Commission Decision of 13 May 2009 in Case COMP/37.990, *Intel*.
43. *See* Case COMP/37.990, *Intel*, at 920-25. The Commission found that Intel had abused its dominant position by relying on the preceding case law and only applied the effect-based approach, which it suggest in the Article 102 Guidance Paper, as supplement to its findings.
44. Case C-23/14, *Post Danmark II*, at 52.

in contrast to a more form-based approach. For that reason, it is necessary first to clarify which approach exclusionary conduct is subject to or, alternatively, which types of exclusionary conduct are subject to which approach.

In the light of this, the answer proposed to the first part contributes to answering the second part. By addressing both questions, it is possible to offer a much-needed clarification of the assessment relating to exclusionary conduct within Article 102 TFEU. Equally important, it is possible to provide suggestions on how to structure the approach. This will create greater legal certainty for dominant firms (and their competitors) which will benefit their competitive behaviour, and hence, the consumer.

Both questions as a whole address the approach taken in connection with the assessment of exclusionary conduct within the meaning of Article 102 TFEU. This area has been the object of attention in the recent decades and does include not only the EU Courts' case law but also both legal and economic literature. This has led to, among other things, uncertainty regarding the assessments of exclusionary conduct within the provision. Therefore, the reached conclusions are not only of practical relevance but also of theoretical relevance. They seek to clarify the uncertainty that dominant firms (and their competitors) are exposed to and will provide a basis for future research.

The aim of the book is to unravel the fundamental aspect of the uncertainty that reigns among both practitioners and academics as regards the assessment of a dominant firm's exclusionary conduct within Article 102 TFEU. This will provide contributions to the development and understanding of that provision. The motivation for this book lies largely in that uncertainty and how it can be clarified. It must be stressed that, according to the research question, the book seeks to contribute to the development and understanding of the assessment of exclusionary conduct within the settings of the current framework of Article 102 TFEU. Therefore, while the aim could have been to provide a fresh start for the assessment of exclusionary conduct, such an aim falls out of the scope of this book. That said, it still "fills in the blanks" meaning that findings on how the assessment of exclusionary conduct ought to be carried out are sometimes required. Accordingly, the aim of this book has both a positive and normative character, i.e., *de sententia ferenda*.[45]

3   METHOD AND THEORY

To reach the aim presented in the research question, the book includes not only one set of theory and method but a multidimensional approach. In consequence, the book will include and combine methods and theories from both the legal and economic framework. Nonetheless, the legal framework will constitute the main methodology, since the aim of the book is to answer the research question in the settings of Article 102 TFEU. In other words, the legal framework will form a foundation for the analyses and discussions throughout the book. This ensures that the provided clarifications and suggestions regarding how to assess exclusionary conduct within the meaning of Article 102 TFEU are in agreement with the legal principles and concepts of that

---

45. *See* below in section 3.1, which addresses the legal method applied in more detail.

provision. If the aim had been an analysis of how economic theory could dictate the assessment of exclusionary abuse [without regard to, for example, case law] then it would have been reasonable to avoid this aspect of setting a legal framework as the foundation.

That being the case, the book will be characterized by a law and economics approach. To a great extent, this will be implemented through analyses and discussions of economic theories in the context of Article 102 TFEU, including how these theories can be applied to the assessment of exclusionary conduct within the legal framework of that provision. These economic theories will be based mainly on industrial organisation theory that has had a great impact on the understanding of competition law.

According to these observations, the book will include, generally speaking, a legal methodology and a law and economics methodology in the pursuit of an answer to the research question. These will be addressed below.

3.1 The Legal Method

Due to the research question, the book includes two different characteristics with regards to the legal method. The primary aim is to deduce how the law is (or likely to be), i.e., *de lege lata*,[46] but at the same time, it does not stop there. It further involves the aim of commenting on how the law ought to be, to some extent, i.e., *de sententia ferenda*.[47]

This is the case when it is needed to "fill in the blanks" to provide an answer to the research question. Take for example the second question (i.e., "how anti-competitive foreclosure effects contrary to Article 102 TFEU can be demonstrated according to the effect-based approach"). It seeks to answer how to assess anti-competitive effects which in some events requires comments on how the assessments ought to be due to a lack of case law. The aim may, therefore, be stated as to provide suggestions on how to apply established legal (and economic) principles and doctrines to the assessment of exclusionary conduct within Article 102 TFEU, i.e., *de sententia ferenda*.[48] This entails that the book will answer how the relevant legislation should be applied and interpreted in specific cases. In essence, the book provides suggestions on which conclusions the EU Courts should arrive at if the author was asked to provide answers.[49]

This is done by first providing clarification on how to understand the EU Courts approach to the assessments of exclusionary abuse. This includes, among other things, the overall goals of Article 102 TFEU which will provide an understanding of what object(s) the provision pursues. Additionally, setting a legal framework for how the EU Courts define anti-competitive foreclosure effects may assist in fitting economic

---

46. *See* Tvarnø, Christina & Nielsen, Ruth, *Retskilder og retsteorier*, 2014, at 31.
47. *See id.*
48. *See id.*
49. *See* Bengoetxea, Joxerramon, *The Legal Reasoning of the European Court of Justice: Towards a European Jurisprudence*, 1993, at 29.

theories onto assessment of exclusionary conduct within the provision. In consequence, the book will involve an analysis made *de lege lata* to support the suggestions made *de sententia ferenda*.

As a result, different sources of law will be analysed and weighted to determine current law (*de lega lata*). Some observations are made below with respect to the sources of law that are relevant to the analyses and discussions in the book (sections 3.1.1 – 3.1.5). The relevant sources of law include the EU Treaty (i.e., primary legislation), case law by the EU Courts (and national courts), the Commission's (and national competition agencies') decisional practice and the *Article 102 Guidance Paper* (i.e., soft law).

3.1.1 Primary Legislation

Without a doubt, the EU Treaty – the TFEU and the Treaty on the European Union (the "TEU") – constitutes the primary legislation. Not only is the Commission bound by it, but the same also goes for national courts and national competition agencies which are bound by the objectives laid out in the EU Treaty.

The EU Treaty presents the objectives of the EU; see e.g., Articles 3–6 of the TEU, Article 119 of the TEUF and Protocol No. 27. More importantly, the regulation of dominant firms' unilateral conduct in the internal market is based on TFEU, namely Article 102 TFEU. Both the general principles and the provision that regulates unilateral conduct are therefore found in the EU Treaty.

3.1.2 The EU Courts' Case Law and the Commission's Decisional Practice

Albeit there is no binding precedent in the EU Treaty, judgments by the EU Courts are considered a source of law. Since Article 102 TFEU merely establishes a general and non-specific legal framework for the assessment of dominant firms' conduct, the EU Courts' case law is of great importance for the book. The case law assists the understanding of Article 102 TFEU in all aspect, which follows from the very first Article 102 TFEU case by the ECJ, namely *Continental Can*[50]. For that reason, the EU Courts' case law will form a primary source of law.

To a large extent, the case law of the EU Courts will, therefore, be applied. This includes judgments of both the ECJ and the GC; however, with the ECJ being the primary source of law in situations where both courts have delivered their verdict in a case. This means that where the ECJ has not provided a verdict (either because it is pending or the case was not appealed), the GC's judgment is subject to a certain degree of uncertainty. For instance, it would have the result that an older judgment by the ECJ will take precedence over a newer case by the GC (if the judgments consider the same topic).[51] It is noteworthy that in some events, the ECJ has not addressed all of the same

---

50. *See* Case 6/72, *Continental Can.*
51. On the relationship between the ECJ and GC see e.g., Arnull, Anthony, *The European Union and its Court of Justice*, 2006, at 633–37.

aspects that the GC have addressed in its judgment or a case may not have been appealed to the ECJ. While the GC's judgment can be applied as current law, caution must be taken with the uncertainty of what the ECJ might have ruled. In some events, it might also be necessary to include the Commission's decisional practice either because the decision was not appealed or if important information was not included in the EU Courts' judgment. In the first event, the decision, or the relevant part of a decision, is to be applied with caution. These decisions feature some uncertainties as to whether the EU Courts would have upheld the decision (i.e., agreeing with the Commission's findings and conclusions).

3.1.3   Case Law/Decisional Practice Apart from the EU Courts/Commission

With a focus on EU Competition law, case law from national courts as well as decisional practice from national competition authorities ("NCAs") is, as a rule, not applied in this book. Neither the EU Courts nor the Commission are bound by such case law or decisional practice, and its relevance is, therefore, limited.[52] The same applies to US case law.

Nonetheless, such case law and decisional practice may provide inspiration to issues which neither the Commission nor the EU Court has addressed. Care has to be taken when especially US case law is applied as inspiration as that case law is built on a different source of law; for instance, the Sherman Antitrust Act (the "Sherman Act")[53].

3.1.4   The Article 102 Guidance Paper (Soft Law)

Besides primary legislation, other types of legislation have relevance. This is especially true for the *Article 102 Guidance Paper*. Since it constitutes soft law and is not intended to constitute a statement of the law,[54] and thereby without prejudice to the interpretations by the EU Courts, it has its primary relevance in areas in which the EU Courts' case law has not addressed.

However, the *Article 102 Guidance Paper* should not be considered to be without any [legal] power. Since the *Article 102 Guidance Paper* sets out enforcement priorities, it is likely to guide the Commission's action in applying Article 102 TFEU to exclusionary conduct by dominant firms.[55] In addition, since the Commission is the primary enforcer of Article 102 TFEU, thereby playing a great role in the shaping of the assessments under the provision, it will provide great guidance on how the assessment is likely to be. In fact, the EU Court will only dismiss the Commission's decision, if there

---

52. National courts and competition agencies are in the same sense not bound by case law or decisional practice in other Member States.
53. The Sherman Antitrust Act (Sherman Act, 26 Stat. 209, 15 U.S.C. §§ 1–7).
54. *See the Article 102 Guidance Paper*, at 3.
55. *See id.* at 2.

has been a manifest error of assessment or a misuse of powers.[56] It is, therefore, not unlikely that the *Article 102 Guidance Paper* will form the basis for future assessments of exclusionary abuses in some aspects. However, it will require that the Commission applies it to its decisions.[57]

3.1.5 The Teleological Interpretation of the EU Court

In respect of the relevant legal sources, it is important to understand the method of legal interpretation of these relevant legal sources that is applied by the EU Courts (when dealing with a subject that has its basis in the EU Courts' interpretation of the law). Accordingly, it is appropriate to address this method in brief.

The method applied by the EU Courts is called "teleological interpretation." This entails that the text of the provision is interpreted according to its purpose as well as the purpose of the EU Treaty.[58] Moreover, it is stressed by Maduro, who has been an Advocate General of the ECJ, that this method is always combined with other legal arguments based on, for example, the wording of the provision (literal interpretation), the legislative history, comparative law and/or the legal context of the provision.[59]

In respect of the literal interpretation,[60] the EU Courts seek to disclose the intentions of the legislator and for this purpose relies on the different language versions of the provisions, since all the languages are official languages.[61] Where the different language versions do shed any light on the interpretation of specific words or provisions, the EU Courts will, when available, resort to other means. This could, for example, be preparatory acts of secondary legislation.[62]

Apart from the role of the provision in its immediate context,[63] the EU Treaty is the context of any legislative act of Community law when dealing with contextual interpretation. Accordingly, a purpose of contextual interpretation is to ensure that the

---

56. *See* e.g., Judgment of 7 September 2007 in Case T-201/04, *Microsoft Corp. v. Commission of the European Communities* ("*Microsoft*"), at 87. The GC stated that "although as a general rule the Community Courts undertake a comprehensive review of the question as to whether or not the conditions for the application of the competition rules are met, their review of complex economic appraisals made by the Commission is necessarily limited to checking whether the relevant rules on procedure and on stating reasons have been complied with, whether the facts have been accurately stated and whether there has been any manifest error of assessment or a misuse of powers."
57. *See* e.g., Case COMP/37.990, *Intel*, at 920-925 (and in particular 920, 921 and 923). The Commission relied primarily on other elements than its *Article 102 Guidance Paper.*
58. *See* Maduro, Miguel Poiares, *Interpreting European Law: Judicial Adjudication in a Context of Constitutional Pluralism*, 1 European Journal of Legal Studies (2007) 137, at 144.
59. *See id.* at 145.
60. For a more in-depth account of literal interpretation see Bengoetxea (1993), at 234–40.
61. *See* Judgment of 6 October 1982 in Case 283/81, *SRL CILFIT and Others v. Ministry of Health* ("*SRL CILFIT*"), at 18.
62. *See* Arnull (2006), at 615–18; Plender, Richard, *The Interpretation of Community Acts by Reference to the Intentions of the Authors*, 2 Yearbook of European Law (1982) 57, at 96.
63. *See* Albors-Llorens, Albertina, *The European Court of Justice, More Than a Teleological Court*, in Cambridge Yearbook of European Legal Studies, Vol 2 (Alan Dashwood & Angela Ward eds.), 1999, at 381.

interpretation of a specific provision does not contradict other provisions of the EU Treaty, Community legislation or the EU Treaty in general.

Teleological interpretation, therefore, is based on the purpose of the provision that is interpretation in the specific case – with Article 102 TFEU being the relevant provision with respect to analyses and discussions in this book. Consequently, when analysing and discussing the EU Courts' case law, this aspect must be taken into account. It may further help to understand the case law and some of the reasons for its different conclusions.

3.2 Law and Economics

Law and economics, also defined as the economic analysis of law,[64] is an important part of the book. This is, among other things, due to the fact that (EU) competition law often combines both legal and economic analyses in assessments of either abuses or illegal coordination; hence, a combination of legal and economic methods/theories is often applied. Therefore, law and economics may be seen as an important and valuable tool for projects that address (European) competition law, be it abuse of dominance or another policy area.

Moreover, one of the main characteristics of this book is the law and economics perspective, especially, in respect of answering the research question. The book will include and combine methods and theories from both the legal and the economic framework, thereby analysing and discussing the law with economic theory. This is illustrated in Figure 1.1. It shows that the legal dogmatic analyses will be used to form the framework for economic analyses with the result of being legal [policy] discussions. In the following, it is provided, in brief, how law and economics is intended to be applied in regards to the research question. Due to the two research questions, law and economics will be applied in two ways.

Figure 1.1. Overview of the Applied Law and Economics-Approach

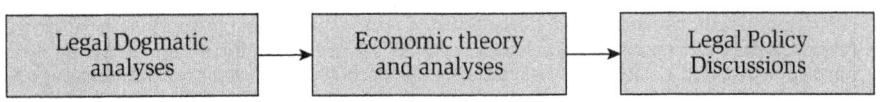

3.2.1 Law and Economics: The First Question

As regards the first part of the research question (*"when to apply the effect-based approach"*), law and economics will be applied to interpret the applicable law and examine when the effect-based approach is to be applied to the assessments of unilateral conduct. This application of law and economics is also called *positive* law

---

64. *See* e.g., Cooter, Robert & Ulen, Thomas, *Law and Economics*, 2011, at 3.

and economics since it by means of analyses and discussions seeks to determine how assessments of unilateral conduct are conducted and not how they ought to be conducted.[65]

Even though this part will involve mainly legal theories and methodologies, economic methodologies and theories will be applied where relevant. Therefore, law and economics is applied with the aim of supporting the arguments and conclusions, and thereby, providing more robust arguments for the reached conclusions. This will further provide a more robust output when the characteristics of (European) competition law are brought to mind.

3.2.2 Law and Economics: The Second Question

While the first part of the research question has its basis in *positive* law and economics, the second part (*"how to assess anti-competitive effects"*) will also apply *normative* law and economics. This entails an approach with the aim of providing suggestions on how anti-competitive effects can be demonstrated. However, it must be noted that the approach will not be strictly normative since the suggestions will still have to be within the legal framework presented in the book.

This part will, to a great extent, involve the application of economic methodologies and theories with the aim of providing suggestions on how anti-competitive effects may be demonstrated in a relevant case. As a result, the legal methodologies and theories will be of less significance in contrast to the first part. Nevertheless, it will be applied within the legal framework for the findings not to contradict the EU Courts' case law.

---

65. *See* e.g., *Id.*; Posner, Richard, *Economic Analysis of Law*, 2007, at 24ff.

PART I The Framework

CHAPTER 2

The Purpose of Article 102 TFEU

1 INTRODUCTION

When firms are making business decisions, it is on the basis that they are the master of their price setting, the level of output which they produce, whether they enter into agreements with another firm, which firms they chose to contract with, the design of their product(s) and so on. Due to competition law,[66] however, firms are under certain conditions *not* free to set prices as they like, choose (freely) who they contract with, freely design the terms of these contracts and so on. Certain types of conduct by firms may have unwanted effects, namely those that have adverse effects on consumers. As a result, these types of conduct are prohibited by competition law. In that respect, Article 101 and 102 TFEU aim at preventing, respectively, firms from preventing, restricting and distorting competition through agreements and prohibiting firms who hold a dominant position in a market from abusing that position. For the latter, which is the provision in focus, such abuse may occur as exclusionary, exploitative and/or discriminatory.[67] Article 102 TFEU's core role is, in other words, the regulation of dominant firms who, by their conduct, restrict competition and produce worse outcomes for that competition, and thereby, consumers. Along with Article 101 TFEU, it is a key provision within EU competition law to ensure that competition in the internal market is not distorted as it is set out in the TEUF.[68] Since Article 102 TFEU then describes the overall restrictions on dominant firms' behaviour, it is of great importance to understand this matter.

It should be remembered that Article 102 TFEU is a legal provision and is based on legal principles. Nevertheless, economic theory and thinking have influenced EU

---

66. Other areas of law also restrict firms conduct; for instance, contract law, environmental law, laws on product safety and consumer protection.
67. Some commentators use four categories, *see*, among others, Padilla & O'Donoghue (2013), at 214.
68. *See* Protocol 27 annexed to the EU Treaty, formerly Article 3 of the TEU.

competition law including Article 102 TFEU. Moreover, competition law assessments have developed over time including the introduction of [new] economic theories and principles. Article 101 TFEU and the EU Merger Regulation are great examples.[69] Both have in recent time seen a reform and are now following a [more] "economic approach."[70] Article 102 TFEU has also received greater economic awareness,[71] but at the same time, it has yet to see a reform in the same extent. However, both the Commission's decisional practice and communications, as well as the EU Courts' case law, includes indications of a greater economic impact regarding the assessment of dominant firms' behaviour.[72]

As a provision within EU competition law, Article 102 TFEU was therefore not able to develop without input from both legal and economic thinking. A consensus in the literature of this matter seems to be that the Freiburg School[73], also known as the Ordoliberal School, provided the [ideological] foundations for Article 102 TFEU while especially the Chicago School[74] provided the [ideological] foundations for section 2 of the Sherman Act in the US. The idea that the Freiburg School has had a profound influence on EU competition law is relatively uncontroversial[75] and is further

---

69. For a background *see*, among others, Jones, Alison, *The Journey toward an Effects-Based Approach under Article 101 TFEU – The Case of Hardcore Restraints*, 55 The Antitrust Bulletin (2010) 783; Wesseling, Rein, *The Modernisation of EC Antitrust Law*, 2000.
70. *See* e.g., Communication of the Commission of 14 January 2011 OJ 2011/C 11/01, *Guidelines on the Applicability of Article 101 of the Treaty on the Functioning of the European Union to Horizontal Co-operation Agreements* ("*the Horizontal Agreements Guidelines*"). Formerly OJ 2001 C 3/2; *the Vertical Guidelines*. Formerly OJ 1999 L 336/21; Communication of the Commission of 19 May 2010 OJ 2010/C 130/01, *Guidelines on Vertical Restraints* ("*the Vertical Restraints Guidelines*"). Formerly OJ 2000 C291/1; Communication of the Commission of 18 October 2008 OJ 2008/C 265/07, *Guidelines on the assessment of non-horizontal mergers under the Council Regulation on the control of concentrations between undertakings* ("*the Non-Horizontal Merger Guidelines*"); Communication of the Commission of 5 February 2004 OJ 2004/C 31/03, *Guidelines on the assessment of horizontal mergers under the Council Regulation on the control of concentrations between undertakings* ("*the Horizontal Mergers Guidelines*").
71. The first serious consideration of a shift from a more form-based approach to an effect-based approach was a rapport by the Economic Advisory Group on Competition Policy, *see* Gual, et al. (2005).
72. Most notably is the Commissions *Article 102 Guidance Paper* on exclusionary conduct published on 24 February 2009. However, the implementation has still to be seen in decisional practice and case law. Take for example Case COMP/37.990, *Intel*. *See* also Case C-549/10 P, *Tomra*; Case T-286/09, *Intel*. In *Intel* an effect-based approach was applied, however, only as a supplement to the traditional legal approach. In spite of this, indications of a greater economic impact can be seen in for example Case T-201/04, *Microsoft*; Case C-52/09, *TeliaSonera*; Case C-209/10, *Post Danmark I*.
73. For a more elaborated reminder of the Freiburg School *see* e.g., Anchustegui, Ignacio Herrera, *Competition Law through an Ordoliberal Lens*, 2 Oslo Law Review (2015) 139; Vanberg, Viktor, *The Freiburg School: Walter Eucken and Ordoliberalism*, 2011, Freiburg Discussion Papers on Constitutional Economics 04/11 available at https://www.econstor.eu/bitstream/10419/4343/1/04_11bw.pdf; Rousseva (2010); Gerber, David, *Law and Competition in Twentieth Century Europe: Protecting Prometheus*, 2001.
74. For a more elaborated reminder of the Chicago School *see* e.g., Fox, Eleanor & Sullivan, Lawrence, *Antitrust – Retrospective and Prospective: Where Are We Coming From? Where Are We Going?*, 62 New York University Law Review (1987) 936; Posner, Richard, *The Chicago School of Antitrust Analysis*, 127 University of Pennsylvania Law Review (1979) 925.
75. *See*, among others, Gerber, David, *Constitutionalizing the Economy: German Neo-Liberalism, Competition Law and the "New" Europe*, 42 The American Journal of Comparative Law (1994)

supported by the structure of the competition provisions of the EC Treaty.[76] It forms, in other words, the basis of EU competition law. Moreover, seminal case law by the EU Courts and decisional practice by the Commission were based on this line of thinking. This is acknowledged by former DG Competition's Director General Philip Lowe:

> The case-law of the European courts and also the decisional practice of the Commission were initially influenced by ordoliberal thought which has its origin in the so-called Freiburg School. Their members advocated a strict legal framework and a strong role for the state in protecting the basic parameters of competition. Competition was understood as a process of economic coordination on the basis of freedom of action. The protection of individual economic freedom – as a value in itself – was regarded as the primary objective of competition policy.[77]

Compared to the Freiburg School, the influence of the three main American schools (i.e., the Harvard School[78], the Chicago School and the Post-Chicago School[79]) on Article 102 TFEU has been less significant. Despite this, some influence can be found. For example, it has been argued that the Harvard School influenced some of the earlier judgments in the EU.[80] This includes, for instance, the *Akzo-test* and the special reasonability which dominant firms are subject to.[81] In regards of the Chicago School, this is limited to a different perspective on competition law and thereby a useful comparison to the one already applied at the time. For instance, the thoughts of the Chicago School can be found in arguments by dominant firms in case law, and they have further been used by academics to criticize the EU Courts' case law.[82] In contrast to the Chicago School, the Post-Chicago School has had a greater impact on Article 102 TFEU. This is for example seen in the Commission's *Article 102 Guidance Paper*. When giving examples of when a low price may constitute anti-competitive conduct, the

---

25, at 73; Hawk, Barry, *Article 82 and Section 2: Abuse and Monopolizing Conduct*, 2008, Fordham Law Legal Studies Research Paper No. 1301690, available at http://papers.ssrn.com/sol3/papers.cfm?abstract_id = 1301690, at 253.

76. Article 101 and 102 TFEU are not a replica of Freiburg School's thought, but their structure bears the imprint of Ordoliberal political philosophy, *see* Miert, Karel Van, *The Future of European Competition Policy*, speech given on 1998 at the Ludwig Erhard Foundation in Bonn; Gerber (2001), at Chapter 9.

77. *See* Lowe, Philip, *Consumer Welfare and Efficiency – New Guiding Principles of Competition Policy?*, speech given on 2007 at 13th International Conference on Competition and 14th European Competition Day, Munich, at 2.

78. For a more elaborated reminder of the Harvard School *see* e.g., Bain, Joe, *Barriers to New Competition: Their Character and Consequences in Manufacturing Industries*, 1956; Stewart, Charles, *Economic Concentration and the Monopoly Problem*, 80 Monthly Labor Review (pre-1986) (1957).

79. For a more elaborated reminder of the Post-Chicago School *see* e.g., Pitofsky, Robert, *How the Chicago School Overshot the Mark: The Effect of Conservative Economic Analysis on U.S. Antitrust*, 2008; Hovenkamp, Herbert, *Post-Chicago Antitrust: A Review and Critique*, 2001 Columbia Business Law Review (2001); Barnett, Randy, *Foreword: Post-Chicago Law and Economics*, *in* Symposium on Post-Chicago Law and Economics (Randy E. Barnett & Jules L. Coleman eds.), 1989.

80. *See* Gormsen, Liza, *The Parallels between the Harvard Structural School and Article 82 EC and the Divergences between the Chicago and Post-Chicago Schools and Article 82 EC*, 4 European Competition Journal (2008) 221.

81. *See id.* at 226

82. *See* e.g., Rousseva (2010), at 41.

Commission states that when the dominant firm is better informed about cost or other market conditions or can distort market signals about profitability, it may engage in predatory conduct to influence the expectations of potential entrants and thereby deter entry.[83] Such theories are the result of the thinking in the Post-Chicago School.[84]

All of this means that while Article 102 TFEU is a legal provision, it is influenced by economic theory and thinking. At the same time, it is not influenced in the same manner as section 2 of the Sherman Act illustrated best by the Chicago Schools [limited] influence on Article 102 TFEU. This has an impact on the protective aim since one must not forget that Article 102 TFEU is a legal provision and that economic theory and thinking ads on top of the legal considerations. As a result, this chapter will analyse first the goals of Article 102 TFEU to create a foundation. After that, the chapter will analyse effective competition as a concept that protects the goals including a discussion of how to understand this concept.

2 THE GOALS OF ARTICLE 102 TFEU

With the aim of answering the research question, it must first be examined which goals Article 102 TFEU, and EU competition law in general, aims at ensuring. Without any thoughts on this matter, it will be difficult to provide any sound answers. As Bork famously stated (in relation to US antitrust law): "Antitrust policy cannot be made rational until we are able to give a firm answer to one question: What is the point of law – what are its goals?"[85] Accordingly, before embarking upon an analysis of the US antitrust rules, he emphasized that knowledge of the goals was required. The same must also apply to EU competition law. If not, any analyses and discussions concerning the assessment of exclusionary conduct being unclear as the end goal of such assessment are uncertain. More importantly, they risk being of no value if they are contrary to what is pursued by the provision.

In consequence, knowing the goals of Article 102 TFEU is essential. The extent of such inquiry can, of course, vary, since a whole book, a PhD thesis or the like can be assigned to such a subject. However, one must as a minimum outline the goal(s). It is therefore not the point of this section to provide an exhaustive analysis of the goal(s),[86] as the aim is to establish guidelines for the analyses and discussions throughout the book. It must also be stressed that this section does not include an analysis or discussion of the theoretical framework of competition law in general.[87] It will not be

83. *See the Article 102 Guidance Paper*, at 68.
84. *See* Bolton, Patrick, et al., *Predatory Pricing: Strategic Theory and Legal Policy*, 88 Georgetown Law Journal (2000) 2239.
85. *See* Bork, Robert, *The Antitrust Paradox: A Policy at War With Itself*, 1978.
86. For a more extensive discussion of the goals of EU competition law, including Article 102 TFEU, *see* e.g., Heide-Jørgensen, Caroline, et al., *Aims and Values in Competition Law*, 2013; William, Allan, *The Effects-Based Approach Under Article 102 Tfeu: History And State Of Play*, in Ten Years of Effects-Based Approach in EU Competition Law: State of Play and Perspectives (Jacques Bourgeois ed.), 2012.
87. For a review of the theoretical framework of competition law *see* e.g., Lianos, Ioannis, *Some Reflections on the Question of the Goals of EU Competition Law*, 2013, CLES Working Paper Series 3/2013 available at http://dx.doi.org/10.2139/ssrn.2235875; Nazzini, Renato, *The Foundation*

discussed why competition law exists or which objectives it ought to pursue from a theoretical and normative perspective.[88] Instead, a positive approach is applied to this inquiry. What is sought is the ultimate goal(s).

From the EU Treaty, it follows that the aim is to ensure a system of free competition within the Internal Market.[89] This can be translated into two overall goals;[90] an "Economic Goal" and an "Integration Goal," respectively.[91] Below, both goals will be discussed in brief with the aim of providing the foundation of Article 102 TFEU.[92]

2.1 Economic Goal

The first goal is the Economic Goal. This goal has been named the basic legitimacy for all competition law enforcement in legal and economic literature.[93] It involves economic efficiency and [consumer] welfare.[94] One commentator has in that respect held that in competition law, the beginning of all wisdom is to understand the true nature of consumer welfare.[95] It should be noted that what was meant here by "true consumer welfare" was consumer welfare within the Chicago School, which have been criticized for not involving consumer welfare but total welfare.[96] The aim of Article 102 TFEU is in that view, generally speaking, that of ensuring the economic efficiency and welfare by prohibiting conduct that has a detrimental effect on competition through the exercise of market power. For that reason, the Economic Goal is seen by many scholars, and in general economists, as the most important goal of Article 102 TFEU (and EU competition law in general).

---

of European Union Competition Law, 2012, at 11–50; Akman, Pinar, *The Concept of Abuse in EU Competition Law: Law and Economic Approaches*, 2012, at 25–47.

88. It may briefly be stated that the primary conclusion of most normative perspectives on Article 102 TFEU – and EU competition law in general – is that total welfare ought to be the goal, and if not the only goal, the primary goal.

89. *See* Protocol No. 27, annexed to the TEU and TFEU. Before the Lisbon Treaty came into force, the objective was found in Article 3(1)(g) TEC. However, it were removed with introduction of the Lisbon Treaty and substituted with Protocol 27. *See* further section 3.

90. *See* Bishop & Walker (2010), at 3. *See* also Whish, Richard & Bailey, David, *Competition Law*, 2015; Padilla & O'Donoghue (2013), at 5–11.

91. Other goals also play a part in Article 102 TFEU, but they are of minor importance and can to some extent be fitted within one of the two goals. For review of some of the other goals *see* e.g., Whish & Bailey (2015), at 19–24.

92. This section will present the two goals of Article 102 TFEU with the aim of preparing the ground for the analyses in the following chapters and further the discussion of the definition for 'exclusionary abuse' in section 3. Consequently, it would be out of scope to make a more comprehensive analysis and discussion. For a more profound analysis of the two goals of EU competition law, reference can instead be made to the literature referred to in the footnotes.

93. *See* Padilla & O'Donoghue (2013), at 6.

94. *See* Bork (1978), at 91.

95. *See* Rule, Charles, *Statement for the Hearing of the Antitrust Modernization Commission: "Treatment of Efficiencies in Merger Enforcement"*, 2005, available at http://govinfo.library.unt .edu/amc/commission_hearings/pdf/Statement-Rule.pdf, at 14.

96. *See* e.g., Lande, Robert, *The Rise and (Coming) Fall of Efficiency as the Rule of Antitrust*, 33 Antitrust Bulletin (1988) 429; Fox & Sullivan (1987).

Even though there is a consensus that economic welfare and efficiency is the main goal of Article 102 TFEU, a complicated debate reigns on what this "welfare" relates to.[97] Normative analyses examining which welfare standards reflect the Economic Goal tend to agree on total welfare.[98] However, this inquiry does not involve a normative approach. Instead, it involves a positive approach as it aims to establish the Economic Goal within Article 102 TFEU and not to discuss what it ought to be. Among the standards of total welfare and consumer welfare, it should be without doubt that consumer welfare represents the Economic Goal within the meaning of Article 102 TFEU. This follows from the seminal case *Continental Can*. In this case, the ECJ held that Article 102 TFEU prohibits conduct that harms consumers either directly or indirectly.[99] This statement has been repeated in case law since then;[100] thereby, confirming this view. The ECJ has further held that Article 102 TFEU aims, in particular, to protect consumers [by means of undistorted competition].[101] According to the ECJ, the aim of Article 102 TFEU is, therefore, that of protecting consumers. This may be done directly or indirectly by protecting effective competition. This latter harm is seen as having an effect to the detriment of consumers due to, for example, the limitation of the choices available to them and, therefore, of the prospect of a long-term reduction of retail prices as a result of competition exerted by [as efficient competitors] competitors.[102]

This is also the Commissions view. In a speech shortly after being nominated as commissioner, Almunia, former vice-president and European Commissioner for Competition Policy, said that:

> [a]ll of us here today know very well what our ultimate objective is: <u>competition policy is a tool at the service of consumers</u>. Consumer welfare is at the heart of our policy and its achievement drives our priorities and guides our decisions.[103] (underlining added)

Moreover, when defining its enforcement activity as well as the anti-competitive foreclosure effect in its *Article 102 Guidance Paper*, the Commission states that:

---

97. *See* Jacobson, Jonathan, *Another Take on the Relevant Welfare Standard for Antitrust*, The Antitrust Source (2015) 1. He lists five options: (1) total welfare, (2) consumer welfare, (3) consumer choice, (4) multiple goals and (5) competitive process. *See* also e.g., Albæk, Svend, *Consumer Welfare in EU Competition Policy*, *in* Aims and Values in Competition Law (Caroline Heide-Jørgensen, et al. eds.), 2013, at 70–74; Padilla & O'Donoghue (2013), at 6; Motta, Massimo, *Competition Policy: Theory and Practice*, 2004, at 18–22.
98. For an overview of different argument for one and the other welfare standards *see* e.g., Nazzini (2012); Motta (2004), at 20–22.
99. *See* Case 6/72, *Continental Can*, at 26.
100. *See* e.g., Judgment of 16 September 2008 in Joined Cases C-468/06 to C-478/06, *Sot. Lelos kai Sia EE and others v. GlaxoSmithKline AEVE Farmakeftikon Proionton, formerly Glaxowellcome AEVE* ("*Sot. Lelos*"), at 68. *See* also Judgment of 14 October 2010 in Case C-280/08 P, *Deutsche Telekom AG v. European Commission* ("*Deutsche Telekom*"), at 170.
101. *See* Case C-280/08 P, *Deutsche Telekom*, at 180.
102. *See id.* at 182; Judgment of 2 April 2009 in Case C-202/07 P, *France Tèlècom v. Commission of the European Communities* ("*France Télécom*"), at 112.
103. *See* Almunia, Joaquín, *Competition and Consumers: The Future of EU Competition Policy*, speech given on 2010 at European Competition Day, Madrid.

[t]he aim of the Commission's enforcement activity in relation to exclusionary conduct is to ensure that dominant undertakings do not impair effective competition by foreclosing their competitors in an anti-competitive way, <u>thus having an adverse impact on consumer welfare, whether in the form of higher price levels than would have otherwise prevailed or in some other form such as limiting quality or reducing consumer choice</u>. In this document the term 'anti-competitive foreclosure' is used to describe a situation where effective access of actual or potential competitors to supplies or markets is hampered or eliminated as a result of the conduct of the dominant undertaking whereby the dominant undertaking is likely to be in a position to profitably increase prices <u>to the detriment of consumers</u>. The identification of likely consumer harm can rely on qualitative and, where possible and appropriate, quantitative evidence. The Commission will address such anti-competitive foreclosure either at the intermediate level or at the level of final consumers, or at both levels.[104] (Underlining added)

In terms of whether the Economic Goal, within the meaning of Article 102 TEFU, refers to total welfare or consumer welfare, it seems therefore tolerably clear that it refers to consumer welfare. However, this is it not strictly "pure" consumer welfare in the economic sense. Such "pure" consumer welfare is understood as the difference between what the consumer would have been willing to pay and what actually is paid or, in other words, the surplus a consumer gets from buying that good. Instead, the standard may be referred to as "in consumers' interest" for a better understanding. This is especially true for exclusionary abuse where it is assessed whether harm to effective competition is in the interest of consumers.[105] Despite the difference, an economist should be able to understand the above attention on consumers as consumer welfare.[106]

In consequence, the Economic Goal refers to the protection of consumers. It involves foreclosure of competition to the detriment of consumers' interest. The focus is not only on a reduction in consumer surplus but further, for example, a limitation of the choices available to consumers.[107] The latter example is based on the idea that the range of options available to consumers should not be impaired or distorted by anti-competitive conduct.[108] How this goal is then achieved is discussed in section 3.

2.2 Integration Goal

Article 102 TFEU is part of the overall goals of the TFEU; hence, the purpose of the provision is also to ensure the goals of the TFEU. One of these, relevant to Article 102

---

104. *See the Article 102 Guidance Paper*, at 19.
105. *See Case C-209/10, Post Danmark I*, at 44. The term consumer welfare is used in paragraph 42 of the same Judgment and Case C-23/14, *Post Danmark II*, at 49. It should be noted that this phrases, however, is a wrong translation of "in consumers' interest" as that phrase features in all other language versions; e.g., the French version refers to "les intérêts des consommateurs" in both paragraphs.
106. *See* Albæk (2013), at 71.
107. *See Case C-202/07 P, France Télécom*, at 112.
108. *See* Lande, Robert, *Consumer Choice as the Ultimate Goal of Antitrust*, 62 University of Pittsburgh Law Review (2001).

TFEU, is the establishment of an Internal Market.[109] In brief, the purpose of the Internal Market is to remove any barriers between the Members States that would prevent goods,[110] services,[111] workers/persons[112] and capital[113] from having complete freedom of movement.

This follows from the EU Courts' case law, which sees Article 102 TFEU as one of the means to establish the Internal Market.[114] When applying Article 102 TFEU, the Commission or the EU Courts may rely on this goal. Examples of such use can be found in the EU Courts' case law and the Commission's decisional practice.[115] Take for example *United Brands*. The Commission and the ECJ held that United Brands' conduct, including price discrimination and export restrictions, were contrary to Article 102 TFEU.[116] One reason for the finding of abuse was that United Brand's conduct made trade between Member States almost impossible.[117]

Therefore, this goal may explain why the Commission and the EU Courts have been hostile towards conduct such as exclusive agreements and refusal to deal, as they may hinder cross-border trade between Member States. Despite the emergence of more economic theory within Article 102 TFEU, it should be noticed that this goal is still important which is illustrated by recent case law. The ECJ continues to note that Article 102 TFEU is an application of the general objective, namely, the institution of a system ensuring that competition in the common market is not distorted.[118] This is also seen in Monti's report to the President of the European Commission.[119] Accordingly, this goal is still important, and the EU Courts may, therefore, be reluctant to change its approach in fear that it may hamper the Internal Market.

The Integration Goal and the Economic Goal are, however, potentially conflicting in some events since they pursue different objectives. Again, exclusive dealing serves as a great example. Such conduct may fulfil the Economic Goal (by being pro-competitive) while it at the same time may be contrary to the Integration Goal (by

---

109. *See* Article 3(3) of TEU. *See* also Ehlermann, Claus-Dieter, *The Contribution of EC Competition Policy to the Single Market*, 29 Common Market Law Review (1992) 257.
110. *See* Article 34 of the TFEU.
111. *See* Article 56 of the TFEU.
112. *See* Article 45 of the TFEU.
113. *See* Article 63 of the TFEU.
114. *See* for example Case C-52/09, *TeliaSonera*, at 20–2; Case C-202/07 P, *France Télécom*, at 103; Judgment of 13 February 1979 in Case 85/76, *Hoffmann-La Roche & Co. AG v. Commission of the European Communities* ("*Hoffman La Roche*"), at 38.
115. For a recent decision *see* Commission Decision of 5 March 2014 in Case AT.39984 *Romanian Power Exchange / OPCOM*, at 1. The Commission found OPCOM had discriminated against firms on the basis of their nationality/place of establishment, thereby restricting competition on the wholesale electricity market in Romania.
116. *See* Commission Decision of 17 December 1975 in Case IV/26.699, *Chiquita*. Upheld in Judgment of 14 February 1978 in Case 27/76, *United Brands Company v. Commission of the European Communities* ("*United Brands*").
117. *See* generally Case 27/76, *United Brands*, at 135, 159, 179, 202 and 232.
118. *See* Case C-52/09, *TeliaSonera*, at 20–2; Case C-202/07 P, *France Télécom*, at 103; Joined Cases C-468/06 to C-478/06, *Sot. Lelos*, at 68.
119. *See* Monti, Mario, *A New Strategy For The Single Market*, 2010, Report to the President of the European Commission José Manuel Barroso.

preventing, for instance, the free movement of goods).[120] The conflict is enhanced by the fact that the Integration Goal is a characteristic of EU competition law and not found in national competition laws around the world; for example, the US.[121] Accordingly, one of the differences between US antitrust law and EU competition law, respectively, is that the latter has two goals while the former only one. However, this difference does not necessarily need to have any impact on the assessments since the same economic reasoning can be applied in both jurisdictions. This requires, however, that the Economic Goal can overrule the Integration Goal. Accordingly, even if conduct may restrict the establishment of the Internal Market, economic efficiencies must still be part of the assessment. If not, this could have adverse outcomes.[122] Even though a conflict may potentially occur between the two goals, an efficient application of Article 102 TFEU should prevent such conflict.

3   EFFECTIVE COMPETITION

In general, it is a widely accepted principle that competition, and especially competition on price, is desirable since it benefits consumers by ensuring, among other things, cost efficiencies, lower prices and on-going innovation.[123] This may be referred to as effective competition.[124] Markets characterized with effective competition tend, therefore, to have higher consumer welfare than markets without effective competition. In consequence, it is apparent that foreclosure (i.e., elimination, marginalization of competitors and deterring of entry) are desired when that foreclosure is the result of legitimate conduct as it is the essence of effective competition.[125] This type of foreclosure ensures the departure of inefficient firms from the market (or that they refrain from entering the market) with the result of consumers benefiting from lower prices, increased quality, innovation, consumer choice or the like. Owing to this principle, not all elimination of competitors – wholly or partially – or deterring their entry infringes Article 102 TFEU since some types of foreclosure, by the definition, are the result of effective competition.[126] On the other hand, some types of foreclosure are not desired. This is the case when foreclosure is not the result of effective competition but is achieved due to the dominant position. When effective competition is harmed, the market will experience the opposite of those benefits mentioned above; for instance, higher prices, less output, lowered quality and/or limited consumer choice.

For those reasons, the impact on competition serves as a good indicator of whether conduct is in breach of Article 102 TFEU. But since the text of Article 102 TFEU merely mentions that abuse of dominance is prohibited the question is whether effective competition can be more than just an indicator; i.e., whether effective

---

120. This may further explain the hostile view on some types of conduct; for example, exclusivity agreements.
121. *See* Bishop & Walker (2010), at 6.
122. *See id.*
123. *See id.* at 15.
124. *See id.*
125. *See the Article 102 Guidance Paper*, at 6.
126. *See* e.g., Case C-209/10, *Post Danmark I*, at 22.

competition may constitute the protective aim of Article 102 TFEU thereby ensuring the goals discussed earlier. In addition, it is far from clear how effective competition shall be understood, or even defined. If effective competition constitutes the protective aim, it is difficult to serve this aim if it is unclear what is meant. As a result, this section aims at answering those questions.

3.1 Effective Competition as the Protective Aim

Case law has applied different concepts in an effort to explain what Article 102 TFEU seeks to protect. This includes, among other things, "performance-based competition", "competition on the merits" and "undistorted competition". As will be shown below, these terms fit under the same protective aim; namely effective competition. Fulfilling these concepts ensures effective competition to the benefit of consumers.

The first concept, performance-based competition, was adapted by Freiburg theorists also known as "Leistungswettbewerb".[127] This concept derived from the nineteenth-century rules on "unfair competition". It described the types of competitive conduct that could not be prohibited as unfair even though it harmed competitors. Even if such conduct had a foreclosure effect, it was not seen as abuse.[128] In that regard, Professor Peter Ulmer proposed a two-step approach for the assessment of exclusionary conduct by dominant firms.[129] This approach involved two conditions: conduct must: (i) significantly affect the competition opportunities for rivals, and (ii) not be within the scope of performance-based competition. If met, conduct constituted abuse of dominance.

This test found its way into the EU Courts' case law. A review of the (early) case law including, for instance, *Hoffman La Roche*, *Michelin I* and *Akzo* illustrates that the ECJ adopted this two-step approach.[130] The ECJ held in all three cases that exclusionary abuse involves conduct: (i) which has the effect of hindering the maintenance of the degree of competition still existing in the market or the growth of that competition, and (ii) where the effect is caused by methods different from those governing normal competition in products or services based on traders' performance.[131]

---

127. See Kallaugher, John & Sher, Brian, *Rebates Revisited: Anti-Competitive Effects and Exclusionary Abuse Under Article 82*, 21 European Competition Law Review (2004) 263, at 270.
128. This correspond to the introductory remarks of the chapters in which it is held that even conduct that may harm competitors does not necessarily harm the effective competition, and thereby, the consumer welfare.
129. See Ulmer, Peter, *Schranken zulässigen Wettbewerbs marktbeherrschender Unternehmen*, 1977.
130. See Judgment of 3 July 1991 in Case 62/86, *AKZO Chemie BV v. Commission of the European Communities* ("*Akzo*"), at 69; Case 322/81, *Michelin I*, at 70; Case 85/76, *Hoffman La Roche*, at 91.
131. It must be noticed that according to the English version of the cases, the wording of the second step is worded in *Hoffman La Roche* and *Akzo* as "on the basis of the transactions of commercial operators", while in *Michelin I* the wording is "based on traders' performance". However, in both the French and German versions, the same wording is repeated in all three cases as the wordings "la base des prestations" and "der Grundlage der Leistungen" is used, respectively. An error of translation is, therefore, present as regards the English versions. The correct translation of the phrases is the one applied in *Michelin I* – and this is also the reason

The second concept, competition on the merits, was adopted by the ECJ to explain which types of conduct Article 102 TFEU prohibits.[132] However, this concept has been criticized for being vague and unclear,[133] since no clear definition has been made by the EU Courts.[134] Help may be found in the first concept (i.e., performance-based competition) which bears great resemblance to competition on the merits since competition in both events are legitimate and desired as long as the dominant firm's conduct is based on its merits/performance. This is only supported by the fact that the reference to competition on the merits is usually made in connection with the two-step test deduced from the concept of performance-based competition.[135]

The third concept, undistorted competition, is based on the EU Treaty objective of ensuring competition in the internal market is not distorted. It should be noticed that before the Lisbon Treaty came into force, this concept was found in Article 3(1)(g) of the then EC Treaty. With the Lisbon Treaty, however, Article 3(1)(g) was repealed and the text transferred to Protocol No. 27, annexed to the EU Treaty. Although Article 51 of the TEU states that the Protocols shall form an integral part of both the TEU and the TFEU, and hence, the legally binding nature should be undisputed,[136] it has been feared that the importance of the concept of Article 3(1)(g) of the then EC Treaty would be reduced with respect the competition rules.[137] Such fear is pointless, however. The ECJ still relies on the concept of undistorted competition,[138] and as a consequence, the relocation of the principle from the fundamental provisions of the EU Treaty to the Protocols seems to be merely symbolic.

The importance of this objective was held in the first case on Article 102 TFEU, *Continental Can*, in which the ECJ had to address the question of how to interpret the provision. The ECJ found that Article 102 TFEU should be interpreted not only in the

---

why it is the one referred to. Nonetheless, this error in translation has not only found it is way into these cases. The error can be found in different cases by the EU Courts including, for example, *British Airways*, *France Télècom*, *Deutsche Telekom*, *TeliaSonera* and *Tomra*. In *Post Danmark I*, however, the wording "on the basis of the performance of commercial operators" was used. Even if an error of translation is present, it should still be clear that the meaning of the phrase is that of "the performance" and not "the transactions" when one compare the phrase with the "Leistungswettbewerb"-concept as well as with the French and German versions.

132. *See* Case 62/86, *Akzo*, at 70.
133. *See* e.g., Akman (2016), at 8.
134. A similar problem is experienced in the US antitrust system. *See* e.g., Werden, Gregory, *The "No Economic Sense" Test for Exclusionary Conduct*, 31 The Journal of Corporation Law (2006) 293. The concept was first invoked in *Northern Pacific Railway Co. v. United States*, 356 U.S. 1 (1958).
135. *See* e.g., Case C-209/10, *Post Danmark I*, at 24–25.
136. *See* Rompuy, Ben Van, *The Impact of the Lisbon Treaty on EU Competition Law: A Review of Recent Case Law of the EU Courts*, 1 CPI Antitrust Chronicle (2011) 1, at 2.
137. *See* e.g., Weitbrecht, Andreas, *From Freiburg to Chicago and Beyond – The First 50 Years of European Competition Law*, 29 European Competition Law Review (2008) 81; Graupner, Frances, *The Battle over the Role of the European Competition Policy: Now you See it, Now You Don't*, 6 Competition Law Journal (2007) 89; Riley, Alan, *The EU Reform Treaty and the Competition Protocol: Undermining EC Competition Law*, 2007, CEPS Policy Brief No. 142, available at http://aei.pitt.edu/7535/.
138. *See* Case C-52/09, *TeliaSonera*, at 20; Judgment of 17 November 2011 2011 in Case C-496/09, *European Commission v. Italian Republic* ("*Italian Republic*"), at 60.

wording of the provision but further in the objectives of the EU Treaty as well.[139] Undistorted competition has since then been a guiding principle in the EU Courts' case law regarding the general objective of Article 102 TFEU.[140] The importance of this concept is illustrated by the fact that it led to the special responsibility that a dominant firm is subject to in consequence of Article 102 TFEU.[141]

In the same manner that competition on the merits and performance-based competition are similar, undistorted competition covers the same protective aim as those two concepts. If conduct by a dominant firm is within, for example, the scope of competition on the merits, it will not distort competition. In other words, undistorted competition involves types of conduct that are within the scope of competition on the merits. Accordingly, these concepts have the same purpose which is to ensure effective competition (the protective aim of Article 102 TFEU is to safeguard effective competition from anti-competitive conduct by dominant firms). This does not mean that the objective is to protect competitors from being excluded from a relevant market or deterred entry to that market since not all foreclosure is detrimental to effective competition. This has become an established principle in recent case law.[142] It is instead the objective to protect (effective) competition by ensuring that competitors are only foreclosed by conduct within the scope of performance/merits.

When assessing exclusionary conduct by a dominant firm, and whether it is abusive, the aim of protecting effective competition in the relevant market forms the basis. That being the case, the analyses and discussions of the EU Courts' case law in the following chapters must include this aspect since the judgments, and hence, the concepts that can be deducted from these cases, have had a basis in this protective aim. If this is not included, it may have the result of erroneous interpretations.

3.1.1   Coherence with the Goals of Article 102 TFEU

In section 2, the goals of Article 102 TFEU were examined which lead to the conclusion that Article 102 TFEU – and EU competition law in general – has two primary goals: The Economic Goal and the Integration Goal. This entails the protection of consumers (consumers' interest) and the Internal Market, respectively. This begs the question of whether effective competition as a protective aim is in coherence with these goals.

3.1.1.1   The Economic Goal

In legal and economic literature, it has been held that when focus is pointed at exclusionary conduct within this provision, it now seems at least tolerably clear that consumer welfare is the overall guiding principle under Article 102 TFEU.[143] However, such statement builds primarily on the Commission's *Article 102 Guidance Paper*, and

---

139. *See* Case 6/72, *Continental Can*, at 22.
140. *See* Case 85/76, *Hoffman La Roche*, at 38; Case C-202/07 P, *France Télécom*, at 103.
141. *See* Case 322/81, *Michelin I*, at 57.
142. *See* Case C-209/10, *Post Danmark I*, at 22; Case C-52/09, *TeliaSonera*, at 43.
143. *See* Padilla & O'Donoghue (2013), at 5 and 273.

consequently, includes some uncertainty in terms of whether such conclusion is true; i.e., whether the EU Courts agree on this aspect. Nonetheless, statements can be found in the EU Courts' case law indicating that the main guiding principle may have shifted towards the protection of consumer welfare. Note that, as concluded in section 2, this involves consumers' interest and not "pure" consumer welfare, though.

According to the ECJ in *Sot. Lelos and others*, exclusionary conduct have to be assessed in the light of the EU Treaty's objectives to protect consumers by means of undistorted competition.[144] In *Deutsche Telekom*, the ECJ stated that Article 102 TFEU aims, in particular, to protect consumers by means of undistorted competition.[145] This aspect has further been included in *Post Danmark I* where the ECJ seems to agree on this point since it stated that "Article [102 TFEU], in particular, covers conduct which has an effect to the detriment of consumers."[146]

In addition, the ECJ has repeatedly rejected the argument that only types of conduct which directly harm consumers are contrary to Article 102 TFEU. This also goes for types of conduct that harm consumers indirectly.[147] In addition, the expression "exclusionary abuse" was defined as such types of conduct (i.e., those harming consumers indirectly) in *Post Danmark I*.[148] In consequence, exclusionary abuse refers to indirect damage on consumers' interest through harmed [effective] competition.

While the protection of consumers may well be the main goal of Article 102 TFEU, the EU Courts still emphasize that effective competition is the means to achieve that this goal. Accordingly, consumer protection is a by-product of ensuring effective competition. This is further apparent in *Post Danmark I*, in which the ECJ defined the anti-competitive effect as being an effect to the detriment of competition, *and thereby*, of consumers' interests.[149] In consequence, it should be clear that the prohibition of conduct that harms effective competition serves as the mean to protect the Economic Goal; i.e., effective competition protects consumer's interest.

3.1.1.2   The Integration Goal

Effective competition also includes the Integration Goal. By safeguarding effective competition, and thereby undistorted competition, a dominant firm is restricted from, for example, creating national or regional markets that would harm the creation of the Single European Market. This features indirectly in the meaning of effective competition. Effective competition can only be present in a relevant market where no firm is allowed to hold or create their own market unless it is due to better performance.

Furthermore, the principle of undistorted competition relates directly to the establishment of an internal market. In Article 3(3) TEU it is clear that the goal of the EU Treaty is to establish an internal market. To establish an internal market, it follows

---

144. *See* Joined Cases C-468/06 to C-478/06, *Sot. Lelos*, at 68.
145. *See* Case C-280/08 P, *Deutsche Telekom*, at 180.
146. *See* Case C-209/10, *Post Danmark I*, at 24.
147. *See* Case 6/72, *Continental Can*, at 26; Case C-280/08 P, *Deutsche Telekom*, at 181–4; Case C-202/07 P, *France Télécom*, at 105.
148. *See* Case C-209/10, *Post Danmark I*, at 20.
149. *See id.* at 44.

from Protocol no. 27 that the internal market as set out in Article 3(3) TEU includes a system ensuring that competition is not distorted. This follows also from the EU Courts' case law.[150] The coherence between effective competition and the Integration Goal follows from both the EU Treaty as well as the EU Courts' case law.

In consequence, the internal market is also included when safeguarding effective competition even though consumer welfare may have a greater influence. This may also explain the strict approach taken by the EU Courts to some types of conduct – for example, exclusive dealing – since this objective is to be considered as well.

3.1.2 Coherence with the Article 102 Guidance Paper and the Other Competition Rules

The *Article 102 Guidance Paper* is meant to represent the Commission's enforcement priorities. Although it is not binding for the EU Courts, it is likely that the Commission will follow it. Since the Commission is the primary enforcer of Article 102 TFEU, it is of great relevance to examine whether there is coherence between this case law established protective aim and the Commission's *Article 102 Guidance Paper*. Moreover, since the objective of Article 102 TFEU must be coherent with those of Article 101 and the EU Merger Regulation,[151] it is also of great importance to assess whether this is the case.

3.1.2.1 The Article 102 Guidance Paper

In the previous sections, the analyses and discussions have taken the departure in the EU Courts' case law rather than the Commission's *Article 102 Guidance Paper* (and its decisional practice). This is owing to the fact that while the Commission interprets the competition law, the EU Courts create it. Nonetheless, since the Commission is the primary enforcer of Article 102 TFEU, it is of great importance to ensure that there is coherence between its *Article 102 Guidance Paper* and effective competition as presented above.[152]

The *Article 102 Guidance Paper* states that the emphasis is on safeguarding the competitive process within the internal market. However, it also noted that what matters is the protection of effective competitive and not the protection of competitors.[153] As a result, the Commission acknowledges that effective competition serves as a method to achieve the goals of Article 102 TFEU. This is only supported by the statement that the aim of the Commission's enforcement in respect of exclusionary abuse within Article 102 TFEU is that of "ensuring dominant firms not impairing effective competition by foreclosing their competitors in an anti-competitive way."[154]

---

150. *See* e.g., Case C-52/09, *TeliaSonera*, at 20.
151. *See* e.g., Rousseva (2010), at 356.
152. Furthermore, many NCAs are likely to rely on the *Article 102 Guidance Paper* when assessing dominant firms' conduct even though they are not obliged to apply it.
153. *See the Article 102 Guidance Paper*, at 6.
154. *See id.* at 19.

This further corresponds to the interpretation made earlier of the EU Courts' case law[155] in regards to effective competition and protecting consumers' interest. The Commission's *Article 102 Guidance Paper* states the same view on effective competition as the EU Courts. As a result, the Commission will seek to safeguard effective competition as a means to protect consumer welfare and the Single European Market.

3.1.2.2   *Article 101 TFEU & the EU Merger Regulation*

The ECJ held in *Continental Can* – when addressing the question of whether the Commission had authority to review mergers and whether it was reviewed correctly in the case at hand – that Article 102 TFEU and Article 101 TFEU seek to achieve the same aim, however, on different levels.[156] It is, therefore, a fundamental principle that the two provisions have the same purpose.[157] For that reason, it is of great importance that the purpose of Article 102 TFEU is not only clarified but also coherent with those of Article 101 TFEU and the EU Merger Regulation. However, as have been mentioned earlier, Article 101 TFEU and the EU Merger Regulation have been subject to modernizations, which included, among other things, a review of their objectives; hence, the objectives of these competition rules have been redefined.[158] It is, therefore, of great importance to ensure, in brief, that the protective aim discussed in regards to Article 102 TFEU also applies to Article 101 TFEU and the EU Merger Regulation.

Regarding Article 101 TFEU, the reform meant a reformulation of the policy objectives.[159] It was emphasized that the main policy objective of the provision is to ensure that firms do not use agreements to restrict competition in the relevant market to the detriment of the consumer;[160] hence, the Integration Goal became only an additional, complementary goal rather than a main goal.[161] Nonetheless, the Integration Goal is still influential.[162] This is seen in for example areas where territorial restrictions are blacklisted or prohibited.[163] Nonetheless, the means to achieve these policy objectives is still the safeguarding of effective competition. This is clear as the Commissions states in the *Vertical Guidelines* that an illegal agreement is one that has restrictive effects on competition,[164] and further the ultimate aim of Article 101 TFEU is to protect the competitive process.[165]

---

155. *See* e.g., Case C-209/10, *Post Danmark I*, at 44.
156. *See* Case 6/72, *Continental Can*, at 25.
157. *See* Rousseva (2010), at 356.
158. *See id.*
159. *See id.* at 305.
160. *See* in general *the Vertical Restraints Guidelines*; Communication of the Commission of 27 April 2004 OJ 2004/C 101/08, *Guidelines on the Application of Article 81(3) of the Treaty* ("*Article 101(3) Guidelines*").
161. *See* Rousseva (2010), at 305.
162. *See the Vertical Restraints Guidelines*, at 7.
163. *See* e.g., *the Vertical Guidelines*.
164. *See id.* at 24 *See* also *the Vertical Restraints Guidelines*, at 133.
165. *See the Vertical Guidelines*, at 105.

On the EU Merger Regulation, an updated regulation[166] was published in 2004 as part of the moderation. This regulation restated the same objectives as the old one.[167] It also included a statement that the Commission must take into account the need to maintain and establish effective competition when reviewing a merger.[168] Likewise, the Commission stressed the importance of effective competition in its *Horizontal Mergers Guidelines*[169] and further elaborated on the term by stating that the term is to be understood as bringing benefits to consumers such as low prices, high-quality products, a wide selection of goods and services and innovation.[170] A similar definition to the one found in the *Article 102 Guidance Paper.*[171]

In consequence, it follows from the analysis above that in respect of both Article 101 TFEU and the EU Merger Regulation, effective competition is the protective aim which serves as a means to protect consumers, and hence, consumer welfare. This being the case, there is coherence between these two sets of competition rules and Article 102 TFEU.

3.2   Understanding Effective Competition

It was established in the previous section that the main objective of Article 102 TFEU is what this book has termed effective competition – which in turn ensures the goals of Article 102 TFEU (protecting consumers' interest and establishing an internal market). Effective competition was not explained, though. Accordingly, this section will analyse how effective competition may be understood and defined. This will serve as the foundation for the definition and understanding of anti-competitive foreclosure effect throughout the following chapters, and hence, why some types of conduct are contrary to Article 102 TFEU. It should also be noticed that there is no single concept that defines effective competition.[172] For that reason, one may benefit from considering oligopoly theory that may provide helpful insights.[173] Case law must also be considered.[174] All of this will assist the inquiry.

On a general level, one might identify three plausible "definitions":[175] the process of rivalry, the absence/presence of restraints and the influence of market price. On an intuitive level, the process of rivalry might correspond to effective competition since it is generally accepted that industries with monopolies tend to be of less interest to consumers. This is at least true for traditionalists who have scepticism towards

---

166. *See* the EU Merger Regulation.
167. *See* e.g., Rousseva (2010), at 315.
168. *See* the EU Merger Regulation, at Article 2(1); *see* also Article 2(3).
169. *See the Horizontal Mergers Guidelines.*
170. *See id.* at 8.
171. *See the Article 102 Guidance Paper,* at 19.
172. *See* Bishop & Walker (2010), at 21.
173. *See* Bender, Christian, et al., *Effective Competition: Its Importance and Relevance for Network Industries,* 46 "Effective competition" in telecommunications, rail and energy markets (2011) 4, at 5. *See* also Bishop & Walker (2010), at 21ff.
174. The primary purpose is to deduce how the law is (or likely to be), i.e., *de lege lata*; thus, the findings must primarily deduce how the law is and not how it ought to be.
175. *See* Bishop & Walker (2010), at 16–20.

dominant firms.[176] Fewer firms further entail a limitation of the choices available to consumers.[177] This is problematic according to case law.[178] For the same reasons, the absence or presence of restraints on a firm's economic activities by any other firm(s) may provide a definition for effective competition. This is supported by the reasoning that restraints will result in non-independent conduct by firms and the fact that it has been applied in earlier cases under Article 101 TFEU.[179] Lastly, effective competition might also be defined as the event where no firm is able to influence the market price. This "definition" stems from the model of perfect competition in which all firms set their prices at marginal costs and consumer welfare is maximized. This means that the elasticity for both the buyers and sellers are infinite. If a buyer offered to pay slightly less, he would not find a seller, and similar, if a seller raised the price slightly he would not find a buyer.

However, all three "definitions" are inadequate for the understanding of effective competition. They are too focused on how the market looks rather than the outcomes. For instance, the number of firms within a market does not necessarily say anything about the level of competition in a market.[180] It does not say how much rivalry is needed to achieve effective competition; must there be a minimum number of firms in a market? An understanding based on the process of competition would have some unwanted consequences. A market with few firms would be viewed with suspicion, and the foreclosure of a competitor would be abusive, even if it that foreclosure were in the interest of consumers. This is obviously problematic since Article 102 TFEU protects competition and not competitors.

The two other "definitions" are also inadequate. Regarding the absence or presence of restraints, every contract involves some degree of restraints (or the absence thereof). More importantly, however, a dominant firm is by its definition able to act independently (to some extent at least) as the firm would otherwise not have been found to hold a dominant position.[181] Accordingly, if this is the definition of effective competition, a firm will restrict effective competition by merely being dominant; thus, a dominant position would be contrary to Article 102 TFEU in itself. This is clearly not suitable as it is too restrictive and further contradicts the fact that a dominant position is not in itself a ground of criticism of the undertaking concerned.[182] Additionally, while the ability to influence the market price (which stems from the model of perfect

---

176. See Monti, Giorgio, *EU Competition Law from Rome to Lisbon – Social Market Economy, in* Aim and Values in Competition Law (Caroline Heide-Jørgensen, et al. eds.), 2013.
177. Regarding the role which "choice" has in competition law, *see* Nihoul, Paul, et al., *Choice – A New Standard for Competition Law Analysis?*, 2016.
178. *See* Case C-202/07 P, *France Télécom*, at 12.
179. *See* Bishop & Walker (2010), at 19.
180. *See id.* at 17.
181. A dominant position has been defined as: "a position of economic strength enjoyed by an undertaking which enables it to prevent effective competition being maintained on the relevant market by affording it the power to behave to an appreciable extent independently of its competitors, its customers and ultimately of the consumers." *See* e.g., Case 85/76, *Hoffman La Roche*, at 38. *See* also *the Article 102 Guidance Paper*, at 10.
182. *See* e.g., Case C-52/09, *TeliaSonera*, at 24.

competition)[183] may provide a good basis for the understanding of welfare maximiza-
tion, it is not suited for policy-making.[184] The main reason is the many assumptions
that the model involves.[185] Perfect competition is not found in any markets, even
though many markets are seen as competitive, and it would therefore not be sensible
to aim at duplicating these market assumptions. The same issue with the definition of
a dominant position arises here.

In the end, effective competition represents the protective aim of Article 102
TFEU due to its benefits for consumers' interest [and the Internal Market]. Protecting
and promoting effective competition is a practice that ensures the goals of Article 102
TFEU (and vice versa).[186] Therefore, the definition ought to reflect this. In other words,
the focus for policy-making should be the outcomes and not necessarily the form of the
market. A dominant firm should not be penalized for how the market is characterized
but only for conduct that are contrary to the goals of Article 102 TFEU. For those
reasons, the positive outcomes which effective competition may deliver, and thereby,
the negative effects which dominant firm's conduct can deliver must be at the heart of
the understanding.

Take, for example the concept of workable competition[187] that was introduced by
Clark[188] in 1940. It is a concept that is recognized, by some,[189] as the basis for what
today is termed effective competition. More importantly, this concept considers market
power explicitly. Clark found market imperfections (e.g., product heterogeneity,
non-transparency and time lags) to be indispensable for economic progress, and hence,
necessary to make competition efficient. Following this approach, the major aim of
regulation should not be to eliminate all excess profits, increase the number of firms
and so on, but rather give competing firms the freedom of discovering more efficient
ways of production and what customers want. Such dynamic approach allows for a
better accounting for dynamic developments in the industry like product innovation
and cost reduction compared to a static approach. In that respect, effective competition
cannot imply the absence of market power. The prospect of having some market power
(and profits) represents a powerful incentive for firms to innovate and invest,[190] and if
that incentive were to be eliminated, firms would be less likely to pursue competitive
behaviour, innovation and so on. As a result, the focus was on the outcome of firm's
conduct and not how the market looked. In that sense, effective competition results in

---

183. All firms set their prices at marginal costs and consumer welfare is maximized. This further
entails that the elasticity for both the buyers and sellers are infinite. That is, if a buyer offered
to pay slightly less he would not find a seller, and similar, if a seller raised the price slightly he
would not find a buyer.
184. See Bishop & Walker (2010), at 20.
185. These include a large number of firms and buyers, homogenous products, complete and perfect
information, no entry or exit costs etc.
186. Bishop & Walker (2010), at 20.
187. When he revised his work later, he changed the wording from "workable" to "effective", see
Clark, John, Competition as a Dynamic Process, 1961.
188. See Clark, John, Toward a Concept of Workable Competition, 30 The American Economic
Review (1940) 241.
189. See Bender, et al. (2011), at 5.
190. See also Motta (2004), at 89.

better products and service as well as lower prices because firms are encouraged to pursue innovation and more efficient ways of production.

As it is well known, a dominant firm may justify its anti-competitive conduct by demonstrating that the anti-competitive foreclosure effect produced is counterbalanced, or outweighed even, by advantages in terms of efficiency that also benefit consumers.[191] One might, therefore, mistake effective competition for an efficiency defence. However, it illustrates that the point that exclusionary conduct might both harm and benefit effective competition. That is, if anti-competitive behaviour leads to better products/service and/or lower costs which outweigh the negative effect(s) then effective competition is ultimately not harmed – again focus is on the (net) outcome and not how the market is characterized.

As can be deduced from the above, effective competition encourages price reduction, innovation and better products.[192] While this is the positive aspect of effective competition (i.e., how conduct benefits effective competition), the negative aspect is found by turning the table. Accordingly, effective competition is harmed if exclusionary conduct prevents better products/services, a lower level of output or results in higher prices. Price and output is, therefore, not the only relevant aspect. Consumer choice constitutes also an important aspect of the assessment of whether conduct is to the detriment of consumers' interest.[193] This has resulted in the ECJ establishing the principle that the lack of increased prices (and a lower level of output) is insufficient to conclude legitimate conduct since "customers [may] suffer loss as a result of the limitation of the choices available to them."[194] That this aspect is important is further illustrated by *Intel*. In showing the anti-competitive effects of Intel's exclusivity rebates (and naked restrictions), the Commission based its assessment on consumer choice.[195] The primary concern for consumers' interest was that the variety of products available was likely to be reduced to the detriment of consumers.

However, any limitation on consumers' choice cannot be to the detriment of consumers. This follows the reasoning for why rivalry as a process cannot define effective competition. In addition, more is not always better. This can be illustrated by three points. First, to the extent products are differentiated, there is less room for economies of scale (differentiation narrows the demand) entailing that product differentiation may lead to higher prices.[196] Second, product differentiation will create some degree of market power that can lead to monopolistic outcomes (e.g., "local monopolies").[197] Third, too much choice can be detrimental to consumers as they get a "choice

---

191. See Case C-209/10, *Post Danmark I*, at 41; Case C-52/09, *TeliaSonera*, at 76.
192. In parts, the same is also true for the three definitions. However, a positive effect on price or the like is assumed rather than observed (or likely to be). For example, lower prices are assumed if there is enough rivalry, no restraints and/or no power over price.
193. For a review of consumer choice and its role within competition law, *see* e.g., Nihoul, et al. (2016).
194. *See* Case C-202/07 P, *France Télécom*, at 112.
195. *See* Case COMP/37.990, *Intel*, at 1598–1611.
196. *See* Carlton & Perloff (2004), at 201.
197. *See* Scherer, Frederic & Ross, David, *Industrial Market Structure and Economic Performance* 1990, at 32–4, 575–6 & 601.

overload" leading to stress, decision-making paralysis and buyers' remorse (i.e., you are unsure whether you found the right product).[198]

Figure 2.1.   Consumer Choice Illustration

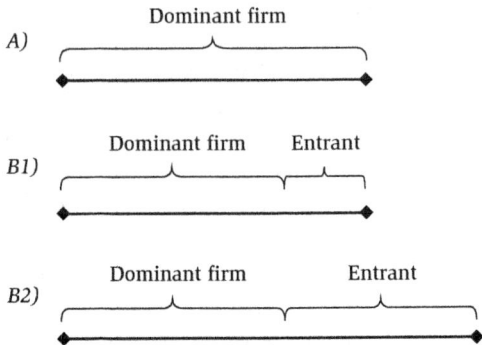

Note: The outcome can differ from the illustration. The outcome in this figure must, therefore, be seen as an example and not an absolute certainty.

This begs the question of how a limitation of the choices available to consumers' is to their detriment. The answer will be whether consumer demand is left unsatisfied.[199] This can be illustrated by the example where the dominant firm is a monopolist and face entry by a competitor. If that competitor is allowed to enter the market then two options are possible regarding choice and consumer demand (see Figure 2.1). It may increase the demand and satisfy that additional amount (and potential take shares from the dominant firm), or it may only steal demand from the dominant firm. If the entrant does not increase demand (i.e., "B1") then there is no detriment of consumers – given that price is not raised, output not reduced and the level of innovation and quality is not reduced. If demand is greater after the entrance (i.e., "B2"), on the other hand, then an effect to the detriment of consumers occurs. It should be noted that this represents a static view as it only focusses on the short-term gains. Considering the long-term effects, the entrance might be able to increase consumer demand through innovation.[200]

An understanding of the term effective competition has been provided above. This involves the outcome that benefits consumers' interest and not how the specific market is formed. In other words, the focus is on prices, output, innovation, the variety or quality of goods or services and so on rather than characteristics of the market. Market characteristics may, of course, assist the assessment whether prices, output, innovation, the variety or quality of goods or services or the like have been or is likely

---

198. *See* Schwartz, Barry, *The Paradox of Choice: Why More Is Less*, 2004.
199. *See* in that respect also the analysis of the condition of a 'new product' in regards of refusal to deal/supply in Chapter 7, section 3.3.2.2.
200. *See* Averitt, Neil & Lande, Robert, *Using the "Consumer Choice" Approach to Antitrust Law, in Choice – A New Standard for Competition Law Analysis?* (Paul Nihoul, et al. eds.), 2016, at 57–9.

to be impacted negatively but a change in, for instance, the process of rivalry (e.g., a competitor is foreclosed) does not necessarily say anything about effective competition. As explained above, a change in the process of rivalry is sometimes even required to foster effective competition. This understanding will assist the understanding of anti-competitive effects in the following chapters, and thereby, how to assess exclusionary conduct.

CHAPTER 3

Defining Anti-competitive Foreclosure Effects

1 INTRODUCTION

As mentioned earlier, merely holding a dominant position is not, and should never be, contrary to Article 102 TFEU. On the other hand, certain types of [exclusionary] conduct may be prohibited under the premise that they are reflections of abuse of that dominant position. In other words, dominant firms are not in themselves a danger to effective competition and consumers' interest, or seen as such, but their conduct can be. The key element is how the dominant firm behaves and whether that conduct is detrimental to effective competition. This indicates that only exclusionary conduct producing a negative effect can be found contrary to Article 102 TFEU.

At the same time, the EU Courts have started to apply the term "anti-competitive [foreclosure] effect" as a required element when assessing whether exclusionary conduct by a dominant firm amounts to abuse within the meaning of Article 102 TFEU.[201] This is also the primary focus of the Commissions *Article 102 Guidance Paper*. Here the Commission states that its enforcement activity "in relation to exclusionary conduct is to ensure that dominant undertakings do not impair effective competition by foreclosing their competitors in an anti-competitive way."[202] In consequence, a greater focus on anti-competitive foreclosure effects has emerged in recent years.

A focus on anti-competitive foreclosure effects, and the demonstration of such effects, raises different questions/issues. First, it is unclear whether the Commission and the EU Courts have always been subject to the requirement of demonstrating an anti-competitive foreclosure effect or if that requirement is a novelty to the approach of

---

201. *See* e.g., Case C-23/14, *Post Danmark II*; Case C-209/10, *Post Danmark I*; Case C-52/09, *TeliaSonera*; Case C-280/08 P, *Deutsche Telekom*.
202. *See the Article 102 Guidance Paper*, at 19 and 20.

exclusionary abuse.[203] Second, a definition of an anti-competitive foreclosure effect is necessary. If a clear definition is not present, then legal certainty is reduced which can negatively affect the coherence of the assessments.[204] Third, demonstrating anti-competitive effects involves a standard of evidence to establish such an effect (i.e., the standard of proof). While it is undisputed that the Commission (alternatively an NCA) has the burden of proof concerning the anti-competitive foreclosure effect,[205] the question in this context is the standard; i.e., what is required to demonstrate an anti-competitive foreclosure effect. For instance, are potential effects sufficient and to what degree is historical evidence useful? This chapter will address the issues outlined above. These answers, along with those from the previous chapter, will provide the needed framework of Article 102 TFEU to answer the research question.

2 THE REQUIREMENT OF ANTI-COMPETITIVE EFFECTS

In *Post Danmark I*, the ECJ concluded that the referring court was required to assess the existence of anti-competitive foreclosure effects to establish abuse.[206] As a result, some commentators have named *Post Danmark I* the landmark case regarding a shift towards the effect-based approach within Article 102 TFEU.[207] This shift involves favouring a more economic approach to the assessments, including the requirement of demonstrating anti-competitive foreclosure effects. This view is held as a contrast to the more form-based approach which relies on the particular form of alleged exclu-sionary conduct to establish abuse.[208] As support for such a shift, the Commissions' *Article 102 Guidance Paper* has further been highlighted as proof.[209] While the *Article 102 Guidance Paper* is not intended to constitute a statement of the law, such proof is not to be undervalued since, when all comes to all, the Commission is the primary enforcer of Article 102 TFEU.

Despite *Post Danmark I* (and the *Article 102 Guidance Paper*) seemingly revolu-tionized Article 102 TFEU, an anti-competitive foreclosure effect has always been required – even under the so-called form-based approach. This will be clear after the

---

203. It is further relevant to examine whether a comprehensive assessment of actual or likely anti-competitive effects is required in all cases or if some types of conduct may be presumed to entail such effect; i.e., whether some types of exclusionary conduct can be categorized as "by object restrictions". This issue will be the inquiry of Chapter 4.
204. It is further risked that both type I and type II errors are made if there is no agreement on how to understand anti-competitive foreclosure effect.
205. Who has the burden of proof in regards of objective justification may be a bit more blurred.
206. See Case C-209/10, *Post Danmark I*, at 44.
207. See, among others, Rousseva & Marquis (2013), at 19. Lundqvist & Ølykke (2013); Bien, Florian & Krah, Matthias, *The Ruling of the CJEU in Post Danmark: Putting an End to Selective Price Cuts as an Abuse Under TFEU Article 102 and Turning Towards a More Economic Approach*, 33 European Competition Law Review (2012) 482; Barazza, Stefano, *Post Danmark: The CJEU Calls for an Effect-Based Assessment of Pricing Policies*, Journal of European Competition Law & Practice (2012).
208. See Chapter 4, which discuss and analysis this issue.
209. The Commission stresses that its object is to ensure that dominant firm do not impair effective competition by foreclosing their competitors in an anti-competitive way. See the *Article 102 Guidance Paper*, at 19.

following analysis. The required effect has instead been refined by the EU Courts' case law meaning that it is now referred to as an anti-competitive foreclosure effect. It is, therefore, reasonable to take the view that the requirement of demonstrating anti-competitive foreclosure effects is nothing revolutionary but merely the result of the general evolution within the provision.[210] In fact, the requirement of demonstrating an effect has been a fundamental principle since the ECJ's very first judgement on Article 102 TFEU, namely *Continental Can*. The ECJ held, among other things, that Article 102 TFEU:

> [...] refers only to practices which have <u>effects on the market and are to the detriment of consumers or trade partners</u>. Further, Article [102 TFEU] reveals that the use of economic power linked with a dominant position can be regarded as an abuse of this position only if it constitutes the means through which the abuse is effected.[211] (underlining added)

The ECJ stated that conduct constitutes abuse only if it is the result of the dominant position (causality), and more importantly if it has effects on the market. A requirement of demonstrating an effect was thereby established. This assigned a responsibility on the Commission, and the EU Courts, to make sure that the finding of abuse is based on a harmful effect. Based on this rationality, the requirement of an effect is no novelty; rather, it may be viewed as standard practice. It follows from that paragraph that the effect may harm either consumers or competitors of the dominant firm. This led to the principle that Article 102 TFEU covers not only conduct that directly cause harm to consumers but also conduct which causes consumers harm through their impact on competition.[212] That principle has thereby evolved into the requirement of an effect detrimental to effective competition.

However, it was not until *Hoffman La Roche* that this requirement became clear. Although it is nearly 40 years since *Hoffman La Roche* was delivered, it still contains the overall definition of abuse of dominance (a definition still relied upon by the EU Courts). In this definition, the ECJ held that the concept of abuse, besides being an objective concept, covers conduct:

> [...] which is such as to influence the structure of a market where, as a result of the very presence of the undertaking in question, the degree of competition is weakened and which, through recourse to methods different from those which condition normal competition in products or services on the basis of the transactions of commercial operators, has the effect of hindering the maintenance of the degree of competition still existing in the market or the growth of that competition.[213] (underlining added)

---

210. How to demonstrate/establish anti-competitive foreclosure effect may be the [contributory] cause for the argument that showing such effects is revolutionary.
211. *See* Case 6/72, *Continental Can*, at 19.
212. *See* e.g., Case C-52/09, *TeliaSonera*, at 24.
213. *See* Case 85/76, *Hoffman La Roche*, at 91.

Even though the ECJ did not specify whether that effect had to be proven or could be presumed due to the specific type of conduct (or the form),[214] whether it is sufficient to prove a likely or actual effect, and so on, *Hoffman La Roche* clarified that the effect caused by a dominant firm's exclusionary conduct is the reason for applying Article 102 TFEU.[215] Without an effect, Article 102 TFEU cannot be applied, and hence, there can be no abuse.

Since then, case law has repeated the requirement established in *Hoffman La Roche*.[216] More recent case law has specified that the requirement involves an anti-competitive [foreclosure] effect. For example, the ECJ has rejected the Commission's argument that there is no need to demonstrate an anti-competitive effect if a foreclosure effect has been demonstrated. In *TeliaSonera*, the ECJ ruled out:

> [...] that the very existence of a pricing practice of a dominant undertaking which leads to the margin squeeze of its equally efficient competitors can constitute an abuse within the meaning of Article 102 TFEU <u>without it being necessary to demonstrate an anti-competitive effect.</u>[217] (underlining added)

Accordingly, even if conduct by a dominant firm produces a foreclosure effect – in this case squeezing the margins of its competitors – such conduct constitutes exclusionary abuse only if it is harmful to effective competition. More precisely, the ECJ held that the anti-competitive effect "must relate to the possible barriers which such a pricing practice may create to the growth on the downstream market of the services offered to end users and, therefore, on the degree of competition in that market."[218] This wording clearly bears resemblances to the paragraph in *Hoffman La Roche* where the effect related to "the impairment of existing competition or the growth of that competition". But this is not merely a coincidence but in fact a deliberate wording. As it follows from *TeliaSonera*, the ECJ directly deduced the requirement of an anti-competitive effect from the concept of abuse established in *Hoffman La Roche*.[219] Accordingly, even if the term anti-competitive foreclosure effect may be relatively new, the requirement of demonstrating such effect is no novelty. Instead, it is merely evidence of the constant evolution in EU competition law which includes, among other things, elaboration of terms.

In consequence, exclusionary conduct constitutes abuse only if it involves a foreclosure effect which is anti-competitive; i.e., an anti-competitive foreclosure effect. Such requirement is consistent with the purpose of Article 102 TFEU. If conduct does not harm effective competition, and thereby, consumers' interest (or is likely to do so)

---

214. *See* e.g., Gormsen, Liza, *Are Anti-Competitive Effects Necessary for an Analysis under Article 102 TFEU?*, 36 World Competition (2013) 223, at 226–7.
215. Advocate General Wahl reached a somewhat similar conclusion in his opinion in *Intel*, *see* Opinion of Advocate General Wahl of 20 October 2016 in Case C-413/14 P, *Intel Corporation Inc. v. European Commission*, at 66.
216. In British Airways the ECJ applied the word "exclusionary effect", *see* Judgment of 15 March 2007 in Case C-95/04 P, *British Airways plc v. Commission of the European Communities* ("*British Airways*"), at 68.
217. *See* Case C-52/09, *TeliaSonera*, at 61. *See also* Case C-280/08 P, *Deutsche Telekom*, at 250–1.
218. *See* Case C-52/09, *TeliaSonera*, at 62; Case C-280/08 P, *Deutsche Telekom*, at 252.
219. *See* Case C-52/09, *TeliaSonera*, at 61. That paragraph refers to paragraph 27 in the same judgement where the former is copied from Case 85/76, *Hoffman La Roche*, at 91.

that conduct is part of competition on the merits which will lead to the departure from the market or the marginalization of competitors who are less efficient and so less attractive to consumers from the point of view of, among other things, price, choice, quality or innovation. The mentioning of anti-competitive (foreclosure) effects in recent case law and the *Article 102 Guidance Paper* is therefore merely amplifications that not every exclusionary conduct is contrary to Article 102 TFEU.[220] As a result, the requirement is a fundamental principle of the application of Article 102 TFEU [with respect to exclusionary abuses].

3 DEFINING ANTI-COMPETITIVE EFFECT

According to the findings above, an anti-competitive foreclosure effect is a prerequisite of finding any exclusionary abuse. The obvious question is then how such effect is demonstrated. Before embarking on that inquiry (see the chapters following this one), it is important to examine what such effects involve. It is, in other words, important to have a definition. In that respect, this section will conduct an analysis of how anti-competitive foreclosure effects can be defined with help from case law, the *Article 102 Guidance Paper,* and legal and economic literature.

Initially, it can be noticed that the term "anti-competitive foreclosure effect" reveals two main elements: (i) an *anti-competitive* element, and (ii) a *foreclosure* element.[221] Both elements can be viewed as screening tools. The foreclosure element screens whether conduct harms actual or potential competitors while the anti-competitive element screens whether the foreclosure effect is detrimental to effective competition and consumers' interest. Accordingly, neither the anti-competitive element nor the foreclosure element is sufficient without the other. Of course, if alleged exclusionary conduct by a dominant firm is anti-competitive then it most likely also features a foreclosure effect. However, not every (unjustifiable) anti-competitive effect is necessarily exclusionary abuse, as it may constitute exploitive or discriminatory abuse. Causality is therefore needed. The foreclosure element ensures that the needed causality is demonstrated. If the dominant firm's conduct does not cause the anti-competitive effect, then no *exclusionary* abuse can be held. The foreclosure element is by this means a tool to examine whether conduct is exclusionary or exploitive (or discriminatory).[222] It should be kept in mind that in practice the foreclosure and anti-competitive element may in some events overlap.

---

220. *See* Case C-209/10, *Post Danmark I*, at 22; Case C-52/09, *TeliaSonera*, at 43.
221. *See the Article 102 Guidance Paper*, at 19. The Commission states: "[...] ensure that dominant undertakings do not impair effective competition by foreclosing their competitors in an anti-competitive way [...]." *See also* Petit, Nicolas, *From Formalism to Effects? The Commission's Communication on Enforcement Priorities in Applying Article 82 EC*, 32 World Competition (2009) 485, at 489 (He centres on the Commissions Article 102 Guidance Paper, and as a result, uses "consumer harm" instead of "anti-competitive effect").
222. If increases in prices are observed, they may either by the product of exclusionary, discriminatory or exploitative conduct. If the dominant firm is able to raise it price without a foreclosure effect, then its conduct cannot be held as exclusionary.

3.1 Foreclosure Element

Article 102 TFEU seeks to limit anti-competitive conduct by dominant firms without chilling pro-competitive conduct by such companies. Since great similarities exist between these two types of conduct, the mentioned object is complicated.[223] In principle, every contract between two firms forecloses alternative sellers or buyers from some portion of the market, namely the portion consisting of what was bought.[224] That is., any conduct that affects competitors, even pro-competitive conduct, can be seen as exclusionary. When a dominant firm wins a sale to a customer or acquires an input from a supplier, competitors are excluded from those sales or purchases. Additionally, even if prices are set above a competitive level, inefficient firms may be either excluded or prevented from entering the market.

Obviously, not all these types of foreclosure are covered by the purpose of limiting anti-competitive conduct. Foreclosure is not necessarily problematic. Foreclosure in the form of, for instance, depriving sales of competitors is a natural consequence of performing [better] in a market. This is clearly within competition on the merits, and it would be foolish to prohibit it. However, foreclosure can be problematic where such deprivation of sales adds an extra benefit besides those steaming from the extra sales made or if it impedes or precludes competitors from additional sales/purchases to/from that customer/supplier besides those made by the dominant firm.[225] Such conduct is exclusionary. It should be stressed that, of course, this does not demonstrate the second element.

More specifically, a dominant firm may either foreclose actual competitors from the market or prevent potential competitors from entering that market. In cases such as *Intel*, *Post Danmark I* and *Akzo* an actual competitor has been in focus,[226] while cases such as *TeliaSonera* and *Deutsche Telekom* has centred more on potential competitors.[227] That the term embraces both types of foreclosure also follows from the *Article 102 Guidance Paper*.[228] In that respect, it is worth mentioning that the markets in *TeliaSonera* and *Deutsche Telekom* were both newly liberalized markets. As a result, the competition had not settled, and hence, competitors were trying to enter the market and gain a foothold at the time of the investigations.[229]

---

223. This is only complicated by the fact that it seeks to prohibit conduct which exclusionary, exploitative and discriminatory.
224. *See* Judge Stephen Breyer's opinion in *Barry Wright Corporation, Plaintiff, Appellant, v. Itt Grinnell Corporation, et al., Defendants, Appellees*, 724 F.2d 227 (1983).
225. *See* Bernheim, Douglas & Heeb, Randal, *A Framework for the Economic Analysis of Exclusionary Conduct, in* The Oxford Handbook of International Antitrust Economics (Roger D. Blair & D. Daniel Sokol eds.), 2015, at 20.
226. *See* Case T-286/09, *Intel*; Case C-209/10, *Post Danmark I*, at 25 & 44; Case 62/86, *Akzo*, at 70.
227. *See* Case C-52/09, *TeliaSonera*, at 88; Case C-280/08 P, *Deutsche Telekom*, at 169.
228. *See the Article 102 Guidance Paper*, at 19.
229. In *Deutsche Telekom*, for example, the German telecommunications markets had been liberalized as of 1 August 1996, while the Commissions investigations took place from 1999 to 2003 (the first complaint was lodged as of 18 March 1999 and the decision was given as of 21 May 2003), *see* Commission Decision of 21 May 2003 in Case COMP/C-1/37.451, 37.578, 37.579, *Deutsche Telekom AG*, at 2 & 7.

Whether the focus is (particularly) on exclusion or preventing entry will depend on whether actual or potential competitors are in focus. Some cases may centre on one of these, while others may consider both. All types of exclusionary conduct can cause both effects.[230] There should, therefore, be no general rule for when one is preferred before the other. On the other hand, it may be relevant to make such distinction in certain situations. This may be the event of newly liberalized markets. In such markets, a dominant firm may hold a first mover advantage or the fruit of a legal monopoly. Even though such advantages are not abusive in themselves,[231] they create special market circumstances. Therefore, such cases differ from the classic example of exclusionary abuse and may warrant a stricter view; i.e., ease on the foreclosure (and anti-competitive) element.

Not only complete foreclosure, i.e., eliminating a competitor from a market or barring a competitor from accessing a market, fulfils the requirement of foreclosure effect. Marginalization of competitors or restricting their access to a part or parts of the market may also constitute abuse.[232] Additionally, the EU Courts have held, in numerous cases, that a foreclosure effect occurs where not only access to the market is made impossible for competitors, but also where that access is made more difficult.[233] With this vague term "made more difficult", any competitive behaviour by a dominant firm runs the risk of being abusive since it makes it more difficult for competitors to compete compared to the event where the dominant firm did not compete. However, since the purpose of Article 102 TFEU is to protect effective competition, it should not matter to what degree one or more competitors are foreclosed. Nevertheless, if there is no foreclosure effect there can be no anti-competitive effect. Accordingly, there must be some degree of foreclosure as harm to competition and consumers' interest will otherwise constitute exploitative or discriminatory abuse. The degree of foreclosure may further serve as guidance on whether competition is harmed; for example, the as efficient competitor test may illustrate that entry is made more difficult, while other factors will be used to determine whether that foreclosure is anti-competitive.

The Commission held recently in its decision in *Telefonica* that demonstrating foreclosure effects does not mean that rivals are forced to exit the market:[234] it is sufficient that the rivals are disadvantaged and consequently led to competing less

---

230. For instance, by making it impossible to generate a profit, margin squeeze conduct can both excluded actual competitors present on the downstream market as well as hinder access by potential competitors to the downstream market.
231. It is well known in economic literature that advantages (and disadvantages) are the essence of competitive process, *see* Porter, Michael, *The Competitive Advantage: Creating and Sustaining Superior Performance*, 1998.
232. *See* e.g., Case C-549/10 P, *Tomra*, at 42; Case C-209/10, *Post Danmark I*, at 22.
233. *See* e.g., Case T-286/09, *Intel*, at 88; Case C-52/09, *TeliaSonera*, at 63; Case C-280/08 P, *Deutsche Telekom*, at 253; Case 322/81, *Michelin I*, at 85.
234. *See also* Case T-201/04, *Microsoft*, at 1089. The GC held that "[i]t must be made clear that the Commission did not state that the tying would lead to the elimination of all competition on the market for streaming media players. Microsoft's argument that, several years after the beginning of the abuse at issue, a number of third-party media players are still present on the market therefore does not invalidate the Commission's argument."

aggressively.[235] However, *disadvantaged* seems at first glance unsuitable with foreclosure effect.[236] It risks embracing too much. For example, any innovation by dominant firms will likely lead to an advantage over its competitors, and hence, disadvantages competitors. However, creating such advantages (and disadvantages) is the essence of competition.[237] Instead, and it is likely the Commission meant so, such (dis)advantages is only deemed contrary to Article 102 TFEU when achieved through other means than competition on the merits – just as exclusion is problematic only when achieved by using methods other than those parts of competition on the merits.[238] It ought, in other words, only to be problematic when anti-competitive.

This was the case in *Microsoft* where Microsoft had tied its Windows Media Player to its Windows Operating System. The GC found Microsoft's competitors were placed in a disadvantageous competitive position compared to Microsoft since the tying prevented developers of third-party media players from competing with Microsoft on "the intrinsic merits of the products."[239] In other words, this disadvantage harmed competition. Additionally, it must be noted that the Commission's statement in *Telefonica* was made in the context of showing that the conduct at hand had had an actual effect on competitors' ability to enter the relevant market and exert a competitive constraint.[240]

Accordingly, four general types of foreclosure effects exist. First, if conduct is successful, it may cause the exit of actual competitors. Second, it may marginalize an actual competitor thereby constraining its ability to compete effectively – for example, a competitor may lose some of its investors or not achieve economies of scale; hence, it may not be able to invest in the competition – or discipline it, so it adapts to the dominant firm's strategy. Third, it may prevent potential competitors from entering the market. Fourth, conduct may slow the entrance of competitors to the market by, for example, allowing firms to enter only a part of the relevant market. Accordingly, the burden of proof in relation to a foreclosure effect present little disadvantage.[241] Most conduct by dominant firms involves a foreclosure effect, and foreclosure effects may even exist where the dominant firm markets shares are decreasing (e.g., by slowing down entrance or expansion by its competitors).[242]

In general, non-pricing conduct (for instance, an exclusivity agreement) is always exclusionary since it prevents the customer[243] from making additional purchases from

---

235. *See* Commission Decision of 4 July 2007 in Case COMP/38.784, *Wanadoo España v. Telefónica*, at 586.
236. *See* Petit (2009), at 489–90.
237. *See* e.g., Porter (1998). *See also* Chapter 3 in which effective competition is discussed.
238. *See* e.g., Case C-209/10, *Post Danmark I*, at 25 (and cited case law).
239. *See* Case T-201/04, *Microsoft*, at 1047. *See also* paragraph 653 in regard of the refusal to license.
240. *See* Case COMP/38.784, *Wanadoo España v. Telefónica*, at 586.
241. *See*, however, Chapter 6 and 7 in which a stricter benchmark for foreclosure is held.
242. *See* e.g., Case T-286/09, *Intel*, at 186; Case C-95/04 P, *British Airways*, at 297; Judgment of 30 September 2003 in Case T-203/01, *Manufacture française des pneumatiques Michelin v. Commission of the European Communities* ("*Michelin II*"), at 297.
243. Or a supplier is prevented from making additional sales.

a competitor to the dominant firm.[244] In other words, if the object was simply to sell its goods to a customer then there should not be any reason, in addition to that sale, to require foreclosure of its competitor(s).[245] Of course, the anti-competitive element is not necessarily demonstrated and, even in that case, pro-competitive effects may justify it.[246] On the other hand, pricing conduct (for instance predatory pricing) is not as clear-cut. It will depend on a comparison of prices and costs in most events. As will be addressed later in Chapter 6, a price above costs will generally not be exclusionary while prices below costs can be viewed as generally exclusionary.[247] In consequence, non-pricing conduct is generally exclusionary while it for pricing conduct, as a rule, is true when the price is below costs. Part 3 will go into detail on this matter.

3.2 Anti-competitive Element

It was concluded in the previous subsection that the foreclosure element is, in general, fairly simple to establish. However, not all types of foreclosure constitute exclusionary abuse within the meaning of Article 102 TFEU. Finding conduct to be exclusionary is a necessary but not a sufficient condition of finding exclusionary abuse.[248] It must also be anti-competitive. The anti-competitive element is, in other words, the decisive element in finding an unlawful restriction of competition as the foreclosure effect otherwise is legitimate competitive behaviour or, in other words, part of competition on the merits. Moreover, Article 102 TFEU is not aimed at hindering competition but rather to prevent conduct from harming effective competition. As a result, some foreclosure must be allowed, as it is the basic mechanism of competition. Some win and some lose.

In contrast to the foreclosure element, the anti-competitive element has been less conspicuous in case law, which was illustrated in section 2. On the other hand, it has been very important in legal and economic literature.[249] Here it has been the synonym

---

244. *See* for that effect Case T-286/09, *Intel*, at 87. The GC held "that exclusivity rebates granted by an undertaking in a dominant position are by their very nature capable of foreclosing competitors." It should be noted that while the GC used this argument to justify its conclusion on finding abuse it illustrates that the EU Courts are aware that some types conduct is in general exclusionary. However, stating that that type of conduct is general anti-competitive seems to be incorrect (or at least imprecise). They may, by their very nature, be capable of foreclosing competitors, but they cannot be regarded as by their very nature being capable of harming competition to the detriment of consumers' interest. *See* below.
245. *See* Bernheim & Heeb (2015), at 20.
246. This aspect (that the anti-competitive effect is not also necessarily demonstrated) may be the reason why *Intel* has caused so much debate. The GC concluded that exclusivity rebates are inherently unlawful due to their foreclosure effect, *see* Case T-286/09, *Intel*, at 89.
247. Moreover, this also raises the question of which costs is relevant.
248. *See* Wright, Joshua, *Simple but Wrong or Complex but More Accurate? The Case for an Exclusive Dealing-Based Approach to Evaluating Loyalty Discounts*, speech given on 2013 at the Bates White 10th Annual Antitrust Conference; Wright, Joshua, *Moving beyond Naive Foreclosure Analysis*, 19 George Mason Law Review (2012) 1163; Jacobson, Jonathan, *Exclusive Dealing, "Foreclosure", and Consumer Harm*, 70 Antitrust Law Journal (2002) 311. *See also* Case C-209/10, *Post Danmark I*, at 44; Case C-52/09, *TeliaSonera*, at 61.
249. *See* for an overview Petit (2009), at 491–3.

of harm to consumers or consumer welfare.[250] It was not until somewhere around the turn of the century, though, that the EU courts began referring to the anti-competitive element.[251] Albeit this lack of explicit references, this element has always been required as concluded in section 2. Here, it was concluded that the anti-competitive effect referred to in *TeliaSonera* has its roots in the concept of abuse laid out in *Hoffman La Roche*. What the anti-competitive entails, therefore, can be traced back to case law as early as *Hoffman La Roche*.

As the anti-competitive element screens whether exclusionary conduct is contrary to Article 102 TFEU, it must relate to the purpose of the provision. The definition of the anti-competitive effect is, therefore, an effect that harms effective competition. The EU Courts' has in some cases stressed that the anti-competitive effect relates to the possible barriers which that type of conduct could create to the growth on the market and, therefore, on the degree of competition in that market.[252] Accordingly, harm to competition involved whether artificial barriers were caused. The aim was to assess whether the dominant firm's conduct was capable of making it more difficult, or impossible, for as efficient competitors to enter the market concerned reducing the competitive pressure on the dominant firm.[253]

Such definition resembles the foreclosure element. However, the key difference is that while most foreclosure [of as efficient] competitors is exclusionary, only foreclosure which harms effective competition is anti-competitive. Though conduct can fulfil both elements concurrently in some events,[254] it is not necessarily the case for all types of conduct. In consequence, the difference between harmed competition and non-harmed competition is important. As argued in Chapter 2, the main concern is that injury to effective competition leads to negative effects for consumers; hence, such harm is where consumers experience higher prices, lower innovation, quality or variety (or is likely to do so). When assessing anti-competitive effects, one must ask whether harm to consumers' interest is likely to happen (if no actual harm has yet occurred). This is further in line with case law and in particular *Post Danmark I*.[255] *Post Danmark I* has further been interpreted as emphasizing impact on competition cannot depend on the narrow question of whether the degree of competition is reduced but rather it must be considered how the reduction of competition harms consumers –[256] which is just another way of saying that only foreclosure which harms *effective* competition can be regarded as abusive. This is clearly in line with the above as the

---

250. *See* in general Padilla & O'Donoghue (2013).
251. The EU Courts first applied the wording *anti-competitive* in cases such as for instance Judgment of 7 October 1999 in Case T-228/97, *Irish Sugar plc v. Commission of the European Communities* ("*Irish Sugar*"); Case T-203/01, *Michelin II*.
252. *See* e.g., Case C-52/09, *TeliaSonera*, at 62.
253. *See id.* at 63.
254. *See* for that effect the discussion of by object restrictions in Chapter 4.
255. *See* Case C-209/10, *Post Danmark I*, at 44.
256. *See* e.g., Rousseva & Marquis (2013), at 43–51.

issue is not the number of competitors or the specific market share of the dominant firm.

It is also in line with the Commission's decisional practice, which has used the term *anti-competitive* in wider extent than case law.[257] The same is true for the *Article 102 Guidance Paper* where an anti-competitive foreclosure effect is defined as the situation "where effective access of actual or potential competitors to supplies or markets is hampered or eliminated as a result of the conduct of the dominant undertaking whereby the dominant undertaking is likely to be in a position to profitably increase prices to the detriment of consumers."[258] It should be noted that the expression "increase prices" refers not only to the power to maintain prices above the competitive level. Instead, it refers to all various type of harm in which the parameters of competition can be influenced to the advantage of the dominant firm and the detriment of consumers.[259] This includes parameters such as prices, output, innovation, the variety or quality of goods or services and so on. Nevertheless, the Commission acknowledge, like the ECJ in *Post Danmark I*, that the anti-competitive effect relates to conduct which harms consumers' interest. Again, not all foreclosure is prohibited.

In consequence, what is to be proven is harm to effective competition in respect of consumers' interest (in the manner effective competition was defined in Chapter 2). In other words, one must assess whether a decline in competition (i.e., foreclosure) leads or is likely to lead to, for instance, higher prices or a lower level innovation. How exclusionary conduct might produce such effects under the effect-based approach is addressed in more detail in Part 3.

3.3 General Definition

From this inquiry, it can be concluded that an anti-competitive effect includes a *foreclosure element* and an *anti-competitive element*. The effect, in total, may be referred to as an anti-competitive foreclosure effect. This aids the understanding of the term as it illustrates the definition of the term including the elements to be examined. That the effect may be termed as anti-competitive foreclosure finds support in not only the EU courts' case law but also the Commission's *Article 102 Guidance Paper*. Figure 3.1 illustrates the definition of the anti-competitive effect.

---

257. *See* e.g., Commission Decision of 14 December 1985 in Case IV/30.698, *ECS/AKZO*, at 83; Commission Decision of 22 December 1987 in Case IV/30.787 and 31.488, *Eurofix-Bauco v. Hilti*, at 81.
258. *See* for that effect *the Article 102 Guidance Paper*, at 19.
259. *See* for that effect *id.* at 11th *Article 102 Guidance Paper*, paragraph 11.

Figure 3.1   Definition of the Anti-Competitive Foreclosure Effect

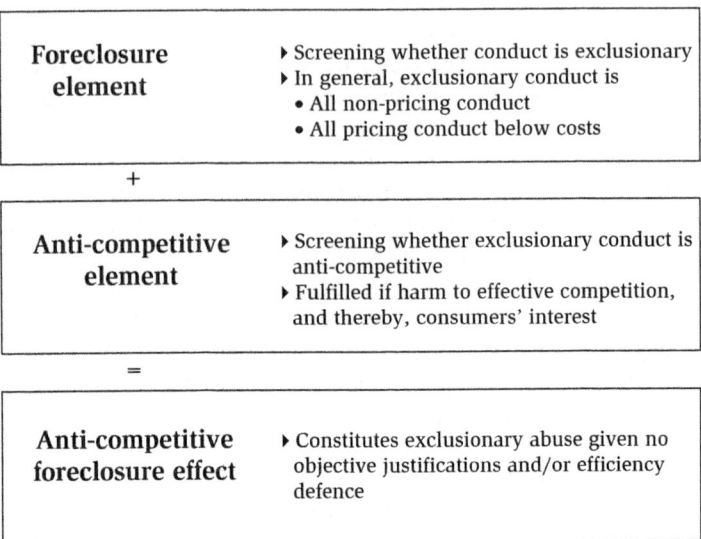

4   THE BURDEN OF PROOF

It was concluded in the previous sections that the assessment of exclusionary abuse is subject to the requirement of demonstrating an anti-competitive foreclosure effect. Such effects were also defined. One question remains, though: what the burden of proof is? This question is probably one of the topics currently generating the highest uncertainty among commentators in respect of Article 102 TFEU. The uncertainty seems to stem from the fact that the EU Courts have used, and continue to use, different terms to refer to the threshold of likelihood of anti-competitive effects that a conduct needs to produce for it to be considered abusive. Therefore, this section will examine whether an actual effect is required including whether historical conduct alters these findings and whether a De Minimis rule applies for exclusionary conduct.

4.1   Actual Versus Potential Effect

It follows from the EU Courts' case law that exclusionary abuse involves an effect detrimental to effective competition. Accordingly, to constitute abuse alleged conduct must have an exclusionary effect on actual or potential competitors to the detriment of effective competition – if the first part is not achieved then it may constitute exploitive or discriminatory abuse. This effect may involve either the exclusion of competitors from the market or the barring of their access to that market. From this outset, prohibiting only actual effects is unfit for demonstrating exclusionary abuse.

The EU Courts' case law, as well as the Commission's decisional practice, is in line with this. It shows that to establish exclusionary abuse within the meaning of Article 102 TFEU, it is not a requirement that there has been an actual or concrete effect. This was made clear in the judgments of the GC in *Michelin II* and *British Airways*. In the first case, Michelin had argued that according to case law[260] the Commission should have carried out an analysis of the actual effects in the specific case. However, the GC disagreed with that argument. It held instead that:

> [t]he "effect" referred to in the case-law cited in the preceding paragraph does not necessarily relate to the actual effect of the abusive conduct complained of. For the purposes of establishing an infringement of Article [102 TFEU], it is sufficient to show that the abusive conduct of the undertaking in a dominant position tends to restrict competition or, in other words, that the conduct is capable of having that effect.[261] (underlining added)

That not only actual effects are sufficient was repeated by the GC in its judgment in *British Airways*. Here the argument was similar to the one applied by Michelin, and the reply of the GC likewise similar. In consequence, the GC established in both cases that a potential effect might be sufficient. If conduct tends to restrict competition or is capable of having such effect, then that is sufficient evidence of an effect. In such events, the GC identifies a likely effect. However, the fact that these statements have come from the GC creates the uncertainty of whether they are truly valid. This depends on whether the ECJ agrees. *Michelin II* was not appealed to the ECJ; hence, we do not know the ECJ's stand on that judgment. However, *British Airways* was appealed. Here British Airways argued that the actual or probable effects should have been examined.[262] The ECJ, indirectly, agreed that an assessment is subject to the requirement of demonstrating, at least, probable effects, but rejected the argument that such effects had not been demonstrated in the case;[263] thereby, confirming a probable effect is sufficient.

The ECJ has since then confirmed that not only actual effects are prohibited. In its recent preliminary ruling in *Post Danmark II*, the ECJ clarified that it suffices to prove a probable anti-competitive effect.[264] Likewise, in *TeliaSonera,* the ECJ held that while an anti-competitive effect must be demonstrated that effect does not necessarily have to be concrete since it is sufficient to demonstrate that there is a *potential* anti-competitive effect.[265] In consequence, a potential effect may be sufficient to establish exclusionary abuse. Behind this argument is the potentially great costs that would incur if a competition authority would have to wait for an actual effect to occur. Re-establishing effective competition will be difficult and may even be impossible. The ability to take precautionary measures against potential negative effects is, therefore,

---

260. The reference was made to the ECJ's definition of the concept of abuse is Hoffman La Roche where that paragraph includes the part "has the effect of hindering", *see* Case 85/76, *Hoffman La Roche*, at 91.
261. *See* Case T-203/01, *Michelin II,* at 239.
262. *See* Case C-95/04 P, *British Airways,* at 92.
263. *See id.* at 98.
264. *See* Case C-23/14, *Post Danmark II,* at 74.
265. *See* Case C-52/09, *TeliaSonera,* at 64.

favourable; also in the view of consumers' interest. That it is important for the Commission (and NCAs) to be able to take precautionary measures is also acknowledged by the Commission itself. In a speech, Neeile Kroes (former European Commissioner for Competition Policy) held that the Commission:

> [...] will not wait until actual effects have manifested themselves. If we wait until rivals are forced to leave the market then we have two serious problems. First, you cannot resuscitate a corpse. No matter how effective the regulatory intervention, if it only happens after exit has occurred, then the damage to the market may be permanent. Second, such intervention will completely miss many examples of consumer harm that weaken competitors, but do not kill them. Competitors may be wounded, confined to a small corner of the market, but not killed. Leaving these cases to one side is a recipe for serious under-enforcement.[266]

As a result, the burden of proof is satisfied if it is demonstrated that there is likely, probable or potential anti-competitive effect. This has also been termed as whether alleged exclusionary conduct tends to have an anti-competitive [foreclosure] effect or is capable of having that effect. "Tend to" has also become the standard of whether alleged conduct constitutes abuse by the ECJ.[267] The two terms (i.e., "tend to" and "capable of") have been used synonymously.[268]

As a result, if alleged conduct is capable of having anti-competitive effects it tends to lead to such effect. "Tend to" and "capable of" can, however, be very different terms with different meanings within the English language; hence, potentially leading to uncertainties and misunderstandings of the burden of proof. The first term refers to something being disposed or inclined to do something or be in the habit of something. The later term, typically, refers to something "having the power or ability to do something". Accordingly, if those meanings are applied, then the terms are fundamentally different. For example, the EU Courts may have the power, and the ability, to annul the Commission's Article 102 TFEU decisions (when appealed), but it may not necessarily be inclined to do so. In fact, there is the opposite tendency. This could cause a low burden of proof. Moreover, "capable of" is more form-based since characteristics determine whether conduct has the ability/power to cause anti-competitive effects. In contrast, "tend to" can be more effect-based as alleged conduct must be inclined to cause an effect and not just have the ability/power to do so. Despite this, both terms can be form-based and further has been so in case law. In both *Michelin II* and *British Airways*, referred to above, exclusionary abuse was established based on characteristics of the dominant firms' conduct.

Nonetheless, "capable of" can be used in the same sense as "tend to". This also seems to be the case concerning case law. This follows from the fact that whether conduct is capable of having such effect requires an assessment done in the context of the circumstances of the case. This was made clear by the ECJ in *Tomra* where it stated

---

266. *See* Kroes, Neelie, *Exclusionary Abuses of Dominance – The European Commission's Enforcement Priorities*, speech given on 2008 at Fordham University Symposium, New York.
267. *See* e.g., Case 322/81, *Michelin I*, at 73. *See also* Case C-209/10, *Post Danmark I*, at 26.
268. *See* e.g., Case C-549/10 P, *Tomra*, at 68; Judgment of 17 December 2003 in Case T-219/99, *British Airways plc v. Commission of the European Communities* ("*British Airways*"), at 293.

that only an analysis of the circumstances of the case might make it possible to establish whether conduct by a dominant firm is capable of excluding competition.[269] In consequence, it is not sufficient that alleged conduct is *generally* capable of having anti-competitive effects.[270] For example, an exclusivity agreement is generally capable of having foreclosure effects since they remove that customers' freedom to choose his supplier and further bar entry of competitors, but it depends on the specific circumstances of the case whether the exclusivity agreement is capable of harming effective competition [to the detriment of consumers]. Some kind of likely anti-competitive effect is, in other words, required. In that context – when the capability is examined within the relevant circumstances of the case – it is reasonable to use the terms synonymously. This includes not only those two terms ("tends to" and "capable of") but also "likely to", "potential effect" and "probable effect".[271] If the relevant circumstances of a case are applied to the inquiry of whether conduct is capable of distorting competition, then a likely/probable/potential effect is shown. This is what the EU Courts do,[272] and hence, that is how the terms are to be understood.

As a result, if it is possible to demonstrate a likely anti-competitive [foreclosure] effect, then actual effects are redundant. Can a likely effect not be demonstrated; an actual effect must be established. This is also the method applied under Article 101 TFEU. Here, actual effects are only required given it has not been established that the agreement is likely to have negative effects.[273] Lastly, in the absence of any effect on effective competition, alleged conduct cannot be classified as exclusionary abuse.[274]

4.2 Historical Effect

As illustrated above, actual effects are not necessary if a likely effect can be demonstrated. This is mainly due to the fact that waiting for actual effects may create serious problems and be costly for consumers. But what if the Commission (or an NCA) does not have to wait? The question is, in other words, whether the Commission is required to prove actual effects if alleged conduct is historic. In such event, the Commission will be able to identify the impact, and it may, therefore, make sense to require actual effects. According to case law, though, the Commission is not required to establish actual effects even when conduct at issue is historic.

---

269. *See* Case C-549/10 P, *Tomra*, at 43.
270. In that respect *see* the discussion in Chapter 4 concerning whether capability in itself is sufficient to establish a by object restriction. This discussion is based to a great extent on recent judgments by the ECJ under Article 101 where it has been ruled that a sufficient degree of harm in the specific case is necessary.
271. *See* Padilla & O'Donoghue (2013), at 269–70.
272. In addition to what have already been discussed, the GC interprets "potential effect" and "capable of" as the same. *See* the reference to *TeliaSonera* (where it is established that a potential effect is sufficient) as the argument for why "capable of" is sufficient, *see* Case T-286/09, *Intel*, at 103.
273. *See* e.g., Judgment of 11 September 2014 in Case C-67/13 P, *Groupement des cartes bancaires (CB) v. European Commission* ("*Cartes Bancaires*"), at 51; Judgment of 4 June 2009 in Case C-8/08, *T-Mobile Netherlands BV and others v. Raad van bestuur van de Nederlandse Mededingingsautoriteit* ("*T-Mobile*"), at 31.
274. *See* Case C-52/09, *TeliaSonera*, at 66.

This was recently held in *Intel* where such an argument was dismissed.[275] On the other hand, it is likely that this only concerns conduct found to have the purpose of harming effective competition. In such events, alleged conduct is prohibited due to its likelihood to harm effective competition as well as the degree of that potential harm. As a result, if the object of a dominant firm's conduct is to harm effective competition, it is prohibited even in the absence of an actual effect. There still need to be a potential effect, obviously, but that is proven by the anti-competitive object. In other words, where a dominant firm actually applies conduct with the purpose of foreclosing effective competition, the fact that the desired result is not ultimately achieved does not alter its categorization as abuse within the meaning of Article 102 TFEU.[276] Not only successful abuse is prohibited but also "attempted abuse".

In the event where conduct has the effect of harming effective competition, this may not be true. Since an effect must be demonstrated, and not just presumed, the actual effect can be important. In consequence, actual effects are likely to be of greater significance when assessing historical conduct. It is important in that context to keep in mind that anti-competitive foreclosure effect does not only cover full exclusion of competitors or barring their entry to the market but also marginalization or making entry more difficult. Accordingly, even if the dominant firm's market share may have remained the same, or even fallen, a partial effect may still be demonstrated. For example, in *Post Danmark I* the plaintiff had been able to win back customers, and the ECJ treated an allegation of abuse with scepticism on that ground.[277] Despite this, the ECJ still acknowledged the possibility of harmful effects if such could be demonstrated.[278] As a result, even though there appears to be an absence of effects, this may not be true. Alleged conduct may have disciplined that competitor from pricing low or invest in innovation; thus, it would be unwise to assume that no effect exists without further examination. In that context, it may be impossible to determine when an effect should have materialized. Therefore, having an absolute requirement of actual effect, even in regards to historical conduct, would be inappropriate.

All things considered, if conduct is historical, it may influence an assessment of whether conduct has the effect of harming effective competition, but it cannot be an absolute requirement. If it has such purpose, instead, it has no relevance as the likely effect is shown through the demonstration of a by object restriction. On the other hand, however, it may be of relevance in regards to justifications or claims of damages.

4.3   De Minimis Threshold and Appreciable Effect

As with historical conduct, the question is further whether insignificant effects can amount to exclusionary abuse. If a dominant firm, for instance, offers an exclusivity agreement or a price below costs to one customer who represents 1% of the relevant market, will such conduct be found contrary to Article 102 TFEU? The question, in

275. *See* Case T-286/09, *Intel*, at 103.
276. *See* for that effect Case C-52/09, *TeliaSonera*, at 65.
277. *See* Case C-209/10, *Post Danmark I*, at 39.
278. *See id.* at 44.

other words, is whether Article 102 TFEU contains a De Minimis Threshold and/or a requirement of an appreciable effect. This has been the subject of examination as early as in *Hoffman La Roche*. Here the ECJ held:

> Moreover since the course of conduct under consideration is that of an undertaking occupying a dominant position on a market where for this reason the structure of competition has already been weakened, within the field of application of Article [102 TFEU] any further weakening of the structure of competition may constitute an abuse of a dominant position.[279] (underlining added)

Due to the dominant position, further weakening of effective competition is prohibited no matter the degree of that weakening. This puts pressure on the assessment of dominance since the finding of dominance has great consequences. However, it also assists in setting a framework for a dominant position. Analogy, therefore, will suggest that if such already weakened competition is not present, then no dominant position can be found. It does, however, raise the question of how to define already weakened competition. Since the dominant position is beyond the scope of this book, it suffices to say that such already weakened competition will be assumed, as a dominant position is presupposed.

Going back to the question of whether a De Minimis Threshold exists, the GC's took the same stance in *Intel* as the ECJ had taken in *Hoffman La Roche*. Intel argued that the Commission ought to have taken into consideration that its conduct concerned only a small part of the market.[280] However, the GC rejected such argument and even directly dismissed a criterion of an appreciable effect or De Minimis Threshold.[281] Similarly, the ECJ rejected a De Minimis Threshold in *Post Danmark II*.[282] However, it is debatable whether this is, and ought to be, entirely true. It makes sense to reject a De Minimis Threshold for conduct having the purpose of restricting competition but not necessarily for those having such effect. In other words, the de Minimis threshold would apply only for by object restrictions. This is similarly the case for Article 101 TFEU.[283] In a recent preliminary ruling, *Expedia*, the ECJ clarified that an agreement, which has an anti-competitive object, constitutes, by its nature and independently of any concrete effect that it may have, an appreciable restriction on competition.[284]

---

279. *See* Case 85/76, *Hoffman La Roche*, at 123.
280. In this context is should be remembered that Intel based this on another market definition than the relevant market defined by the Commission which, of course, was larger; hence, made the impact look smaller than the Commission findings.
281. *See* Case T-286/09, *Intel*, at 116.
282. *See* Case C-23/14, *Post Danmark II*, at 73.
283. *See* e.g., Communication of the Commission of 30 August 2014 OJ 2014/C 291/01, *Notice on agreements of minor importance, which do not appreciably restrict competition under Article 101(1) of the Treaty on the Functioning of the European Union* ("*De Minimis Notice*"), at 2 & 13. In the latter paragraph the Commission states that the De Minimis Notice "does not cover agreements which have as their object the prevention, restriction or distortion of competition within the internal market."
284. *See* Judgment of 13 December 2012 in Case C-226/11, *Expedia Inc. v. Autorité de la concurrence and Others* ("*Expedia*"), at 37.

This is justified by the fact that by object restrictions can be regarded, by their very nature, as being injurious to the proper functioning of normal competition.[285] Accordingly, since there is no need to take account of the effects of an agreement once it appears it has as its object the restriction of competition, there is no need to consider whether the effect is significant. Moreover, it risks removing the purpose of the by object categorization if it was a requirement to show a significant effect. Otherwise, the assessment would be closer to the one under by effect restrictions since the effect must be known before it can be concluded whether it is significant. Following the example of Article 101 TFEU, it is logical to dismiss a De Minimis Threshold, or an appreciable effect threshold, under Article 102 TFEU concerning by object restrictions.

Concerning by effect restrictions, it is less logical. It depends on, among other things, whether competition is really believed to be so disadvantaged that it cannot endure even the slightest damage. This seems unlikely. Nevertheless, drawing lines for when conduct may cause anti-competitive effects based on, for instance, the percentages of customer affected is also likely to be unfit for Article 102 TFEU. Such thresholds will depend on each case. This is also acknowledged by the ECJ which has found it to be artificial to establish, without prior analysis, the portion of the tied market beyond which conduct by a dominant firm may have an exclusionary effect on competitors.[286] Accordingly, a De Minimis threshold like the one known from Article 101 TFEU does not fit Article 102 TFEU; this is only more obvious when it is remembered that the De Minimis Threshold in Article 101 TFEU concerns market shares of the parties.[287] Article 102 TFEU does already include a sort of De Minimis Threshold as only conduct by dominant firms can be subject to the provision. Adding an additional De Minimis rule would, accordingly, seem odd since anti-competitive conduct is liable to give rise to not insignificant restrictions of competition.[288]

Even if a De Minimis Threshold is unfit for Article 102 TFEU, the question of whether the effect is significant should be considered in terms of by effect restrictions – at least indirectly. This could be achieved, for instance, by assessing whether any effect is likely in the case at hand rather than just whether alleged conduct is generally likely to lead to such effects. Therefore, while a potential effect is sufficient,[289] a purely hypothetical effect cannot be held as a likely effect.[290] Additionally, it could be achieved when assessing justifications by a dominant firm. Here one of the conditions, which need to be demonstrated, is whether alleged conduct has not eliminated effective competition by removing all or most existing sources of actual or potential competition.[291] Accordingly, if the effect is insignificant, it is likely that fulfilling this condition is easier.

---

285. *See* Chapter 4.
286. *See* Case C-23/14, *Post Danmark II*, at 73; Case C-549/10 P, *Tomra*, at 43.
287. *See De Minimis Notice*, at 8.
288. *See* Case C-23/14, *Post Danmark II*, at 73.
289. *See* e.g., *Id.* at 66; Case C-52/09, *TeliaSonera*, at 64.
290. *See* Case C-23/14, *Post Danmark II*, at 65.
291. *See the Article 102 Guidance Paper*, at 30.

Despite this, the ECJ has explicitly held that there is no need to show an anti-competitive effect is of a serious or appreciable nature.[292] However, this is attributable to the dominant position.[293] Due to the dominant position, competition is already seen as hampered instead of being harmed by conduct, which justifies the lack of a requirement of appreciable effects. Conduct by a dominant firm does not always affect the market, which is dominant on, though. Conduct such as especially tying and bundling, refusal to supply or deal and margin squeeze will foreclose competition on a distinct market where the firm is not necessarily dominant. In that event, the assumption of an already weakened market cannot be applied.[294] This accord with economic theory that for such types of conduct, a significant effect is required. Therefore, if existing competition is not hampered, exclusionary conduct must have a significant effect. However, where competition is already hampered, protecting competition requires a stricter approach since it is not able to withstand that conduct. As a result, any harm on competition under Article 102 TFEU is seen as significant.

It should be noticed that the discussion above referred to the anti-competitive foreclosure effect in whole, which indirectly supposes that an effect has been demonstrated.[295] That is, if such effect has been demonstrated, the degree of which it affects the relevant market is irrelevant. On the other hand, the question of appreciable effect may matter for demonstrating the anti-competitive foreclosure effect in the first place.[296]

4.4 Concluding Remarks

Summarizing (see Table 3.1), it is not required to show an actual anti-competitive foreclosure effect since a likely or potential effect is sufficient. If a likely effect can be demonstrated, it will be pointless to require proof of actual effects as competition might suffer irreversible injuries. In that context, historical evidence may assist either if it can confirm that the likely effect, in fact, did occur or if there was no effect. Two points must be noticed, though. First, anti-competitive foreclosure effects do not only cover the event where the dominant firm gains market power but also where it preserves it or slows a decline in that market power. Accordingly, a decline in market shares cannot disprove an anti-competitive foreclosure effect. Second, if a dominant firm applies

---

292. *See* Case C-23/14, *Post Danmark II*, at 74.
293. *See id.* at 70.
294. *See* for that effect *Streetmap.EU Limited v. Google Inc., Google Ireland Limited and Google UK Limited*, EWHC 253 (Ch) (2016).
295. *See* Case C-23/14, *Post Danmark II*, at 70. The ECJ stated: "As regards, in the second place, the serious or appreciable nature of an anti-competitive effect, although it is true that a finding that an undertaking has a dominant position is not in itself a ground of criticism of the undertaking concerned [...], the conduct of such an undertaking may give rise to an abuse of its dominant position because the structure of competition on the market has already been weakened [...]."
296. For a discussion of appreciability and likely effects, *see* e.g., Colomo, Pablo Ibáñez, *Appreciability and De Minimis in Article 102 TFEU*, 7 Journal of European Competition Law & Practice (2016) 651.

exclusionary conduct with the purpose of foreclosing effective competition, the fact that the desired result is not ultimately achieved does not alter its categorization as abuse.

Furthermore, a De Minimis threshold to determine whether there is an abuse of a dominant position is not justified within Article 102 TFEU. As the provision only applies to dominant firms, a threshold is already applied. On the other hand, it may be relevant whether the effect is appreciable. When alleged conduct affects the market on which the dominant firm holds its dominant position the effect is, by its very nature, liable to be appreciable. However, if it affects a distinct market, on which that firm is not dominant, then the effect must be appreciable.

Albeit the lack of a requirement of showing an appreciable effect or consider historic effects, this does not equal abuse. If a dominant firm is restricting competition due, for instance, its object, it is not certain that the case will be pursued. This may be due to the resources that are required compared to possible benefits of penalizing the firm. Even if a case is pursued, the dominant firm may be able to justify its conduct. If the effect is insignificant, the chance of justifying that conduct may be greater compared to a scenario where that conduct affected the whole market. Lastly, it may have an impact on claims of damages and the fine that is imposed on the dominant firm.

Table 3.1   Overview: The Burden of Proof

	By Object Restriction	*By Effect Restriction*
– Are actual effects required?	– No, a potential effect is sufficient.	– No, a likely effect is sufficient.
– Do historical effects matter?	– No, if the purpose is to harm competition the result does not matter.	– It may assist, but it is not adequate alone.
– Does Article 102 TFEU include a De Minimis Threshold?	– No, the notion of dominance already includes one.	– No, the notion of dominance already includes one.
– Must the effect be appreciable?	– No, such conduct is by its very nature appreciable.	– If conduct affects a distinct market without dominance, then yes – If conduct affects the dominant market, then no.

PART II Research Question No. 1

CHAPTER 4

By Object Restrictions Within Article 102 TFEU

1 INTRODUCTION

Article 102 TFEU, or more precisely the case law of Article 102 TFEU, has stirred up a debate in recent decades and one of the most debated aspects is the approach taken to exclusionary abuse.[297] That debate, as will be discussed in more detail later, concerns criticism of the so-called form-based approach with the result that that approach should be abandoned in favour of the effect-based approach. At the same time, the proponents of the effect-based approach have a tendency to present a choice between the two approaches.[298] While there is no doubt that anti-competitive effects have been subject to increased attention by the EU Courts and the effect-based approach, in that way, has gained increased acceptance, it would be wrong to conclude that the effect-based approach is the only way to assess exclusionary conduct.

On the contrary, the effect-based approach is merely one out of two different approaches that can be applied. In other words, exclusionary conduct can be assessed according to either the form-based approach or the effect-based approach. The fact that not all types of exclusionary conduct are subject to the effect-based approach – i.e., an analysis of the actual or likely effects – is due to the fact that these types of conduct are by their very nature capable of being harmful to effective competition. In this regard, Advocate General Kokott's drunk driving analogy serves as an illustrative example. In her opinion in *T-Mobile*, Kokott explained why drunk driving is always illegal as our

---

297. One just has to take a look at the debated caused by the GC's judgment in *Intel*. Here a number of articles have been devoted to criticising the approach taken by the GC. *See*, among others, Peeperkorn (2015); Petit (2015); Geradin, Damien, *Loyalty Rebates After Intel: Time for the European Court of Justice to Overrule Hoffman-La Roche*, 11 Journal of Competition Law and Economics (2015) 579; Venit (2014); Nihoul (2014). It should be pointed out that the approach has also been defended. *See*, among others, Whish (2015); Wils (2014).
298. *See e.g.*, Wils (2014), at 410 (Who addresses this aspect).

experience warns us of the likelihood to cause harm. The risk of harm is sufficiently great to warrant an outright prohibition, rather than judging infringements on a case-by-case basis. With this example, the reason behind by object restrictions in Article 101 TFEU was explained.[299]

Contrary to Article 101 TFEU, the text of Article 102 TFEU does not include such a distinction.[300] Instead, conduct is unlawful if it constitutes abuse that "may affect trade between Member States." This difference between Article 101 and 102 TFEU has further been addressed by the GC. It held that Article 102 TFEU, unlike Article 101 TFEU, "contains no reference to the anti-competitive aim or anti-competitive effect of the practice referred to. However, in the light of the context of Article [102 TFEU], conduct will be regarded as abusive only if it restricts competition."[301] As will be addressed in the next section, such distinction is, nevertheless, evident in the application the provision – and even in that case. While only Article 101 TFEU contains a direct reference to such categorization, it should be remembered that both provisions seek to achieve the same aim.[302] Therefore, it is only logical that they do so through the same means meaning by object restrictions are not limited to Article 101 TFEU. Experience and (economic) theory may also warn us of the likelihood of some types of conduct to cause harm within Article 102 TFEU in the same way it warns us of some types of agreements.

For that reason, it will be illustrated that a distinction between by object restrictions and by effect restrictions exists within Article 102 TFEU. This will build on the EU Courts' case law since the inquiry is whether such distinction exists and not whether it should exist. In addition to this, by object restrictions will be defined. Such definition explains when the effect-based approach is to be applied; i.e., through the process of elimination (conduct that does not fall within the by object category is subject to the effect-based approach).

2   FORM TO EFFECT

One area which has triggered a wide-ranging debate, and still continues to do so, is the so-called form-based approach[303] (and the effect-based approach).[304] The discussion

---

299. See Opinion of Advocate General Kokott of 19 February 2009 in Case C-8/08, *T-Mobile Netherlands BV and Others*, at 47.
300. Some commentators have reasoned the divergence between Article 101 and 102 TFEU in the fact that the term also had to catch conduct that exploits consumers, *see* Sinclair, Duncan, *Abuse of Dominance at a Crossroads – Potential Effect, Object and Appreciability under Article 82 EC*, 25 European Competition Law Review (2004) 491; Loewenthal, Paul-John, *The Defence of "Objective Justification" in the Application of Article 82 EC*, 28 World Competition (2005) 455.
301. See Case T-203/01, *Michelin II*, at 237.
302. See Case 6/72, *Continental Can*, at 25.
303. The origin of the term "form-based approach" appears to be in the 1990s debate on the reform of the block exemption regulations for vertical agreements under initially Article 85(3) EEC and then Article 81(3) EC (now Article 101(3) TFEU), *see* Whish, Richard, *Regulation 2790/99: The Commission's "new style" Block Exemption for Vertical Agreements*, 37 Common Market Law Review (2000) 887; Wils (2014).
304. See Ahlborn, Christian & Padilla, Jorge, *From Fairness to Welfare: Implications for the Assessment of Unilateral Conduct under EC Competition Law*, in European Competition Law Annual 2007 (Claus-Dieter Ehlermann & Mel Marquis eds.), 2008.

has primarily centred on a shift that would take the approach to exclusionary abuse from being formalistic to be based on (anti-competitive) effects.[305] In this regard, the form-based approach is criticized for being unsuitable concerning the assessment of exclusionary abuse since it is not able to take into account and properly evaluate the specific economics-based factors, which feature in each exclusionary abuse case.[306] Alongside this criticism, EU competition law has seen a modernization over the last decades; in particular true for Article 101 TFEU and in the EU Merger Control. Those provisions are recognized as being subject to the effect-based approach. As a result, it has been argued that time has come to consider a fresh reform for Article 102 TFEU.[307] Such reform would entail a shift towards the effect-based approach.

That criticism may be unfounded in the sense that the so-called formalistic case law is evidence of by object restrictions within Article 102 TFEU rather than lack of attention towards anti-competitive effects. This would certainly fit the findings in the previous chapter in which it was concluded that an anti-competitive foreclosure effect is, and has been, required in every case concerning exclusionary abuse. However, before that analyse can begin, it is appropriate to understand the two approaches. This is particularly important as the two terms can cause some confusion owing to the inconsistent meanings applied to the terms.[308]

2.1 Form-Based Approach

By its definition,[309] a form-based approach entails an assessment based on the form or the nature of a given type of exclusionary conduct.[310] The analysis, in other words, centres on whether alleged conduct matches a given type of conduct held as exclusionary abuse. If this is the case, then that particular conduct infringes Article 102 TFEU. One scholar has even defined the approach as an interpretation of competition law that requires courts to discount and even disregard relevant competitive effects.[311]

The first source for the form-based approach may be the text of Article 102 TFEU. As it is well known, the founders of the EU Treaty did not provide a clear definition of abuse, though. Instead, a non-exhaustive list of examples of abuse of dominance was provided. The analysis may rely on testing whether alleged conduct in the case at hand

---

305. *See e.g.,* Geradin, Damien, et al., DG Comp's Discussion Paper on Article 82: Implications of the Proposed Framework and Antitrust Rules for Dynamically Competitive Industries 2006, available at http://papers.ssrn.com/sol3/papers.cfm?abstract_id = 894466; Gual, et al. (2005).
306. Padilla & O'Donoghue (2013), at 68–69; Gual, et al. (2005).
307. *See e.g.,* Arezzo, Emanuela, *Is there a Role for Market Definition and Dominance in an Effects-Based Approach?,* in Abuse of Dominant Position: New Interpretation, New Enforcement Mechanisms? (Mark-Oliver Mackenrodt, et al. eds.), 2008, at 22.
308. For a great example, *see* the discussion between Rey & Venit (2015); Wils (2014).
309. Formalism is defined by Merriam-Webster dictionary as "a method, style, way of thinking, etc., that shows very careful attention to traditional forms and rules".
310. In *Intel* the GC applied such approach to its assessment as it held the alleged exclusivity rebates were "by their very nature capable of restricting competition", *see* Case T-286/09, *Intel,* at 85.
311. *See* Orbach, Barak, *The Durability of Formalism in Antitrust,* 100 Iowa Law Review (2015) 2197, at 2198.

resembles one of the four examples. In fact, different criticism has centred on such reliance,[312] which indicates such actual reliance by the Commission and the EU Courts. In consequence, the characteristics of a given type of conduct are the key element of the form-based assessment. If conduct can be characterized as, for example, predatory pricing – as in unfair selling prices mentioned in Article 102 TFEU (a) – it will be abuse of dominance within the meaning of Article 102 given no objective justifications can be presented.

The core of the form-based approach is further the limited amount, or even a lack,[313] of attention to whether the conduct generates actual or likely anti-competitive effects on the relevant market to reach a finding of abuses. Instead, following an examination of the formal features a capability to cause anti-competitive foreclosure effects on the market by alleged exclusionary conduct is inferred;[314] or in other words, a potential anti-competitive effect is inferred.[315]

This is due to the fact that Article 102 TFEU has been constructed in such a way that conduct cannot be allowed if its purpose is to strengthen the dominant position and thereby abuse it.[316] Purpose is not the subjective intention of the dominant firm, but the objective meaning and purpose of its conduct.[317] Subjective intention is not a necessary requirement for a finding of abuse,[318] but it can be a relevant factor.[319] Conduct that is found to have as its purpose the strengthening of a dominant position is, in other words, capable of restricting competition.[320] It is, by that token, deemed liable to produce harmful anti-competitive effects based on its form and/or because of its opposition to a fundamental aim of competition law. This approach has allowed the Commission to apply Article 102 TFEU by inferring anti-competitive effects without the necessity of proving those effects.[321] Such approach has resemblance to the Freiburg School, and as a result, the approach is also referred to as the "orthodox-approach".[322]

This approach can also be viewed as the preferred approach by "traditionalists".[323] According to this view, competition law protects more than economic welfare. As a result, a scepticism toward monopolies outweighs the (potential) benefits which they may produce owing to a strong belief in competition as a structure.[324] In the example of a merger leading to a monopoly with lower costs, those supporting an

---

312. See e.g., Eilmansberger, Thomas, *Dominance – The Lost Child? How Effects-Based Rules Could and Should Change Dominance Analysis*, 2 European Competition Journal (2006) 15; Niels, Gunnar & Jenkins, Helen, *Reform of Article 82 EC: Where the Link Between Dominance and Effects Breaks Down*, 11 European Competition Law Review (2005) 605.
313. See Gormsen (2013), at 232.
314. See e.g., Case C-549/10 P, *Tomra*, at 68.
315. See for that effect Case C-52/09, *TeliaSonera*, at 64.
316. See Case 27/76, *United Brands*, at 189.
317. See Case 85/76, *Hoffman La Roche*, at 90–1.
318. See Case C-549/10 P, *Tomra*, at 21.
319. Take for instance test for predatory pricing, see Case 62/86, *Akzo*, at 71–2.
320. See Judgment of 30 January 2007 in Case T-340/03, *France Télécom SA v Commission of the European Communities* ("*France Télékom*"), at 195. Upheld by Case C-202/07 P, *France Télécom*, at 48. See also Case C-549/10 P, *Tomra*, at 13.
321. See Gormsen (2013), at 228.
322. See e.g., *Id.*
323. See Monti (2013).
324. See *id.* at 45.

effect-based approach will assess whether the pro-competitive effects (increase in productive efficiencies) offsets the anti-competitive effects (reduction in allocative efficiencies). In contrast, the "traditionalist" would argue that the merger must be blocked as economic freedom and structure of competition is more important than productive efficiencies owing to the argument that monopolies are less likely to benefit competition and it is difficult to predict the actual welfare impact.[325]

Such an approach can be justified by, mainly, two arguments. First, such approach provides legal certainty.[326] Dominant firms, as well as other interested parties, will have reliable expectations regarding the outcome of different types of exclusionary conduct when the form-based approach reigns. The dominant firm, in other words, knows *ex ante* whether it is abusing that position. In the extreme case, dominant firms will have a checklist of different types of conduct that it must refrain from – unless justifications can be provided. It can be argued that with such knowledge this will lead to more aggressive competition since dominant firms will not need a "buffer" for the price since it knows where the line between abuse and legitimate conduct is. On the other hand, it may lead to less aggressive competition since firms, when being dominant, are refrained from applying conduct which are/can be pro-competitive; hence, actually being harmful to consumers instead of benefiting them.[327] This, however, requires pro-competitive types of conduct to be banned.

Second, enforcement costs are reduced.[328] When abuse can be determined by a limited analysis, the needed resources are less than compared to applying an extensive analysis of the actual or likely anti-competitive effects. Moreover, a form-based approach softens the knowledge problem for competition agencies and courts compared to the one an effect-based approach can cause. The approach makes it both easier and less costly to find abuse. However, such approach may have other costs. It risks leading to both Type I errors (false positives) and Type II errors (false negatives). A pure form-based approach is, therefore, often considered to provide legal certainty and timely enforcement, but at a too high cost of false positives and false negatives.[329]

Accordingly, the approach assumes, which it has been criticized for,[330] easily the existence of anti-competitive effects.[331] The form-based approach is by some scholars held as resembling the per se-approach known from US antitrust law.[332] However, they are not the same. While this is discussed in more detail in section 5.1.3, one comment

---

325. *See* Künzler, Adrian, *Economic Content of Competition Law: The Point of Regulating Preferences*, *in* The Goals of Competition Law (Daniel Zimmer ed., 2012).
326. *See e.g.*, Østerud, Erik, *Identifying Exclusionary Abuses by Dominant Undertakings under EU Competition Law: the Spectrum of Tests*, 2010, at 67.
327. *See* Gual, et al. (2005).
328. *See e.g.*, Østerud (2010), at 67.
329. *See* Petit (2009), at 486; Gual, et al. (2005).
330. *See* Roeller, Lars-Hendrik & Stehmann, Oliver, *The Year 2005 at DG Competition: The Trend towards a More Effects-Based Approach*, 29 Review of Industrial Organization (2006) 281, at 282.
331. The ECJ has held that "prices below average variable costs must be considered prima facie abusive inasmuch as, in applying such prices, an undertaking in a dominant position is presumed to pursue no other economic objective save that of eliminating its competitors", *see* Case C-202/07 P, *France Télécom*, at 109.
332. *See e.g.*, Petit (2009), at 485 (and references).

is worth making. Contrary to the per se-approach, dominant firms found infringing Article 102 TFEU has always been able to justify their conduct. In consequence, the form-based approach may instead be viewed as a "burden-shifter"; i.e., shifting the burden from the Commission to the dominant firm in demonstrating whether its alleged conduct infringes Article 102 TFEU.

Additionally, the findings of abuse in the so-called formalistic case law, as explained in more detail in Chapter 3, have been based on anti-competitive effects. There is, however, the issue of whether the lack of actual anti-competitive effects can be justified as conduct caught by the form-based approach.[333] One the one hand, the ECJ has dismissed a decrease in the dominant firm's market shares as evidence for disproving abusive conduct.[334] On the other hand, it may be a question of how actual effects are understood as the ECJ has stated that in the absence of any effect on the competitive situation of competitors, conduct cannot be classified as an exclusionary conduct,[335] and that the anti-competitive effect of a particular practice must not be of purely hypothetical.[336] However, if the purpose of a given type of conduct is that of restricting competition, the fact that the desired result is not ultimately achieved does not alter its categorization as abuse within the meaning of Article 102 TFEU.[337] In other words, there is a potential effect, which is not purely hypothetical, if a purpose of restricting competition is established. This can be illustrated by the extreme example of a firm with 100% market shares that succeeds in deterring entry. Market shares are not increased, but effective competition may still be harmed to the detriment of consumers. Alternatively, the firm may preserve its dominant position by only foreclosing a part of the market – for example, letting its competitor increase its market share from 5% to 10% (it has then doubled its market share) but not more than that – which the ECJ has established as contrary to Article 102 TFEU.[338]

2.2 Effect-Based Approach

In contrast to the form-based approach, the effect-based approach does not rely on an assessment of the form. Instead, it centres on the actual or likely anti-competitive effect caused by a dominant firm's conduct.[339] In that matter, it weighs all of the circumstances of a case in deciding whether conduct should be prohibited. In practice,

---

333. See Gormsen (2013), at 232–33.
334. See Case C-95/04 P, British Airways, at 293; Case T-203/01, Michelin II, at 239.
335. See Case C-52/09, TeliaSonera, at 66.
336. See Case C-23/14, Post Danmark II, at 65.
337. See for that effect Case C-52/09, TeliaSonera, at 65.
338. In Tomra, the ECJ held that "the foreclosure by a dominant undertaking of a substantial part of the market cannot be justified by showing that the contestable part of the market is still sufficient to accommodate a limited number of competitors. First, the customers on the foreclosed part of the market should have the opportunity to benefit from whatever degree of competition is possible on the market and competitors should be able to compete on the merits for the entire market and not just for a part of it. Second, it is not the role of the dominant undertaking to dictate how many viable competitors will be allowed to compete for the remaining contestable portion of demand." See Case C-549/10 P, Tomra, at 42.
339. See Gual, et al. (2005).

however, it employs a burden-shifting framework entailing courts will rarely be required to balance effects;[340] i.e., if an actual or likely anti-competitive effect is established, the burden of proving pro-competitive effects which offset the negative then shifts to the dominant firm. This means that the plaintiff (in practice the Commission) has the initial burden of demonstrating the alleged conduct produced or threatens to produce anti-competitive effects. If successful, then the burden shifts to the defendant (i.e., the dominant firm) who must provide justifications for its exclusionary conduct. If successful, the Commission or the EU Courts then has to decide whether these effects do, in fact, offset the negative effects. Accordingly, if no effect can be demonstrated, no exclusionary abuse can ever be established.

While this has some resemblance to the form-based approach, the difference lies in the careful examination of the actual or likely effects. By focusing on the effects of alleged conduct rather than on the form, an effects-based approach is argued to make the circumvention of competition policy constraints more difficult for companies.[341] At the same time, this approach provides a more consistent treatment of practices. As recalled from above, one characteristic of the form-based approach was its limited consideration of effects. Accordingly, the effect-based approach takes into account that many types of conduct may have different effects depending on the specific settings; hence, distorting competition in some cases and promoting efficiencies and innovation in others.[342] As the assessment is not based on the form of particular conduct but the anti-competitive effect, the competition authority needs to identify a theory of harm and assess the extent to which such a negative effect on consumers is potentially outweighed by potential efficiency gains proved by the dominant firm.[343] There needs to be a story, a coherent narrative which explains harm to consumers backed by facts and evidence.[344] Accordingly, the effect-based approach is comparable to the rule of reason-approach known in the US.

Furthermore, while the form-based approach presents some advantages for both firms (legal certainty) and competition authorities (reduction of enforcement costs), respectively, its shortcomings are argued as almost certainly more significant compared to the effect-based approach.[345] Under the form-based approach, competition enforcers run the risk of committing type-I and type-II errors. Type-I errors waste not only taxpayers money but also send undesirable signals to dominant firms, which may be deterred from adopting efficient (or unproblematic) courses of conduct.[346] Instead, an effect-based approach is more likely to reduce the risk of type-I errors due to its more in-depth analysis; i.e., the assessment of the effect.

---

340. *See* Orbach (2015), at 2216.
341. *See* Roeller & Stehmann (2006), at 282.
342. *See id.* at 2216.
343. *See* Gual, et al. (2005), at 3.
344. *See* Mosso, Carles, *The More Economic Approach Paradigm: An Effects-based Approach to EU Competition Policy, in* Structure and Effects in EU Competition Law: Studies on Exclusionary Conduct and State Aid (Wolfgang Wurmnest & Jürgen Basedow eds.), 2011, at 19.
345. *See e.g.*, Østerud (2010), at 67; Petit (2009), at 486; Roeller & Stehmann (2006).
346. *See* Petit (2009), at 486.

The core of the effect-based approach is, therefore, the case-by-case assessment in contrast to the more "static" assessment under the form-based approach. In consequence, a presumed anti-competitive effect is, in contrast to the form-based approach, insufficient. This entails a need for a [more] economic-based analysis since a limited analysis will be inadequate. The effect-based approach is sometimes also referred to as the "[more] economic approach".[347] The application of the term "effect-based approach" will in the following include the term "economic approach". In other words, the terms are used synonymously.

2.3 Has a Shift Happened?

As illustrated above, Article 102 TFEU case law is generally considered as formalistic. The starting point is, therefore, that a form-based approach has been the norm for the assessment of exclusionary abuse. This ought not to be too controversial, as economic models often rely on different features; for example, the nature of the products, what kind of information customers have, entry barriers and so on.[348] There is, of course, a great difference between checking off the features of an economic model and simply looking at the alleged conduct and checking whether it is a specific type of conduct not including the features of, for instance, the market. Nevertheless, some degree of formalism may be required to structure a meaningful decision-making process.[349]

An attempt to shift, or even modernize, the approach towards an effect-based one has then been attempted. This attempt has its origins in the gap between the EU Courts' case law and the expressed need to ensure that even dominant companies can compete where doing so would be beneficial for consumers.[350] The attempt has, however, not been successful if it measured in terms of whether a full shift has taken place.[351] Steps toward implementing the effect-based approach have, nonetheless, been taken. Possibly, the first step, or milestone, was a report issued July 2005 by a committee of economists, the Economic Advisory Group on Competition Policy (the "EAGCP Report"). Unsurprisingly, the EAGCP Report heavily advocated an effect-based approach.[352]

This was followed by the Commission's *Article 102 Discussion Paper*[353] and its *Article 102 Guidance Paper*, respectively. Both papers indicated, generally, a shift away from the EU Courts' [formalistic] case law and advocated, for example, the as efficient

---

347. *See e.g.*, Gual, et al. (2005); Nihoul (2014); Wils (2014). Some commentators argue, however that they are two different things, *see e.g.*, Peeperkorn (2015), at 45–6.
348. The same is also true for e.g., the stability of cartels. For instance, the number of firms in a market, all things being equal, will affect the stability; the more firms the less stable a cartel will be due to the increased gain of deviating from the cartel and vice versa.
349. *See* Orbach (2015), at 2199–2200.
350. *See* Rey & Venit (2015), at 5.
351. *See* Akman (2016).
352. *See* Gual, et al. (2005), at 8.
353. *See* Communication of the Commission of December 2005, *DG Competition discussion paper on the application of Article 82 of the Treaty to exclusionary abuses* ("*Article 102 Discussion Paper*").

competitor-test to be applied to all pricing conduct.[354] The proposed shift towards a greater devotion on the effects of alleged conduct was illustrated by its definition of exclusionary conduct contrary to Article 102 TFEU. This entailed that only exclusionary conduct with adverse effects on consumers was viewed contrary to Article 102 TFEU.[355]

However, the *Article 102 Guidance Paper* features an important reference to its role as merely enforcement priorities,[356] and more importantly, that it is not "intended to constitute a statement of the law and is without prejudice to the interpretation of Article [102 TFEU] by the Court of Justice or the Court of First Instance of the European Communities."[357] This, of course, gave rise to some concern, and even scepticism, that the method used for selecting cases might not be identical with the one employed once the case had been selected for enforcement action.[358] In other words, it was feared that the Commission would still rely on existing [formalistic] case law rather than the analyses advocated in the *Article 102 Guidance Paper*.

This concern for whether a shift would take place is aggravated by case law following the publications of the *Article 102 Guidance Paper*. Here *Tomra* and *Intel* are great examples –[359] while *TeliaSonera* and *Post Danmark I* stand as supporting cases for the *Article 102 Guidance Paper*.[360] One must, nevertheless, keep two facts in mind. First, *Tomra* and *Intel* were both appeal cases and the Commission decisions were initiated before the *Article 102 Guidance Paper* was published – and so had no legal relevance for the judgments –[361] while *TeliaSonera* and *Post Danmark I* were preliminary rulings. This meant that the ECJ was able, in the latter cases, to give its view on the appropriate assessment and not (just) whether the Commission's assessment was adequate. Second, the types of conduct assessed in *Tomra* and *Intel* differ from the types of conduct assessed in *TeliaSonera* and *Post Danmark I*. The alleged types of

---

354. *See e.g.*, the *Article 102 Guidance Paper*, at 23–7. *See* also paragraph 41 in regards of conditional rebates.
355. *See id.* at 19.
356. *See id.* at 2 "This document sets out the enforcement priorities that will guide the Commission's action in applying Article [10]2 to exclusionary conduct by dominant undertakings. Alongside the Commission's specific enforcement decisions, it is intended to provide greater clarity and predictability as regards the general framework of analysis which the Commission employs in determining whether it should pursue cases concerning various forms of exclusionary conduct and to help undertakings better assess whether certain behaviour is likely to result in intervention by the Commission under Article [102]."
357. *See id.* at 3.
358. *See* Geradin, Damien, *Is the Guidance Paper on the Commission's Enforcement Priorities in Applying Article 102 TFEU to Abusive Exclusionary Conduct Useful?*, in Competition Law and the Enforcement of Article 102 (Ioannis Kokkoris ed., 2010; Gormsen, Liza, *Why the European Commission's Enforcement Priorities on Article 82 EC Should Be Withdrawn*, 31 European Competition Law Review (2010) 45.
359. *See* generally Padilla & O'Donoghue (2013). *See* also e.g., Venit (2014); Federico (2011); Miralles, Graciela, *Tomra: Exclusive Dealing and Rebates in the Light (and Shadows) of Dominance*, 2 European Journal of Risk Regulation (2011) 129.
360. *See* Rousseva & Marquis (2013); Lundqvist & Ølykke (2013). For an overview of the case, *see* also Bergqvist, Christian, *Final Curtain or another Around on Post Danmark?*, 34 European Competition Law Review (2013) 287.
361. *See* Case C-549/10 P, *Tomra*, at 81.

conduct in the two former cases had a history of being unlawful.[362] Similar types of conduct had been established as capable of restricting competition by former case law thereby constituting abuse of dominance. In contrast to those, the alleged conduct in *Post Danmark I* had no "unlawful pedigree".[363]

In consequence, a complete shift away from the form-based approach known in [earlier] case law by the EU Courts to an effect-based approach has not taken place. Such complete shift is further unlikely. As will be shown in the following sections, the form-based approach constitutes one of two approaches which the Commission can apply to the assessment of alleged exclusionary conduct; i.e., finding a restriction of competition either by object or by effect – similar to Article 101 TFEU. In addition, the ECJ's preliminary ruling in *Post Danmark II* confirms that a more formalistic approach can suffice in showing a likely anti-competitive effect.[364]

Despite the fact that the form-based approach still has some merits, it is still open for improvements; for example, acknowledging more directly that conduct may or may not be detriment to consumers in different markets.[365] It would be welcomed, among other things, if it were explicitly acknowledged that exclusivity agreements and prices below variable costs cannot always be subject to a presumption of anti-competitive effects even when applied by dominant firms. Such false presumption would, clearly, be the case where competition is for the customer (for the former) or in a two-sided market (for the latter).[366] In these events such types of conduct are part of the market and the competition; hence, prohibiting such conduct would disable the dominant firm from competing [on the merits]. Additionally, a similar fine-tuning as the one that has

---

362. *See* in more detail section 4.
363. CMBT (Judgment of 16 March 2000 in Joined Cases C-395/96 P and C-396/96 P, *Compagnie Maritime Beige Transports SA and others v. Commission of the European Communities* ("*CMBT*").) cannot be consider as similar case to *Post Danmark I*. The fact that it was conduct carried out by a cartel and not by a single firm was a main influencer on the finding of abuse. This is illustrated by the Commission as it held "[i]n this regard, a distinction must be made between a concerted decision by several undertakings forming, in this case, a shipping conference aimed at fixing, within the framework of a plan, a special price to remove a competitor, and the case already examined by the Commission and the Court of Justice of abusively low prices established by a single undertaking acting unilaterally, where it was necessary to distinguish between predatory prices and aggressive competition." *see* Commission Decision of 23 December 1992 in Case IV/32.448 and IV/32.450, *Cewal*, at 80.
364. *See* Chan, Sunny, *Post Danmark II: Per Se Unlawfulness of Retroactive Rebates Granted by Dominant Undertakings*, 37 European Competition Law Review (2016) 43. For an opposite standpoint *see e.g.*, Colomo, Pablo Ibáñez, *Post Danmark II: The Emergence of a Distinct 'Effects-Based Approach to Article 102 TFEU*, 7 (2016) 113.
365. After all, Jean Tirole received his Nobel Prize "for his analysis of market power and regulation" since "[b]efore Tirole, researchers and policymakers sought general principles for all industries. They advocated simple policy rules, such as capping prices for monopolists and prohibiting cooperation between competitors, while permitting cooperation between firms with different positions in the value chain. Tirole showed theoretically that such rules may work well in certain conditions, but do more harm than good in others [...] The best regulation or competition policy should therefore be carefully adapted to every industry's specific conditions." *See* Nobel Prize Committee press release, http://www.nobelprize.org/nobel_prizes/economic-sciences/laureates/2014/press.html.
366. *See* the discussion of sufficient degree of harm in section 5.1.2.

been seen in the recent years concerning by object restrictions under Article 101 TFEU would be welcome to avoid "capability" and "potential effect" embracing too much.[367]

3   THE STANDARD IN ARTICLE 101 TFEU

A distinction between by object restrictions and by effect restrictions will have obvious resemblances to Article 101 TFEU; i.e., if by object restrictions can be found within Article 102 TFEU, they are likely to share many similarities with by object restrictions within Article 101 TFEU. It is for that reason appropriate to have an overview of by object restrictions within that provision. The point is not to give an exhaustive analysis but to illustrate, briefly, the rationale for by object restrictions, the criteria for determining by object restrictions and the relationship between by object and by effect restrictions within Article 101 TFEU.[368]

In this provision, infringements include agreements[369] having "as their object or effect the prevention, restriction or distortion of competition." Agreements having an anti-competitive object are exempted from an analysis of the anti-competitive effect since such effect is presumed.[370] In general, by object restrictions are those that can be regarded, by their very nature, as being injurious to the proper functioning of normal competition.[371] That can be assumed to be the case where an agreement, also having regard to its legal and economic context, has the specific capability (or tendency) to have a negative impact on competition. If the agreement does not restrict competition by object, it is then prohibited under Article 101 TFEU only if it is shown, based on an analysis of the actual and/or likely effects, it has the effect of restricting competition. In other words, by object restrictions may be held as being a presumption rule since the actual or likely effect is redundant.[372]

Different rationales for by object restrictions exist. There are three overall reasons (note that the second and third rationales are the same as those governing the form-based approach).[373] First, economics and experience tell us that some types of agreements are so likely to be harmful that the harm can be presumed. For instance, a horizontal agreement on setting prices is seen as harmful to consumers since the firms

---

367. See e.g., Case C-67/13 P, *Cartes Bancaires*.
368. For a more exhaustive analysis of restrictions by object within Article 101 TFEU *see*, among others, Bailey, David, *Restrictions of Competition By Object under Article 101 TFEU*, 49 Common Market Law Review (2012) 559. *See* also Sng, Yi Heng Alvin, *The Distinction Between "Object" and "Effects" in EU Competition Law and Concerns after Groupement des Cartes Bancairs (C-67/13 P)*, 37 European Competition Law Review (2016) 179; Calzado, Javier Ruiz & Scordamaglia-Tousis, Andreas, *Groupement des Cartes Bancaires v Commission: Shedding Light on What is not a 'by object' Restriction of Competition*, 6 Journal of European Competition Law & Practice (2015) 495. Kolstad, Olav, *Object Contra Effect in Swedish and European Competition Law*, 2009, Report on behalf of the Swedish Competition Authority.
369. Agreements are used in this context to describe the practices included in Article 101 TFEU. Consequently, the term agreements in this context also include collusion, concerted practice or the like.
370. See e.g., Case C-67/13 P, *Cartes Bancaires*, at 49.
371. See e.g., *Id.* at 50; Case C-226/11, *Expedia*, at 36.
372. See Kolstad (2009), at 5. *See* also e.g., Bailey (2012), at 563.
373. See Bailey (2012), at 562–70.

will rationally choose a price which achieves the monopoly price (or at least above the price which would have been set under competitive settings).[374] Moreover, analogies have been drawn between by object restrictions and "risk offences" by Advocates General Trstenjak and Kokott.[375] This involves that the experience of certain dangerous behaviour (for instance, drunk driving) leads to the prohibition of such. This entails, in other words, that such an offence applies irrespective of whether the accused drove safely and irrespective of whether his or her drunk driving did, in fact, result in any harm (for instance, a traffic collision). The risk of the anticipated danger is sufficient to commit the offence.[376] However, it is argued that this experience may not merely be based on experience acquired in the EU. Three other factors may inform the classification a by object restriction.[377] This include, insights of industrial organization involving empirical research demonstrating that an agreement is very likely to distort the competitive process,[378] experience from another jurisdiction,[379] and policy goals (for instance, conduct that impairs the creation of an internal market).[380]

Second, by object restrictions promote legal certainty. One of the advantages of by object restrictions is that they enable firms to have a relatively clear understanding of the legal consequences of their actions and adapt their behaviour accordingly.[381] Firms know the types of agreements they must refrain from unless they can justify them by satisfying the conditions set out in Article 101(3) TEUF. This also leads to deterrent effects.

Third, by object restrictions provide an analytical framework that facilitates an effective enforcement. Since actual effects are not required, the enforcement of such restrictions is less resourceful. It is clear that it avoids complex matters of demonstrating an actual or likely effect by merely finding a potential effect. Of course, this requires that the use of by object restriction is appropriate in the case; i.e., the agreement, having regard to its legal and economic context, has the specific capability/tendency to have a negative impact on competition.

As already mentioned, it follows [from case law] that for an agreement to be regarded as having an anti-competitive object, it is sufficient if it has the potential of having a negative impact on competition, that is to say, it is capable of resulting in the

---

374. See e.g., Bishop & Walker (2010).
375. See Opinion of Advocate General Trstenjak of 4 September 2008 in Case C-209/07, *The Competition Authority v. Beef Industry Development Society Ltd and Barry Brothers (Carrigmore) Meats Ltd*, at 46; Opinion of Advocate General Kokott in Case C-8/08, *T-Mobile*, at 47.
376. See Bailey (2012), at 563–4.
377. See id. at 564–5.
378. For empirical works see, among others, Levenstein, Margaret & Suslow, Valerie, *What Determines Cartel Success?*, 44 Journal of Economic Literature (2006) 43; Hay, George & Kelley, Daniel, *An Empirical Survey of Price Fixing Conspiracies*, 17 Journal of Law and Economics (1974) 13; Lande, Robert & Connor, John, *How High Do Cartels Raise Prices? Implications for Reform of the Antitrust Sentencing Guidelines*, 80 Tulane Law Review (2005) 513. (And the cited litterature).
379. See Opinion of Advocate General Roemer of 27 April 1966 in Case C-56/64, *Consten and Grundig v. Commission of the European Communities*, at 358 (who referred to the treatment of vertical territorial restrictions under US law).
380. See Goyder, Joanna, *Cet Obscur Objet: Object Restrictions in Vertical Agreements*, 2 Journal of European Competition Law & Practice (2011) 327, at 333 & 338.
381. See e.g., Motta (2004), at 191; Hay & Kelley (1974), at 151–2; Bailey (2012), at 565.

restriction of competition.[382] Accordingly, a by object restriction involves an agreement capable of restricting competition. The fact that some types of agreement are capable thereof is further the reasoning behind a distinction between by object and by effect restrictions.[383] Capability may, however, be held as only the starting point for finding a by object restriction;[384] i.e., capability is not in itself sufficient for the finding of a by object restriction.

The core criterion is, instead, whether an agreement reveals a sufficient degree of harm to competition. This was recently stressed by the ECJ in *Cartes Bancaires*.[385] If there is not a sufficient degree of harm to competition, an agreement cannot be regarded as being, by its very nature, harmful to the proper functioning of normal competition;[386] irrespective of its capability. Whether sufficient degree of harm is present depends on an assessment of the relevant circumstances of the case including the content of the agreement, its objectives and the economic and legal context of which it forms a part.[387] In consequence, whether an agreement can be regarded as by object restriction cannot only rely on the fact that it looks like such an infringement. However, it must be stressed that such an assessment is not as comprehensive as the one that is needed regarding actual or likely effects. The purpose is to assess whether that agreement is, in fact, a by object restriction within the context of the case, not whether it produces an actual or likely effect.

Summarized, by object restrictions are those which can be regarded, by their very nature, as being harmful to competition. This involves an assessment of the agreement in terms of whether it: (i) is capable of restricting competition, and (ii) shows a sufficient degree of harm in the individual case. Accordingly, demonstrating such restriction requires an assessment of the capability in the individual case at hand.

4 EVIDENCE FROM CASE LAW

The idea of by object restrictions within Article 102 TFEU, obviously, does not stem from a vivid imagination but from the EU Courts' case law.[388] It is, therefore, appropriate to analyse that case law with the purpose of presenting the evidence of such restrictions including the distinction between by object and by effect restrictions. In that context, it is important to divide this section into different subsections. This serves the purpose of providing an overview plus a list of examples. As a result, the

---

382. *See e.g.*, Judgment of 14 March 2013 in Case C-32/11, *Allianz Hungária Biztosító Zrt and others v. Gazdasági Versenyhivatal* ("*Allianz Hungária*"), at 38; Case C-8/08, *T-Mobile*, at 31.
383. *See e.g.*, Case C-226/11, *Expedia*, at 36.
384. Capability has in the literature after *Cartes Bancaires* been named "the lower benchmark" (while "sufficient degree of harm" is a higher benchmark) for finding by object restrictions, *see e.g.*, Murray, Grant, *In Search of the Obvious: Groupement Des Cartes Bancaires and "by Object" Infringements under EU Competition Law*, 36 European Competition Law Review (2015) 47.
385. *See* Case C-67/13 P, *Cartes Bancaires*, at 49.
386. *See id.* at 75.
387. *See id.* at 53 (and case law cited).
388. The idea of by object restrictions has also been addressed in recent literature, *see e.g.*, Colomo (2016), at 714–721; Østerud (2010), at 59. *See* also Opinion of Advocate General Wahl in Case C-413/14 P, *Intel*, at 80 & 82.

following subsections will consist of different types of conduct including: (i) exclusivity agreements and rebates, (ii) loyalty-inducing rebates, (iii) predatory pricing, (iv) tying (and bundling), and (v) margin squeeze. It must be stressed that this is neither an exhaustive list of types of exclusionary abuse within Article 102 TFEU nor a list of types of conduct that is always by object restrictions. Instead, the subsections below provide examples conduct that may be by object restrictions.

4.1 Exclusivity Agreements/Rebates

Evidence of by object restrictions can easily be found in case law.[389] One area where evidence is particularly noticeable is that of exclusivity agreements and rebates. In the seminal case *Hoffman La Roche*, the ECJ established that exclusivity agreements and rebates are unlawful when performed by a dominant firm.[390] While this in itself is a strong indication of by object restrictions, the illustrative evidence comes from the argument behind this strict view. In regards to exclusivity agreements, the ECJ held that "they are not based on an economic transaction which justifies this burden or benefit but are designed to deprive the purchaser of or restrict his possible choices of sources of supply and to deny other producers access to the market."[391] In similar veins, the ECJ held that a fidelity rebate (i.e., exclusivity rebate) "is designed through the grant of a financial advantage to prevent customers from obtaining their supplies from competing producers."[392] Accordingly, these types of conduct were abusive due to their anti-competitive nature and not their actual or likely anti-competitive effect. This is illustrated especially by the term "designed to" which reveals an anti-competitive purpose.

On the other hand, this case could merely be evidence of carelessness toward anti-competitive foreclosure effects, and hence, just old, formalistic case law. On the contrary, however, case law has since then confirmed the standpoint.[393] In *Intel*, exclusivity rebates were held as being anti-competitive by their very nature.[394] When compared to the definition of by object restrictions in Article 101 TFEU it is clear that the exclusivity rebate constituted a by object restriction. In other words, the purpose of these rebates is to prevent customers from obtaining their supplies from competitors.[395] In *Intel*, the GC also found that the "naked restrictions" (payment on the condition that the launch of competing products was either postponed or cancelled) "pursued an anti-competitive object."[396] In that context, the GC stated that:

> for the purposes of applying Article [102 TFEU], showing an anti-competitive object and an anti-competitive effect may, in some cases, be one and the same

389. *See* Colomo (2016).
390. *See* Case 85/76, *Hoffman La Roche*, at 89.
391. *See id.* at 90.
392. *See id.*
393. *See e.g.*, Case C-23/14, *Post Danmark II*, at 27.
394. *See* Case T-286/09, *Intel*, at 85.
395. *See id.* at 86.
396. *See id.* at 204.

thing. If it is shown that the object pursued by the conduct of an undertaking in a dominant position is to restrict competition, that conduct will also be liable to have such an effect.[397]

Thus, the GC – besides repeating *Michelin II* and *France Télékom* (*see* below) – established that there exist both by object and by effect restrictions and that Intel's exclusionary conduct fell within the first category. While this statement concerned the naked restrictions, one can argue in favour of it being applicable for exclusivity rebates as well. Both types of conduct involve exclusivity. In their extreme form, exclusivity rebates/agreements require the customer to buy only from the dominant firm while naked restrictions require the customer not to buy from other suppliers. Therefore, the result is the same; i.e., exclusivity. In consequence, case law concerning exclusivity agreements and rebates serves as evidence of by object restrictions within Article 102 TFEU.

Since the definition of these types of conduct are discussed in more detail in Chapter 5, section 2 it suffices to define exclusivity agreements as "an obligation or promise to obtain all or most of one's requirements exclusively from the dominant firm"[398] and exclusivity rebates (also known as fidelity – or loyalty rebates)[399] as "rebates the grant of which are conditional on the customer's obtaining all or most of its requirements from the dominant firm".[400] The "all or most of its requirements" are generally accepted when customers are obliged to buy 80% or more of its requirement from the dominant firm.[401] Accordingly, both types of conduct concerns either exclusivity or quasi-exclusivity from the customer. This requirement of exclusivity or quasi-exclusivity from the customer is further the reason why they fall within the by object category. According to the ECJ, such behaviour is not based on an economic transaction that justifies this burden or benefit but is designed to deprive the purchaser of or restrict his possible choices of sources of supply and to deny other producers access to the market.[402]

Of course, this raises the issue of whether this can truly be true even when a dominant firm applies an exclusivity agreement, for example, to only one customer who represents 1% of the market.[403] One could certainly frame a strong argument. However, there exists no requirement of an appreciable effect when dealing with by object restrictions (*See* Chapter 3, section 4.3). In the extreme form, this means that even if the desired result, namely that of foreclosing competitors, is not ultimately achieved that fact does not alter the finding of a by object restriction.[404] When a

---

397. *See id.* at 203.
398. *See e.g.*, Case 85/76, *Hoffman La Roche*, at 89.
399. *See e.g.*, Case C-23/14, *Post Danmark II*, at 27. *See* also Case T-286/09, *Intel*, at 76.(the GC defined exclusivity rebates as "fidelity rebates within the meaning of Hoffmann-La Roche").
400. *See e.g.*, Case T-286/09, *Intel*, at 76.
401. *See the Vertical Restraints Guidelines*, at 129. *See* also Colomo (2016), at 714–5. In *Intel* the lowest percentage was 80% (in the case NEC), *see* Case T-286/09, *Intel*, at 79.
402. *See* for that effect Case 85/76, *Hoffman La Roche*, at 90.
403. A famous argument against by object restrictions for exclusivity agreements and rebates, *see* e.g., Petit, Nicolas, *The Advocate General's Opinion in Intel v. Commission: Eight Points of Common Sense for Consideration by the CJEU*, Forthcoming Concurrences (2017).
404. *See* for that effect Case C-52/09, *TeliaSonera*, at 65.

dominant firm pursues an anti-competitive purpose, the actual or likely effect is by its definition redundant. While a dominant firm is restricting competition due to its object, it is not given that it will be found to have abused its position, though. First, it may be that the case will not be pursued due to enforcement priorities, and second, the chance of providing an objective justifying may be greater compared to a scenario where that conduct affected the whole market.[405]

All of this is, of course, not to say that exclusivity agreements and rebates are always by object restrictions, but rather that case law has found abuse of dominance according to this approach. In other words, these types of conduct within the relevant settings of the cases are examples of by object restrictions. While it is evident that such conduct is generally capable of restricting competition by tying customers,[406] it is not always the case. The relevant circumstances are therefore still important. For instance, it is highly important that the firm is an unavoidable trading partner. A recurrent circumstance of the cases has been the fact that the dominant firm has been an unavoidable trading partner.[407] If that relevant circumstance is not established a by effect restriction may be a better approach.

4.2 Loyalty-Inducing Rebates

Evidence can also be found in case law concerning loyalty-inducing rebates. Within this case law, some of the first direct evidence of by object restrictions can be found;[408] i.e., the first time anti-competitive versus anti-competitive effect has been addressed. For instance, the GC stated in *Michelin II* that:

> for the purposes of applying Article [102 TFEU], establishing the anti-competitive object and the anti-competitive effect are one and the same thing [...]. If it is shown that the object pursued by the conduct of an undertaking in a dominant position is to limit competition, that conduct will also be liable to have such an effect.[409] (Underlining added)

As is apparent from this statement, an anti-competitive effect is presumed if an anti-competitive object has been established. In other words, conduct can be viewed liable of producing an anti-competitive effect due to its anti-competitive object. By holding the object and effect as "one and the same thing", this could be interpreted as Article 102 TFEU only being relevant if a dominant firm's conduct has an anti-competitive object. However, such an interpretation would be too far-reaching. Conduct that does not have an anti-competitive object may still be harmful to effective competition (and conduct that restricts competition by effect does not necessarily

---

405. It may also affect the potential penalty and damages claims.
406. *See* Case T-286/09, *Intel*, at 86–7 in which the GC explains why exclusivity rebates is capable of restricting competition.
407. *See id.* at 91–3; Case 85/76, *Hoffman La Roche*, at 41. *See* also section 5.1.2.
408. *See* Case T-228/97, *Irish Sugar*, at 170.
409. *See* Case T-203/01, *Michelin II*, at 241.

restrict competition by object). As will be demonstrated in the following subsection, this was corrected by the GC in *France Télékom*.[410]

Tomra serves as additional evidence. The ECJ has been criticized for not applying the same [effect-based] approach in *Tomra* which it suggested in *Post Danmark I* (*see* below), and hence that it took a step back in terms of implementing the effect-based approach. However, the two cases differ substantially. In contrast to *Post Danmark I*, the focus was on the anti-competitive nature of the rebate scheme and not its likely effect. This follows clearly from the judgment as the ECJ held:

> [...] it must be observed that, according to the Commission, the failure in the judgment under appeal to examine the arguments on whether the prices charged by the Tomra group were lower than their long-run average incremental costs had no effect on the conclusion reached by the General Court that <u>the Commission's analysis of the abusive nature of the rebates applied by Tomra was well founded</u>.[411] (Underlining added)

The ECJ concluded subsequently that the rebate scheme had an anti-competitive nature.[412] As a result, it was not necessary to undertake an effect-based approach in this case. It was sufficient to demonstrate that the rebate scheme was capable of restricting competition in the case at hand; i.e., it was by its very nature anti-competitive. When comparing *Tomra* with *Michelin II* it clearly follows that the assessment concerned whether the rebate scheme restricted competition by object and not by effect.

It is, therefore, not only exclusivity agreements and rebates that may fall within the by object category. This may also occur to other types of rebate schemes; those that are loyalty-inducing rebates. As with exclusivity agreements and rebates, the definition of loyalty-inducing rebates is discussed in more detail in Chapter 5, section 2. It suffices, therefore, to define them as "rebates the grant of which is *not* directly linked to a condition of exclusive or quasi-exclusive supply, but where the mechanism for granting the rebate can have that effect (i.e., a loyalty-inducing effect)"[413]. A rebate that has the same effect as predatory pricing falls for that reason outside this category.[414]

An example of loyalty-inducing rebates is individualized target rebates.[415] This category embraces more than just individualized target rebates, though. In the above, it was shown that the rebate scheme assessed in *Michelin II* constituted a by object restriction. That rebate scheme was not individualized, but a standardized rebate scheme; i.e., the rebate scheme applied to all customers. Therefore, this category embraces both individualized and standardized target rebates. It should be noticed that this category also extends to cases such *Michelin I*, *British Airways* and *Tomra* despite these cases not including the object and effect vocabulary.[416] For instance, in *Tomra*

---

410. *See* also Case T-286/09, *Intel*, at 203.
411. *See* Case C-549/10 P, *Tomra*, at 67.
412. *See id.* at 73.
413. *See e.g.*, Case T-286/09, *Intel*, at 78.
414. *See* Chapter 5, section 2.
415. *See* Case T-286/09, *Intel*, at 78.
416. *See* Colomo (2016), at 67.

the Commission had focused on establishing the anti-competitive object of the rebate scheme since the analysis concerned the abusive nature of the rebate scheme rather than its effect.[417]

This also goes for *Post Danmark II*, which confirmed the standing case law that if a rebate scheme operated by a dominant firm, which is not an exclusivity rebate, "nevertheless tends to make it more difficult for those customers to obtain supplies from competing undertakings, produces an anti-competitive exclusionary effect."[418] The ECJ laid out a two-step test including: (i) the "nature and operation" of the rebate scheme, and (ii) the context of the market including the extent of the dominant position.[419] While this two-step test has been argued to follow an effect-based approach,[420] it resembles the assessment of by object restrictions under Article 101 TFEU. The second aspect is applied to ensure that the rebate scheme reveals a sufficient degree of harm. For example, the ECJ used the extent of Post Danmark's dominant position and the condition of competition in the market to establish an unavoidable trading partner-status.[421] That position helped, including the extent of the rebate scheme,[422] to confirm a sufficient degree of harm. Accordingly, case law reveals a focus on the abusive nature (object) of the rebate scheme rather than the effect that it may produce.

4.3 Predatory Pricing

Evidence can also be found in predatory pricing case law. In *Akzo*, the ECJ established that "prices below average variable costs" (i.e., to say, those which vary depending on the quantities produced) by means of which a dominant undertaking seeks to eliminate a competitor must be regarded as abusive."[423] Again, the reason behind that approach serves as the illustrative example. Since such pricing behaviour generates a loss on each sale, a dominant firm, according to the ECJ, has no interest in applying such prices except that of eliminating it competitors and subsequently taking advantage of its increased market power.[424] In other words, such prices have the purpose of distorting effective competition.

That such prices are considered by object restrictions was made clear in *France Télékom*. In the process of explaining the applicable test for the prices in question, the GC stated:

---

417. *See* Case C-549/10 P, *Tomra*, at 67. ("[...] had no effect on the conclusion reached by the General Court that the Commission's analysis of the abusive nature of the rebates applied by Tomra was well founded.").
418. *See* Case C-23/14, *Post Danmark II*, at 42.
419. *See id.* at 29–30.
420. *See* Colomo (2016), at 114 (who compares this approach to that under margin squeeze. However, as is shown in Section 4.5 margin squeeze can also be a by object restricton).
421. *See* Case C-23/14, *Post Danmark II*, at 39–41.
422. *See id.* at 46 (the rebate scheme covered the majority of customers in the market).
423. *See* Case 62/86, *Akzo*, at 71.
424. *See id.*

As regards the conditions for the application of Article 82 EC and the distinction between the object and effect of the abuse, it should be pointed out that, for the purposes of applying that article, showing an anti-competitive object and an anticompetitive effect may, in some cases, be one and the same thing. If it is shown that the object pursued by the conduct of an undertaking in a dominant position is to restrict competition, that conduct will also be liable to have such an effect.[425] (Underlining added)

The GC added that a price below average variable cost is deemed abusive according to that framework.[426] This line of text brilliantly illustrates that by object restrictions exist within Article 102 TFEU. Moreover, the text also shows that there is a distinction between by object and by effect restrictions; thereby, correcting the GC's paragraph in *Michelin II*.

What is also important regarding that judgment is the fact that *France Tèlèkom* was appealed to the ECJ.[427] Since the GC's ruling was upheld, this alone indicates a mutual understanding between the ECJ and the GC. Besides this aspect, the ECJ confirmed the GC's statement on by object restrictions. This is illustrated by how the *Akzo-test* was explained, and hence, why abuse was found. As shown above, the GC explained the test on the basis that some types of conduct might have an anti-competitive object. The ECJ did not apply the same wording. Instead, the ECJ stated", as a principle of case law, that prices below average variable costs (AVC) must be considered prima facie abusive since a dominant firm is then presumed to pursue no other economic objective save that of eliminating its competitors."[428] The fact that the ECJ did not refer directly to by object restrictions, but prima facie abuse should not be interpreted as the ECJ rejecting such restrictions, though. The wording means the same and merely illustrates that prices below AVC is a by object restriction (prima facie abuse) but not automatically abuse since a dominant firm has the right to justify its conduct.[429] In consequence, it confirmed the stand on by object restrictions.

It should be noted that this is not only true for prices below variable costs. The same is true for prices that are above AVC but below average total costs ("ATC") "if they determined as part of a plan for eliminating a competitor."[430] Instead of relying on an anti-competitive object steaming from the dominant firm's conduct, it comes from the dominant firm itself. That is, the predatory intent cannot be presumed but must be demonstrated.[431] As a result, the famous *Akzo-test* is in fact evidence of by object restrictions within Article 102 TFEU.

---

425. *See* Case T-340/03, *France Télékom*, at 195.
426. *See id.* at 195.
427. Both statements in *Michelin II* and *Intel* were provided by the GC and since the Michelin II was not appealed and the ECJ has yet to deliver its ruling in *Intel* one could sow doubt about value of these statements since the ECJ is the higher authority.
428. *See* Case C-202/07 P, *France Télécom*, at 109.
429. *See* section 5.1.3. *See* also Colomo (2016).
430. *See* Case 62/86, *Akzo*, at 72.
431. Case T-340/03, *France Télékom*, at 197.

When *Post Danmark I* is then introduced, the distinction between by object and by effect restrictions becomes clear-cut. While the alleged conduct in *Post Danmark I*[432] can be seen as distinct conduct from predatory pricing,[433] this book does not distinguish between predatory pricing and selective pricing. It may be true that "classic" predatory pricing conduct concerns prices applied to all customers and that a selective price, therefore, does not correspond to that definition. However, if predatory pricing is to be defined that narrowly, predatory pricing might only exist in theory. Additionally, the prices dealt with in *Akzo* were not applied to all customers but rather only to its competitors' customers.[434] In consequence, such a narrow definition would not correspond to the case law.[435] It would further be unwise to treat such types of conduct differently.[436] Selectivity should instead act as a factor that may influence the outcome of the assessment.[437] Accordingly, *Post Danmark I* is treated as a predatory pricing case in the following.

To understand *Post Danmark I*, the referred questions, which the ECJ had to give its position on, are important. The ECJ had to provide an answer on whether: (i) prices below above the "ATC" but above the average incremental costs ("AIC") could constitute abuse if they were *not* part of a plan for eliminating a competitor, and (ii) if so, how abuse could be established.[438] Accordingly, the prices in question fell outside the scope of the *Akzo-test* as they were neither: (i) below "AVC" nor (ii) part of a plan for eliminating a competitor (i.e., no predatory intent)[439]. If, on the other hand, the prices had been below AVC (alternatively the AIC benchmarks applied)[440] or part of a plan for eliminating a competitor, the ECJ would most likely have found the prices to be contrary to Article 102 TFEU, as the ECJ took its starting position in *Akzo*.[441]

The ECJ proceed by finding that prices above ATC are unable to produce anti-competitive effects[442] and that prices between the AIC and ATC without predatory intent can constitute abuse *if* an anti-competitive effect is demonstrated through an actual or likely exclusionary effect to the detriment of competition and, thereby, of

---

432. For an overview on the background of the cases, which was more complex than illustrated in the preliminary ruling, *see* Bergqvist (2013).
433. This even true for the ECJ in *Post Danmark II*, *see* Case C-23/14, *Post Danmark II*, at 55.
434. *See* Case IV/30.698, *ECS/AKZO*, at 81.
435. In that context, it worth mentioning that there is no distinguish between exclusivity agreement and selective exclusivity agreement, refusal to deal selective refusals to deal, tying and selective tying, and so on.
436. Since the ECJ build its judgment on *Akzo* (*see* below), selective prices seem to be required the same treatment as "classic" predatory pricing.
437. *See* Chapter 5, section 3.
438. *See* Case C-209/10, *Post Danmark I*, at 18.
439. *See id.* at 29.
440. The ECJ noticed that AIC had been used instead of AVC but seemed to accept it as the lower cost benchmark in the present case. For a discussion of cost benchmarks, *see* Chapter 7.
441. *See* for that effect Case C-209/10, *Post Danmark I*, at 27. The ECJ build its judgment on Akzo as it held that "[...] prices below the average of 'variable' costs (those that vary depending on the quantities produced) must, in principle, be regarded as abusive, inasmuch as, in charging those prices, a dominant undertaking is deemed to pursue no economic purpose other than that of driving out its competitors."
442. *See id.* at 36.

consumers' interests.[443] Accordingly, even though an anti-competitive object could not be established due to the lack of predatory intent, abuse was still possible if a by effect restriction were demonstrated. Therefore, the requirement of an anti-competitive effect is not evidence of a new approach by the ECJ but rather further development of the already established *Akzo-test*.[444] In other words, it was the result of a price which did not constitute a by object restriction but could constitute a by effect restriction; thereby, confirming the distinction than abandoning preceding case law and the principles herein.

Accordingly, predatory pricing may constitute a by object restriction. Moreover, it was established that the *Akzo-test* constitutes a "by object-test"; i.e., prices below AVC and prices between AVC and ATC with a predatory intent constitutes by object restrictions. As it follows from the wording, a by object restriction can be found due to either objective or subjective intent. The first types of prices are deemed anti-competitive due to that conduct's anti-competitive object while the second is due to the dominant firm's anti-competitive object (i.e., predatory intent). In other words, the ECJ finds it reasonable to infer that the price has no plausible explanation other than an anti-competitive matter.

4.4 Tying and Bundling

Tying has generally been viewed as abusive conduct in the same way as exclusivity agreements and rebates have been viewed as abusive conduct.[445] This type of conduct has generally been seen as conduct that is designed to deprive the purchaser of, or restrict his possible choices of, sources of supply and to deny other producers access to the market. In *Hilti*, the GC's assessment of abuse included a title "Improper nature of Hilti's behaviour".[446] In the same case, the Commission also concluded that "these policies all have the object or effect of excluding independent nail makers who may threaten the dominant position Hilti holds."[447] A similar approach was taken in *Tetra Pak II*.[448] In consequence, case law on tying and bundling suggests that the rationale for this type of conduct is not fundamentally different from the logic underlying that of exclusive agreements and rebates.[449]

The Commission (and the GC) took a different approach in *Microsoft*. Here the Commission famously concluded that:

---

443. *See id.* at 44.
444. *See* Rousseva & Marquis (2013), at 37. ("As we don't find indications that the approach in *Akzo* has been overruled, we believe that, where the price is between ATC and average incremental cost, an abuse can be established if intent is shown").
445. *See e.g.,* Judgment of 6 October 1994 in Case T-83/91, *Tetra Pak International SA v. Commission of the European Communities* ("*Tetra Pak II*"), at 140 (the GC stated that the tying "were intended to strengthen Tetra Pak's dominant position by reinforcing its customers' economic dependence on it").
446. *See* Judgment of 12 December 1991 in Case T-30/89, *Hilti AG v. Commission of the European Communities* ("*Hilti*"), at 95.
447. *See* Case IV/30.787 and 31.488, *Eurofix-Bauco v. Hilti*, at 75.
448. *See* Case T-83/91, *Tetra Pak II*, at 135 & 140.
449. Colomo (2016), at 724.

> While in classical tying cases, the Commission and the [EU] Courts considered the foreclosure effect for competing vendors to be demonstrated by the bundling of a separate product with the dominant product, in the case at issue, users can and do to a certain extent obtain third party media players through the Internet, sometimes for free. There are therefore indeed good reasons not to assume without further analysis that tying WMP constitutes conduct which by its very nature is liable to foreclose competition.[450]

On these grounds, the Commission wanted to explain "why tying in this specific case ha[d] the potential to foreclose competition."[451] All this may be interpreted as a step towards the effect-based approach;[452] i.e., Microsoft conduct was abusive as a by effect restriction. Arguments can certainly be made that the findings were based on the theory of harm of Raising Rival's Costs (which according to Chapter 7 forms the foundation for this kind of exclusionary conduct). Accordingly, the finding of abuse relied on Microsoft's conduct raising the costs of its competitors thereby distorting competition. This was illustrated by showing that original equipment manufacturers ("OEM") were reluctant to add a second media player owing to the facts that, first, it would take up additional hard disk capacity and consumers would not be prepared to pay a higher price for this addition as it offered similar functionalities, and second, the presence of several media players on the same PC created a risk of confusion on the part of users and an increase in customer support and testing costs.[453] As a result, competitors would have had to compensate OEMs for these additional costs thereby raising competitors' costs.

Another important point was the fact that Windows Media Player could not be removed by OEMs (or users).[454] This meant that competitors were prevented from competing on the merits, since competitors competed to have their products pre-installed while Microsoft, owing to its conduct, "evade[d] that competition and the significant additional costs which it entail[ed]."[455] On these grounds, one might, therefore, conclude that Microsoft's conduct constituted a by effect restriction since it was proven that it raised competitors cost and thereby significantly weakened those competitors' ability to compete.[456]

While the assessment can be seen as following an effect-based approach, it may just as easily be seen as the opposite;[457] i.e., Microsoft's conduct constituted a by object restriction. When comparing the paragraph 'in this specific case ha[d] the potential to

---

450. *See* Commission Decision of 24 March 2004 in Case COMP/C-3/37.792, *Microsoft*, at 841.
451. *Id.* at 842.
452. *See e.g.*, Rousseva (2010), at 250; Këllezi, Pranvera, *Rhetoric or Reform: Does the Law of Tying and Bundling Reflect the Economic Theory?*, in *Article 82 EC: Reflections on its Recent Evolution* (Ariel Ezrachi ed., 2009, at 147).
453. Case T-201/04, *Microsoft*, at 1044-5; Case COMP/C-3/37.792, *Microsoft*, at 852.
454. *See* Case T-201/04, *Microsoft*, at 1047.
455. *See id.*
456. *See* Rousseva (2010), at 253.
457. Some commentators have criticized the judgment for rejecting the effect-based approach, *see e.g.*, Ahlborn, Christian & Evans, David, *The Microsoft Judgment and Its Implications for Competition Policy towards Dominant Firms in Europe*, 75 Antitrust Law Journal (2009), at 888 (They stated that "the [GC] declined the Commission's invitation to consider an effects-based analysis of tying.").

foreclose competition' with the case law of Article 101 TFEU (i.e., sufficient degree of harm in the individual case), one can draw the analogy that tying is a type of exclusionary conduct that was seen as generally capable of restricting competition, but it was not perfectly clear whether that would also be true in this particular case. In other words, the Commission had to assess whether the relevant circumstances of the case either proved or disproved a potential to foreclose competition in the specific case. One of those relevant circumstances was whether users would download alternative media players.[458] Other relevant circumstances related to the market including how that market functioned. As further support for the argument that Microsoft's conduct constituting a by object restriction, and not a by effect restriction, the GC upheld the Commission's conclusion on the basis that the "findings [were] not based on any new or speculative theory, but on the nature of the impugned conduct, on the conditions of the market and on the essential features of the relevant products."[459]

In the end, while it can be argued in favour of both sides the tying conduct in *Microsoft* must be seen as by effect restriction – although the robustness of the assessment is open for criticism.[460] Neither the Commission nor the EU Courts merely presumed an anti-competitive foreclosure effect but rather concluded that there was "a reasonable likelihood that tying WMP with Windows w[ould] lead to a lessening of competition so that the maintenance of an effective competition structure w[ould] not be ensured in the foreseeable future."[461] While this paragraph has been interpreted as the GC reaffirming that no effects-based analysis is required,[462] it shows that the [likely] effect on effective competition was considered. One can, of course, criticize it for not being more specific on the particular harm, which it causes consumers, but as concluded earlier, effective competition and not consumer welfare is the protective aim of Article 102 TFEU. Therefore, it was sufficient for the Commission and the GC to find that Microsoft was in a position, due to its conduct, to profitably increase prices, reduce innovation or customers' choice to prove likely anti-competitive foreclosure.[463]

4.5 Margin Squeeze

With especially *Deutsche Telekom* and *TeliaSonera*, margin squeeze is often seen as a type of exclusionary conduct that can only constitute abuse if it is done through the effect-based approach.[464] This is due to ECJ's confirmation that that margin squeeze constitutes abuse only insofar as it has an anti-competitive effect –[465] the Commission

---

458. Case COMP/C-3/37.792, *Microsoft*, at 845 (The Commission found that users who had Windows Media Player pre-installed on their PCs were in general less likely to use alternative media players).
459. Case T-201/04, *Microsoft*, at 1058.
460. *See* Padilla & O'Donoghue (2013), at 612–3.
461. *See* Case T-201/04, *Microsoft*, at 1089; Case COMP/C-3/37.792, *Microsoft*, at 984.
462. *See* Ahlborn & Evans (2009), at 900.
463. *See* for that effect Case AT.39230, *Rio Tinto Alcan*, at 67.
464. *See* for that effect e.g., Colomo (2016), at 719 & 724–5.
465. *See* Case C-52/09, *TeliaSonera*, at 61; Case C-280/08 P, *Deutsche Telekom*, at 250.

had contended the contrary in *Deutsche Telekom*.[466] As was concluded in Chapter 3, however, an anti-competitive foreclosure effect is required for all types of exclusionary abuse. Therefore, the requirement of an anti-competitive effect cannot serve as proof that margin squeeze should be assessed under the effect-based approach.

On the contrary, case law serves as evidence that margin squeeze may constitute a by object restriction. In *Deutsche Telekom*, the ECJ concluded (despite the Commission was wrong to argue that there was no need to demonstrate an anti-competitive effect) that an anti-competitive effect had been demonstrated by the Commission, since: (i) the input was indispensable to competitors' effective penetration of the downstream markets, and (ii) the margin between the upstream and downstream prices was either negative or insufficient to cover the appellant's product-specific costs.[467] Based on these findings, the ECJ concluded in *TeliaSonera* that when both conditions are met an "at least potentially anti-competitive [foreclosure] effect of a margin squeeze is probable."[468] In case law of Article 101 TFEU, the ECJ has stated in similar terms that "in order for the agreement to be regarded as having an anti-competitive object, it is sufficient that it has the potential to have a negative impact on competition."[469] Accordingly, the potential effect recurs in both examples. Therefore, when parallels are drawn to that case law, it follows that margin squeeze is further evidence of by object restrictions within Article 102 TFEU.

The fact that margin squeeze may constitute a by object restriction is only supported by the principle that when "a dominant undertaking actually implements a pricing practice resulting in a margin squeeze on its equally efficient competitors, with the purpose of driving them from the relevant market, the fact that the desired result, namely the exclusion of those competitors, is not ultimately achieved does not alter its categorisation as abuse within the meaning of Article 102 TFEU."[470] Consequently, even if the negative impact of that conduct does not materialize, it is still abusive due to its *purpose*. All in all, the approach to margin squeeze resembles that of predatory pricing. That is, prices below costs are likely to be viewed as by object restrictions. This ensures consistency within Article 102 TFEU. Lastly, it should be noted that case law concerning margin squeeze deviates from that of an outright refusal to deal (which follows a more effect-based approach) since a duty to deal had already been established.[471] The issue was therefore not whether a duty to deal should be imposed, but whether that duty was abused. This is touched upon in more detail in Chapter 5, section 2.2.2.

---

466. *See* Case COMP/C-1/37.451, 37.578, 37.579, *Deutsche Telekom AG*, at 179–80.
467. *See* Case C-280/08 P, *Deutsche Telekom*, at 255.
468. Case C-52/09, *TeliaSonera*, at 71.
469. *See e.g.,* Case C-32/11, *Allianz Hungária*, at 38; Case C-8/08, *T-Mobile*, at 31.
470. *See* Case C-52/09, *TeliaSonera*, at 65.
471. This was not the case in *TeliaSonera* (a preliminary ruling), *see id.* at 6.

5   THE "BY OBJECT" CATEGORY

The previous section showed that Article 102 TFEU includes by object restrictions and that a distinction between restriction of by object and by effect exists. This means that in some cases, anti-competitive effects have been assumed to result from alleged conduct while, in other cases, alleged conduct is abusive only insofar as a negative impact on competition is proven. The challenge is then to make sense of this divided case law which includes the question of when conduct constitutes a by object restriction. This section will address this by seeking the definition for by object restrictions.

Figure 4.1   Defining by a Object Restriction

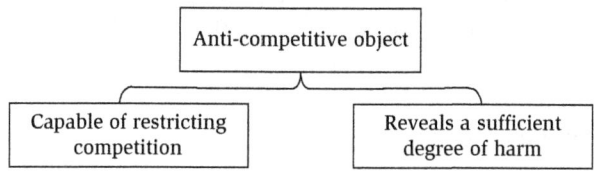

5.1   Defining by Object Restrictions

A common feature appears from the types of conduct found restricting competition by object in case law. They are, in the eyes of the EU Courts (and the Commission), not part legitimate competition, or in other words, without the scope of competition on the merits.[472] The purpose of these types of conduct is inherently anti-competitive. Since the concept of abuse is an objective concept,[473] it must be recognized for not involving a subjective object to restrict competition, though. The intention by the dominant firms is not a decisive element. This is illustrated by the fact that while some cases have relied on direct evidence of anti-competitive intent,[474] most cases seem to presume such intent due to the type of conduct. This further means that even the existence of an intention to compete on the merits, even if it were to be established, cannot prove the absence of abuse.[475] Therefore, the definition takes its departure in objective criteria; i.e., the dominant firm's conduct.

The (presumed) anti-competitive effect relates to the restriction of competition, or in other words, the harm to effective competition. It will be shown in the following subsections that finding such restrictions involves a dominant firm's exclusionary conduct that: (i) tends to restrict competition (not competitors), or in other words, is

---

472. *See* Colomo (2016), at 65.
473. *See* Case 85/76, *Hoffman La Roche*, at 91.
474. *See e.g.*, Case 62/86, *Akzo*, at 72.
475. *See* for that effect Case C-549/10 P, *Tomra*, at 22.

capable hereof, and that (ii) it reveals a sufficient degree of harm.[476] This overall definition is illustrated in Figure 4.1 which illustrates two conditions which must be met to demonstrate a by object restriction. If conduct is capable of restricting competition, it can only be held as having an anti-competitive object given the relevant circumstances of the case supports this/does not disprove such capability.

Take for example an exclusivity agreement/rebate. While case law has established such conduct as being capable (generally) of restricting competition,[477] certain market conditions may disprove this view. For instance, the dominant firm may not be an unavoidable trading partner, and hence, competitors should be able to compete for the customers' total demand and not just a part of that demand. In that event, the dominant firm does not possess a non-contestable share of the market which it can (ab)use in its favour. Since the conditions of the market do not reveal a sufficient degree of harm on competition in that particular case, the exclusivity agreement cannot constitute a by object restriction. This further means that the status as an "unavoidable trading partner" forms a supporting factor for the finding of by object restrictions for this type of conduct.

5.1.1 Capable of Restricting Competition

By having the option to establish abuse through a by object restriction, certain types of exclusionary conduct can be regarded, by their very nature, harmful to effective competition. As a result, the first condition must involve capability (or tendency). In other words, if the object pursued by a dominant firm's exclusionary conduct[478] is not that of restricting competition then there can be no presumption of an anti-competitive effect. If conduct is only capable of (or tends only to) foreclosing competitors, but not necessarily competition, an actual or likely anti-competitive effect is then required. Accordingly, if the dominant firm's conduct is capable of, for instance, restricting a competitor's access to the market, it does not necessarily fulfil the capability requirement.

As a result, the object of alleged pricing conduct is likely to be viewed in context with an as efficient competitor-standard for pricing conduct[479] since the departure from the market of competitors who are less efficient compared to the dominant firm, alternatively the marginalisation of such competitors, are attractive to consumers from the point of view of, among other things, price, choice, quality or innovation.[480] For non-pricing conduct, the focus will be whether alleged conduct, for instance, deprives competitors the incentive and ability to compete; thereby, distorting effective competition.

---

476. According to case law capability is sufficient. But, it is argued in the following that capability in general cannot suffice (as under Article 101 TFEU).
477. See Case 85/76, *Hoffman La Roche*, at 89 & 90.
478. Note that focus is on the dominant firm's conduct and not the dominant firm itself; i.e., objective intent versus subjective intent.
479. This is further the approach the Commission has indicated that it will apply in its assessment on pricing conduct, *see the Article 102 Guidance Paper*.
480. See Case C-209/10, *Post Danmark I*, at 22.

In determining whether exclusionary conduct is capable of restricting competition, the ECJ has specified how such a restriction of competition can be found.[481] In *Michelin I*, it held that it had to be examined whether conduct:

> [...] tends to remove or restrict the buyer's freedom to choose his sources of supply, to bar competitors from access to the market, to apply dissimilar conditions to equivalent transactions with other trading parties or to strengthen the dominant position by distorting competition.[482]

According to the ECJ's statement, four different types of restriction of competition exist.[483] However, the third restriction – discrimination – does not apply to exclusionary abuse,[484] and cannot constitute a by object restriction when assessing exclusionary conduct. Instead, discriminatory abuse can constitute an abuse in itself or support the finding of exclusionary abuse.

The statement further illustrates that this condition cannot only be termed as "capable of", but also as "tends to restrict competition". The ECJ has also applied "designed to restrict competition".[485] Accordingly, this condition does not distinguish between "capable of", "tend to" or "designed to". The use of "tend to restrict" also illustrates the EU Courts' (and the Commissions) perception of such types of exclusionary conduct normally being harmful to competition. Since such perception exists among them, it only then seems rational for an assessment of actual or likely effect to be regarded redundant. However, and as will be addressed below, it must be stressed that the tendency must relate to the specific case which is why it is only the first step.

Moreover, it must still be demonstrated that alleged conduct has the specific capability/tendency to have a negative impact on competition. Otherwise, chilling pro-competitive conduct is risked. Take the example of predatory pricing. It follows from case law that a price below AVC (alternatively AAC) has the specific capability/tendency to have a negative impact on competition. While some may argue the same goes for a price above AVC, it does not have such specific capability/tendency. It is true in regards of individual competitors but not effective competition. Since the negative impact must relate to effective competition, such price does not fulfil the requirement unless a predatory intent exists.

This can further be illustrated with the approach taken to margin squeeze conduct. If a potential anti-competitive effect can be demonstrated by having regarded the purpose of the dominant firm's conduct, case law has established that a concrete

---

481. *See* alternatively Østerud (2010), at 60-1. (Who finds three different categories for which the form-based approach can be applied: conduct which (i) restricts customers' freedom, (ii) fails a price/cost-test and (iii) discriminates).
482. *See* Case 322/81, *Michelin I*, at 73.
483. This paragraph has been repeated in case law since then. *See e.g.,* Case C-23/14, *Post Danmark II*, at 64; Case C-209/10, *Post Danmark I*, at 26; Case C-549/10 P, *Tomra*, at 71.
484. *See* Case C-209/10, *Post Danmark I*, at 30. *See* also Case C-549/10 P, *Tomra*, at 71 (In which the ECJ did not include this type of discrimination in the overall test for whether the retroactive rebates were abusive).
485. In *Hoffman La Roche* for example, the ECJ explained that the rebates were contrary to Article 102 TFEU since they were designed to restrict competition, *see* Case 85/76, *Hoffman La Roche*, at 90. *See* also Case T-286/09, *Intel*, at 86.

anti-competitive effect is not necessary.[486] It may be sufficient to look at whether, first, the spread between the upstream price and the downstream price(s), and second, whether the upstream input/service is indispensable.[487] If the spread between the upstream price and downstream price(s) is negative,[488] an effect that is at least potentially exclusionary towards (as efficient) competitors is probable. However, it is not necessarily capable of having a negative impact on competition. This is the case if the upstream input/service is indispensable; thus, in that event such prices reveal a potential anti-competitive effect.[489] In other words, negative prices are not enough to establish a presumption of an effect (i.e., a by object restriction) even though they may be capable of foreclosing (as efficient) competitors.[490] This is only logical. If an actual or potential substitute on which competitors can rely on is present, a dominant firm's squeeze of margins cannot have a tendency to restrict competition since a negative impact on effective competition cannot be presumed. However, such squeeze of competitors' margin may, depending on the actual case, still restrict competition due to its effect.

5.1.2 Sufficient Degree of Harm

If exclusionary conduct is found to constitute a by object restriction, it constitutes a *prima facie* abuse. Such prima facie abuse, in other words, presumes that the dominant firm pursues no other economic objective save that of restricting effective competition.[491] Accordingly, abuse within the meaning of Article 102 TFEU is established unless the dominant firm can provide an objective justification or efficiency defence for its conduct. This illustrates the great consequences of finding a by object restriction. The first step presented in the previous section, therefore, cannot be sufficient to establish a by object restriction.

As recalled from section 3 by object restrictions within Article 101 TFEU can be established when an agreement, *having regard to its legal and economic context*, has the specific capability/tendency to have a negative impact on competition. A similar requirement must apply for Article 102 TFEU as well. The Commission must assess whether the specific capability or tendency of restricting competition is true *in the case at hand*; i.e., whether it reveals a sufficient degree of harm. In other words, the presumption must be challenged in the specific circumstances of the case. If not, a too strict approach including false positives is risked. It should be noticed that it does not entail an analysis of all the circumstances of the case but rather whether there are

---

486. *See e.g.,* Case C-52/09, *TeliaSonera*, at 64.
487. *See id.* at 69–74.
488. According to *TeliaSonera* the same applies in the case where competitors operate on the downstream market with reduced profitability, *see id.* at 70 The Commission, however, seems to have interpreted this as entailing a positive margin does not fulfil this condition since the exclusionary effect is not probable, *see* Commission Decision of 15 October 2014 in Case AT.39523, *Slovak Telekom*, at 826.
489. *See* for that effect Case C-52/09, *TeliaSonera*, at 70–1.
490. *See* for that effect Case C-280/08 P, *Deutsche Telekom*, at 250.
491. *See* for that effect Case C-202/07 P, *France Télécom*, at 48.

(relevant) circumstances that can confirm or reject the finding. For example, a price below AVC may, in general, be capable of restricting competition but if information shows that that price is offered to a customer, which would not have considered other suppliers, then that piece of information will reject the finding of a by object restriction.[492] Likewise, a two-sided market may force a (dominant) firm to price below costs on one side (maybe even free of charge).

It follows from case law that the Commission is obliged to consider all the *relevant* circumstances of the case. In the previous subsection, a reference was made to *Michelin I* regarding how to assess the capability/tendency. The same reference also includes a requirement of considering all the circumstances of the case.[493] Furthermore, in *Irish Sugar* the GC held that it is an established principle of case law that regards to the relevant circumstance must be taken when the Commission assesses whether conduct is abusive,[494] and also, that this principle also resulted from case law before *Michelin I*. Lastly, any doubt should be removed by the ECJ's judgment in *Tomra*, in which it was stated:[495]

> None the less, the Commission, as part of its examination of the conduct of a dominant undertaking and for the purposes of identifying <u>any abuse</u> of a dominant position, <u>is obliged to consider all of the relevant facts surrounding that conduct</u> [...][496](underlining added)

Despite this, there still seem to be some confusion regarding the importance of demonstrating a sufficient degree of harm. In other words, it seems to be less important in Article 102 TFEU compared to Article 101 TFEU. This difference can be illustrated with *Intel* (by the GC) and *Cartes Bancaires* (by the ECJ). In *Intel,* the GC rejected the argument that it was required to assess all the circumstances surrounding the case.[497] In *Cartes Bancaires*, in contrast, the ECJ reminded the GC and the Commission (as well as everybody else) of the importance of proving a sufficient degree of harm. The agreement at issue was found capable of restricting competition, but the Commission and the GC were found to have in no way explained in what respect that conduct revealed a sufficient degree of harm for it to be characterized as a by object restriction.[498] As a result, the ECJ set aside the judgment of the GC since regard to all relevant circumstance of the case had not been taken.

---

492. *See* for that effect Decision by Ofcom of 20 June 2013 in CW/988/06/08: *Complaint from THUS plc and Gamma Telecom Limited against BT about alleged margin squeeze in Wholesale Calls pricing* (which rejected a margin squeeze complaint (after initial finding anti-competitive effects). Here, one customer was removed from the analysis since its demand was not open for competition. If it had not received the low price from BT it had vertical integrated and handled the service internally. That special circumstances changed the negative margin to a positive margin entailing anti-competitive effect could not be held as being likely).
493. *See* Case 322/81, *Michelin I,* at 73.
494. *See* Case T-228/97, *Irish Sugar,* at 114.
495. *See* also paragraph 43: "[...]only an analysis of the circumstances of the case, such as the analysis carried out by the Commission in the contested decision, may make it possible to establish whether the practices of an undertaking in a dominant position are capable of excluding competition."
496. *See* Case C-549/10 P, *Tomra,* at 18.
497. *See* Case T-286/09, *Intel,* at 84.
498. *See* Case C-67/13 P, *Cartes Bancaires,* at 69.

Concerning the demonstration by object restrictions a lesson, therefore, must be learned from the ECJ's judgment in *Cartes Bancaires* – even though it concerned Article 101 TFEU. While some types of conduct have the specific capability/tendency to have a negative impact on competition that presumption must be challenged. This entails taking into account the relevant circumstances surrounding a case. This does not mean that every single fact should be examined – that would be impossible and it would further conflict with the purpose of a by object restriction. Rather it must be assessed whether there are circumstances that either confirm or disconfirm the presumption. In *Intel*, such relevant circumstance could be, for instance, whether Intel was an unavoidable trading partner, whether competition was for the customer or its demand, whether a competitor would have been able to enter contracts with the tied customer(s) in the absent of the exclusivity rebate and so on.

The lesson learned from *Cartes Bancaires* entails that the GC's judgments in *Intel* and *Cartes Bancaires*, respectively, share some resemblance. One may, therefore, ask whether the ECJ's judgments will share resemblance; i.e., whether the ECJ will find the GC in *Intel* to have errored in law by not examining whether Intel's conduct revealed a sufficient degree of harm for it to be characterized as a by object restriction and thereby set aside the judgement of the GC. Having regard to the analyses in the following sections, the obvious answer would be yes.[499]

On the other hand, it seems unlikely. This is due to the fact that the GC's reasoning involved a main assumption with regards to the market conditions, which were actually true.[500] This assumption involved Intel being an unavoidable trading partner; a part of the customers' demand constituted a non-contestable share. Intel had thereby ensured a part of the customers' demand no matter what. Such a special circumstance is of great importance since an exclusivity rebate (or agreement) thereby enables a dominant firm to use its non-contestable share as an advantage in securing [a part of] the contestable share.[501] By requiring customers to obtain all or most of their demand from the dominant firm, the contestable share of the market is secured since customers are dependent on Intel. They have not much of a choice but to accept exclusivity. In consequence, Intel was able to secure all or a part of the contestable share of the customers' demand without having to compete on the merits with its competitors; hence, effective competition was distorted.

While it is unlikely that the GC's judgment will be set aside, it is, on the other hand, advisable for the ECJ to comment on the statement that an assessment of all circumstance is not necessary. As stressed above, a lesson should be learned from *Cartes Bancaires*. It may also be that the ECJ do not agree with the GC interpretation of *Tomra*. In brief,[502] the GC rejected the argument that *Tomra* entails a requirement of

---

499. Such conclusion was reached by e.g., Colino, Sandra Marco, *All Eyes on Intel: A Stepping Stone to a Fresh Legal Framework for the Analysis of Rebates Under EU Competition Law*, Forthcoming Concurrences (2017).
500. *See e.g.*, Case T-286/09, *Intel*, at 103 (In which the GC explains why Intel's conduct was capable of restricting competition in the case at hand based on the fact that Intel was an unavoidable trading partner).
501. This element is also important under by effect-approach, *see* Chapter 7.
502. *See* Case T-286/09, *Intel*, at 97; Case C-549/10 P, *Tomra*, at 72.

assessing all circumstances since, the GC argued, that requirement only applied for retroactive rebates and not exclusivity rebates. However, the requirement embraced wider than merely retroactive rebates. When one takes a closer look at the ECJ's judgment in *Tomra*, it follows that it referred to a paragraph in the GC's judgment. This included, among other things, a reference to loyalty rebates within the meaning of *Hoffman La Roche* – the kind of rebates which "exclusivity rebates" are based on. In that paragraph, the GC stated:

> [...] that a rebate system in which the rate of the discount increases according to the volume purchased will not infringe Article [102 TFEU] unless the criteria and rules for granting the rebate reveal that the system is not based on an economically justified countervailing advantage but tends, following the example of a loyalty and target rebate, to prevent customers from obtaining their supplies from competitors (*see* Hoffmann-La Roche v Commission, paragraph 90, and Michelin II, paragraph 59).[503] (underlining added)

The GC further concluded in its judgment

> [...] that in order to determine whether exclusivity agreements, individualised quantity commitments and individualised retroactive rebate schemes are compatible with Article [102 TFEU], it is necessary to ascertain whether, following an assessment of all the circumstances and, thus, also of the context in which those agreements operate, those practices are intended to restrict or foreclose competition on the relevant market or are capable of doing so.[504] (underlining added)

As is apparent from those paragraphs, they did not only concern retroactive rebates but further exclusivity agreements (and quantity commitments). Since an exclusivity rebate is, basically, an exclusivity agreement with financial compensation,[505] the statement is also applicable for *Intel*. Accordingly, it was incorrect to state, as the GC did, that the reference in the ECJ's judgment in *Tomra* did not apply to exclusivity rebates. This is even clearer when it is recalled that it was established in the very same judgment that the Commission, as part of its examination of the conduct of a dominant undertaking and for the purposes of identifying *any abuse* of a dominant position, is obliged to consider all of the relevant facts surrounding that conduct.[506]

While it, therefore, should be without any doubt that it is necessary to consider all the *relevant* circumstances of an individual case, the GC could also be saved by the fact that it referred to "all circumstances". As this requirement only involves an examination of whether there a circumstances which confirm or disconfirm the presumption, it would be unfit to assess all circumstances.[507] However, it would be

---

503. *See* Judgment of 9 September 2010 in Case T-155/06, *Tomra Systems ASA and others v. European Commission* ("*Tomra*"), at 213.
504. *See id.* at 215.
505. *See* Case T-286/09, *Intel*, at 76. The GC held that "rebates the grant of which is conditional on the customer's obtaining all or most of its requirements from the undertaking in a dominant position."
506. *See* Case C-549/10 P, *Tomra*, at 18.
507. It is possible that the ECJ will make a similar comment as it did in *Toshiba* where it held that a by object restriction could be found *"without a more detailed analysis of the relevant economic and legal context being necessary"*, *see* Judgment of 20 January 2016 in Case C3-373/14 P,

appropriate for the ECJ to take advantage of the opportunity and clear any confusion which the judgment of the GC may have created – as the ECJ has done before.[508] That would not only mean that the approach will be in agreement with the findings made in this chapter but further the approach in Article 101 TFEU creating a transversal consistency (i.e., consistency across competition rules).[509] While such constituency may be most important regarding their purpose (i.e., protecting effective competition), such general constituency cannot be created if the approach within the different provisions differs too much. Hopefully, this will be clarified by the ECJ delivers its judgment in *Intel*. Thereby, legal certainty is further created which allows dominant firms to adapt their conduct accordingly.

In consequence, demonstrating a by object restriction involves demonstrating exclusionary conduct being capable of harming effective competition *in the individual case*. Such demonstration must have regard to all relevant circumstances of the case at hand and cannot only rely on the character of the dominant firm's conduct. However, it should be stressed that such assessment does not include a comprehensive analysis since such analysis is reserved for the demonstration of actual or likely anti-competitive effects. Rather the relevant circumstances can either confirm or disconfirm the presumption of negative impact on effective competition.

5.2   Per se Abuse?

By object restrictions can be compared to per se prohibitions within US antitrust law. If conduct falls within the per se-rule conduct, there is no need for an elaborate enquiry as to the precise harm nor is there any business excuse for such practice.[510] An important question, therefore, is whether a by object restriction equals a per se abuse. However, such opinion can only be dismissed as follows below. First, it should be recalled that it is a general principle that conduct found contrary to Article 102 TFEU constitutes an abuse only if it lacks justification.[511] This also applies in the event where conduct is found having an anti-competitive object.[512] In particular, a dominant firm may demonstrate, for that purpose, either that its conduct is objectively necessary,[513]

Toshiba Corporation v. European Commission ("*Toshiba*"), at 34. That would fit the findings of the GC and the Commission had already done such a limited analysis.

508. *See* Case C-280/08 P, *Deutsche Telekom*, at 250. The Commission had argued – which had been rejected by the GC – that it was not necessary to demonstrate an anti-competitive effect. The ECJ rightly rejected such argument.

509. For a discussion of transversal consistency *see e.g.,* Petit, Nicolas, *The Future of the Court of Justice in EU Competition law*, *in* The Court of Justice and the Construction of Europe: Analyses and Perspectives on Sixty Years of Case-law (The European Court of Justice ed., 2013).

510. *See Northern Pacific Railway Co. v. United States.*

511. *See* the seminal judgment in Case 27/76, *United Brands*, at 184. *See* also Case C-209/10, *Post Danmark I*, at 40. Østerud (2010), at 60.

512. *See* Case T-286/09, *Intel*, at 81; Case C-202/07 P, *France Télécom*, at 111. The acknowledgement was not directly visible, but in, for instance, *France Tèlècom* the ECJ stated that showing no recoupment of cost can "assist in excluding economic justifications other than the elimination of a competitor." Accordingly, the ECJ held indirectly that economic justifications can offset the anti-competitive effect with respect to a conduct with an anti-competitive object.

513. *See* Case C-209/10, *Post Danmark I*, at 41.

or that the exclusionary effect produced may be counterbalanced or outweighed by advantages in terms of efficiency that also benefit consumers.[514] In that last regard, it is for the dominant firm to show (i) that the efficiency gains, which is likely to result from its conduct, counteract any likely negative effects on competition and consumers[515] in the affected markets, (ii) that those gains have been, or are likely to be, brought about as a result of that conduct, (iii) that such conduct is necessary for the achievement of those gains in efficiency and (iv) that it does not eliminate effective competition, by removing all or most existing sources of actual or potential competition.[516] In other words, even if an anti-competitive object (or an anti-competitive effect) is established, a dominant undertaking can justify its conduct the same way an agreement can be justified under Article 101(3) TFEU.

Furthermore, the aspect of per se abuses within Article 102 TFEU has been addressed. In *Sot. Lelos and others* the General Advocate did address the issue (the ECJ did not explicitly address the question of per se abuses within Article 102 TFEU).[517] In the Opinion, the General Advocate concluded that it was not suited to have a per se rule since such a principle does not sit well with Article 102 TFEU even when it is clear from the circumstances of the case that there is both intent and an anti-competitive effect.[518] The conclusion was reached on the foundation that a dominant firm's anti-competitive conduct may have pro-competitive effects, and as a consequence thereof, a dominant firm must have the opportunity to demonstrate justifications. The considerations by the General Advocate corresponds therefore with the consideration presented above, meaning that even if an anti-competitive object can be established, conduct only constitutes an abuse if there are no objective justifications. In other words, per se abuse does not exist under Article 102 TFEU.

5.3 Concluding Remarks

As have been illustrated above, the finding of abuse under Article 102 TFEU is not limited to a finding of a by effect restriction. Abuse can also be established by the finding of a by object restriction. Here, the Commission looks at inherently harmful infringements. This is done, primarily, by focusing on the content and the objectives of that specific conduct to see whether it reveals a sufficient degree of harm to competition.[519] The other case (i.e., by effect restrictions) concerns types of conduct that are not always harmful to competition. This begged the question of where to draw the line between these two cases. It is not always easy to decide but, all things being equal, it

---

514. *See e.g.,* Case C-95/04 P, *British Airways*, at 86; Case C-52/09, *TeliaSonera*, at 31 & 75.
515. It should be noted while the English versions applies the term "consumer welfare" other langue versions such as French, German and Danish applies the them "consumers" interest'.
516. *See* Case C-209/10, *Post Danmark I*, at 42.
517. *See* Opinion of Advocate General Colomer, Ruiz-Jarabo of 1 April 2008 in Joined Cases C-468/06 to C-478/06, *Sot. Lelos kai Sia EE and others v. GlaxoSmithKline AEVE Farmakeftikon Proionton*, at 37–77.
518. *See id.* at 76.
519. *See* Italianer, Alexander, *The Object of Effects*, speech given on 2014 at CRA Annual Brussels Conference, Brussels, at 2.

must depend on whether the dominant firm's conduct reveals a sufficient degree of harm to competition. The importance of this aspect to find a by object restriction was stressed above; hence, its importance should come as no surprise.

By object restrictions come with some important consequences. Most obviously, this concerns procedural aspects and a burden of proof-shifter. When finding a by object restriction, the Commission will be able to conclude anti-competitive effects more promptly. This saves enforcement costs.[520] More importantly, it also shifts the burden. With the finding of a by object restriction the burden goes from the Commission, which must demonstrate an anti-competitive effect, to the dominant firm who, in turn, must then justify its conduct. By having a presumed effect, it may also be more difficult to justify conduct. When counterbalancing the negative effect if it is not certain how much is needed since only a potential effect has been established. As a result, by object restrictions demands an open view on efficiency defences and objective justifications. Economic literature shows that they are possible but with current case law justifying anti-competitive conduct may be practically impossible.[521]

Additionally, a by object restriction entails less focus on effects. Accordingly, following a cursory examination of alleged conduct's formal features, one can infer it is likely to harm effective competition. Since such examination follows the form-based approach, similar critic is to be expected for by object restrictions. However, some of this criticism is unfounded due to a wrong understanding of the concept.[522] This can be illustrated by a misuse of a, rather famous, remark from one scholar. It held that by object restrictions "[are] like banning the sale of Ferrari cars, because it is highly probable that drivers will not respect the speed limits."[523] The quote has been used to criticize the form-based approach.[524] However, this is a wrong interpretation of Article 102 TFEU (and the quote). Buying a Ferrari cannot be compared with exclusionary conduct but rather that of acquiring dominance – which is also what the quote is intended for. Therefore, a better quote would be that the form-based approach (finding by objection restrictions) is like banning speeding (or drunk driving) due to the risks of personal and material injuries. This is, on the other hand, quite reasonable.

---

520. There is always the argument that can be made against this which involves the complexity of calculating costs. Even if anti-competitive effects are not needed to be demonstrated when a dominant firm is pricing below AVC, and thereby saves time and resources, it has to allocate a lot of time and resources to calculate the costs. However, this does not change the fact that the part of demonstrating anti-competitive effect is redundant; hence, resources and time is saved.
521. See for that effect the GC's comment in *Intel* where it held: "Although exclusivity conditions may, in principle, have beneficial effects for competition, so that in a normal situation on a competitive market, it is necessary to assess their effects on the market in their specific context […],those considerations cannot be accepted in the case of a market where, precisely because of the dominant position of one of the economic operators, competition is already restricted", see Case T-286/09, *Intel*, at 89.
522. See also section 2.
523. See Heimler, Alberto, *Below-Cost Pricing and Loyalty-Inducing Discounts: Are They Restrictive and If So, When?*, 1 CPI Journal (2005), at 172.
524. See e.g., Petit (2009), at 485.

PART III Research Question No. 2

CHAPTER 5

Predation Versus Exclusion

1 INTRODUCTION

The most important consequence of applying an effect-based approach to the assessment of exclusionary conduct is perhaps the need for a sound and economic theory of harm.[525] This entails an explanation for why a given type of conduct is harmful to effective competition, and thereby, to the detriment of consumers' interest.[526] However, the importance of a theory of harm raises the question of whether every type of exclusionary conduct is subject to the same theory, and if not, which types of exclusionary conduct are subject to which theory. For that reason, this chapter will analyse, first, the difference between Predation and Exclusion (section 2); also known as pricing versus non-pricing conduct. This includes why it is necessary to distinguish between those two overall types of exclusionary conduct when assessing exclusionary conduct and which types of conduct fall into which category.

Although Predation and Exclusion are different analyses, some aspects of the assessment of anti-competitive foreclosure effect will recur in all or most cases. Therefore, the chapter will address these factors (section 3). This will allow the two following chapters to focus on the special aspects of their respective theory of harm. Altogether, this chapter will address the assessment of anti-competitive foreclosure effects in a more general matter while the following two chapters will focus on the specific approach for their respective types of conduct.

---

525. These are discussed in more details in Chapters 6 and 7.
526. The more traditional approach in the EU Courts' case law has also relied on a theory of harm but, as it was discussed in Chapter 3 & 4, the underlying rationality has not necessarily been very explicit. This is also due to the fact that that traditional case law has generally found restrictions by object rather than by effect (i.e., the effect-based approach has generally not been applied).

2 PREDATION OR EXCLUSION?

It should come as no surprise – due to, for instance, Chapters 6 and 7 of this book – that exclusionary conduct is advocated to be divided into two overall categories; i.e., Predation and Exclusion. There should also be no doubt that the assessment, despite the two different categories, must still focus on the same end goal; i.e., assessing anti-competitive foreclosure effects.[527] In other words, despite two different approaches can be applied they still seek to assess whether exclusionary conduct harms effective competition to the detriment of consumers' interest. The difference between Predation and Exclusion, due to their differences regarding how harm to effective competition is achieved, must still be respected.

While this book denotes those two categories as Predation and Exclusion, referring to them as pricing versus non-pricing conduct, respectively, may in some events help to see the difference, and hence, understand the advocated distinction better. On the other hand, however, naming them pricing and non-pricing conduct is not always the most informative term since a rebate and margins squeeze, as will be shown in section 2.2, can be subject to both categories depending on the case.[528] Nevertheless, both sets of terminology will be applied. Following this, the purpose of this section is: (i) to illustrate why it is necessary to distinguish between Predation or Exclusion, and (ii) to provide an overview of which types of conduct (likely) falls within which category.

2.1 A Necessary Distinguish

In its text, Article 102 TFEU does not distinguish between Predation and Exclusion – or pricing and non-pricing conduct for that matter. Instead, abuse as a whole is prohibited with four examples being mentioned. These are by no means exhaustive, though.[529] Despite this, it has been noticed earlier that the assessment of different types of conduct differs in some aspects (see e.g., Chapter 3). In addition, when dealing with exclusionary conduct in both theory and practice, a distinction is also made between conduct that focus on the price and those that focus on other elements.

The EU Courts' case law is a case in point.[530] For example, the need to distinguish between different types of exclusionary conduct was made clear by the GC in *Intel*. The GC based its assessment on cases involving non-pricing conduct (or at least cases not involving a price/cost test) with the argument that different treatment is required since

---

527. *See* Crane, Daniel & Miralles, Graciela, *Toward a Unified Theory of Exclusionary Vertical Restraints*, 84 Southern California Law Review (2011) 605. (Who propose a unified test for all exclusionary conduct by claiming substantial foreclosure must rule but, at the same time, forgets to explicitly acknowledge the importance difference between Predation and Exclusion).
528. In principle, this is true for every type of conduct.
529. *See e.g.,* Case C-52/09, *TeliaSonera*, at 26.
530. The case law shows that a case will seek guidance in cases with similar issues; e.g., a case which focuses on whether a price is abusive will apply principles from cases which had also focused on a price (*see e.g., Post Danmark I*) and a case concerning a loyalty inducing rebate will rely on cases dealing with a similar issue (*see e.g., Intel* and *Post Danmark II*).

"unlike an exclusive supply incentive, the level of a price cannot be regarded as unlawful in itself."[531;532] The GC rejected, thereby, the relevance of [recent] pricing conduct-cases, including *Deutsche Telekom*, *TeliaSonera* and *Post Danmark I*, as applicable for the assessment of the rebate scheme in question.[533]

Legal and economic literature also distinguishes between pricing and non-pricing conduct.[534] It was also seen earlier that this aspect is important. For example, Chapter 3 found the definition of an anti-competitive (foreclosure) effect – although an overall definition fits all – to involve different elements depending on whether the assessment concerns pricing or non-pricing conduct. In consequence, before assessing whether a dominant firm's conduct causes any harm to effective competition, and thereby consumers' interest, it must be considered whether alleged conduct classifies as pricing or non-pricing conduct; i.e., whether the issue is a matter of Predation or Exclusion.

The main reason for this distinction is the element that is in focus. Regarding pricing conduct (i.e., Predation), the assessment of anti-competitive foreclosure effects is centred on a low price. More precisely, the price is the principle levering customers' behaviour.[535] In contrast, a low price is *not* the centre of attention in regards to non-pricing conduct (i.e., Exclusion). The issue will be that of tying up (alternatively foreclosing access to) customers or suppliers by, for example, creating a loyalty inducing effect.[536] In consequence, a rebate or margin squeeze, for example, may be contrary to Article 102 TFEU even if the (effective) price is above the dominant firm's relevant costs, i.e., even if it satisfies a price/cost test. Besides illustrating the difference, this also highlights that exclusionary conduct is not always easily identified as one or the other – and it illustrates why the terms pricing and non-pricing conduct is not always the most informative. This will be addressed in more detail below.

The difference, and the need to distinguish, between different types of exclusionary conduct is perhaps best illustrated by how anti-competitive effects in the form of higher prices are achieved (i.e., how the dominant firm can raise its price due to a foreclosure effect). As can be recalled from Chapter 1, the end-result of any exclusion-

---

531. *See* Case T-286/09, *Intel*, at 99.
532. Two remarks are worth making. First, exclusivity supply incentive are not necessarily unlawful, *see e.g.,* Judgment of 28 September 2006 in Case C-552/03 P, *Unilever Bestfoods (Ireland) Ltd v. Commission of the European Communities,* ("*Van den Bergh Foods*"); Judgment of 23 October 2003 in Case T-65/98, *Van den Bergh Foods Ltd v. Commission of the European Communities* ("*Van den Bergh Foods*"). Second, the level of a price can be regarded as unlawful in itself according to the *Akzo-test*. Therefore, there is some inconstancy in this statement.
533. *See* Case T-286/09, *Intel*, at 98–9.
534. *See e.g.,* Whish & Bailey (2015). Chapter 17 addresses non-pricing conduct while Chapter 18 addresses pricing conduct; Padilla & O'Donoghue (2013 *See* also Bernheim & Heeb (2015), at 4–5. (Who divides conduct into those involving exclusionary conditions – e.g., exclusive dealing and loyalty rebates – and those which do not involve such condition - e.g., predatory pricing, "simple bundling", volume discount and conventional tying – but, nonetheless, justify this separation on the ground that for the latter price lever over the customers' behaviour). *See* in contrast Akman (2016), at 66. (Who argue it is a major problem with equating the AEC-test with Predation as it is then only applicable to pricing conduct; thereby, indirectly indicating a dislike towards separating conduct into pricing and non-pricing categories.).
535. *See* Case C-209/10, *Post Danmark I*, at 27–28. *See* also Bernheim & Heeb (2015), at 5.
536. *See e.g.,* Case 322/81, *Michelin I*, at 85; Case C-549/10 P, *Tomra*, at 75. For a different type of case, *see* Case T-201/04, *Microsoft*.

ary abuse will be some type of exploitative conduct (or an attempt thereof). Harm to consumers' interest covers not only an "excessive price" (and a lower level of output) but also, for instance, reduction in innovation and the variety of goods.[537] For illustrative purposes, however, an "excessive price" is applied to this example. Here, the dominant firm's exclusionary conduct forecloses effective competition which then allows it to raise its price (potentially the monopoly price). This may be achieved be one of two methods (see Figure 5.1).

Figure 5.1   The Difference Between Predation and Exclusion

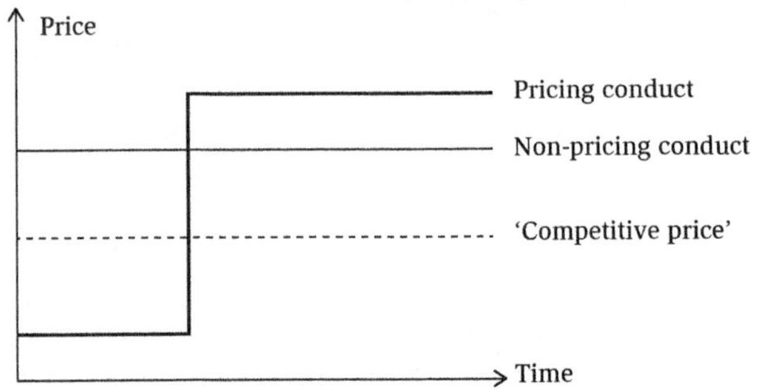

Caption: Note: This is merely an illustration and should not been viewed as statement that Predation always leads to higher prices than Exclusion. It may be the opposite event. However, for illustrative purposes (and to separate the lines) this is chosen.

First of all, the "excessive price" is, for reasons of simplicity, defined as a price set above the "competitive price".[538] This "excessive price" is achieved differently depending on whether Predation or Exclusion is applied. In terms of Predation, this is achieved by means of a low price-period; i.e., pricing below the "competitive price".[539] If the low pricing-period is successful – i.e., competition is foreclosed – then it is followed by a period of "excessive prices" (also known as recoupment). The dominant firm is, in other words, able to raise the price to the detriment of consumers due to a period of low prices. Accordingly, the issue in regards to pricing conduct is whether the dominant firm is able to recoup its loss in the low pricing-period.[540]

---

537. *See* for that effect *the Article 102 Guidance Paper*, at 11 & 19.
538. In a competitive market, a "competitive price" is set. In this illustration, it shows the price offered to consumers if competition is not distorted. For simplicity, this price may be held as representing the dominant firm's costs. In a concrete case, this competitive price is likely to be above costs, though, since markets characterized as perfect competition is even more unlikely in a market which contains a dominant firm.
539. Except special circumstances, pricing conduct will only be found contrary to Article 102 TFEU given price is below the costs of the dominant firms costs due to legal certainty and that inefficient competitors are not protected, see Case C-280/08 P, *Deutsche Telekom*, at 202; Case C-209/10, *Post Danmark I*, at 22 & 36. For a special circumstance *see e.g.*, Joined Cases C-395/96 P and C-396/96 P, *CMBT*.
540. This is discussed in more detail in Chapter 6.

In terms of Exclusion, the dominant firm succeeds in raising its price from the beginning. A low pricing-period is not required. The main difference is therefore how the "excessive price" is achieved. The increase in price is still achieved by foreclosing effective competition but not due to a low price. Instead, the excessive price is achieved by, for instance, tying up the markets most effective distribution channel(s) or preventing them from achieving economies of scale. This raises competitors' costs and forces them to raise their price which, in the end, enables the dominant firm to raise its price and profits (given that a similar increase in costs does not incur).[541]

As illustrated, the end-result of a dominant firm's conduct is the same independent of whether the issue is Predation or Exclusion. The road differs, however. Depending on the likely success, a dominant firm may choose to apply conduct under either the Predation or Exclusion framework. The difference between the two categories is also found in both case law and the *Article 102 Guidance Paper*. According to the *Article 102 Guidance Paper*, the Commission will apply a price/cost analysis when assessing pricing conduct.[542] Additionally, the EU Courts have favoured a price/cost test when dealing with pricing conduct; namely, predatory pricing[543], selective low prices[544] and margin squeeze[545]. This follows the logic from above since the essence of the analysis has been Predation. The assessment, therefore, needed to show whether competitors were unable to compete with the price. When a dominant firm instead applies non-pricing conduct, it would be incorrect to apply a price/cost-test since effective competition may be harmed while the price is above costs – as illustrated in Figure 5.1. A price/cost-test would not shed any light on the potential anti-competitive foreclosure effects. If anything, it may result in false negatives. Which type category applies to which type of exclusionary conduct does not follow clearly from the *Article 102 Guidance Paper* or case law, though.[546] Nonetheless, there should be no doubt that the issue is Exclusion if not Predation.

In consequence, it is of great importance to clarify whether exclusionary conduct relates to Predation or Exclusion. The most solemn consequence can be an incorrect conclusion when assessing the dominant firm's conduct. For example, if a price/cost test is applied to assess exclusionary conduct within Exclusion that assessment may reach the conclusion that there is no abuse although the dominant firm has abused its dominant position. Therefore, it is important that it is assessed whether conduct falls within Predation or Exclusion. This further has the consequence that Chapters 6 and 7 deal with Predation and Exclusion, respectively. Which type of conduct, in general, fits under each category is analysed in the following.

---

541. This is discussed in more detail in Chapter 7.
542. *See the Article 102 Guidance Paper*, at 23–7. In such cases, the Commission will apply an AEC-test where the object is to examine whether the dominant firm would have been able to compete against itself.
543. *See e.g.*, Case C-202/07 P, *France Télécom*, at 107–8; Case 62/86, *Akzo*, at 70 & 73.
544. *See* Case C-209/10, *Post Danmark I*, at 28–35.
545. *See* Case C-52/09, *TeliaSonera*, at 40–6; Case C-280/08 P, *Deutsche Telekom*, at 197–203.
546. The *Article 102 Guidance Paper* features a section explaining how the Commission intends to deal with pricing conduct, see *the Article 102 Guidance Paper*, at 23–7. Such section does not feature for non-pricing conduct. This creates uncertainty concerning the approach the Commission is likely to take and, moreover, little assistance for NCAs.

2.2   Do Rebates and Margin Squeeze Always Constitute Pricing Conduct?

Categorizing a type of exclusionary conduct as one or the other is simple in some events (see section 2.3). For instance, it is apparent that exclusionary conduct such as exclusivity agreements, tying & bundling and refusal to deal/supply are in the category of Exclusion while exclusionary conduct such as predatory and selective prices fall within Predation. However, for other types of exclusionary conduct it may not be that obvious. It may also depend on the structure of the plaintiff's allegations.[547] This is especially true for rebates and margin squeeze. The question is whether the anti-competitive foreclosure effect that, for example, a rebate may produce is due to a pricing or non-pricing element; i.e., whether it is predatory pricing or exclusivity (or even bundling) in disguise.[548] In other words, it is possible to assess this type of conduct within both Predation and Exclusion. This fosters some formidable ambiguity regarding how to assess their legality. Therefore, the question is whether some guidelines can be provided for when such types of conduct fall within Predation or Exclusion, respectively.

2.2.1   Rebates

Rebates – in particular, those that have been termed as loyalty-inducing or exclusivity rebates (also known as market-share rebates in the US) – are a widely debated topic.[549] Rebates in this context may, in general terms, be characterized as conditional rebates since the reduction in price is achieved by, for example, meeting a specified threshold – or seen from the customer's point of view; the rebate is withdrawn if the customer does not meet a specific threshold.[550] A rebate that is not conditional but is a deviation from a standard price will most likely be viewed as the same type of conduct as those assessed as pricing conduct; for instance, a selective low price.[551] This type of "rebate" is not included in the analysis below.

Conditional rebates can take many forms but varies upon mainly three dimensions.[552] The first dimension is how the rebate is achieved. For example, a customer may trigger a rebate by satisfying a threshold based upon volume, volume growth over the previous period, the percentage of the customer's requirement is purchased from the supplier or the percentage of shelf space it commits to the supplier's product. In regards of mixed bundling (see the third dimension), the rebate is typical triggered by buying the bundle. If the products are not used in fixed proportions, it can be triggered

---

547. *See* Salop, Steven, *The Raising Rivals' Cost Foreclosure Paradigm, Conditional Pricing Practices and the Flawed Incremental Price-Cost Test*, 2016, Georgetown Law Faculty Publications and Other Works, available at http://scholarship.law.georgetown.edu/facpub/1620, at 2.
548. For margin squeeze, the issue is whether it resembles predatory pricing or refusal to deal.
549. *See*, for an overview, Padilla & O'Donoghue (2013).
550. *See* for that effect Case C-23/14, *Post Danmark II*.
551. *See* in that context Case C-209/10, *Post Danmark I*. Here the ECJ determined that the selective prices were to be assessed within Predation, even though they technically were a rebate. For an overview of the case, which was more complex than illustrated in the preliminary ruling, see Bergqvist (2013).
552. *See e.g.*, Wright (2013), at 3–4.

when a certain amount/percentage of the demand is bought or the like. As already mentioned, a rebate is conditional in some way or the other but it may be on different grounds. Overall, the granting of a rebate may contain an obligation to obtain all or a given proportion of supplies from the dominant undertaking or it may depend on the attainment of, for example, sales objectives.[553]

The second, and an important one according to the EU Courts' case law, is which units the rebate is applied to; i.e., whether the rebate is applied only to the incremental units (an incremental rebate) or to all units (a retroactive rebate). The former is the "classic" rebate where purchases exceeding a specified threshold are sold at a lower price. This contrasts with the latter, which is calculated by applying the rebate to all units purchased. This further cause the rebate to become more significant since the price reduction for the incremental units will include the price reduction for the units purchased up to the threshold. The effective rebate percentage received on the incremental units exceeds the rebate percentage. Accordingly, these rebates are more likely to cause anti-competitive harm than incremental rebates.[554] That a retroactive rebate may be more likely to cause anti-competitive harm can also be found in the EU Courts' case law, which has focused on retroactive rebates.[555]

The third dimension is the number of products included in the rebate; i.e., whether the rebate is a single-product rebate or a multi-product rebate.[556] The latter is also known as a mixed bundling (or bundle rebate).[557] This type of rebate refers to situation where a dominant firm offers a rebate to customers purchasing two or more distinct products together (i.e., a primary and secondary product) than to customers who do not purchase the bundle. As it is the case with single-product rebates, there is an uncertainty of whether these rebates are subject to an assessment with Predation or

---

553. *See* for that effect Case C-23/14, *Post Danmark II*, at 28; Case T-286/09, *Intel*, at 74–8. Here, a distinction between rebates featuring an obligation to deal exclusively and those depending on, for instance, sales targets is made.

554. *See e.g., the Article 102 Guidance Paper*, at 40.

555. The EU Courts case law has so far only addressed rebates that were retroactive. Moreover, this is also evident in the Commissions decisional practice which had had little focus on incremental rebates. One example on incremental rebates is the Velux case which was opened in 2007 due to a complaint by one of Velux's competitor. The competitor claimed Velux's incremental rebates created anti-competitive foreclosure effects. However, the case was closed shortly after since the inspections did not confirm the allegations: Commission Decision of 2009 in Case COMP/39.451, *Velux (Closing of invistigation)* – Not published. For a review of the case see Albaek, Svend & Claici, Adina, *The Velux Case – An In-Depth Look at Rebates and More*, 2 Competition Policy Newsletter (2009) 44. Or Batchelor, Bill & Jebelli, Kayvan Hazemi, *Rebates in a State of Velux: Filling in the Gaps in the Article 102 TFEU Enforcement Guidelines*, 32 European Competition Law Review (2011) 545.

556. In its *Article 102 Guidance Paper*, the Commission treats single-product rebates under the category "exclusive dealing" and multi-product rebates under the category "tying and bundling" which illustrates that the Commission also separates these two types of rebates.

557. For discussion of multi-product rebates see, among others, Gates, Sean, *Antitrust by Analogy: Developing Rules for Loyalty Rebates and Bundled Discounts*, 79 Antitrust Law Journal (2013) 99; Elhauge, Einer, *Tying, Bundled Discounts, and the Death of the Single Monopoly Profit Theory*, 123 Harvard Law Review (2009) 397; Hovenkamp, Herbert & Hovenkamp, Erik, *Complex Bundled Discounts and Antitrust Policy*, 57 Buffalo Law Review (2009) 1227.

Exclusion (as a matter of tying).[558] Categorizing mixed bundling as either Predation or Exclusion would be wrong, though, as it depends on the specific case (as with conditional rebates). A single-product rebate (a traditional conditional rebate) can also be seen as two different products as these rebates normally involve a contestable (the amount the customer would have bought from the dominant firm under all circumstance) and a non-contestable share. When a reference is made to a rebate, it will generally include both types of rebates.

2.2.1.1   The Clash Between Different Views

When speaking of rebates, it is not controversial to say that this subject is controversial. A great dispute on how to assess such rebates has and is taken place. This refers not only to the EU Courts case law but also to case law within the US (see section 2.2.1.2). A major factor in this dispute is the fact that a rebate is, technically, a low price,[559] and consequently, is open for the same assessment that is applied to other types of conduct within Predation while the ECJ, on the other hand, rejects such assessment as a prerequisite for finding abuse. Since rebates can be assessed within Predation, the as efficient competitor-test has been heavily advocated as the relevant assessment tool in legal and economic literature.[560] This also includes the Commission who advocates the as efficient competitor-test ("AEC-test") in its *Article 102 Guidance Paper*.[561]

On the other hand, rebates are also open to the assessment that is applied within Exclusion (i.e., as an analogy to exclusivity agreements or tying and bundling).[562] First of all, a rebate may constitute a punishment mechanism directed at disloyal customers,[563] and research has shown that (retroactive) rebates do not necessarily imply lower prices for consumers.[564] Second, a dominant firm may apply a rebate scheme as a subtle alternative to requiring or obliging its manufacturer or distributor to deal exclusively or quasi-exclusively or enter into a tying agreement;[565] i.e., making the

---

558. *See* Elhauge (2009), at 450 (who argues that that bundled discounts are a form of product tying, and "one can think of tying as simply a special case of bundled discounts"); Hovenkamp & Hovenkamp (2009), at 1230 (who mixed bundling "thus has some, but not all, of the characteristics of predatory pricing").

559. It may to be true reduction in price, though. *See* section 2.2.1.3.

560. *See*, among others, Padilla & O'Donoghue (2013); Federico (2011); Miralles (2011).

561. *See the Article 102 Guidance Paper*, at 37–45.

562. *See* Moore, Derek & Wright, Joshua, *Conditional Discounts and the Law of Exclusive Dealing*, 22 George Mason Law Review (2015) 1205.

563. *See* Economides, Nicholas, *Tying, Bundling, and Loyalty/Requirement Rebates*, *in* Research Handbook on the Economics of Antitrust Law (Einer R. Elhauge ed., 2013, at 130–1 (Who states that a "loyalty 'discount' is equivalent to a 'disloyalty penalty'"); Elhauge, Einer, *How Loyalty Discounts Can Perversely Discourage Discounting*, 5 Journal of Competition Law and Economics (2009) 189, at 216 ("The word 'discounts' deceptively suggests otherwise, but the nominal 'discount' is just the difference between the compliant and noncompliant prices that a firm chooses, and does not indicate prices lower than the levels").

564. *See* Maier-Rigaud, Frank & Schwalbe, Ulrich, *Do Retroactive Rebates Imply Lower Prices for Consumers?*, 2013, LEM 2013-11, available at http://papers.ssrn.com/sol3/papers.cfm?abstract_id = 2276396.

565. *See e.g.*, Tom, Willard, et al., *Anticompetitive Aspects of Market-Share Discounts and Other Incentives to Exclusive Dealing*, 67 Antitrust Law Journal (2000) 615.

rebate a de facto exclusivity agreement (alternatively creating de facto tying conduct). The *Article 102 Guidance Paper* even notices that conditional rebates can have anti-competitive foreclosure effects "similar to exclusive purchasing obligations".[566] From such a statement, one would expect exclusivity agreements and conditional rebates to be assessed in the same way. If the issue is the same, it would be sensible to apply the same analytical tool. All in all, the above shows that categorizing a rebate may not be as simple as it might seem since the price is not necessarily the exclusionary tool, and hence, neither the key element in determining whether a rebate [scheme] is contrary to Article 102 TFEU.

According to the EU Courts' case law, the price is not, necessarily,[567] the key element when assessing conditional rebates. The AEC-test has been rejected numerous times.[568] It has even been held that the test is "only one tool amongst others for the purposes of assessing a rebate scheme."[569] The focus has been on whether the rebate created a loyalty-inducing effect by analysing other factors such as, in particular, how the threshold is determined, the items that the rebate is calculated on, and the duration of the reference period.[570] This analysis has only been carried out when the rebate did *not* contain an obligation or promise on the customer's side to obtain all or most of its requirements from the dominant firm, though. In the event of a direct link to exclusivity or quasi-exclusivity, a loyalty-inducing effect has been presumed.[571] Accordingly, the EU Courts distinguish between those rebates which are conditional in the way that they contain an obligation or promise,[572] and second, those where the granting of the rebate (or whether the rebate is withdrawn) depends on the attainment of, for instance, sales objectives.[573] Nonetheless, in both events, the AEC-test has been determined as not being a prerequisite to a finding the rebate scheme abusive.[574] Such statements indicate that these rebates are viewed as non-pricing conduct.

This contrasts with the *Article 102 Guidance Paper* – as mentioned earlier. In this communication, the Commission embraces the AEC-test as the applicable test for conditional rebates including mixed bundling.[575] Besides being inconsistent with case law, it is further inconsistent with its initial comment that conditional rebates can have actual or potential anti-competitive foreclosure effects similar to exclusivity agreements. Therefore, one would have expected an approach to rebates that resembles the

---

566. *See the Article 102 Guidance Paper*, at 37. In the same sense, mixed bundling is treated within the category of "Tying and bundling" and not "Predation", see *id.* at 59–61.
567. *See* Case C-23/14, *Post Danmark II*, at 58.
568. The AEC-test was rejected as late as in *id.* at 61; Case T-286/09, *Intel*, at 142–6; Case C-549/10 P, *Tomra*, at 73–4. The question remains whether the ECJ will uphold the GC's judgment in *Intel*.
569. *See* Case C-23/14, *Post Danmark II*, at 61.
570. *See e.g.*, Case 322/81, *Michelin I*, at 75–86.
571. *See* Case T-286/09, *Intel*, at 85. The GC held "exclusivity rebates granted by an undertaking in a dominant position are by their very nature capable of restricting competition."
572. *See id.* at 76-7 *See* also Case T-155/06, *Tomra*, at 210; Case T-203/01, *Michelin II*, at 56.
573. *See* Case T-286/09, *Intel*, at 78. *See* also Case T-155/06, *Tomra*, at 211; Case T-203/01, *Michelin II*, at 57.
574. *See e.g.*, Case C-23/14, *Post Danmark II*, at 62; Case T-286/09, *Intel*, at 143–144; Case C-549/10 P, *Tomra*, at 79.
575. *See* the the *Article 102 Guidance Paper*, at 41 & 59–61.

one applied to exclusivity agreement (and tying/bundling for mixed bundling). A price/cost test cannot be an absolute condition – although it may be relevant in some cases – for the assessment of anti-competitive foreclosure effects since price is not necessarily the exclusionary tool. Instead, such test best serves as one tool among others. Despite this, the Commission specifies that a low price will be the key element in determining whether a rebate is anti-competitive rather than relying on other factors.[576] This inconsistency can only worsen the confusion that reigns: you just have to look at legal and economic literature in which many perceive rebates as pricing conduct; thus, advocating a price/cost test.[577] This has resulted in strong criticism as they, obviously, does not share the view of the EU Courts' case law. Despite all of this, the Commission is still to apply the AEC-test as the decisive test in a case –[578] at least for retroactive rebates,[579] which begs the question of whether the Commission believe the AEC test is right for the assessment of conditional rebates.

2.2.1.2 Inspiration from the US

Nonetheless, a different view may slowly appear due to debate caused by recent case law in the US.[580] Before continuing, it is worth mentioning that while the approach in the EU is also criticized for being formalistic and rejecting economic considerations, this is not the case in the US. It is instead quite the opposite as the argumentation concerns a "rule of reason"-approach versus a price/cost-test. Some commentators have even held the price/cost-test as being formalistic.[581] Difference between the EU and US approach, regarding conditional rebates, seems, therefore, to be that a by object approach[582] is applied in the EU (Chapter 4 which showed that exclusivity rebates and

---

576. *See id.* at 41.
577. For a general overview *see e.g.*, Whish & Bailey (2015); Padilla & O'Donoghue (2013). *See* also, among others, Geradin (2015); Peeperkorn (2015); Venit (2014); Nihoul (2014); Federico (2011); Waelbroeck, Denis, *Michelin II: A per se Rule against Rebates by Dominant Companies?*, 1 Journal of Competition Law and Economics (2005).
578. *See* Case COMP/37.990, *Intel*. The Commission applied the AEC-test; however, only as a supplement.
579. The Commission applied the AEC-test in a case regarding an incremental rebate scheme by Velux, and as result of the test, closed the investigation. However, the decision is not public available and the facts of the case is, therefore, unclear. *See*, nonetheless, Albaek & Claici (2009).
580. *See* in particular *ZF Meritor, LLC v. Eaton Corp.*, 696 F.3d 254 (2012). *LePage's Inc. v. 3M*, 324 F.3d 141 (2003) (en banc)). *See* in contrast *Eisai Inc. v. Sanofi-Aventis U.S., LLC et al.*, No. 08-4168 (MLC) (2014). An assessment which focused on the price was applied.
581. *See* Salop, Steven, *Exclusionary Conduct, Effect on Consumers, and the Flawed Profit-Sacrifice Standard*, 73 Antitrust Law Journal (2006) 311.
582. Some prefer using the word "per se". However, in this book it has been explained that this word is unfit for Article 102 TFEU as it might risk being misunderstood in the context that no justifications are allowed. Moreover, "by object" differ from "per se" in the sense that it requires some sort of analysis, meaning conduct cannot be held abusive due to its form only, but rather that a potential anti-competitive effect must be shown. *See* Chapter 4.

loyalty-inducing rebates have historically been viewed a by object restriction) and a by effect-approach is applied in the US.[583]

The US antitrust distinguishes between Predation and Exclusion;[584] hence, there exists a similar debate of how to assess conditional rebates.[585] Simplified, the discussion concerns whether they ought to be assessed according to a price/cost-test (i.e., Predation)[586] or a rule of reason approach (i.e., Exclusion)[587]. Especially one recent case is reflective of this debate; namely *Eaton v. ZF Meritor*[588] (2012).[589] The plaintiff, ZF Meritor, had argued that the rebate applied in the case was to be assessed as an exclusivity agreement while the defendant, Eaton, argued in favour of a price/cost-test (known as the Brook Group-test) since case law, traditionally, had applied such test in similar cases.[590] In the end, the Third Circuit Court found that a price/cost test was irrelevant in the case. A price/cost-test was only relevant if the price had been the predominant mechanism of exclusion.[591] Accordingly, whether a rebate [scheme] is subject to a price/cost test depends on whether the price is under review.

Another case in similar lines from the US is *LePage's v. 3M*[592] (2003). Here the alleged abusive conduct was a bundled rebate. As with *Eaton v. ZF Meritor*, it was concluded that a price/cost test was inappropriate for the assessment since the case could not be regarded as a matter of unlawful pricing but rather a matter of unlawful bundling.[593] Accordingly, US case law distinguishes between pricing and non-pricing conduct. This was further seen in *Eisai v. Sano-Aventis*[594] (2014). In contrast to the two other cases, the price was found to be central to the assessment; thus, a price/cost test was applied as the relevant assessment tool.

Because of these cases, Joshua Wright, FTC Commissioner at the time, jumped into the debate over the proper approach for analysing the potential anti-competitive

---

583. Whether this will continue to be true is likely to be made clear in the ECJ's upcoming judgment in *Intel*.
584. *See e.g.*, Moore & Wright (2015); Salop (2006).
585. *See* Wright (2013). *See* also the debate between Steven Salop, Daniel Crane and Thomas Lambert at truthonthemarket.com which stems from Wright's speech.
586. For those advocating a price/cost test see, among others, Fumagalli, Chiara & Motta, Massimo, *On the Use of Price-Cost Tests in Loyalty Discount: Which Implications From Economic Theory*, 2015, CEPR Discussion Paper No. DP10550 available at http://papers.ssrn.com/sol3/papers.cfm?abstract_id=2596630; Areeda, Phillip & Hovenkamp, Herbert, *Antitrust Law: An Analysis of Antitrust Principles and Their Application*, 2015; Bishop & Walker (2010); Crane, Daniel, *Mixed Bundling, Profit Sacrifice, and Consumer Welfare*, 55 Emory Law Journal (2006) 423; Lambert, Thomas, *Evaluating Bundled Discounts*, 89 Minnesota Law Review (2005) 1688.
587. For those advocating the exclusive dealing test see, among others, Moore & Wright (2015); Gates (2013); Economides, Nicholas, Loyalty/Requirement Rebates and the Antitrust Modernization Commission: What is the Appropriate Liability Standard?, 2009, NET Institute Working Paper No. #09-02 available at http://papers.ssrn.com/sol3/papers.cfm?abstract_id=1370699; Jacobson (2002); Tom, et al. (2000).
588. *See ZF Meritor, LLC v. Eaton Corp.*
589. For a review of the case see Wright (2013), at 12–6; Fumagalli & Motta (2015), at 2–4.
590. *See Brooke Group Ltd. v. Brown & Williamson Tobacco Corp.*, 509 U.S. 209 (1993).
591. *See ZF Meritor, LLC v. Eaton Corp.*, at 275.
592. *See LePage's Inc. v. 3M*.
593. *See id.* at 154–5.
594. *See Eisai Inc. v. Sanofi-Aventis U.S., LLC et al.*

effects of loyalty rebates.[595] He approved the approach in *Eaton v. ZF Meritor*, stating that he believes Exclusion better accords with current economic research.[596] In other words, he recommends Exclusion when the price is not the exclusionary tool. Accordingly, it may be that the EU and the US are converging on the assessment conditional rebates.[597] Whether he agrees with *Eisai v. Sano-Aventis* does not follow since it was delivered after his speech, but it is reasonable to consider he agrees on the fact that that case concerned a matter of price.[598]

2.2.1.3 The (Ir)relevance of a Price/Cost-Test

The analysis above highlighted the different mechanisms that Predation and Exclusion have for causing anti-competitive foreclosure effects, and hence, why conditional rebates cause debate. These differences apply specifically to the role of a price/cost-test. According to case law, a price/cost-test is needed for pricing conduct (i.e., conduct falling within Predation). For conduct within Exclusion, such test is not needed. Some commentators have argued that conditional rebates are, although a concern for Exclusion, only abusive when price is below cost.[599] However, a price below cost cannot constitute an absolute requirement for the finding of abuse.[600]

This can be illustrated by its (ir)relevance for demonstrating anti-competitive foreclosure effect (i.e., why it can cause false negatives). The first argument for why a price below cost cannot be an absolute precondition can be illustrated through an example where a monopolist faces emerging entry by an [as efficient] entrant.[601] Before entry (i.e., period one), the monopolist is charging a price of EUR 100 and selling 400 units with [marginal] costs of EUR 50, so that its profit margin is EUR 50 per unit and a total profit of EUR 20,000. After the entrant (also with costs of EUR 50) enters (i.e., period two), the price falls to EUR 60. Suppose that at a price of EUR 60 both firms will sell 300 units, earning a profit margin of EUR 10 per unit and total profits of EUR 3,000 each.

In fear of this loss of profits (EUR 20,000 to EUR 3,000), the monopolist provides a rebate conditional on exclusivity. While the entrant may engage in a bidding war, the monopolist is likely to prevail. It is paying to maintain its market power, whereas the entrant can only pay to achieve viability. The market power funds a higher bid. This

---

595. *See* Wright (2013).
596. *See id.*
597. *See* Davie, Yann, *EU and US Antitrust: Converging Approaches to Monopolies?*, 2014; Fogt, Howard, *US and EU Converging on Dominant-Firm-Abuse Theory*, 2013.
598. *See* Wright (2013), at footnote 59.
599. *See e.g.*, Klein, Benjamin & Lerner, Andres, *Price-Cost Tests in Antitrust Analysis of Single Product Loaylty Contracts*, 80 Antitrust Law Journal (2016) 631.(Who argues that a price-cost test is an appropriate threshold test required to establish whether a loyalty discount amounts to de facto exclusive dealing, and thus, should be evaluated under exclusive-dealing law); Crane, Daniel, *The Paradox of Predatory Pricing*, 91 Cornell Law Review (2005) 1. (Who argues that a price below cost is a necessary condition of anti-competitive effects, and thus, a safe harbor for prices above cost is appropriate no matter the allegedly harmful conduct).
600. *See e.g.*, Salop (2016); Moore & Wright (2015).
601. This example is derived from Salop (2016).

means that the entrant would be willing to bid up to its EUR 3,000 (i.e., its profit if it enters) to prevent its exclusion while the monopolist would be willing to bid an amount up to EUR 17,000 (EUR 20,000 minus EUR 3,000) to maintain its monopoly. The monopolist would prevail with a bid of EUR 3,001 and end up with a profit of EUR 16,999. The reduction in price would be EUR 100 minus approx. EUR 7.50 (EUR 3,001/400 units)[602] EUR 92.50 which is well above costs. While this example is simple, it illustrates why a rebate, even though it may look as a Predation, is not a matter of low pricing but rather Exclusion. It must be noted that, while not directly stated, the example relies on the entrant only being able to take half the market in period two. The dominant firm is only able to outbid the entrant due to the entrant's expectation of viability; i.e., it expects only to steal some of the dominant firm's share rather than potentially all. If the entrant were able to enter and compete for exclusivity, the dominant firm would have to set its price below costs to achieve foreclosure.

While this stylish example illustrates why the classical price/cost-test can fail to show anti-competitive effects, a price/cost-test focusing on the effective price[603] might fit as an analytical tool.[604] The effective price, which the competitor must match, is therefore not the average price of the dominant firm, but the standard price less the rebate, which the customer loses by switching to the competitor.[605] However, this price/cost-test has a serious flaw (the second point). To calculate the effective price, a contestable share is required. That contestable share is defined by the Commission as the incremental purchases for incremental rebates and the amount of a customer's purchase requirements that can realistically be switched to a competitor for retroactive rebates. While it is to some degree simple to calculate a contestable share in respect of incremental rebates it is inherently complex in terms of retroactive rebates. In addition, the two sides (i.e., the dominant firm and the competitor(s)) will often disagree on the magnitude of the contestable share because they are relying on different source documents, estimations and other calculations.[606] For these reasons, the test will often be somewhat subjective and depend on the party calculating the price. The predictions of the test could, therefore, be incorrect, leading to implementation errors. Considering the fact that case law, so far, has only dealt with retroactive rebates, it is therefore not surprising that the price/cost-test has been rejected. Note also that the effective price is EUR 85 in the example under the assumption that the contestable share is 50%.[607] This is clearly above costs.

Regarding the third point, a conditional rebate (both single- and multi-product rebates) needs not to represent a true rebate at all.[608] As noted above in section 2.2.1.1,

---

602. That is, a rebate at 7.5%.
603. Note that the effective price is $\approx$ EUR 85 which is above costs under the assumption the contestable share is 50%. That is, EUR 100 * (1 − (7.5%/50%)).
604. *See* Klein & Lerner (2016).
605. *See the Article 102 Guidance Paper*, at 41.
606. *See* Rummel, Per, *Rebate schemes under Article 102 TFEU: Post Danmark II*, 53 Common Market Law Review (2016) 1121, at 1122; Salop (2016), at 45.
607. That is, EUR 100 * (1 − (7.5%/50%)). *See* the formula in Federico, Giulio, *The Antitrust Treatment of Loyalty Discounts in Europe: Towards a more Economic Approach*, 2 Journal of European Competition Law & Practice (2011) 277, at 284.
608. *See* Elhauge (2009), at 450.

it can be turned around in the sense that the dominant firm charges higher prices to buyers who will not comply with the exclusivity or bundling condition than to buyers who will. This presupposes an ability to set the stand-alone prices at whatever level above that which it would have priced at absent the rebate; for instance, because the dominant firm's product is a must-stock product for customers. In that event, the stand-alone price can exceed the prices that would have prevailed absent the rebate. The stand-alone price is in that sense a penalty.[609] Given the dominant firm is able to set a monopoly price in the primary market, or for the contestable share, it can set a stand-alone price equalling the monopoly price plus the rebate.[610] Although the customer receives a lower price (and may prefer to buy) due to the rebate, it does not really represent a rebate, and the customer is not better off. It ends up paying the same price and loses a potential supplier.

Since the rebate acts as a penalty, Exclusion is the best fit. The purpose is not to provide a low price followed by recoupment. Instead, it is to foreclose competitors from the market by raising their costs by, for instance, preventing economies of scale. To find a rebate being a penalty rather than a true rebate requires a "but-for price"; i.e., the price without the rebate.[611] This means that the Commission must be able to prove that the rebate is not a reduction in the price that would have prevailed otherwise (but rather an indirect increase). In the perfect world, the Commission could observe a price before the dominant firm started offering its rebate. However, such information is not necessarily available which leaves the Commission in a situation where it must estimate the "but-for price". An exact price would be unrealistic, though. As long as it is able to demonstrate that the rebate represents an increase and not reduction, it should suffice.

The above analysis shows that a price/cost is not necessarily adequate for the assessment of rebates. However, this is not to conclude that a price/cost-test is always irrelevant. For example, if the incremental price is below costs the AEC-test can be applied as presented in the *Article 102 Guidance Paper*.[612] This will then require a careful examination of the dominant firm's costs that would otherwise have been saved by assessing the rebate as Exclusion.

2.2.1.4 Concluding Remarks

It has been shown that case law, when dealing with conditional rebates, has focused on elements other than price; consequently, rejecting the AEC-test as a prerequisite of finding a rebate abusive. However, it must be stressed that this has been in the events of exclusivity rebates and rebates with similar effects (i.e., loyalty-inducing rebates). More specifically, these rebates have been given retroactively (also known as an all

---

609. *See* Economides (2013), at 130–1.
610. *See* Rubinfeld, Daniel, *3M's Bundled Rebates: An Economic Perspective*, 72 The University of Chicago Law Review (2005) 243. *See* also Greenlee, Patrick, et al., *An Antitrust Analysis of Bundled Loyalty Discounts*, 26 International Journal of Industrial Organization (2008) 1132.
611. *See* Economides (2013); Elhauge (2009); Greenlee, et al. (2008).
612. *See e.g., the Article 102 Guidance Paper*, at 70.

unit-rebate) and conditional in some way or the other.[613] In contrast, non-conditional rebates have been subject to Predation.[614] Concerning a conditional rebate that is given as an incremental rebate, the EU Courts have not been given a chance to express their stance. Instead, the Commission has had the chance. As explained earlier, the Commission applied a price/cost-test that indicates that this type of rebate belongs to the Predation category.

It was also shown why a price/cost-test might cause false negatives when applied to conditional rebates. This was due to three points that all showed, individually and combined, why a price/cost-test might fail to show anti-competitive foreclosure effects. The most robust of point was the one illustrating that a conditional rebate can represent a penalty rather than a truer rebate. Based these findings, some conclusions can be made.[615]

First, exclusivity rebates (also known as loyalty or fidelity rebates) falls within the category of Exclusion. This type of rebate is defined by the EU Courts as a rebate which involves "financial advantages [that] tends to prevent [customers] from obtaining all or most of their requirements from [competitors]."[616] That definition is quite ambiguous, however. As a result, this definition must be read in connection with other parts of the judgments if these rebates are to be defined. By doing so, one discovers that these rebates involve an obligation or promise by the customer to obtain all or most of his supplies from the dominant firm.[617] The "all or most of its requirements" are generally accepted when customers are obliged to buy 80% or more of its requirement from the dominant firm.[618] In *Intel*, for instance, the lowest percentage was 80% (in the case of NEC).[619] Setting a certain threshold for the requirement would be too inflexible as it must depend on the specific case, though.[620] Accordingly this type of rebate concerns either exclusivity or quasi-exclusivity from the customer; hence, the name exclusivity rebates. Regarding retroactive versus incremental, the EU Courts have not dealt with an incremental exclusivity rebate. Despite this, it is likely to be the same outcome as it does not change the fact that exclusivity is the issue of matter and not the price.

Second, loyalty-inducing rebates also fall into the category of Exclusion. This type of rebate is also a conditional rebate. It is absent of a direct link to a condition of exclusive or quasi-exclusive supply but is rather, for instance, depending on the

---

613. Either: (i) linked to an obligation or promise to obtain all or a given proportion of supplies from the dominant firm, *or* (ii) depending on the attainment of sales objectives.
614. *See* Case C-209/10, *Post Danmark I*.
615. All this requires of course that the case law continue to set the precedent for rebates that depends on, especially, the forthcoming ECJ judgment in *Intel*.
616. *See e.g.*, Case C-23/14, *Post Danmark II*, at 27. *See* also Case C-549/10 P, *Tomra*, at 70; Case 322/81, *Michelin I*, at 71; Case 85/76, *Hoffman La Roche*, at 89.
617. *See* Case C-23/14, *Post Danmark II*, at 28. The ECJ stated that: "Moreover, [the rebate] was not coupled with an obligation for, or promise by, purchasers to obtain all or a given proportion of their supplies from Post Danmark, a point which served to distinguish it from loyalty rebates within the meaning of the case-law referred to in paragraph 27 above." Paragraph 27 included the definition mentioned in the text above. *See* also Case 322/81, *Michelin I*, at 72.
618. *See the Vertical Restraints Guidelines*, at 129. *See* also Colomo (2016), at 714–5.
619. *See* Case T-286/09, *Intel*, at 79.
620. *See* for that effect Case C-549/10 P, *Tomra*, at 43.

attainment of individual sales objectives.[621] In other words, it is a rebate which falls out of the scope of exclusivity rebates but has a similar effect. In general, a loyalty-inducing rebate has been held when the rebate [scheme] was retroactive with a reference period of one year.[622] Other factors such as the customers targeted[623], the sales objectives being individualized[624], the wide divergence between the dominant firm's market share and those of its main competitors[625] and a lack of transparency[626] have also been part of the assessment but has not been recurring factors in every case. Although it has not been stated by the EU Courts or the Commission it is likely that the consideration made above regarding the irrelevance of a price/cost-test has had an influence on the assessment of loyalty rebates; especially, the complexity and uncertainty surrounding retroactive rebates and the effective price.

According to these conclusions, retroactive rebates are to be assessed as either an exclusivity or loyalty-inducing rebate. That may not always be the case, though. In the analysis above, the dominant firm is presumed to be an unavoidable trading partner.[627] In all the case referred to above, the dominant firm has been found to hold an unavoidable trading partner-status. Case law has even gone the length of finding a dominant position [almost] always equals an unavoidable trading partner.[628] However, a dominant firm may not always be an unavoidable trading partner. This will depend on many factors; for instance, the market characteristic, the nature of the goods, the number and size of customers and competitors, the differentiation of the firms' goods and so on. Accordingly, a firm may be dominant but not necessarily an unavoidable trading partner; the former does not entail the latter, but the latter may be a factor in determining a dominant position since such position is likely to allow the firm to act independently.[629] If a dominant firm is *not* an unavoidable trading partner, then it and its competitors are competing, or at least able to do so, for exclusivity on, all things being equal, equal terms. The winner, in other words, is the firm who can offer the best price, product or so; hence, the dominant firm cannot (ab)use a position as an unavoidable trading partner. In such events, the price may become the exclusionary tool and the rebate may then fall within Predation since price competition is enhanced.[630] Nevertheless, the assessment can revert to Exclusion if other factors than the price represent the exclusionary tool.

---

621. *See id.*; Case C-95/04 P, *British Airways*; Case 322/81, *Michelin I*.
622. *See e.g.,* Case C-23/14, *Post Danmark II*, at 32–35 (in particular 35).
623. *See* Case C-549/10 P, *Tomra*, at 75.
624. *See* Case C-95/04 P, *British Airways*, at 71; Case 322/81, *Michelin I*, at 64.
625. *See* Case 322/81, *Michelin I*, at 82.
626. *See id.* at 83.
627. The same is generally true theories within Raising Rivals' Costs (i.e., Exclusion), see Wright (2013), at 21.
628. *See* Case C-23/14, *Post Danmark II*, at 40; Case T-286/09, *Intel*, at 91. *See also* Case T-155/06, *Tomra*, at 269; Case C-95/04 P, *British Airways*, at 75; Case 85/76, *Hoffman La Roche*, at 41.
629. As it was the case in Case 85/76, *Hoffman La Roche*, at 41.
630. This is also true if the reference period corresponds to the frequency of purchased. For example, if customers purchase every six month and the reference period of which the rebate is calculated is six month. In that event, the retroactive rebate becomes effectively an incremental

As with exclusivity rebates, the EU Courts have not been given the chance to give it stance on incremental non-exclusivity rebates. But the Commission has. As explained earlier, the Commission applied a price/cost-test which indicates that this type of rebate belongs to the category of Predation. Given that the EU Courts agree with the Commission, this means that incremental non-exclusivity rebates fall outside the scope of loyalty-inducing rebates while retroactive non-exclusivity rebates fall within the scope of loyalty-inducing rebates. Such conclusion should be reached with care, however. If the rebate constitutes a penalty for disloyal customers rather than a true rebate, it will more likely be an issue for Exclusion rather than Predation.

Regarding mixed bundling, such rebates may fall within one or the other category depending on the specific case. If the rebate represents a penalty for customers who will not accept the bundle, then that rebate falls within Exclusion. If on the other hand, it represents a true rebate, then it falls within Predation since the (potential) issue is a low price. This means that mixed bundling in the former event will resemble tying and pure bundling. The same analogy can be applied for single-product rebates above. This applies to those rebates that are retroactive as wells as those that are incremental.

All in all, single-product rebates in the form of exclusivity rebates and loyalty-inducing rebates (those having the same effect as an exclusivity rebate) fall with Exclusion. The also goes for mixed bundling when the rebate represents a penalty rather than a true rebate. The same principle also applies to single-product rebates in regards of whether they constitute a loyalty-inducing rebate, and it may be a helpful to tool to distinguish between predatory and loyalty-inducing rebates. Other types of rebates fall within Predation as the exclusionary mechanism relates then to a low price and not the tying of customers. These rebates will be referred to as Predatory rebates.

2.2.2 Margin Squeeze

As with rebates, margin squeeze is subject to controversy. This originates from the divergences between the approach taken in the US and the on in EU.[631] In the US, margin squeeze can be caught by either refusal to deal or predatory pricing.[632] In contrast, margin squeeze qualifies as a standalone abuse from refusal to deal and predatory pricing in EU focusing on the spread between the upstream and downstream price.[633] As a result, it is debated whether margin squeeze should be recognized as a

---

rebate. However, such scenario is unlikely, as the incentive to create a retroactive rebate scheme would be little. Instead, the dominant firm would have an incentive to apply exclusivity rebates.

631. *See* Hay, George & McMahon, Kathryn, *The Diverging Approach to Price Squeezes in the United States and Europe*, 8 Journal of Competition Law & Economics (2012) 259; Meisel, John, *The Law and Economics of Margin Squeezes in the US versus the EU*, 8 European Competition Journal (2012).
632. This was established in *Pacific Bell Telephone Co. v. linkLine Communications, Inc.*, 555 U.S 438 (2009).
633. *See* Case C-52/09, *TeliaSonera*, at 34 & 56. *See* also Gaudin, Germain & Mantzari, Despoina, *Margin Squeeze: An Above-Cost Predaotry Pricing Approach*, 12 Journal of Competition Law and Economics (2016) 1, at 2.

distinct, stand-alone category of abuse or whether it should be treated in an equivalent fashion to other established forms of abuse such as refusal to deal and predatory pricing exist.[634]

A closer look at the EU Courts' case law reveals the reason for qualifying margin squeeze as a standalone abuse. This is because, first, the so-called "Bronner condition" (i.e., a product or service that is indispensable) does not act as a precondition for finding unlawful margin squeeze,[635][636] and second, that the downstream price needs not to be predatory.[637] Instead, focus in on the margin. Thus, unlawful margin squeeze can be found without neither the test for refusal to deal nor the test for predatory pricing being satisfied.

That margin squeeze (or other types of contrastive refusal)[638] does not presuppose an indispensable upstream input to be unlawful ought not to be that controversial, though. That requirement may entail "double work". This is the case when the dominant firm has already been imposed a duty to deal. It will be over the top to require the finding of an indispensable upstream input if national authorities have already imposed an obligation to deal – given that the necessary balancing of incentives has already been made by the national authorities.[639] And as it "happens" to be with margin squeeze cases within the EU they have primarily concerned former state monopolies with an obligation to deal[640] and, in regards to the cases handled by the Commission, and afterwards the EU Courts, the market for broadband services in which the dominant firm had been imposed a duty to deal.[641] While it does not follow directly from the EU Courts' case law that the rejection of the "*Bronner* condition" is caused by the fact that the dominant firms were former state monopolies obliged to deal with its downstream competitors, recent Commission decisions have been more explicit.[642]

---

634. See e.g., Heimler, Alberto, *Is a Margin Squeeze an Antitrust or a Regulatory Violation?*, 6 Journal of Competition Law & Economics (2010) 879; Carlton, Dennis, *Should "Price Squeeze" be a Recognised Form of Anticompetitive Conduct?*, 4 Journal of Competition Law and Economics (2008) 271; Jones, Alison, *Identifying an Unlawful Margin Squeeze: The Recent Judgments of the Court of Justice in Deutsche Telekom and TeliaSonera*, in *Cambridge Yearbook of European Legal Studies* (Alan Dashwood & Angela Ward eds.), 2010.

635. See Case C-52/09, *TeliaSonera*, at 58.

636. There is also the question of whether the condition of a "new product" is or is not a precondition for the finding of unlawful margin squeeze.

637. See Case C-52/09, *TeliaSonera*, at 34.

638. See e.g., Commission Decision of 22 June 2011 in Case COMP/39.525, *Telekomunikacja Polska*.

639. See for that effect the *Article 102 Guidance Paper*, at 82.

640. See Veljanovski, Cento, *Margin Squeeze: An Overview of EU and National Case Law*, e-Competitions: Competition Laws Bulletin (2012) 1, at 1. (Who suggest that, out of 41 margin squeeze cases, 29 (nearly 71%) of the case were in the telecommunications sector, followed by three in the postal sector, two in the water sector, and one decision each in the gas, electricity, aviation, railway, pharmaceuticals, entertainment and construction sectors).

641. See Case AT.39523, *Slovak Telekom*; Commission Decision of 16 July 2003 in Case COMP/ 38.233, *Wanadoo Interactive*; Case COMP/C-1/37.451, 37.578, 37.579, *Deutsche Telekom AG*. See in contrast TeliaSonera, that was not deal with by the Commission, (preliminary ruling) where the dominant frim was not under any regulatory obligation to deal, see Case C-52/09, *TeliaSonera*, at 6.

642. See Case AT.39523, *Slovak Telekom*, at 363. ("The Commission considers that the circumstances of the present case, and in particular the existence of a regulatory framework for the

In those circumstances, it makes perfect sense that margin squeeze qualifies as a standalone abuse from refusal to deal (in the sense that indispensability does not need to be proven), since a duty to deal is already imposed. It is then not a matter of whether a duty to deal should be imposed but whether the dominant firm is breaching its obligation. In other words, the difference between margin squeeze and refusal to deal in case law have been that for the former a duty deal has already been imposed while it for the latter was necessary to examine whether such obligation could be imposed by a competition authority.

This might be viewed as controversial since the rejection of the "Bronner condition" comes from *TeliaSonera* – a case in which the dominant firm was not under any regulatory obligation to deal.[643] But, on the other hand, it is exactly in those circumstances that it was relevant for the ECJ to provide indispensability as a way to demonstrate the anti-competitive element. As pointed out above, when an obligation to deal is already imposed, it is a matter of whether that obligation is abused. When that is not the case, it is relevant to assess whether the upstream input is indispensable to competitors' effective penetration of the downstream market. While this may be seen as margin squeeze being treated in an equivalent fashion to refusal to deal it is better understood as a method to prove a reasonable prospect of recoupment (see Chapter 5, section 5 for more details). In effect, it shows whether the dominant firm will be able to benefit from the foreclosure. In consequence, the ECJ was correct to reject indispensability as an absolute condition for unlawful margin squeeze while it is, as the ECJ pointed out, still an important aspect.

One could argue that this aspect should not be reserved exclusively for the case of indispensability, but that it should also apply to cases in which the upstream input has been developed under the protection of special/exclusive rights or has been financed by state resources – which seems to be the standpoint if the Commission in it *Article 102 Guidance Paper.*[644] This would at least help understand what is meant when the ECJ in *TeliaSonera* held that "taking into account the dominant position of the undertaking concerned in the upstream market, the possibility cannot be ruled out that, by reason simply of the fact that the upstream input is not indispensable for the supply of the downstream product, a pricing practice which causes margin squeeze may not be able to produce any anti-competitive effect, even potentially." Moreover, this aspect is further important in regards to the event where there already is a duty to deal. In other words, while the dominant firm may be imposed a duty to deal, its product/service may not necessarily be indispensable according to the test presented in *Bronner*. But even it that event, an anti-competitive effect must be shown as it would

---

access to ULL market and the existence of ST's obligation to give access to its local loop are different from the circumstances in the Bronner case"). For constructive refusals, see Case COMP/39.525, *Telekomunikacja Polska.*

643. *See* Case C-52/09, *TeliaSonera*, at 6 & 47.
644. *See* the *the Article 102 Guidance Paper*, at 82 ("This could also be the case where the upstream market position of the dominant undertaking has been developed under the protection of special or exclusive rights or has been financed by state resources.").

otherwise be a matter of regulation (and not competition law). In *Telefónica*, for example, it was found that competitors on the downstream market did not have a viable alternative input (Telefónica was a former state monopoly who benefited from that position);[645] thus limiting the competitive pressure on Telefónica.

In effect, the analysis above shows that margin squeeze can be held as an independent form of abuse from that of refusal to deal. The question is then whether that goes for predatory pricing as well. A review of case law and decisional practice shows that these have relied on the AEC-test. The relevance of the AEC-test has further been confirmed by the ECJ.[646] As a result, margin squeeze has been termed as a form of pricing conduct by the EU Courts.[647] One might, therefore, conclude that the issue has been a matter of Predation since the price has been the exclusionary tool; i.e., that margin squeeze has been viewed as a tool that enables the dominant firm to increase its profits following the foreclosure effect.

In fact, margin squeeze is slowly being accepted as a form of "above-cost-predatory pricing" where opportunity costs [of not selling to its downstream competitors] are added to the assessment of whether the dominant is pricing unlawfully low;[648] thus part of Predation. In effect, that is what is proposed by the ECJ when it is examined whether the dominant firm's downstream arm could operate with a profit if it had to pay the upstream price charged to its competitors.

However, it seems most sensible to apply Predation when [a duty to deal is imposed and] the dominant firm is unable to adjust its upstream price as it wishes. This is even an assumption behind the argument of viewing margin squeeze as "above cost-predatory pricing".[649] The price may, for instance, be fully or partly regulated by a national regulatory authority;[650] i.e., either an absolute or maximum price is set. Additionally, even if the upstream price is not regulated, adjusting (i.e., raising) it may be seen as excessive pricing, and this may refrain a dominant firm from engaging in such conduct as it may lead to (increased) regulation or a competition law case. In other words, such feared intervention may create a de facto regulated upstream price. If this is not the case, the dominant firm would be better off by raising its upstream price allowing it to capture the surplus of the most efficient downstream firm (either

---

645. *See* Case COMP/38.784, *Wanadoo España v. Telefónica*, at 223–242. Upheld in Judgment of 29 March 2012 in Case T-336/07, *Telefónica SA v. European Commission* ("*Telefónica*"), at 275; Case C-295/12 P, *Telefónica*, at 119.
646. *See* Case C-52/09, *TeliaSonera*, at 31–4; Case C-280/08 P, *Deutsche Telekom*, at 200–4.
647. *See e.g.*, Case T-286/09, *Intel*, at 98–9.
648. *See e.g.*, Gaudin & Mantzari (2016); Petzold, Daniel, *It Is All Predatory Pricing: Margin Squeeze Abuse and the Concept of Opportunity Costs in EU Competition Law*, 6 Journal of European Competition Law & Practice (2015) 346; Heimler (2010).
649. Gaudin & Mantzari (2016), at 13–6 (who assummes a duty to deal plus opreates with a [maximum] price for the wholesale product/service).
650. This was the case in Deutsche Telekom, see Case COMP/C-1/37.451, 37.578, 37.579, *Deutsche Telekom AG*, at 5; Judgment of 10 April 2008 in Case T-271/03, *Deutsche Telekom AG v. Commission of the European Communities* ("*Deutsche Telekom*"), at 11. *See also* Case AT.39523, *Slovak Telekom*, at 41.

itself or a competitor).[651] Therefore, when the dominant firm is restricted or refrained from adjusting its upstream price, it is sensible to adjust the downstream price and thereby sacrifice profits in the short run for increased profits in the long run.

If the dominant firm is not imposed a duty to deal and neither restricted or refrained from adjusting its upstream price it would be more sensible to increase its downstream price [to the monopoly profit level] and instead increase the upstream price creating a margin for its competitors that does not allow them to operate profitable in the market; i.e., engaging in de facto refusal to deal. By doing so, the dominant firm does not have to sacrifice profits to achieve greater profits. In other words, it is able to increase its price and profits by engaging in Exclusion rather than Predation. This means that margin squeeze goes from conduct similar to predatory pricing to conduct similar to refusal to deal. The dominant firm effectively hinders its competitors' access to the market or alternatively makes it more difficult. This is achieved in the same way as above by making it unprofitable for competitors to enter the market (i.e., competitors must price below cost to match the dominant firm's downstream prices). Accordingly, the AEC-test is still useful despite the issue being Exclusion and not Predation. That is, if, because of the adjusted upstream prices, the dominant firm's downstream price does not allow even an as an efficient competitor to trade profitably (covering LRAIC)[652] in the downstream market then the dominant firm is effectively engaging in refusal to deal. The difference is that profit is not sacrificed. For the motivation behind such margin squeeze, see Chapter 7.

Accordingly, whether competitors can compete with the downstream price does not necessarily reveal a pro-competitive effect; neither does it tell whether margin squeeze is a matter Predation or Exclusion (or even exploitive conduct). One would instead benefit from taking a starting point in Figure 5.1. What matters is whether the downstream or the upstream price is the issue. If the former is the subject of matter, the issue is a period of low downstream prices (potentially below the upstream price) followed by a period of high downstream prices. If the latter is the subject of matter, the issue is a high upstream price that forces the downstream price up to the detriment of consumers. The latter may happen even where a positive margin is unable to cover the relevant costs (or even the downstream price) as the dominant firm, for example, is facing competitors who are more efficient as itself.[653] As a result, if the downstream price is the issue then margin squeeze is a concern for Predation (Chapter 6). If on the other hand, the upstream price is the issue then it is a concern for Exclusion (Chapter 7) – or exploitive abuse if it is not exclusionary. Therefore, it is important to be clear on the exclusionary tool.[654]

---

651. This type of margin squeeze has also been termed as exploitive margin squeeze, see Jullien, Bruno, et al., The Economics of Margin Squeeze, 2014, CEPR Discussion Paper No. DP9905 available at http://papers.ssrn.com/sol3/papers.cfm?abstract_id = 2444927.
652. *See* Case AT.39523, *Slovak Telekom*, at 860; *the Article 102 Guidance Paper*, at 80.
653. *See e.g.*, the example used in Gaudin & Mantzari (2016).
654. *See* Jullien, et al. (2014). (Who also recognizes that exclusionary margin squeeze can either viewed under Predation or Exclusion).

2.3   Categorizing Types of Conduct

According to the above, some guidelines on how to divide different types of exclusionary conduct into the two overall categories can be made. Initially, it must be stressed that the results reached are non-exhaustive; i.e., it is not an exhaustive list of the possible types of exclusionary abuse that may be caught by Article 102 TFEU but merely examples. Additionally, whether a type of exclusionary conduct falls within Predation or Exclusion depends on the specific case. Exclusionary conduct that is classified, generally, as Predation in one case may be found to be a better fit for Exclusion in another case and vice versa. For instance, an exclusivity agreement may be a better fit for Predation if a review of the circumstances of the case reveals that a low price is the tool that is applied to tie up customers.

Categorizing different types of conduct may seem formalistic. Since the "form" decides the test to be applied, it may not be directly evident that focus is actually on effects. As stressed above, however, to determine which category exclusionary conduct falls into one must consider the circumstances of the specific case. Just looking at the form of a dominant firm's conduct is not enough. This was illustrated with rebates and margin squeeze. In addition, the (potential) anti-competitive effect is actually the primary reasons for this categorization. It recognizes that anti-competitive harm differs from conduct to conduct which justifies the categorization. Should it, nevertheless, be held that having two overall categories forms a form-based approach, then everything within competition law is form-based. For instance, prohibited conduct is categorised as either an illegal agreement, abuse of dominance, illegal state aid and so on. Moreover, within Article 101 TFEU a distinction between vertical and horizontal agreements are made. Therefore, it is impossible to get rid of the form-based approach if it is defined as narrowly. Competition law – and all law in generally – is built on form-based elements and principles.

Table 5.1   Examples of Types of Conduct within Predation and Exclusion

Predation	Exclusion
– Predatory pricing	– Exclusivity agreements & rebates
– Predatory rebates	– Tying & bundling
– Margin squeeze	– Loyalty-inducing & bundled rebates
	– Refusal to deal/supply

Note: This list is non-exhaustive (and, for example, margin squeeze may fall within Exclusion and bundled rebates can fall with Predation)

Although the definitive conclusion depends on the specific case, the findings above provide a general overview of which types of conduct fits under which category.

This overview is illustrated in Table 5.1.[655] Predatory pricing[656], selective pricing[657], predatory rebates[658] and margin squeeze[659] fall within the pricing category; i.e., Predation. On the other side, conduct such as tying/bundling[660], exclusivity agreements,[661] loyalty/bundle rebates[662] and refusal to supply[663] fall within the non-pricing category; i.e., Exclusion. For the first types of conduct, a low price is the exclusionary tool. When applying such conduct, the aim is to foreclose effective competition through a low pricing-period that then allows the dominant firm to raise its price. For the latter, raising the input costs constitutes the exclusionary tool. In consequence, the exclusionary tool decides the test applied to the assessment of anti-competitive effects.

3   IMPORTANT FACTORS

There are many differences between finding abuse through the object-approach and the effect-approach. For example, the former does not consider whether alleged conduct is likely to produce negative effects (they are by their very nature always serious, although not necessarily obvious) while the latter sees anti-competitive effects as something which depends on many factors related both to the particular features of the conduct itself and of the market in which it takes place.[664] Accordingly, the effect-based approach is influenced by different factors.[665] Since the assessment, in other words, must be carried out in the light of all the circumstances of a particular case,[666] it is not possible to provide an exhaustive list of factors which may or may not be important. Nevertheless, some factors are likely to be important in many, if not all, cases. It is, therefore, possible to provide a list of some the more important factors that can be considered.

---

655. It should be noted that the cases referred to in the previous footnotes does not necessarily represents cases involving an effect-based approach.
656. *See e.g.*, Case 62/86, *Akzo*; Case C-202/07 P, *France Télécom*.
657. *See e.g.*, Case C-209/10, *Post Danmark I*. In the view of this Author, predatory pricing and selective pricing are the same type of conduct in the same sense that exclusivity and quasi-exclusivity agreements are the same type of conduct. Due to the ECJ's distinction between them in *Post Danmark II*, however, they are also separate here; see Case C-23/14, *Post Danmark II*, at 55.
658. *See* for that effect Albaek & Claici (2009).
659. *See* Case C-295/12 P, *Telefónica*; Case C-52/09, *TeliaSonera*; Case C-280/08 P, *Deutsche Telekom*.
660. *See* Case T-201/04, *Microsoft*; Judgment of 2 March 1994 in Case C-53/92 P, *Hilti AG v. Commission of the European Communities* ("*Hilti*").
661. *See* Case C-552/03 P, *Van den Bergh Foods*; Case T-65/98, *Van den Bergh Foods*.
662. *See* Case C-23/14, *Post Danmark II*; Case T-286/09, *Intel*; Case C-549/10 P, *Tomra*; Case C-95/04 P, *British Airways*; Case T-203/01, *Michelin II*; Case 322/81, *Michelin I*; Case 85/76, *Hoffman La Roche*.
663. *See* Case T-201/04, *Microsoft*; Judgment of 26 November 1998 in Case C-7/97, *Oscar Bronner GmbH & Co. KG v. Mediaprint Zeitungs- und Zeitschriftenverlag GmbH & Co. KG* ("*Bronner*").
664. *See* Italianer (2014), at 2–3.
665. *See* Case C-549/10 P, *Tomra*, at 18. (The ECJ stated that "the Commission [...] is obliged to consider all of the relevant facts surrounding that conduct").
666. *See* Case C-23/14, *Post Danmark II*, at 68.

121

These factors can be found in the EU Courts' case law. Moreover, in its *Article 102 Guidance Paper*, the Commission has been advocating an effect-based approach.[667] Doing so, the Commission has listed different factors that might be relevant for the assessment of actual or likely anti-competitive effects. This includes seven factors that the Commission considers relevant.[668] Therefore, this section will focus on these seven factors and discuss why they might be important for the assessment. This list is of course not intended to be an exhaustive list. Neither is it intended to suggest a hierarchy among the listed factors since none of the factors can suffice in them self to confirm or disconfirm anti-competitive effects and some of the factors will even overlap in some or most events.

3.1   The Position of the Dominant Firm

The first factor is the position of the dominant firm. This may be expressed more precisely as the degree of dominance. Since abuse of dominance within Article 102 TFEU requires, first of all, the establishment of dominant position, it is not a question of whether the firm holds a dominant position. Instead, this aspect concerns the strength of that dominant position. The Commission's statement in its *Article 102 Guidance Paper* illustrates this. Here, the Commission take the position that, in general, the stronger the dominant position, the higher the likelihood that conduct protecting that position leads to anti-competitive foreclosure.[669]

The degree of dominance has also been important in older case law. For example, the divergence between the dominant firms' market shares and those of its competitors has been applied as a relevant factor in finding a rebate scheme abusive.[670] This balance of power strength meant that the retroactive rebate obtained by customers was artificially enlarged.[671] In practice, this resulted in a situation where a competitor had to offer a higher rebate than the dominant firm since the competitor could only win a part of the customers demand; hence, it would need to compensate the customer for the rebate lost on the part still supplied by the dominant firm, but without a rebate. The degree of dominance illustrated, thereby, the increased likelihood of anti-competitive effects in the specific case. Accordingly, the aspect overlapped other relevant factors such as the position of the dominant firm's competitors (see section 3.3).

Additionally, the concept of "super-dominance" or a "quasi-monopoly" has in a few cases been a relevant factor for the assessment of abuse. This was for the first time referred to by Advocate General Fennelly in *Compagnie Maritime Belge Transport*.

> "To my mind, [Article 102 TFEU] cannot be interpreted as permitting monopolists or quasi-monopolists to exploit the very significant market power which their superdominance confers so as to preclude the emergence either of a new or

---

667. *See the Article 102 Guidance Paper*, at 19; Italianer (2014), at 3.
668. *See the Article 102 Guidance Paper*, at 20.
669. *See id.* at 20 (first article).
670. *See* Case 322/81, *Michelin I*, at 82.
671. Owing also to the fact that the rebate was retroactive and the dominant firm an unavoidable partner.

additional competitor. Where an undertaking, or group of undertakings, or group of undertakings whose conduct must be assessed collectively, enjoys a position of such overwhelming dominance verging on monopoly, comparable to that which existed in the present case at the moment when G & C entered the relevant market, it would not be consonant with the particularly onerous special obligation affecting such a dominant undertaking not to impair further the structure of the feeble existing competition for them to react, even to aggressive price competition from a new entrant, with a policy of targeted, selective price cuts designed to eliminate that competitor."[672]

The rationale behind super-dominance is that if a firm with 50% market shares is found to hold a dominant position, then a firm with 90% market shares, everything else being equal, must be consider to posesing an even stronger position. This logic further expands to the special responsibility that entails a stricter responsibility for super dominant firms.[673] In contrast to the Advocate General, the ECJ did not apply the wording "super dominance" (but still found abuse of dominance although prices were above costs). Abused were found on the grounds of the special responsibility.[674]

In *Irish Sugar*, the GC seemingly relied on that concept, to some degree at least. According to the GC, exclusionary conduct, which bring about great obstacles, by a firm holding a dominant position as extensive as that enjoyed by Irish Sugar had to be viewed as contrary to Article 102 TFEU.[675] In other words, the considerably strong position constituted a reinforcing factor.[676] By the same token, the ECJ considered Tetra Pak's quasi-monopoly a relevant factor for the assessment of abuse,[677] and Microsoft's market shares of over 90% were an important factor for the Commission' assessment of Microsoft's exclusionary conduct since such position approaches that of a complete monopoly, and hence, is an overwhelmingly dominant position.[678] However, in these situations the degree of dominance has primarily been used to imply that a dominant position could easily be identified due to the enjoyed super-dominance or a quasi-monopoly.[679] Therefore, it is no surprise that the concept has not been entirely embraced.[680]

---

672. See Opinion of Advocate General Fennelly of 29 October 1998 in Joined Cases C-395/96 P and C-396/96 P, *Compagnie Maritime Belge NV and Dafra-Lines v. Commission of the European Communities*, at 137.
673. See Geradin, Damien, et al., The Concept of Dominance in EC Competition Law, 2005, Research Paper on the Modernization of Article 82 EC, available at http://papers.ssrn.com/sol3/papers .cfm?abstract_id = 770144, at 73.
674. See Joined Cases C-395/96 P and C-396/96 P, *CMBT*, at 37.
675. See Case T-228/97, *Irish Sugar*, at 185.
676. A market share of over 90% had been held from 1985 to 1995, see Commission Decision of 14 May 1997 in Case IV/34.621, 35.059/F-3, *Irish Sugar pic*, at 108.
677. See Judgment of 14 November 1996 in Case C-333/94 P, *Tetra Pak International SA v. Commission of the European Communities* ("*Tetra Pak II*"), at 31 & 48.
678. See Case COMP/C-3/37.792, *Microsoft*, at 435.
679. See Case C-333/94 P, *Tetra Pak II*, at 31. The ECJ held: "Accordingly, the [GC] was right to accept the application of Article [102 TFEU] in this case, given that the quasi-monopoly enjoyed by Tetra Pak on the aseptic markets and its leading position on the distinct, though closely associated, non-aseptic markets placed it in a situation comparable to that of holding a dominant position on the markets in question as a whole."
680. See e.g., Szyszczak, Erika, *Controlling Dominance in European Markets*, 33 Fordham International Law Journal (2011) 1738, at 1757; Geradin, et al. (2005), at 6.

The importance of the degree of dominance has, however, been given less importance by recent case law. In *TeliaSonera*, the ECJ had to consider several questions including whether the degree of market dominance held by the undertaking concerned is relevant to establish whether conduct constitutes an abuse. The answer by the ECJ was concise and clear. According to the ECJ, Article 102 TFEU does not envisage any variation in form or degree in the concept of a dominant position. Where a firm has an economic strength, such as that required by Article 102 TFEU to establish a dominant position in a particular market, its conduct must be assessed in the light of that provision.[681] This, however, did not prevent the ECJ from acknowledging that situations such as those in *Irish Sugar* and *Compagnie Maritime Belge Transports* (i.e., super-dominance or a quasi-monopoly) might be relevant to the assessment in other cases.[682] Nonetheless, this acknowledgement related more to the extent of the effects of the dominant firm's conduct than to the question of whether abuse as such exists. The degree of dominance in this regard is, in other words, relevant for determining the amount of any fine and for claims of damages.

Therefore, when dominance has been established, the degree of dominance is a question of the level of fines and the actual impact (i.e., claims of damages). This is only logical. However, facts such as the dominant position originating in a former legal monopoly[683] or that it is due to a cartel[684] may be factors worth considering in regards to the "conditions on the relevant market". In the former event, the position is the fruit of investments that were undertaken well before the liberalization of the market. Those original investments were undertaken in a context where the dominant firm benefited from special or exclusive rights that shielded it from competition. The investment criteria used by the former monopoly at that time would have led to the investment being made even if there would have been a duty to supply. Coupled with such markets –[685] generally being categorized by markets requiring great investments, and hence, prone to high entry barriers with economies of scale/scope and network effects being important – a dominant firm possess a special position in that market.

In consequence, the degree of dominance has little, and possible no, the influence of whether abuse exists within Article 102 TFEU. If a firm is found dominant within the meaning of Article 102 TFEU, the specific strength of that position has no say in whether abuse exists. On the other hand, how the dominant position has originated may be a relevant factor. Nevertheless, this will be something that is included under the conditions on the relevant market. As a result, the degree of dominance is instead relevant for determining the fine and assessing any claims for damages.

---

681. *See* Case C-52/09, *TeliaSonera*, at 80.
682. *See id.* at 81.
683. This is the case for most of the margin squeeze cases, see e.g., Case C-295/12 P, *Telefónica*; Case C-52/09, *TeliaSonera*; Case C-280/08 P, *Deutsche Telekom*. *See* also e.g., Case AT.39523, *Slovak Telekom*; Case COMP/39.525, *Telekomunikacja Polska*. The same is true for Case C-23/14, *Post Danmark II*, at 59; Case C-209/10, *Post Danmark I*, at 23.
684. This was the case in *Compagnie Maritime Belge Transport*. This was stressed by the Commission in its decision as the argument for prohibition of above cost-pricing in the case, see Case IV/32.448 and IV/32.450, *Cewal*, at 80.
685. This is, for example, markets for broadband (*Deutsche Telekom, France Télécom, TeliaSonera* and *Telefonica*) and postal services (*Post Danmark I* and *Post Danmark II*).

3.2   The Conditions in the Relevant Market

As touched upon above, the conditions in the relevant market will be [highly] relevant. For instance, this could be whether the market is a newly liberalized market. The consequences of such markets were covered above. More importantly, however, this factor includes, generally, the conditions of entry and expansion, such as the existence of economies of scale and scope and network effects.[686] The aspect may also explain how competition works on the market. For instance, whether competition is for the customers' whole demand or a part of customers' demand. If the former is the case, then exclusivity agreements are a natural part of effective competition.

In a market with economies of scale, increasing the output produced enables firms with high fixed costs to accomplish lower ATC. When a firm with high fixed costs produces a lot, the share of the fixed cost which each produced unit bears decreases, and in turn, so does the ATC. Economies of scale are, in other words, a source of productive efficiency. If a market is characterized with economies of scale, an incumbent dominant firm has an advantage over competitor planning to enter the market (or recently entered competitors).[687] Additionally, competitors are less likely to enter or stay in the market if the dominant undertaking forecloses a significant part of the relevant market.[688] Equally important is the likelihood of re-entry that is also reduced in the event of economies of scale/scope. Re-entry is especially important in cases where the dominant firm seeks to recoup a loss made to exclude competitors.[689]

Similarly, conduct may allow a dominant firm to tip a market characterized by network effects in its favour or to further entrench its position in such a market.[690] In such markets, the value of a firm's product depends on the number of customers that firm has.[691] The number of users is, in other words, crucial. Network effects have resemblance to economies of scales. The difference, however, is that while economies scale relates to the supply side of a market, network effects are related to the demand side.[692] A telephone, for example, may become cheaper to produce after reaching a certain scale but looking at the demand side, it is only useful to an individual if others have one as well. The value of the phone is dependent on the number of individuals using it. A market characterized by network effects are also likely to be categorized by economies of scale but this is not necessarily the case and it may even be the case that the effects of economies of scale are minor in comparison with the network effect;[693]

---

686. *See the Article 102 Guidance Paper*, at 20.
687. *See* Coscellia, Andrea & Edwards, Geoff, *Dominance and Market Power in EU Competition Law*, *in* Handbook on European Competition Law: Substantive Aspects (Ioannis Lianos & Damien Geradin eds.), 2013, at 365.
688. *See the Article 102 Guidance Paper*, at 20 (second article).
689. *See* Chapter 6.
690. *See* for that effect Case COMP/C-3/37.792, *Microsoft*.
691. *See* Rohlfs, Jeffrey, *A Theory of Interdependent Demand for a Communications Service*, 5 The Bell Journal of Economics and Management Science (1974) 16.
692. *See* Shapiro, Carl, *Exclusivity in Network Industries*, 7 George Mason Law Review (1999) 673.
693. *See id.* at 673.

i.e., in terms of the competitive advantage. Markets characterized by network effects are especially found in many high-tech sectors.[694]

An important feature of economies of scale/scope and network effects is that foreclosure can be successful even where competitors are still in the market. If competitors are prevented from reaching, for instance, economies of scales, a dominant firm may be able to raise its price over the competitive price [and recoup its loss]. How such strategy can work is discussed in more detail in Chapter 6 and 7. Another important feature of such market conditions is that effective competition will only allow a certain number of firms in the market. In consequence, when assessing whether foreclosure is anti-competitive one must consider this. It must be considered, in other words, whether the foreclosure is in fact due the dominant firm's conduct and not due to the market being unable to sustain the foreclosed competitor(s).

As mentioned, the conditions in the relevant market may also explain how and why market functions in a certain way. For example, the conditions for competition in a one-sided market differ from those of a two-sided market.[695] In the former, certain types of conduct is abuse by object; for example, pricing below AVC.[696] However, in a two-sided market, such below-cost pricing (even giving the product away for free) may be required to compete effectively. This may be illustrated by free newspapers that earn their revenue through advertising. In consequence, the condition of the relevant market is highly important as it can explain certain types of observed conduct.

In the end, the conditions on the relevant market come down to, primarily, the conditions of entry and expansion.[697] This includes the existence of economies of scale and scope and network effects addressed above, but it may also include great sunk costs in the form of required investments and/or research and development, certain know how/knowledge, intellectual property rights, government regulations and the like.

3.3 The Position of the Dominant Firm's Competitors

While the degree of dominance is less important for the existence of abuse, the position of the dominant firm's competitors may be (more) relevant. The weaker competitors are, the more likely it is for conduct to be an anti-competitive. For example, one theory of harm concerning predatory pricing, which the Commission recognizes in its *Article 102 Guidance Paper*, is "Financial Predatory Pricing".[698] Such conduct is targeted at a competitor dependent on external financing, where low-pricing conduct by a dominant firm may adversely affect the competitor's performance so its access to further

---

694. This is the case of Google who is currently under investigation by the Commission. *See* also Evans, David, *The Online Advertising Industry: Economics, Evolution, and Privacy*, 23 The Journal of Economic Perspectives (2009) 37.
695. *See* Pablo, Alfonso Lamadrid de, *The Double Duality of Two-sided Markets*, 64 Competition Law Journal (2015) 5.
696. *See e.g.,* Case C-202/07 P, *France Télécom*, at 109.
697. *See the Article 102 Guidance Paper*, at 20 (second article).
698. *See* also Chapter 6, section 3.3.1.

financing may be seriously undermined.[699] This requires the competitor to possess a weak position on the market (compared to the dominant firm). However, this does not necessarily equal a competitor less efficient than the dominant firm. It may be a recent, or potential, entrant who requires substantial financial support for entering the market. If the competitor, on the other hand, is less efficient foreclosure is normally unproblematic. Such intervention should therefore only be in the event of special circumstances since it is not the purpose of Article 102 TFEU to protect less efficient competitors but rather to protect effective competition. It is, for that reason, importance to distinguish between a weak competitor and a less efficient competitor.

In certain circumstances, however, a (at the moment) less efficient competitor may also exert a constraint which should be considered when considering whether conduct leads to anti-competitive foreclosure. The Commission may take a dynamic view of the competitor's competitive constraint on the dominant firm – and thereby protect that competitor – given that in the absence of the dominant firm's conduct such competitor may benefit from, for instance, demand-related advantages such as network and learning effects which will tend to enhance its efficiency.[700] Therefore, such protection of effective competition will relate to both the first and second factor discussed above. Everything else equal, the stronger the dominant firm's position is, the weaker the position of its competitors is. More important is the connection to the conditions on the relevant market. According to the Commission, this factor includes the importance of competitors for the maintenance of effective competition.[701] If for example, there are high entry barriers and little likelihood of (re)entry then even the exclusion of a non-as efficient competitor may warrant intervention. It could be the case that the competitor foreclosed is the closest competitor to the dominant undertaking, a particularly innovative competitor, or a competitor with the reputation of systematically cutting prices (i.e., a "maverick competitor").[702] The Commission may intervene in such situations since a specific competitor may play a significant competitive role even if it only holds a small market share.[703] However, the cause of the foreclosure and likelihood of, for example, re-entry either from that competitor or another must be considered.

Additionally, this factor also includes the counterstrategies available to competitors; i.e., whether competitors are able to correspond to the dominant firm's conduct. The more aggressive firms are, including the dominant firm, the more effective is the competition and, everything else equal, consumers will benefit. For instance, the more aggressive a dominant firm is allowed to price, the more consumers benefit thanks to lower prices. From the example of "Financial Predatory Pricing" above will in that event relate to the access to finance. Another example relates to refusal to deal/supply

---

699. *See the Article 102 Guidance Paper*, at 68.
700. *See id.* at 24 This Commissions statement is related to pricing conduct, but it should also be applicable to non-pricing conduct.
701. *See id.* at 20 (third article).
702. Regarding maverick competitors, the EU Merger Regulation also focus on such competitors. Here, the worry is that such competitors will be bought by larger firm to chill competition, see *the Non-Horizontal Merger Guidelines*, at 85.
703. *See the Article 102 Guidance Paper*, at 20 (third article).

where it will be relevant to examine whether it is possible to duplicate the input produced by the dominant undertaking in the foreseeable future.[704]

3.4 The Position of Customers and Input Suppliers

When a dominant firm forecloses effective competition, it usually does so by preventing competitors from contracting with customers and suppliers. For example, it may tie up suppliers with exclusivity agreements or offer prices below cost to customers. In this regard, targeting certain customers or suppliers may be an important strategy. As will be shown in Chapter 7, by foreclosing low cost-suppliers a dominant firm may succeed in raising its competitors' costs and potentially gain the power to raise the output price and, at the same time, its profit. Some customers or suppliers may further be of particular importance for the entry or expansion of competitors, and by applying its conduct to those, the dominant firm enhances the likelihood of anti-competitive foreclosure.[705] It may also be easier for a dominant firm to engage in predatory pricing conduct if it selectively targets specific customers with low prices, as this will limit the losses incurred.[706] However, it must be stressed that targeting selective suppliers or customers by, for instance, selective pricing cannot, by itself, constitute exclusionary abuse within the meaning of Article 102 TFEU.[707]

Accordingly, this factor includes the consideration of the possible selectivity of the dominant firm's conduct.[708] Some customers or suppliers may be important for either entry or expansion. In the case of customers, they may, for example, be the ones most likely to respond to offers from alternative suppliers, they may represent a particular means of distributing the product that would be suitable for a new entrant, they may be situated in a geographic area well suited to new entry or they may be likely to influence the behaviour of other customers. In the case of suppliers, they may, for example, be the ones most likely to respond to requests by customers who are competitors of the dominant undertaking in a downstream market or may produce a grade of the product or produce at a location particularly important for a new entrant. In case law, the ECJ has, for example, held the targeting of the largest customers as a supporting factor in finding abuse of dominance.[709]

3.5 The Extent of the Allegedly Abusive Conduct

Besides the selective nature of exclusionary conduct, conduct may vary in length. In general, the Commission considers that the higher the percentage of total sales in the relevant market is affected by the conduct, the longer its duration and the more

---

704. *See id.* at 83.
705. *See* Case T-228/97, *Irish Sugar*, at 188.
706. *See the Article 102 Guidance Paper*, at 72.
707. *See* Case C-209/10, *Post Danmark I*, at 30.
708. *See the Article 102 Guidance Paper*, at 20 (fourth article).
709. *See e.g.,* Case C-549/10 P, *Tomra*, at 75.

regularly it has been applied, the more likely is a foreclosure effect.[710] On the other hand, the Commission further consider it less likely that a dominant firm engages in Predation if its conduct concerns a low price applied for a long period.[711] Accordingly, the longer the period a price is offered between AAC and LRAIC the more likely it is to exclude a financial weak, but as efficient, competitor since it is more likely that competitor runs out of funds. On the other hand, it may, as the Commission rightly acknowledge, be a sign of strong competition and the market has found its level.

Since a long period may indicate either anti- or pro-competitive conduct this factor must be viewed in connection with other factors; for example, evidence of actual foreclosure and the market conditions. If an as efficient competitor is excluded from the market, that fact may support the "Financial Predatory Pricing-theory". Likewise, the longer an exclusivity agreement extends over, the more likely it is for that conduct to be anti-competitive. Again, it must be stressed that it must be considered in the context of other factors; for instance, the conditions in the relevant market may explain the relatively long duration of an exclusivity agreement.

Nevertheless, the extent of the allegedly abusive conduct has been applied as an important factor in case law. This is true for conditional rebates. Since *Michelin I*,[712] the reference period (i.e., the period of time for which the sales are collected and the rebate calculated on) has been an important factor.[713] This factor has been important since a retroactive rebate has the inherent effect, at the end of the period, of increasing pressure on the customer to reach the target needed to obtain the rebate or to avoid suffering a loss for not reaching the target.[714] The longer the period, the stronger the effect is. Accordingly, a retroactive rebate with a long reference period creates a so-called suction effect.[715] Such effect makes it easier for a dominant firm to tie its own customers to itself and so harm effective competition.

In consequence, the extent of the allegedly abusive conduct is important for the assessment of abuse. Despite "the longer the duration, the more likely it is to be anti-competitive" is the rule of thumb this should be viewed in the context of the relevant case. Therefore, it must be viewed in the context of the other factors. When unaccompanied this factor is, like the other factors, inadequate.

3.6 Evidence of Actual Foreclosure

If conduct has been in place for a sufficient period, the market performance of the dominant undertaking and its competitors may provide direct evidence of anti-competitive foreclosure. This could, for instance, be the exclusion of competitors. The

---

710. *See the Article 102 Guidance Paper*, at 20 (fifth article).
711. *See id.* at 73.
712. *See* Case 322/81, *Michelin I*, at 78 & 81.
713. *See* Case C-23/14, *Post Danmark II*, at 34. This factor has been less obvious in other cases; however, still there indirectly, *see e.g.,* Case C-549/10 P, *Tomra*, at 75; Case C-95/04 P, *British Airways*, at 73.
714. In *Post Danmark II* customers whose volume of mailings proved to be lower than the quantity estimated had to reimburse Post Danmark, see Case C-23/14, *Post Danmark II*, at 32.
715. *See id.* at 35; Case C-549/10 P, *Tomra*, at 78 & 79.

opposing argument can also be held; i.e., if there is evidence of foreclosure not occurring it might tell us that there is no harm to effective competition.[716] As will be recalled from Chapter 3, it is not required to demonstrate a decrease in the dominant firm's market share. It is important to keep in mind that anti-competitive foreclosure effect does not only cover complete exclusion of competitors or barring their entry to market but further marginalization or making entry more difficult. Accordingly, even if the dominant firm's market share may have remained the same, or even fallen, an anti-competitive effect may still be demonstrated.

If evidence of actual foreclosure does exist it will, obviously, aid the assessment of exclusionary abuse. The first place to look would be the market shares of the dominant firm. It may show that market shares have risen or a counterfactual analysis may reveal a decline in market shares has been slowed.[717] For similar reasons, actual competitors may have been marginalized or exited the market or potential competitors may have tried to enter the market without success or only entered with limited success. It must be stressed that evidence of actual foreclosure cannot amount to abuse on its own – see Chapter 3. It must be shown that actual foreclosure effects are attributable to the allegedly abusive conduct and that it is detrimental to effective competition. In consequence, while evidence of foreclosure may [strongly] indicate exclusionary abuse, it cannot establish such on its own.

3.7 Direct Evidence of any Anti-competitive Strategy

Besides evidence of actual foreclosure, evidence of an anti-competitive strategy might also be available. Such strategy may reveal the purpose of that conduct; thus, it may assist the assessment of whether alleged conduct was within the scope of "competition on merits". Such evidence includes, for instance, internal documents that contain direct evidence of a strategy to exclude competitors, such as a detailed plan to engage in certain conduct to exclude a competitor, to prevent entry or to pre-empt the emergence of a market, or evidence of concrete threats of exclusionary action.[718] This factor has especially been applied in case law dealing with predatory pricing.[719] It is further included in the second part of the *Akzo-test*; i.e., prices between AVC and ATC constitute abuse where they are determined as part of a plan for eliminating a competitor ("anti-competitive intent").[720] In *France Télécom*, for example, the Commission relied on internal documents, email correspondence, framework letters, internal presentations and internal strategy plans to attest the existence of an anti-

---

716. *See* for that respect Case C-209/10, *Post Danmark I*, at 39. The ECJ held that "it is worth noting that it appears from the documents before the Court that Forbruger-Kontakt managed to maintain its distribution network despite losing the volume of mail related to the three customers involved and managed, in 2007, to win back the Coop group's custom and, since then, that of the Spar group."
717. *See the Article 102 Guidance Paper*, at 20 (sixth article).
718. *See id.* at 20 (seventh article).
719. *See* Case C-202/07 P, *France Télécom*, at 97–8; Case C-333/94 P, *Tetra Pak II*, at 42; Case 62/86, *Akzo*, at 102, 107–9 & 115.
720. *See* Case 62/86, *Akzo*, at 72.

competitive strategy.[721] It is clear that such direct evidence may be helpful in interpreting the dominant undertaking's conduct.

However, evidence of anti-competitive intent does not have to be direct in the sense that it must be internal documents, emails or the like. Instead, other types of "indirect" evidence may be applied. The ECJ clarified this in *France Tèlècom*. It found that despite recoupment is not a precondition for finding abuse such evidence may "assist in establishing that a plan to eliminate a competitor exists."[722] Such indirect evidence may further assist in excluding economic justifications other than the elimination of a competitor;[723] i.e., it may potentially serve as a tool for the dominant firm to justify its conduct.

Although evidence of predatory intent may be helpful for the assessment, it cannot be held as prerequisite of finding abuse within the meaning of Article 102 TFEU.[724] As may be recalled, exclusionary abuse is an objective concept;[725] hence, the subjective intention of a dominant firm is irrelevant for the assessment if abuse is demonstrated in another way. The existence of any anti-competitive intent constitutes only one of several facts that may be considered to determine that a dominant position has been abused.[726] Instead, the main issue when demonstrating abuse is the objective purpose of the dominant firm's conduct; i.e., the importance lay on whether it has anti-competitive effects or is likely to have such effects.

3.8 The Counterfactual

As hinted above, the counterfactual scenario is highly important. If foreclosure cannot be attributed to the dominant firm's exclusionary conduct that firm cannot be held to have abused its dominant position (at least in terms of an exclusionary abuse). For example, competitors may have been unable to keep up with an innovating dominant firm, consumers demand may have shifted (e.g., two products which used to be distinct product are now seen as one product), investments by a competitor may have failed etc. Likewise, an exclusivity agreement may correspond to the amount that the customer would have bought from the dominant firm absent the exclusivity agreement.

This factor may also be affected by some of the other factors. For instance, the market conditions may reveal that the market can only sustain a limited number of firms, which explains an unsuccessful entrance. If a market cannot sustain further entry, entrance by a firm may make pricing below costs indispensable.[727] While this may lead to the exclusion of as efficient competitors, a counterfactual scenario can reveal that this foreclosure effect cannot be attributed to the dominant firm. Anything

---

721. *See* Case COMP/38.233, *Wanadoo Interactive*, at 110. *See* also Case C-202/07 P, *France Télécom*, at 199.
722. *See* Case C-202/07 P, *France Télécom*, at 111.
723. *See id.*
724. *See* Case C-549/10 P, *Tomra*, at 21.
725. *See* Chapter 2.
726. *See* Case C-549/10 P, *Tomra*, at 20.
727. *See* Bishop & Walker (2010), at 304.

else would be absurd. The same result can occur if a competitor enters the with an unstainable business model or make investment choices that, for example, do satisfy consumers' demand.

3.9 Summarizing

Above, different important factors have been discussed. Again, it must be stressed that while they can assist the assessment of exclusionary abuse, they cannot suffice alone. In other words, they will work together as they may be moving in opposite directions. The factors can be summarized as follows:

- *The degree of dominance* is of little or no importance as it is a matter for whether a firm holds a dominant position and, potentially, for determining the seriousness of the dominant firm's conduct.
- *The conditions in the relevant market* will be highly important. This generally concerns whether there are economies of scale/scope and network effects.
- *The position of the dominant firm's competitors* will be relevant if, for instance, the success of a given type of conduct depends on the competitors' strength. Additionally, how a competitor acts in the market may indicate the impact on effective competition.
- *The position of the customers or input suppliers* might be important if selective conduct can enhance or make it easier to produce the anti-competitive effect.
- *The extent of the alleged abusive conduct* is important as the longer the duration and the more it embraces, the more likely conduct is to be anti-competitive. However, it must be viewed in the context of the other relevant factors.
- *Evidence of actual foreclosure* will provide an indication of exclusionary abuse, but it cannot alone suffice as it only tells something about the foreclosure effect. The opposite argument can also be held, but one must be careful since anti-competitive effect does not only arise where, for instance, the dominant firm it increases market share.
- *Direct evidence of any anti-competitive strategy* can assist in finding abuse. However, most firms have intent to win market shares.

CHAPTER 6
Predation

1 INTRODUCTION

The previous chapter included a general analysis concerning the effect-based approach. It was concluded that one must distinguish between Predation and Exclusion. While the next chapter focuses on the latter, this one will centre on anti-competitive foreclosure effects in regards to Predation. As indicated in earlier chapters, the assessment will rely on a price/cost-test. This is because the exclusionary tool here is the price, more particular, whether it is set too low (the issue of whether it is set too high is a matter of exploitive abuse). As will be covered throughout this chapter, a low price is a necessary condition for finding pricing conduct abusive under the effect-based approach, but not sufficient alone.[728]

Competition law is aimed at encouraging low prices since they reflect competitive markets and benefit consumers.[729] However, low prices may be harmful to effective competition and the detriment of consumers' interest in some situations. As it was illustrated in Figure 5.1 in Chapter 5, the theory of harm concerning abusive pricing conduct is that the dominant firm aims at achieving a price above the "competitive price" by means of a low price-period. The difficulty, however, is how to separate conduct benefiting consumers from those that harms effective competition (and thereby consumers). Under the by object-approach, such harm is assumed while it must be demonstrated under the effect-based approach. Accordingly, the assessment must be able to identify whether harm to effective competition and consumers has occurred or is likely to do so.

---

728. This is not the same for abuse under the object-approach, though. As explained in Chapter 4, a price below AVC (alternatively AAC) will be sufficient.
729. *See* e.g., Hovenkamp, Herbert, *Federal Antitrust Policy: The Law of Competition and Its Practice*, 2016, at 3–7 (Who explains why, as a matter of basic economic theory, competitive markets are a chief goal of antitrust law). *See also* Crane (2005), at 1 (Who states that Predation is a paradoxical offense).

Therefore, the aim of this chapter is to analyse how anti-competitive foreclosure effects under the effect-based approach can be demonstrated when dealing with conduct that falls within Predation. More precisely, this entails an enquiry of: (i) which theory of harm may explain when these types of conduct produce an actual or likely anti-competitive foreclosure effect, and (ii) how different types of exclusionary conduct that fall within this category can be assessed according to this theory of harm.

2 THE THEORY OF HARM

That different types of conduct can be fit into a category named Predation was explained in Chapter 5. As a result, one overall theory of harm can be attached to these types of conduct explaining how they may produce anti-competitive foreclosure effects. The EU Courts, in regards to a margin squeeze case, has explicitly stated that pricing policies applied by a dominant firm, as a general rule, are subject to a price/cost-test.[730] Additionally, in its *Article 102 Guidance Paper*, the Commission advocates one overall test for all types of pricing conduct.[731] Accordingly, whether that conduct takes the form of predatory pricing, margin squeeze, a rebate or something else, an overall test applies – according to this view.[732] The specific assessment, of course, will differ depending on the specific type of pricing conduct. This will be addressed in section 3. Nevertheless, it should be possible to outline a general test regarding conduct for which price is the exclusionary tool. Since the focus is an unlawful low price, this entails a natural focus on predatory pricing-theory in the following.

The theory of harm relating to Predation is fairly straightforward and uncontroversial. The purpose of such anti-competitive pricing conduct is, in its most basic form, a two-step strategy for attaining monopoly profits.[733] These two steps can be termed the "Predation-period" and the "Recoupment-period",[734] respectively. The simplicity of the theory of harm is illustrated in Figure 6.1. During the first step, the dominant firm charges a low price (normally below its costs) in the hope of driving its competitor(s) out of the market or deter their entry to the market by forcing them to sell at a loss. If the first step is successful, the firm can then proceed to the second step. Since it now has the market to itself (in its extreme form of this example), the firm is able to charge a monopoly price to recoup the losses it sustained in the Predation-period and subsequently earn a steady stream of monopoly profits into the future. If the profits made in the second period are greater than the losses made in the first period – i.e., if "box B" is greater than "box A" – then that conduct is restricting effective competition to the detriment of effective competition as the dominant firm' conduct is successful.

---

730. *See* Case C-52/09, *TeliaSonera*, at 41.
731. *See the Article 102 Guidance Paper*, at 23–7.
732. Note that rebates and margin squeeze does not necessarily fall within Predation, *see* the conclusion reached from the analysis in Chapter 5.
733. *See* e.g., Leslie, Christopher, *Predatory Pricing and Recoupment*, 113 Columbia Law Review (2013) 1695, at 1697.
734. Concerning the relevance of proof of [likely] recoupment in relation to the EU Courts standpoint on that issue, *see* section 2.3.

Figure 6.1 The Theory of Harm for Predation

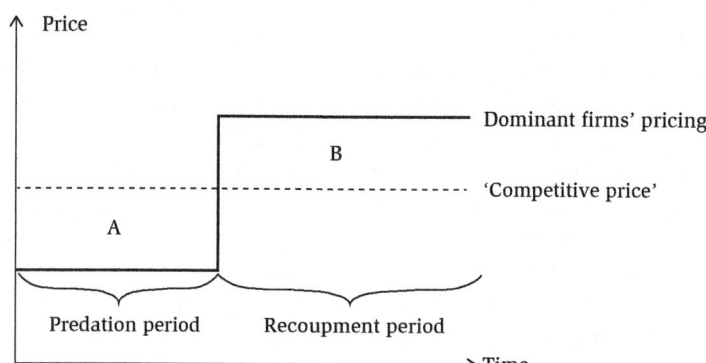

While the overall theory of harm is uncontroversial, Predation is still a contro-versial area of competition law.[735,736] Different aspects may explain this. First, Preda-tion is a paradox since, on the one hand, history and economic theory tells us that Predation can be an instrument of abuse but, on the other hand, price reductions are the hallmark of competition and the tangible benefit that consumers perhaps most desire from competition.[737] Therefore, and in contrast to Exclusion (see Chapter 7), Predation has a beneficial effect on consumers' interest in the short term and a detrimental effect in the long term. Second, the real world does not always correspond to the economic models used to explain Predation, which can create some friction. Third, there is no requirement of recoupment within EU competition law.[738] Case law has rather rejected recoupment as a prerequisite. Fourth, Predation is subject to a disagreement within legal and economic literature (see below). The last aspect is of course strongly influence by the first three.

The controversial aspect is perhaps best illustrated by the influence of the Chicago School. According to this view, it is believed that successful Predation simply does not occur, since such conduct is a high-risk strategy that entails significant up-front losses (also termed as costs) and a low likelihood of sustained profitability.[739] In other words, it is unlikely to be profitable for a firm to engage in Predation. This

---

735. *See* Fumagalli, Chiara & Motta, Massimo, *A Simple Theory of Predation*, 56 The Journal of Law & Economics (2013) 595, at 595.
736. This is also illustrated by famous quote by Easterbrook which illustrates the elusiveness of the concept of Predation: "we have so many theories [of Predation] for the same reason that 600 years ago there were a thousand positions on what dragons looked like." *See* Easterbrook, Frank, *Predatory Strategies and Counterstrategies*, 48 The University of Chicago Law Review (1981) 263, at 264.
737. *See* Bolton, et al. (2000), at 2241.
738. Recoupment is an essential element of the burden of proof in the US antitrust system regarding unlawful prices, *see* Brooke Group Ltd. v. Brown & Williamson Tobacco Corp.
739. *See* Posner (1979). *See also* Baker, Jonathan, *Predatory Pricing After Brooke Group: An Economic Perspective*, 62 Antitrust Law Journal (1994) 585, at 586. (Who notice that Predation has been termed as both a white tiger and an unicorn since it has been viewed as very unlikely or even as a myth).

scepticism is greatly illustrated by the famous study by John McGee[740] where he studied a case from 1911, *Standard Oil*,[741] which before then was considered the classic example of Predation (in the US).[742] McGee found little indication of (likely) recoupment which had been the argument in finding unlawful conduct,[743] and he further held it to be economically irrational for a large firm to engage in Predation against a smaller rival given the larger market share over which the predator must cut the price. These findings were based on two main arguments.[744] First, the predator will not be able to sustain such losses indefinitely; hence, the prey will not be induced to leave the market. Second, nor will a lack of funds exclude even the smallest prey, since, as it was argued, capital markets would step in to supply funds to an efficient producer. Moreover, even if the prey were excluded the predator would gain little since an attempt to raise prices would trick the event of entry by either the prey or a potential competitor (who reopens the prey's plant).[745] As it is clear, the arguments made by McGee rely on strong market assumptions – for instance, there are no entry barriers and no capital market imperfections – which are unlikely to be true. Nonetheless, it illustrates that Predation is necessarily neither profitable nor common conduct.

Economic theory has since then shown us that Predation may be successful, and thus, this scepticism has been criticized. This criticism came most notably from the Post-Chicago School. In brief, this point of view refused to rule out the possibility of Predation being a rational strategy although it may not be a common strategy.[746] The Chicago scepticism still influenced the courts in the US and led them to impose a recoupment requirement for finding abusive pricing conduct under the Sherman Act section 2.[747] This requirement coupled with the scepticism of successful Predation had a negative impact on the success rate of plaintiffs alleging Predation since the burden of proving recoupment became very difficult.[748]

Such approach is in stark contrast to the EU Courts' case law. Here, a strong scepticism does not exist, and proof of recoupment is further not a prerequisite of finding abusive pricing conduct.[749] The Chicago scepticism and the requirement of

---

740. *See* McGee, John, *Predatory Price Cutting: The Standard Oil (N. J.) Case*, 1 The Journal of Law & Economics (1958) 137.
741. *See Standard Oil Co. of New Jersey v. United States*, 221 U.S. 1 (1910). The case has since then been re-examined with the conclusion that the case was anti-competitive since Standard Oil raised competitors' costs thereby also raising the output price. That is, its conduct was not evidence of Predation but rather Exclusion, Granitz, Elizabeth & Klein, Benjamin, *Monopolization by "Raising Rivals' Costs": The Standard Oil Case*, 39 The Journal of Law & Economics (1996) 1.
742. *See* Bolton, et al. (2000), at 2244.
743. *See* McGee (1958), at 138.
744. *See id.* at 139–41.
745. *See id.* at 140–1.
746. For a brief overview of the difference between the two schools views concerning Predation *see* e.g., Baker (1994), at 586–92.
747. *See Matsushita v. Zenith Ratio Corp.*, 475 U.S. 574 (1986); *A.A. Poultry Farms, Inc. et al. v. Rose Acre Farms, Inc.*, 683 F. Supp. 680 (1888); *Brooke Group Ltd. v. Brown & Williamson Tobacco Corp. See also* Leslie (2013), at 1695.
748. *See* Bolton, et al. (2000), at 2258–62.
749. *See* Case C-202/07 P, *France Télécom*, at 110.

recoupment[750] seem therefore not to have found its way into EU competition law. As will be shown below, however, the test developed by the EU Courts (i.e., the *Akzo-test*) does not preclude recoupment and may even be held as, indirectly, requiring proof of (likely) recoupment.

While the approach taken in the US antitrust law relies on an effect-based approach (known as the rule of conduct-approach) following the *Brooke*-case,[751] the EU Courts' case law, before *Post Danmark I*, is to a large extent based on a by object restrictions (see Chapter 4). Accordingly, the difference between the two jurisdictions may be that the EU has two approaches while the US only has one (and that the effect-based approach has yet to be fully applied in the EU). While this may explain (some of) the divergence between the EU and US, it also provides indications for how to assess exclusionary conduct falling within Predation. In other words, guidance in terms of how the effect-based approach can be applied can be sought in how Predation is assessed in the US. As a result, the following subsections will to a great extent rely on that theory to fill in the "blanks".

2.1 The Standard: The "as Efficient Competitor-Test"

A blizzard of tests defining Predation has been developed in legal and economic literature.[752] Some of these depend on the relationship between price and cost (which will be referred to as a price/cost-test in the following),[753] some on the relationship between price and time,[754] and some on the relationship between quantity sold and time.[755] One approach even avoids dependence like those mentioned altogether and, instead, suggests that the totality of the circumstances is examined.[756]

While different methods have been proposed in legal and economic literature the ECJ has established that a price/cost-test is to be applied (i.e., the *Akzo-test*).[757] This

---

750. Recoupment is an essential element for both the Chicago School and the Post-Chicago School. The difference lies in how likely Predation is seen. *See* e.g., Baker (1994), at 586–92.
751. The Areeda/Turner-test that was applied before the *Brooke*-case is based on a per se-rule where prices under AVC are unlawful while prices over AVC is lawful, *see* Bolton, et al. (2000), at 2250–5.
752. The modern tests of abusive predatory pricing is generally believed to have started with the Areeda/Turner-test, *see* Areeda, Phillip & Turner, Donald, *Predatory Pricing and Related Practices under Section 2 of the Sherman Act*, 88 Harvard Law Review (1975) 697.
753. *See* e.g., Ordover, Janusz & Willig, Robert, *An Economic Definition of Predatory Product Innovation*, 91 The Yale Law Journal (1981) 8; McGee, John, *Predatory Pricing Revisited*, 23 Journal of Law and Economics (1980) 289; Posner (1979); Joskow, Paul & Klevorick, Alvin, *A Framework for Analyzing Predatory Pricing Policy*, 89 The Yale Law Journal (1979) 213; Areeda & Turner (1975).
754. *See* e.g., Baumol, William, *Quasi-Permanence of Price Reductions: A Policy for Prevention of Predatory Pricing*, 89 The Yale Law Journal (1979) 1.
755. *See* e.g., Williamson, Oliver, *Williamson on Predatory Pricing II*, 88 Yale Law Journal (1979) 1183; Williamson, Oliver, *Predatory Pricing: A Strategic and Welfare Analysis*, 87 The Yale Law Journal (1977) 284.
756. *See* e.g., Scherer, Frederic, *Predatory Pricing and the Sherman Act: A Comment*, 89 Harvard Law Review (1976) 869; Scherer, Frederic, *Some Last Words on Predatory Pricing*, 89 Harvard Law Review (1976) 901.
757. *See* Case 62/86, *Akzo*, at 74.

goes both for margin squeeze[758], selective pricing[759], predatory pricing[760] and presumably rebates[761]. The Commission also advocates a price/cost-test in its *Article 102 Guidance Paper* for all types of pricing conduct;[762] a test that has been named the as efficient competitor-test (the "AEC-test")[763]. With support from both the EU Courts and the Commission, it is likely that future cases will rely on the AEC-test. As repeated heavily throughout this book, the aim is to provide suggestions and answers on how to apply the effect-based approach within the framework of Article 102 TFEU, not just how to apply such approach in general. In consequence, the findings in this chapter must fit into the framework presented throughout this book. Therefore, it is no surprise that the AEC-test will form the starting point for the discussions in this chapter. This is not to say that other standards such as the ones that focus on the relationship between price and time or relationship between quantities sold and time cannot ever be applied.[764] It is merely a statement that the starting point will be a price/cost-test in the form of the AEC-test. As a result, the following subsections will centre on the AEC-test and how it can be applied under the effect-based approach.

The AEC-test, as its name suggest, tests whether a competitor who is as (or more) efficient as the dominant firm (an "as efficient competitor") is likely, in the circumstances of the case, to be foreclosed.[765] If such effect is shown, the dominant firm can rebut this effect by proving its conduct is, on balance, efficient.[766] It examines, in other words, whether these competitors are able to compete with the dominant firm's prices. The test is based on, among other things, the rationale that a firm should not be punished for having lower costs than its competitors have, but allowed to price accordingly.

> It would be absurd to require the firm to hold a price umbrella over less efficient entrants [...]. [P]ractices that will exclude only less efficient firms, such as the monopolist's dropping his price nearer to (but not below) his cost, are not actionable, because we want to encourage efficiency.[767]

Besides being a test – i.e., testing whether the price is above or below costs – it further forms a standard. This is clear when the test is altered into an answer for the question: "whose exclusion should be prevented against exclusionary pricing conduct

---

758. *See* Case C-52/09, *TeliaSonera*, at 41; Case C-280/08 P, *Deutsche Telekom*, at 198.
759. *See* Case C-209/10, *Post Danmark I*, at 28.
760. *See* Case C-202/07 P, *France Télécom*, at 108; Case C-209/10, *Post Danmark I*, at 28.
761. The Commission applied a price/cost-test in a recent case which unfortunately was not published, *see* Albaek & Claici (2009).
762. *See the Article 102 Guidance Paper*, at 23–7.
763. While the test/standard is referred to as the "as efficient competitor-test", the Commission has also applied the term "equally efficient competitor-test" in decisional practice, *see* e.g., Case AT.39523, *Slovak Telekom*, at 828. The tests, nevertheless, are the same test despite their different names.
764. For example, it may support the argument of non-predation behaviour if the price has been applied for a long period of time, *see* for that effect *the Article 102 Guidance Paper*, at 73.
765. *See* Posner, Richard, *Antitrust Law*, 2001, at 194–5.
766. *See id.* at 195.
767. *See id.* at 196.

by dominant firms?" The answer cannot sensibly be rivals in general;[768] thus, a reasonable answer becomes as efficient competitors.[769] Moreover, when competition is effective, firms more efficient gain at the expense of less efficient firms. As a result, the AEC-test, as a standard, appears to accord with protecting effective competition.[770] This further helps countering the critique surrounding Article 102 TFEU involving the protection of competitors instead of competition.[771] This is also stressed in the *Article 102 Guidance Paper.*[772]

While the AEC-test may be seen as a European concept, it has its origin in the US;[773] namely an article from 1974 by Richard Posner.[774] He argued that, for reasons of economic efficiency, only two forms of pricing conduct should be deemed unlawful. First, prices below short-run marginal cost (i.e., the cost incurred by a sale) is not in the interest of efficiency and can only have the purpose and effect of excluding an equally or more efficient rival.[775] Second, a price below long run marginal cost (i.e., the costs which has to be recovered to stay in business indefinitely) does not imply anti-competitive harm, but if there is intent to exclude, such price will have the purpose and likely effect of excluding an as efficient competitor.[776] This resembles the two-step test established in *Akzo.*[777] Note that the test is also referred to as the equal efficient competitor-test ("EEC-test").

It is sometimes argued that the *Akzo-test* is the product of the Areeda/Turner-test[778] that was based on the profit sacrifice standard as well as on objective intent.[779] They argued that (short-run) profit sacrifice by a dominant firm should be a necessary condition for unlawful pricing conduct instead of, like Posner, focusing on as efficient competitors.[780] The test, nevertheless, had similarities with Posner's view as they focused on short-run marginal costs. In their view prices below such costs are unlawful

---

768. *See* Vickers, John, *Abuse of Market Power*, 115 The Economic Journal (2005) F244, at F256. *See also* Chapter 2.
769. *See* in that respect also Case C-209/10, *Post Danmark I*, at 21 (Where the ECJ held that Article 102 TFEU does not "seek to ensure that competitors less efficient than the undertaking with the dominant position should remain on the market").
770. *See* Vickers (2005), at F256.
771. *See* Nazzini (2012), at 72–3.
772. *See the Article 102 Guidance Paper*, at 23.
773. *See* Marty, Frederic, *As-Efficient Competitor Test in Exclusionary Pricing Strategies: Does Post-Danmark Really Pave the Way Towards a More Economic Apporach?*, 2014, GREDEG Working Paper, available at http://www.gredeg.cnrs.fr/working-papers/GREDEG-WP-2013-26.pdf, at 13.
774. *See* Posner, Richard, *Exclusionary Practices and the Antitrust Laws*, 41 The University of Chicago Law Review (1974) 506.
775. *See id.* at 519.
776. *See id.*
777. *See* e.g., Nazzini (2012), at 224 (Who states that the test for predation in the case law is unequivocally based on the as efficient competitor principle).
778. *See* Areeda & Turner (1975).
779. *See* Baumol, William, *Predation and the Logic of the Average Variable Cost Test*, 39 The Journal of Law & Economics (1996) 49, at 53. *See also* Mandorff, Martin & Sahl, Johan, *The Role of the "Equally Efficient Competitor" in the Assessment of Abuse of Dominance*, 2013, Konkurrensverket Working Paper Series in Law and Economics, available at http://www.konkurrensverket.se/globalassets/english/publications-and-decisions/the-role-of-the-equally-efficient-competitor-in-the-assessment-of-abuse-of-dominance.pdf, at 4–5.
780. *See* Areeda & Turner (1975), at 703.

since it greatly increases the possibility of rivalry being extinguished or prevented for reasons unrelated to the efficiency of the monopolist. Due to the difficulties of the concept of marginal costs, it led them to argue a price below AVC should be presumed to be predatory.[781] Moreover, the test referred, indirectly, to Posner's standard as it was argued that pricing above ATC is competition on the merits and excludes only less-efficient rivals.[782]

The difference between the two tests lies in the view of prices between AVC and ATC. The Areeda/Turner-test concluded these as per se lawful contrary to what Posner (and the *Akzo-test*) proposed. The Areeda/Turner-test did recognize the issue (i.e., that there is a profit sacrifice), but worrying more about false positives, they could see no satisfactory method of eliminating the risk while not at the same time unwarrantedly protecting less efficient rivals.[783] When compared to the *Akzo-test*, the ECJ seems to have relied on both the EEC-test and the Areeda/Turner test.[784] The first part of the *Akzo-test* resembles the Areeda/Turner-test (applying an AVC standard), while the second part deviated from it since the ECJ was not ready to risk the elimination as efficient competitors.[785] One could make the case that the *Akzo-test* combines the principles of the AEC-standard proposed by Posner with the profit-sacrifice approach in the Areeda/Turner-test.[786]

In consequence, the AEC-test, as a test, constitutes a price/cost-test.[787] The purpose is to compare the dominant firm's prices with its relevant costs. The quantity sold or the period of time is, as a starting point, irrelevant. The AEC-test serves, therefore, the purpose of protecting competition within that standard; i.e., whether an as efficient competitor can compete with the specific price. Besides being consistent with general welfare considerations (in so far as it protects competition in the form of as or more efficient competitors as opposed to less efficient ones), it is consistent with the principle of legal certainty, as it is based on the dominant firm's own prices and costs.[788] However, when assessing anti-competitive effects under the effect-based approach, a price/cost-test is not sufficient in itself. When a price is below the relevant cost, foreclosure can at most be proven. Applying the AEC-test requires, therefore, proof of, first, a foreclosure effect (section 2.2), and second, an anti-competitive effect (section 2.3).

---

781. *See id.* at 712.
782. *See id.* at 707.
783. *See id.* at 710-1.
784. *See* Lang, John Temple & O'Donoghue, Robert, *Defining Legitimate Competition: How to Clarify Pricing Abuses Under Article 82 EC*, 26 Fordham International Law Journal (2002) 83, at 126 (who find that the Akzo-test broadly endorses the approach advocated by Areeda & Turner); Buttigieg, Eugène, *Competition Law: Safeguarding the Consumer Internet. A Comparative Analysis of Uk Antitrust Law and EC Competition Law*, 2009, at 173 (who argue the ECJ added a strategic element to the Areeda/Turner-test for prices between AVC and ATC). *See*, in contrast, Jones, Alison & Sufrin, Brenda, *EU Competition Law: Text, Cases, and Materials*, 2014, at page 406 (who argues the Akzo-test differs significantly from the Areeda/Turner-test).
785. *See* Buttigieg (2009), at 174.
786. For a similar view *see* Mandorff & Sahl (2013), at 7.
787. *See the Article 102 Guidance Paper*, at 25. *See also* Posner (1974), at 519.
788. *See* Case C-295/12 P, *Telefónica*, at 124; Case C-52/09, *TeliaSonera*, at 41–8; Case C-280/08 P, *Deutsche Telekom*, at 167–8, 192 & 200–3.

2.2 The Foreclosure Effect

Proof of actual or likely foreclosure is the first step of demonstrating unlawful Predation. Besides being the first step of finding a by effect restriction, a foreclosure effect [on existing or potential competitors] is the means whereby pricing conduct ultimately harms consumers. If no foreclosure effect exists then that conduct cannot constitute exclusionary abuse (it can at most be discriminatory or exploitive). To prove a foreclosure effect, it is proposed that two conditions must be fulfilled: (i) a below-cost period must be demonstrated and (ii) a Theory of Predation must be relied on. The aim is to provide an explanation as to why a competitor is foreclosed due to the below-cost price i.e., why it chooses to partial or fully exit (alternatively stay out of or only enter parts of) the market rather than to compete effectively. Such explanation cannot be made with just a below-cost period[789] and, as a result, a Theory of Predation must be relied on. While both aspects are important, the latter is not discussed in this subsection but instead in the section 3. This is due to the fact that margin squeeze differs from predatory pricing and rebates.

2.2.1 A Below-Cost Period

It is a well-known principle in the EU Courts' case law that unlawful pricing conduct presupposes proof of a below-cost price.[790] Predation is an action that is only profitable due to its exclusionary effects (i.e., the Predation period); thus, Predation cannot occur through static profit maximisation as it would otherwise be exploitive behaviour. In other words, Predation must involve some sort of profit sacrifice, which in turn forecloses competition thereby enabling increased or sustained profits in the long term. A literal application could allow for intervention where a dominant firm sets prices above costs, but below the optimal price, since profits can be sacrificed without pricing below costs.[791,792] However, such foreclosure would concern competitors who are less efficient and such foreclosure is part of effective competition.[793] In addition, the EU Courts have established that the legal test is based on a comparison of prices and

---

789. See in contrast those types of pricing conduct which fall within the by object category.

790. See e.g., Case C-209/10, *Post Danmark I*, at 36; Case C-52/09, *TeliaSonera*, at 32 & 41.

791. Motta (2004).(who also notice that however sophisticated mangers might be, it is unlikely that they could have a notion of what the optimal price is; hence, it becomes impossible to establish in a real case whether profit has been sacrificed). *See also* Edlin, Aaron & Farrell, Joseph, *The American Airlines Case: A Chance to Clarify Predation Policy, in* The Antitrust Revolution: Economics, Competition, and Policy (John E. Kwoka & Lawrence J. White eds.), 2004, at 510–17 (who points out that a below-cost price could mean simply non-profit-maximizing pricing or it might mean actually losing money on average).

792. *See also* the *Article 102 Guidance Paper*, at 64–6. The Commission's test requires a profit sacrifice and not necessarily a price below costs. This would allow intervention where a dominant firm prices above costs but below the optimal price. On the other hand, the Commission are of the opinion that only prices below LRAIC are problematic, *see id.* at 67.

793. *See* Case C-209/10, *Post Danmark I*, at 22.

costs.[794] Accordingly, a below-cost period is in line with the "standard" which the AEC-test provides. The question is then what is the appropriate cost benchmark; i.e., when will a price be below costs?

2.2.1.1   The Cost Benchmark

As the foreclosure element is based on a price/cost-test, it must rely on cost benchmarks. If the price exceeds its cost, then that conduct will not be condemned.[795] The question is then: what is the relevant cost benchmark(s)? While costs benchmarks can be discussed in lengths – especially if one asks what the benchmark(s) ought to be – that is not the purpose of this book. The purpose of this subsection is instead to establish the relevant cost benchmark(s) according to case law. While the object of Predation can also be achieved by other means (the best example is perhaps excess capacity),[796] the focus is on a low-cost price period. Additionally, in the event where it is argued that a dominant firm has been overspending on advertising, R&D or the like the method is still the same; do the costs (including the increased spending) surpass the price (alternatively revenue).[797]

First of all, it must be noticed that case law has historically relied on average costs; i.e., AVC and ATC with ATC being the relevant benchmark for by effect restrictions since prices below AVC constitute a by object restriction (see Chapter 4). Due to recent developments, however, it is likely that this will change to AAC and LRAIC. The Commission is the primary enforcer, and it is likely that those costs will be preferred in future decisions since they are advocated in its *Article 102 Guidance Paper*.[798] The ECJ has also accepted other types of cost benchmark than AVC and ATC,[799] and when it comes to a complex economic assessment, the EU Courts has established that the Commission must be afforded a broad discretion.[800] Not only does this allow the Commission to adjust its analysis to cope with the developments in [legal and] economic literature, but it also paves the way for AAC and LRAIC. What is also important is that it is generally accepted by legal and economic literature that AAC and

---

794. *See* Bishop & Walker (2010), at 302.
795. *See* Bolton, et al. (2000), at 2239–41 (who reaches a similar conclusion).
796. For examples *see* e.g., Bishop & Walker (2010), at 318–20; Padilla & O'Donoghue (2013), at Chapter 12.
797. If such conduct is used to raise competitors' cost (i.e., recoupment is not sought) then Exclusion is a better framework for that conduct.
798. *See the Article 102 Guidance Paper*, at 26.
799. *See* Case C-209/10, *Post Danmark I*, at 31.
800. *See* Case C-295/12 P, *Telefónica*, at 54; Case C-280/08 P, *Deutsche Telekom*, at 41 & 271; Case C-202/07 P, *France Télécom*, at 129 & 163. *See also* Judgment of 28 May 1998 in C-7/95 P, *John Deere Limited v. Commission of the European Communities* ("*John Deere*"), at 34; Judgment of 17 November 1987 in Joined Cases 142 and 156/84, *British American Tobacco Company Ltd and R. J. Reynolds Industries, Inc. v. Commission of the European Communities* ("*BATC*"), at 62; Judgment of 11 July 1985 in Case 42/84, *Remia BV and others v. Commission of the European Communities* ("*Remia*"), at 34.

LRAIC is a better match for the assessment of Predation.[801] Lastly, AAC and LRAIC are good proxies for AVC and ATC, respectively,[802] which means that they can still be used in the same context. This means that prices below AAC can be considered as by object restrictions and prices above LRAIC as a general safe harbour.[803] The relevant cost benchmark then becomes LRAIC since a competitor who is as efficient as the dominant firm should be able to compete effectively with such prices.

2.2.1.2 Level of Detail and Periods

When addressing the relevant cost benchmark there is also the questions of whether to assess the below-cost period on a detailed (i.e., at the level of each individual offer) or an aggregated level (i.e., at the mix of the products sold/offered) and whether to assess each period individually (i.e., period-by-period) or together (i.e., multi-period). While it is not for this book to review this in detail in terms of how it ought to be, it suffices to say that, concerning the latter, the Commission has considered both methods; i.e., a period-by-period approach[804] and a Discounted Cash Flow method ("DCF-method")[805]. Nevertheless, assessments of the profitability have relied on the period-by-period approach,[806] while the DCF-method has been used as support for the finding from the period-by-period analysis.[807] The lack of reliance of a DCF-method may be attributable to the result, which such a method can provide. The Recoupment-period may be included in the analysis of whether there is a Predation-period. This may allow a high price in the latter stage to distort the assessment of the first stage. The finding may imperfectly reflect the actual conduct. On the other hand, it may then assist in showing likely recoupment.

Concerning whether to assess conduct at a detailed or aggregated level, the aggregated level must apply when looking for by effect restrictions. For by object

---

801. *See* e.g., Baumol (1996), at 57–9 (who concludes AAC is better fit than the AVC standard proposed in the Areda/Turner-test and reject the use of ATC due its lack of economic sense for multi-product firms).

802. The main difference between AVC and AAC is that AVC only includes variable costs, while AAC includes all those cost that could have been avoided independent of whether they are variable or fixed. In most cases, however, AAC and AVC will be the same, as it is often only variable costs that can be avoided. Similarly, LRAIC and ATC are good proxies for each other, and they are the same in the case of a single product firm. If a multi-product firm has economies of scope, LRAIC will be below ATC for each individual product, as true common costs are not considered in LRAIC.

803. Note however section 2.2.1.3 in which it is discussed when the general safe harbour does not apply.

804. The period-by-period approach consists of determining profits or losses incurred during specific periods. Some costs are allocated only to the period in which they were incurred and other costs being capitalized and allocated to more than one time period, typically through the use of straight-line depreciation, *see* Case AT.39523, *Slovak Telekom*, at 845.

805. The DCF-method, on the other hand, consists of assessing the overall profitability over an adequate period to arrive at a single measure, the net present value (NPV), *see* Decision of 15 November 2014 in Case AT.39523, *Slovak Telekom*, paragraph 846.

806. *See* Case C-295/12 P, *Telefónica*, at 110–5.

807. *See* Case T-336/07, *Telefónica*, at 213. Upheld in Case C-295/12 P, *Telefónica*, at 112.

restrictions, on the other hand, a detailed level will suffice to establish an abuse.[808] This is based on the principle that an as efficient competitor is able to replicate the dominant firm's conduct at least; i.e., to bid for the same customers.[809] This, of course, presupposes a correct market definition (especially the geographical market) and that the dominant firm is not an unavoidable trading partner. If the dominant firm is setting prices, which on average are above LRAIC, then competitors are, as a rule, able to compete effectively. If on the other hand, competitors are not able to bid for the same customers,[810] certain important customers are targeted or the like, then it may be necessary to adjust the aggregated level and potentially LRAIC.

2.2.1.3   Less Efficient Competitors

When prices are compared to costs, the relevant costs are those of the dominant firm.[811] By doing so, it is assessed whether the dominant firm can compete with its own pricing policy. This ensures that the competitor(s) who might be foreclosed cannot be considered to be less efficient than the dominant firm. It further conforms to the general principle of legal certainty since considering the costs and prices of the dominant firm enables that firm to assess the lawfulness of its own conduct. While a [dominant] firm knows its own costs and prices, it does not, as a rule, know those of its competitors (knowledge of competitors' prices and costs could even be problematic in regards to Article 101 TFEU).

Despite its clear advantages, the AEC-test is not exempted from criticism.[812] The AEC-test has, for example, been criticized for not acknowledging the positive effects stemming from the (potential) entry of less efficient competitors or the anti-competitive effects caused by excluding a less efficient competitor.[813] As it was discussed in Chapter 5, section 5.4 the position of the dominant firm's competitors is likely to be an important element when assessing anti-competitive foreclosure effects. In a market where a dominant firm is present competition is already weakened, and that fact may have a natural limitation on the number and the strength of competitors. This criticism is, therefore, of no surprise as the reason for competitors being less efficient may be due to the dominant firm itself.

The criticism includes not only competitors who are less efficient than the dominant firm, but further those competitors who this book refers to as "weak

---

808. Even if only one offer is below AAC, the firm will have breached Article 102 TFEU as there is neither a De Minimis rule nor a requirement of applicability. However, it may affect the enforcement priorities, the potential fine and claimed damages, *see* Chapter 4.
809. The aggregated approach is consistent with a hypothetical entrant's internal decision-making process in that it assesses the profitability of its investment based on not only customer but the whole market as such, *see* for that effect Case AT.39523, *Slovak Telekom*, at 832.
810. For example, if the dominant firm has monopoly. If competitors are excluded from customers due to the dominant firm offering a better service, quality or so there is no need for intervention as it is merely performing better.
811. *See* Case C-52/09, *TeliaSonera*, at 46.
812. For an overview of the different points of criticism *see* e.g., Padilla & O'Donoghue (2013), at 232–3.
813. *See id.* at 232-3; Salop (2006), at 328.

competitors".[814] This involves a firm who is yet to become as efficient as the dominant firm but can become so given it, for instance, achieves economies of scale.[815] Such firms may, as an example, be found in newly liberalized markets where the dominant firm is enjoying a head start owing to the former monopoly. Distinguishing between these weak competitors and less efficient competitors is important. Weak competitors have the qualifications to be as efficient and intervention seems, therefore, more justified.[816] However, intervention in both events must rely on special circumstances. A weak competitor may be foreclosed simply due to the fact, for example, that the market cannot sustain further entry or that the firm made a bad business decision. Accordingly, there should be good reasons to intervene in both events.

Even though there can be justified intervention in the event where the foreclosed firm is less efficient than the dominant firm, or has yet to become as efficient, legal and economic literature generally tries to dissuade enforcers from prohibiting above-cost prices –[817] where ATC constitutes the relevant benchmark due to the *Akzo-test*.[818] Pricing above costs, in other words, is proposed to constitute a safe harbour rule. The logic goes that if prices remain above ATC, an as efficient competitor cannot be foreclosed by having to compete at the same price.[819] The safe harbour rule then prevents competition law from chilling [aggressive] price competition, which is ultimately desired. Clearly, however, intervention is in some circumstances relevant as it can improve or ensure consumers' interest (i.e., lower prices, better products and so on) despite being more restrictive on dominant firms' conduct than the AEC-test would normally imply.[820] Nevertheless, even where intervention seems justified it still has adverse effects.[821] Besides promoting the entry of firms to strengthen effective competition, it adds further restrictions on dominant firms' conduct and risks keeping prices up – especially if they had the effect of telling a dominant firm to hold an umbrella of

---

814. *See* Chapter 5, section 5.4.
815. *See* for that effect *the Article 102 Guidance Paper*, at 24.
816. *See* Schmalensee, Richard, *On the Use of Economic Models in Antitrust: The ReaLemon Case*, 127 University of Pennsylvania Law Review (1979) 994, at 1021.
817. *See*, among others, Padilla & O'Donoghue (2013), at 334–42; Bishop & Walker (2010); Posner (2001), at 302–7. Other commentators have advocated intervention in the event of prices above costs, *see* e.g., Edlin, Aaron, *Stopping Above-Cost Predatory Pricing*, 111 The Yale Law Journal (2002) 941. (proposing a rule that where an entrant charges at least 20 % below the prevailing price, a monopolist cannot respond with any price cut at all for twelve–eighteen months or until its loses its monopoly); Baumol (1979). (Proposing a rule that a dominant firm is allowed to make reactive price cuts, but forbid reduced prices from being raised after the entrant leaves the market unless costs of demand have changed. *See* next footnote, though); Williamson (1977). (proposing a rule that a dominant firm is allowed to make reactive price cuts, but forbid increasing output for twelve to eighteen months after entry).
818. In US antitrust, a cost benchmarks lower than ATC is often advocated as a safe harbour. *See* e.g., Areeda & Turner (1975). (who proposes AVC since, given the institutional limitations of courts and agencies, there was no reliable way to condemn such behaviour without chilling pro-competitive conduct); Baumol (1996). (who supports the Areada/Turner-test but ultimately prefer AAC as the benchmark). *See also* Bishop & Walker (2010), at pages 302–307.
819. *See* Baumol (1996), at 57 (He applies AVC instead of ATC but the logic is the same).
820. *See* Vickers (2005), at F256.
821. *See* Elhauge, Einer, *Why Above-Cost Price Cuts to Drive out Entrants Are Not Predatory: And the Implications for Defining Costs and Market Power*, 112 The Yale Law Journal (2003) 681.

monopoly prices over its competitors.[822] Accordingly, even if there a beneficial effect there is [almost certainly] also an adverse effect.

A safe harbour rule seems like a logic consequence of the AEC-test as the purpose is only to intervene where competitors as efficient or more than the dominant firm are [likely to be] foreclosed. On the other hand, it is difficult to ignore the fact that foreclosure of less efficient competitors may have anti-competitive effects. However, such anti-competitive effects are produced in special circumstances. Just take the infamous *Compagnie Maritime Belge Transport* case. This was not a "normal" case. Instead, it was a cartel, forming almost a monopoly, which attempted to exclude the single competitor outside the cartel.[823] The Commission even emphasized this in its decision as the argument for prohibiting the above cost-prices in the case.[824] In some events, it may even be obvious that the AEC-test has no relevance since the structure of the market makes the emergence of an as efficient competitor practically impossible.[825] That could be the case in a newly liberalized market, a market where the dominant firm has been given legal rights/obligations or the like. In such markets, deviating from the AEC-test is justified as the presence of a less efficient competitor contributes to intensifying the competitive pressure on that market and exerting constraints on dominant firm's conduct which would otherwise not have been there. What is characterized by both examples is that they deviate from a "normal" case.

The question then remains whether the requirement of a below-cost period is abandoned in the cases or whether costs are adjusted. The latter seems to be favoured by the ECJ where the costs and prices of competitors then become the subject of examination.[826] While this may be a practical option, it raises different issues. Therefore, it may be more sensible to apply, for example, a profit sacrifice-test; i.e., whether the dominant firm is forgoing profits. Such tests ask whether allegedly anti-competitive conduct would be profitable for the dominant firm and would make good business sense even if it did not foreclose competitors and thereby created or preserved market power.[827] If that conduct is not profitable, the firm sacrificed short-run profits and might have been investing in an exclusionary scheme, seeking to secure monopoly power and recoup the foregone profits later.[828] Such approach will be

---

822. See Posner, Richard, *Antitrust Law: An Economic Perspective*, 2001, 2nd ed., University Of Chicago Press, page 238.
823. See Case IV/32.448 and IV/32.450, *Cewal*, at 80.
824. The Commission held: "In this regard, a distinction must be made between a concerted decision by several undertakings forming, in this case, a shipping conference aimed at fixing, within the framework of a plan, a special price to remove a competitor, and the case already examined by the Commission and the Court of Justice of abusively low prices established by a single undertaking acting unilaterally, where it was necessary to distinguish between predatory prices and aggressive competition." *See id.*
825. See Case C-23/14, *Post Danmark II*, at 59.
826. *See* Case C-52/09, *TeliaSonera*, at 45. In *Post Danmark II* the ECJ stated that the AEC-test is of no relevance when the structure of the market makes the emergence of an as-efficient competitor practically impossible, but did not expand further on the issue.
827. *See* Melamed, Douglas, *Exclusionary Conduct under the Antitrust Laws: Balancing, Sacrifice, and Refusals to Deal*, 20 Berkeley Technology Law Journal (2005) 1247, at 1255; Padilla & O'Donoghue (2013), at 185.
828. *See* Areeda & Turner (1975); Ordover & Willig (1981).

in line with the *Article 102 Guidance Paper*.[829] Again, one need to take careful steps as short-term profit sacrifice alone, obviously, is insufficient to make conduct exclusionary since much procompetitive conduct entails the sacrifice of current profit in the pursuit of greater profit over the longer term. For example, investing in R&D sacrifice current profit to obtain what is expected to be a significantly greater future profit.[830] In consequence, short-term profit sacrifice may be the first step, but that finding must be assessed in connection with, first, the circumstances of the case (i.e., are there any special circumstances that warrant intervention), and second, a Theory of Predation. They will tell whether the foreclosure effect is due to the dominant firm.

2.3   The Anti-competitive Effect

The most important part of the assessment of unlawful exclusionary conduct is what follows proof of foreclosure; i.e., the anti-competitive effect. As emphasized earlier, foreclosure alone is insufficient. It is, therefore, necessary to evaluate whether that foreclosure effect is likely to result in harm to effective competition (thereby to the detriment of consumers' interest) before a violation can be established.[831]

According to the EU Courts' case law, the dominant firm's strategy is to be relied on when evaluating the anti-competitive effect.[832] As recalled from above, the AEC-test has its roots in both the Areeda/Turner-test and the EEC-test. Under the first test, a price below AVC was presumed to be anti-competitive since such conduct revealed a Predation strategy.[833] Moreover, the ECJ took the view, similar to Posner's, that prices above AVC but below ATC may also be anti-competitive if a Predation strategy was demonstrated. Accordingly, a Predation strategy is presumed with prices below AVC while such strategy must be demonstrated with prices above AVC [and below ATC]. The anti-competitive element may, therefore, be termed as the "Predation strategy". Following this, it is only logical that proof of a Predation strategy has been required in pricing case law following *Akzo*. What is less clear is what such strategy entails and how such is demonstrated. In the EU Courts' case law, such strategy has been demonstrated through predatory intent. However, in that event, a by object restrictions is found and not a by effect restriction. The question is therefore what is required to

---

829. *See the Article 102 Guidance Paper*, at 64–6.
830. *See* for that effect Elhauge, Einer, *Defining Better Monopolization Standards*, 56 Stanford Law Review (2003) 253, at 274–9.
831. *See* Case C-209/10, *Post Danmark I*, at 44; Case C-52/09, *TeliaSonera*, at 61.
832. *See* Case C-209/10, *Post Danmark I*, at 28; Case T-336/07, *Telefónica*, at 190; Case C-52/09, *TeliaSonera*, at 41; Case C-280/08 P, *Deutsche Telekom*, at 198; Case C-202/07 P, *France Télécom*, at 108; Case 62/86, *Akzo*, at 74.
833. It should be noted that this related to recoupment despite it being less directly stated. Even though the test is known as price/cost-test, it was based on a second condition; namely, the possibility of recoupment. For example, it was stressed in that "[...] predatory pricing would make little economic sense to a potential predator unless he had (1) greater financial staying power than his rivals, and (2) a very substantial prospect that the losses he incurs in the predatory campaign will be exceeded by the profits to be earned after his rivals have been destroyed." *See* Areeda & Turner (1975), at 698.

prove a Predation strategy under the effect-based approach. In the following, it will be argued that recoupment it the tool to assess anti-competitive effects.

2.3.1 Recoupment as the Predation Strategy

It follows, at least implicit, from the definition of Predation that the dominant firm is trading short-term losses for long-term profits. On that basis, recoupment is generally viewed as the anti-competitive element when assessing exclusionary conduct within Predation.[834] As stated by one scholar, the low price-period "is an investment on (future) monopoly profits."[835] The rationality for a recoupment rule is that "[w]ithout recoupment, even if predatory pricing causes the target painful losses, it produces lower aggregate prices in the market, and consumer welfare is enhanced."[836] A competitor may have suffered harm, but effective competition has not. Accordingly, when a dominant firm applies unlawful pricing conduct the purpose is to earn future monopoly profits which offset the losses made in the Predation-period; ultimately, providing an aggregated profit greater than that without unlawful Predation. Since economic theory tells us that Predation is only rational with recoupment (and harm to consumers is achieved through recoupment), it is only sensible to require proof of recoupment for the finding of a by effect restriction. In contrast to by object restrictions where recoupment is presumed,[837] it must be demonstrated to show a by effect restriction.

The related justifications can illustrate the importance of recoupment for imposing a requirement of proving recoupment. They illustrate why recoupment should be favoured but also why it can create controversy within Article 102 TFEU. The justifications can be divided into three main aspects. First, recoupment is said to minimize false positives. Second, it is argued that a requirement of recoupment avoids more complicated issues like intent and price-cost relationships. Third, it is argued that there can be no anti-competitive harm absent recoupment.

A false positive exists if a dominant firm (defendant) is found liable when it, in fact, has not abused its dominant position. In that case, intervention is obviously an unbidden guest. Such intervention is almost certainly detrimental to consumers since they risk chilling competition. This will, of course, have a greater impact on risk adverse firms due to their risk profile.[838] As a result, if the EU Courts (and the Commission) are not careful, Predation can easily be confused with merely low prices which benefit consumers; thus, dominant firms may refrain from lowering their prices, investing in innovation or other conduct that may raise costs. This is especially likely

---

834. *See* e.g., Padilla & O'Donoghue (2013), at 311–2; Bishop & Walker (2010), at 308; Bolton, et al. (2000), at 2267.
835. *See* Bork (1978), at 145.
836. *See Brooke Group Ltd. v. Brown & Williamson Tobacco Corp.*
837. *See* Case 62/86, *Akzo*, at 71 ("A dominant undertaking has no interest in applying such prices except that of eliminating competitors so as to enable it subsequently to raise its prices by taking advantage of its monopolistic position").
838. *See* Brodley, Joseph & Hay, George, *Predatory Pricing: Competing Economic Theories and the Evolution of Legal Standards*, 66 Cornell Law Review (1981) 738, at 790.

in these times where dominant firms (and their advisors) are unsure on how to assess exclusionary conduct. By requiring proof of likely recoupment, Predation only constitutes abuse when a dominant firm is likely to profit from it's below-cost behaviour. Such approach has its obvious advantage. On the other hand, however, recoupment is not as simple as a high price and not necessarily as simple as it is advocated; thus, requiring proof of requirement may even cause false negatives if it is not understood correctly. This will be addressed in section 3.1.2.

A requirement of recoupment operates further as a screening tool to distinguish pro-competitive from anti-competitive pricing conduct. The requirement, in other words, is designed to screen out cases where Predation appears unprofitable, and hence, irrational.[839] Additionally, it has been argued (in the US) that a requirement of recoupment has the effect that courts avoid having to evaluate the below-cost period;[840] in other words, if there is no likelihood of recoupment, the firm must not be pricing below cost and vice versa.[841] This is advocated due to the fact that the matter of determining costs is complex. Recoupment is not merely another element, as it is the case in EU competition law, but is elevated to a threshold element where failure to prove the probability of recoupment eliminates the need to consider a case.[842] In other words, recoupment is argued to be a step before demonstrating a below-cost period. As explained above, however, a below-cost price period is the first step according to the EU Courts' case law. In addition, prices below AVC and those between AVC and LRAIC with a predatory intent constitute a by object restriction; thus, it would contradict this legal rule if recoupment could make the price/cost-test redundant. On the other hand, this does not preclude the Commission from using it as a tool in its enforcement priorities. If it seems unlikely that recoupment is possible, it may be wise for the Commission to priorities its resources to other cases. Additionally, the ECJ has established that it can assist the Commission in excluding economic justifications.[843] Note, however, that it is unlikely that it can exclude justifications such as, for example, selling of the obsolete products.[844]

The first two aspects rely on the assumption that there can be no anti-competitive effects absent recoupment. If this assumption is not applied, then the two arguments above are obviously flawed. The requirement cannot constitute a screening tool if consumers can be harmed in other ways and the requirement will not minimize false positive but may instead "maximize" false negatives since abuse can be rejected even when conduct is to detriment consumers' interest. While the logic behind the assumption is straightforward (as consumers are not harmed if their gain in the Predation period offsets their loss in the recoupment-period) it has some pitfalls relating to how recoupment is understood (these will be addressed below in section 3.1.2). For many

---

839. *See* Bolton, et al. (2000), at 2263.
840. *See* Leslie (2013), at 1710–2.
841. *See* for that effect *A.A. Poultry Farms, Inc. et al. v. Rose Acre Farms, Inc.*, at 1401.
842. *See* Leslie (2013), at 1711.
843. *See* for that effect Case C-202/07 P, *France Télécom*, at 111.
844. *See* Rousseva (2010), at 170–1.

scholars, recoupment involves the ability to raise prices.[845] Recoupment is not that simple, though. It may instead allow the dominant firm to cut costs (e.g., costs related to innovation) thereby allowing for recoupment. While consumers do not experience a higher price – and is not harmed according to this narrow view on recoupment – they will likely experience a lower level of innovation, variety or quality.

Moreover, it is important to note that the third aspect also addresses effective competition. While competitors, even as efficient competitors, may incur losses on each sale made (or if they decline to match the loss inducing price, may lose sales as consumers take advantage of the below-cost prices by the dominant firm) it is argued that in the absence of recoupment, no anti-competitive harm takes place. I.e., if recoupment is not possible, effective competition exists since the foreclosed competitor will re-enter or a potential competitor will enter denying recoupment.[846] Consequently, according to this view harm to effective competition only occurs in the event of (successful) recoupment – even in the event where as efficient competitors are foreclosed.[847] Again, this is fairly logical as the simple explanation for such foreclosure is otherwise related to those competitors or the market; for instance, bad business decisions or that the market could only sustain a certain number of firms. However, as stressed above, one should be aware of the pitfalls relating to the understanding of recoupment.

According to the above, proof of recoupment is the key element in demonstrating the anti-competitive element of the anti-competitive foreclosure effect. While recoupment of losses initially incurred, therefore, constitutes the rational objective associated with Predation, one should be aware of how recoupment is understood and applied.[848] It is especially important that the *Akzo-test* is not forgotten, and hence, that the requirement of recoupment relates to by effect restrictions and not by object restrictions.

2.3.2 Recoupment and Case Law

While a requirement of recoupment constitutes a logical condition for finding unlawful Predation under the effect-based approach, it begs the question of whether it fits with case law.[849] At first glance, case law reveal a negative answer. In both *Tetra Pak II* and

---

845. *See* e.g., Bishop & Walker (2010), at 310. ("In summary, a strategy that involves lower prices to consumer in the short run with no corresponding higher prices in the longer run should not be considered anti-competitive.")
846. *See* Leslie (2013), at 1709.
847. *See* Wagle, Steven, *Predatory Pricing, A Case Study: Matsushita Electric Industries Co. v. Zenith Radio Corporation*, 22 Creighton Law Review (1988) 89, at 119.
848. *See* for that effect Case COMP/38.233, *Wanadoo Interactive*, at 334 (which led the Commission to state that "while the recoupment of losses initially incurred may constitute a rational objective associated with predation, other scenarios are perfectly conceivable").
849. It should be noted that this does not alter the *Akzo-test*; i.e., prices below AAC and prices between AAC and LRAIC with a predatory intent will still constitute by object restrictions.

France Télécom, the ECJ rejected recoupment as a precondition for finding unlawful predatory pricing.[850] Similarly, the ECJ also rejected such requirement in *TeliaSonera* in regards of margin squeeze.[851]

However, it would be wrong to conclude that recoupment is unfit for Article 102 TFEU on that basis. It must be remembered that in both *Tetra Pak II* and *France Télécom* the *Akzo-test* was fulfilled.[852] That is, the dominant firm's conduct constituted a by object restriction. Concerning *TeliaSonera*, the ECJ rejected recoupment as a requirement since margin squeeze does not necessitate a loss for the dominant firm.[853] In other words, margin squeeze is not necessarily an issue of Predation, but may instead be an issue of Exclusion. A requirement of recoupment would, therefore, be unfit for these cases. With this important point in mind, one will discover that recoupment is, in fact, an important element in case law; though it may be less evident.

First, it should be noted that the ECJ does not preclude the finding of unlawful Predation to occur on other grounds than the *Akzo-test*. This was settled in *Post Danmark I*. Here the ECJ concluded that unlawful Predation does not only include intent to foreclose competitors.[854] The significance of the judgment is, therefore, that anti-competitive foreclosure effects can be demonstrated without the *Akzo-test*.[855] In consequence, the judgment removed any doubt, should it have existed, that abuse can be established on other grounds than a by object restriction.

However, this should have been clear already from the ECJ's judgment in *France Télécom*. Here, France Télécom had argued that the demonstration of likely recoupment was a precondition for finding predatory pricing. While the ECJ rejected such obligation to include recoupment in the assessment since the *Akzo-test* was fulfilled (see above), it recognized that that interpretation does not preclude the Commission from finding unlawful Predation on the grounds of recoupment since such proof may assist in establishing the Predation strategy.[856] Therefore, while the ECJ has rejected recoupment as a requirement, it should be understood as a rejection in that specific setting.

Such conclusion is supported by *Tetra Pak II* even though the ECJ also here rejected recoupment as a requirement. As with *France Télécom*, the rejection is limited to the circumstances of the case.[857] This was even explicitly stated by the ECJ as it found that "it would not be appropriate, in the circumstances of the present case, to require in addition proof that Tetra Pak had a realistic chance of recouping its

---

850. *See* Case C-202/07 P, *France Télécom*, at 110; Case C-333/94 P, *Tetra Pak II*, at 44.
851. *See* Case C-52/09, *TeliaSonera*, at 103.
852. *See* Chapter 4.
853. *See* Case C-52/09, *TeliaSonera*, at 101.
854. The ECJ noticed it had not, in the national proceedings, been possible to establish that Post Danmark had deliberately sought to drive out its competitor, while at the same time recognizing that its pricing conduct could be unlawful given it produced an actual or likely anti-competitive effect.
855. *See* Rousseva & Marquis (2013), at 3 & 5 (who argue the judgment did not overrule the Akzo-test but proof of adverse effects becomes an alternative to the condition of intent).
856. *See* Case C-202/07 P, *France Télécom*, at 111.
857. *See* Rousseva (2010), at 164.

losses."[858] In other words, by finding unlawful Predation according to the *Akzo-test* recoupment was not required.[859] Accordingly, case law reveals that recoupment is not required if Predation is assessed according to the *Akzo-test* and that if the *Akzo-test* is not fulfilled, then recoupment can be a method to show anti-competitive effects.

Additionally, despite recoupment not being required when finding unlawful Predation according to the *Akzo-test*, it is, in fact, the rational basis for such conduct being by object restrictions. When explaining the *Akzo-test*, the ECJ reasoned the unlawfulness of price below AVC on the grounds that the purpose of such conduct is "that of eliminating competitors so as to enable it subsequently to raise its prices by taking advantage of its monopolistic position."[860] Clearly, the ECJ did not accept such prices, as it would foreclose competitors and subsequently allow recoupment. This also explains why the ECJ would not allow prices between AVC and ATC with an intention to foreclose a competitor. Following the reasoning for banning prices below AVC, such intention to foreclose competitors was presumed to have roots in a purpose of recoupment. As a result, the Predation strategy referred to in the second step of the Akzo-step refers indirectly to recoupment. However, recoupment is in that event proved by intent to foreclose competitors since such foreclosure, following the analogy of the first step, has the purpose of recoupment. Therefore, it is safe to say that recoupment is the general idea of anti-competitive harm not only in legal and economic literature but also, more importantly, in the *Akzo-test*.

Additionally, exclusionary conduct falling within Predation (at least for predatory pricing) has only been condemned where recoupment was either established or probable on the facts.[861] In *Wanadoo* (*France Télécom*) the Commission undertook a detailed assessment of whether recoupment was likely and concluded it was. In both *Akzo* and *Tetra Pak II* recoupment was probable. Both firms were dominant in a wide range of products, but only engaged in selective price cuts and, given their dominant position, it has been argued that this would lead to a reputation building effect allowing for recoupment.[862]

In consequence, when case law is analysed in the context of recoupment one can conclude the following. First, recoupment is the general idea of anti-competitive effects within the *Akzo-test*, and thereby, the motive for banning these types of conduct. Second, the rejection of recoupment being a requirement is limited to the circumstances of these cases; more particularly, when conduct falls within the *Akzo-test*. Third, and lastly, recoupment is accepted as a method to find unlawful Predation when conduct does *not* fall within the *Akzo-test*. This means that recoupment is redundant when Predation constitutes a by object restriction, while it is necessary in the finding of a by effect restriction.

---

858. *See* Case C-333/94 P, *Tetra Pak II*, at 44.
859. In addition, the ECJ may have misunderstood the concept of recoupment since it supported its conclusion on the grounds that the aim to protect effective competition "rules out waiting until such a strategy leads to the actual elimination of competitors." *See id.*
860. *See* Case 62/86, *Akzo*, at 71.
861. *See* Padilla & O'Donoghue (2013), at 318.
862. *See* Lang & O'Donoghue (2002), at 144. *See also* Padilla & O'Donoghue (2013), at 318; Rousseva (2010), at 163.

3 FRAMEWORK FOR ASSESSING DIFFERENT TYPES OF PREDATION

In the preceding subsection, it has been analysed how exclusionary conduct falling within Predation can be assessed according to an effect-based approach. This revealed, among other things, that the foreclosure effect requires a below-cost period; i.e., a price below LRAIC. Besides the below-cost period a Theory of Predation is also required. This was not analysed above as will be in the following. It further revealed that the anti-competitive element is demonstrated if the dominant firm has a reasonable prospect of recoupment. While it has been rejected as an absolute requirement in case law, the analysis above showed that is line with case law as recoupment has been, indirectly, presumed in case law (due to by object restrictions). The findings from the analysis are therefore in accordance with how Predation was presented in Chapter 5; i.e., as a mechanism to increase the price.

In this section, it will be analysed how this framework of an effect-based approach can be applied to different types of exclusionary conducts. This include: (i) predatory pricing, and (ii) margin squeeze. Note that this is not an exhaustive list.

3.1 Predatory Pricing

For many commentators, Predation equals predatory pricing. Section 2 did indeed heavily lean on the principles of predatory pricing when analysing and discussing Predation. Nevertheless, predatory pricing can be viewed as a distinct type of conduct within Predation. The end-result may be the same as the others, but the means to get there can differ. As a result, this section analyses how to demonstrate the foreclosure and anti-competitive effect, respectively, when dealing with predatory pricing.

3.1.1 Foreclosure Effect

As concluded in section 2.2.1 the foreclosure effect is based on a below-cost period. Such proof is not sufficient alone, though. Pricing between AAC and LRAIC represents commonly observed conduct by both dominant and non-dominant firms in a wide variety of markets.[863] As it is not uncommon for firms to incur losses from time to time on grounds other than Predation, it would raise issues if such a low pricing-period would suffice to establish a foreclosure effect. It is the nature of most businesses to remain operating even in times of losses;[864] and if a firm comes under suspicion merely due to this circumstance it may discourage firms to innovate, enter new markets or other events which may require a low pricing-period. By throwing suspicion on dominant firms in such events, effective competition may be harmed rather than protecting it. Of course, that is not to say that this type of conduct cannot have foreclosure effects, and in the end anti-competitive effects, but rather that a low-pricing

---

863. *See* Bishop & Walker (2010), at 305.
864. *See* Baumol (1996), at 56.

period cannot constitute sufficient evidence. Instead, it should be demonstrated that it forecloses such competitors, or at least is likely to do so.

This is where the Theory of Predation is brought into play. In the following three main theories of how predatory pricing can occur are discussed:[865] (i) "Financial Predation", (ii) "Signalling Predation," and (iii) "Reputation Predation". Moreover, these three strategies are explicitly referred to in the *Article 102 Guidance Paper* as methods that can investigate whether suspected conduct reduces the likelihood that competitors will compete.[866] It is, therefore, reasonable to expect that future assessments will rely on one of these methods.

3.1.1.1 *Financial Predation*

Within EU competition law, the most famous method to demonstrate anti-competitive effects is perhaps the deep pocket theory. It was the issue pointed out by the ECJ in *Akzo*.[867] The deep pocket theory states that a richly endowed predator would charge low prices to drive out a poorly endowed competitor.[868] Financial Predation, however, is not to be confused with this traditional deep pocket theory. That theory ignores the possibility that profit-seeking investors may finance the prey; thus, the theory is no longer accepted –[869] except in certain regulatory circumstances.[870]

In contrast to the deep pocket theory, the modern theory of Financial Predation centres on the dominant firm's ability to manipulate the relationship between the prey and its investors.[871] In general, this works by the predator taking advantage of the prey's reliance on external financing and subsequently impairs the prey's ability to compete or removes the prey from the market entirely. Accordingly, this strategy becomes viable due to capital market imperfections.[872] This may occur since the prey's investors can mitigate these problems by extending financing only in staged commitments, thereby, imposing an explicit or implicit threat of termination in case of poor

---

865. A more comprehensive review can be found in e.g., Bolton, et al. (2000).
866. *See the Article 102 Guidance Paper*, at 68. These was further advocated in the EAGCP report leading to the *Article 102 Guidance Paper*, *see* Gual, et al. (2005), at 20–21.
867. *See* Case 62/86, *Akzo*, at 72 (it was feared an as efficient competitor might be foreclosed due to its smaller financial resources may be incapable of withstanding the competition waged against him).
868. *See* Milgrom, Paul & Roberts, John, *New Theories of Predatory Pricing*, *in* Industrial Structure in the New Industrial Economics (Giacomo Bonanno & Dario Brandolini eds.), 1990.
869. *See* above section 2 in regards of McGee's paper.
870. *See* e.g., Viscusi, Kip, et al., *Economics of Regulation and Antitrust*, 2005, at 564–7 (arguing a firm may conduct cross-subsidization of below-cost pricing in one market by setting regulated price in second market above socially efficient level).
871. *See* e.g., Bolton, Patrick & Scharfstein, David, *A Theory of Predation Based on Agency Problems in Financial Contracting*, 80 The American Economic Review (1990) 93; Fudenberg, Drew & Tirole, Jean, *A "Signal-Jamming" Theory of Predation*, 17 The RAND Journal of Economics (1986) 366.
872. *See* Bolton, et al. (2000), at 2286.

performance.[873] Therefore, by lowering the prey's profit, the predator may succeed in destroying or hampering the relationship between the prey and its investors.

This is done by placing the investor(s) in a dilemma.[874] If it provides a continuing supply of funds sufficient to deter Predation, it invites agency misconduct. Such agency misconduct is invited since it is impossible to sign a financial contract explicitly contingent on realized profit.[875] On the other hand, if it attempts to impose financial discipline on the prey with repayment obligations and collateral requirements, it may induce Predation since the predatory pricing conduct may make the prey unable to earn enough within a particular time period to successfully pay back its investor(s);[876] thus, leading to foreclosure. In addition, reduced earnings aggravate future agency problems by forcing the prey to pledge a bigger share of future profits to its outside investors and creditors; thus, the prey's manager has less incentive to maximize profits.

Accordingly, successful Financial Predation relies on different assumptions. Proof of a plausible Financial Predation is subject to five essential conditions:[877]

(1) The prey depends on external financing.[878]

(2) The prey's external financing depends on time-specific performance.[879]

(3) Predation reduces the prey's time-specific performance, thereby hampering the prey's ability to gain external financing or forcing the prey to renegotiate external financing contracts less favourably.[880]

(4) The dominant firm knows the prey depends on external financing.[881]

---

873. This can happen in three overall examples. First, if the investors are debtholders, they may threaten to liquidate the firm or deny new credit in the event of default. Second, if they are venture capitalists, they may refuse to extend additional financing if early performance is poor. Third, if they are shareholders, they may decline to purchase additional equity if expected returns are low due to disappointing initial performance. See id.

874. See id. at 2288.

875. There are two alternative interpretations of this assumption. One is that at the end of each period, the firm privately observes profit. The other is that profit is observable but not verifiable; although both the firm and investor(s) can observe profit, the courts cannot; hence, these parties cannot write an enforceable profit-contingent contract. See Bolton & Scharfstein (1990), at 95.

876. Less drastically, the predator may be able to lower the prey's earnings, and thus impair the prey's debt capacity, by limiting the amount of collateral it can offer. Or the lower earnings may cause investor(s) to believe wrongly that the firm's profits are likely to be lower or riskier in the future and therefore to stiffen their lending terms, see Bolton, et al. (2000), at 2287.

877. See id. at 2290-2.

878. Without such dependents agency problems and contractual responses that expose the prey to Predation are not created.

879. This relationship is an essential condition because, if the prey's financing does not depend on initial performance, then the financial relationship between the prey and its investors and creditors would be insensitive to a strategy of price Predation.

880. The dominant firm's pricing conduct must be of sufficient magnitude and probability to affect the supply of further financing, thereby threatening the prey's financial viability. This may be demonstrated through the prey's business plan which can reveal the requirements to stay in business and/or become viable.

881. Without actual or imputable knowledge that the prey's viability depends on outside funding, Financial Predation is not rational. Such knowledge may come from aspect such as common industry knowledge, discoverable through simple investigation, inferable from the predator's conduct or its internal documents.

(5) The dominant firm can finance the Predation-period of sufficient length to adversely affect a prey's financing through its own financing, or through an external source that is stronger than the prey's source.[882]

3.1.1.2   Signalling Predation

In regards of Signalling Predation, the dominant firm attempts to mislead the prey, and any other potential entrants, into believing market conditions are unfavourable. Such conduct may be plausible since a firm's decision to enter or leave a market is based on its evaluation of expected future revenues and costs.[883] There are, generally, two types of Predation that are associated with signalling strategies: Demand[884] and Cost Signalling Predation. In Demand Signalling Predation, a dominant firm reduces the price to prevent the prey from learning about market conditions. In contrast, in Cost Signalling Predation, the dominant firm reduces its price to mislead the prey into believing it has lower costs.

Demand Signalling. In its simple form, Demand Signalling Predation aims at reducing the prey's sales in the entered market by cutting prices that prevent the entrant from discovering whether demand is sufficiently strong to justify its continued presence in the market.[885] This form of Predation requires the dominant firm to be informed of the actual market conditions while the prey does not have accurate information. It may be difficult, as misleading information, regarding demand conditions, may require the dominant firm to sacrifice profits for an extended period of time to make market conditions seem unfavourable for entry. Accordingly, it will, typically, only occur when an entrant either enters only a portion of the market or is only established in a portion thereof and seeks to expand gradually. Secret price cuts are further the best option for such strategy, as the purpose is to distort true information.

All this information indicates that for a demand-side signalling strategy, the following four conditions must hold.[886]

(1) The prey is either entering a limited product or geographic market or is gradually expanding from a limited product/geographic market.[887]

---

882. Without superior financing, the dominant firm will face agency risks and financing constraints similar to those that confront the prey.

883. *See* Creane, Anthony, *An Informational Externality in A Competitive Market*, 14 International Journal of Industrial Organization (1996) 331; Kreps, David & Wilson, Robert, *Reputation and Imperfect Information*, 27 Journal of Economic Theory (1982) 253.

884. Demand signalling may also be termed as 'test market Predation' as the competitor can be said to be entering its product into a test market (either as potential entrant or market expansion by current competitor) where the dominant firm misleads the actual condition.

885. *See* Bolton, et al. (2000), at 2311.

886. *See id.* at 2313–4.

887. If the prey is not attempting to test the market response to its product on a limited basis but entering on a full scale, then other form Predation must be applied foreclose – e.g., Financial Predation.

(2) The dominant firm secretly offers prices lower than what the prey can rationally offer.[888]

(3) The dominant firm's secret price-cutting is only established in the limited markets, whereas in other markets prices stay at their original levels.[889]

(4) The prey should rationally believe that demand for its product is weak in the target market.[890]

Cost Signalling. In its simple form, Cost Signalling Predation attempts to misinform the prey that the dominant firm has a lower cost structure than is true. This kind of Predation is designed to make the prey believe it cannot compete against the dominant firm, and hence, it should not enter the market or expand.[891] Besides focusing on costs, it is similar to demand signalling. In contrast to Demand Signalling, secret price cuts are not necessary. Instead, the dominant firm's true cost must be secret.

Therefore, for a cost signalling strategy to be effective, four conditions need to hold.[892]

(1) The prey should believe that the dominant firm's costs are significantly lower than its own.[893]

(2) The dominant firm must decrease its price at or about the time the prey would observe the information.[894]

(3) The prey must believe the dominant firm has lower cost according to the lowered price (the true costs are secret).[895]

(4) The possible belief of cost reduction must be sufficient to induce the prey to leave the market or limit expansion into other markets.[896]

---

888. This may include price reductions made in anticipation of entry, as well as following entry.
889. Below-cost pricing in only one market is strongly consistent with Signalling Predation. Otherwise, conduct would resemble Financial Predation better.
890. Signalling Predation will injure competitors only if it prevents them from learning that demand for its product has strength sufficient to warrant its continued presence in the test market or expansion into new markets. For example, this precondition might be satisfied if the incumbent cuts its price to such a low level that very few consumers buy the victim's product.
891. *See* Bolton, et al. (2000), at 2318.
892. *See id.* at 2320-1.
893. Besides pricing low, this may be done through/assisted by different events which bring the information to the prey. For example, the dominant firm may signal (e.g., publications) it has made an important innovation, hired a new management team or CEO, engaged in extensive downsizing, or obtained exclusive access to a cheap source of foreign supply or other scarce input etc.
894. If there is no reaction from the dominant firm, it will not have the intended purpose of misleading the prey.
895. The prey must believe there is a connection between the lowered price and lower costs. Such belief will be reliable where, for instance, the dominant has in the past actually reduced its prices when costs fell, and/or the price reduction followed an announcement by the predator that it had reduced its costs.
896. The reason for a lack of entering or expansion by the prey must relate to the cost signalling as the dominant firm's conduct, otherwise, cannot be Cost Signalling Predation.

3.1.1.3   Reputation Predation

The purpose of Reputation Predation is to build a reputation, and hence, in a way misleading competitors into believing that market conditions are unfavourable. It has, accordingly, similarities with Signalling Predation. To engage in Reputation Predation, the dominant firm reduces the price in one market (or one time-period) to establish a reputation as a price cutter in other markets (or periods).[897] Observing this conduct, a competitor in another market (or period) or a potential entrant may rationally believe the dominant firm will engage in Predation if it engages in aggressive competition or enters the market.[898] This reputation-induced belief of a fierce competition may deter entry for the potential entrant and market expansion by current competitors. The biggest difference from Signalling Predation is therefore that while Signalling Predation performs better under secret price cuts (or secret cost), Reputation Predation cannot be strategical if the price cut is secret.

In consequence, Reputation Predation also serves as an entry barrier.[899] It is on that basis argued that Reputation Predation better serves as a tool to either enhance or intensify another plausible Predation strategy.[900] It may assist in finding foreclosure where, for instance, Financial Predation has been found unsuccessful. That is, the dominant firm's conduct may be unlikely to result in a foreclosure effect according to Financial Predation, but a foreclosure effect is likely according to Reputation Predation. Similarly, it can reinforce the likelihood of successful recoupment.

Accordingly, for Reputation Predation to be successful four conditions is required.[901]

(1) The dominant firm must operate in multiple markets (either in terms of products or in terms of geographic areas) and face competition in some of those markets or a single market with probable entry over time.[902]

(2) The dominant firm must engage in a financial or signalling strategy to predate.[903]

(3) The dominant firm must deliberately pursue a reputation.[904]

---

897. *See* Bolton, et al. (2000), at 2300.
898. It may also work as method to discipline actual competitors.
899. *See* Milgrom & Roberts (1990), at 280–1.
900. *See* Bolton, et al. (2000), at 2301.
901. *See id.* at 2302–4.
902. With multiple markets or periods reputation cannot be build. Reputation Predation requires, therefore, a Predation market/period to build the reputation and a recoupment market/period to take advantage of the reputation.
903. If the dominant firm does not engage in either financial or Signalling Predation, then the dominant firm does not build up a Predation reputation. Competitors may observe it lowers its price, but still above cost; however, such reputation will not deter an as efficient competitor.
904. To avoid an over inclusive rule, it will be sensible to require proof 'intent' by, for instance, a corporate plan to engage in Reputation Predation; publication or dissemination of information likely to create a reputation effect; suppression of information that might reveal bluffing by the predator or acquirement of a complaining victim in the demonstration market; or repetition of its conduct in multiple markets or over successive time periods.

(4) Potential entrants must receive a signal of the dominant firm's conduct, which influences their decision to enter the market or stay out.[905]

3.1.2 Anti-competitive Effect

Three main methods of proving foreclosure have been presented in the previous subsection. However, for predatory pricing (and all other exclusionary conduct) to be unlawful, it must, ultimately, include an anti-competitive effect. As concluded in section 2.3, recoupment is the method to demonstrate anti-competitive effects when dealing with Predation under the effect-based approach. At the same time, it is a complex matter and one that is subject to controversy and debate. While this controversy has caused some commentators to go to the length of claiming recoupment as unnecessary and inappropriate,[906] it does not have such effect on this conclusion. As pointed out earlier, some of the controversy surrounding recoupment can be attributed to how recoupment is understood (i.e., how recoupment is proven). Creating an understanding of recoupment is, therefore, highly important to analysis how it can be proven. As a result, different aspects are analysed below with the purpose of providing a framework for how recoupment can be proven.

3.1.2.1 A Paradox

Initially, to understand recoupment and the controversy surrounding it (to some extent at least) it should be noted that recoupment represents a paradox. Firms are usually considered rational, and the further a price is below cost the more suspicious it is. One just has just to look at case law in which a dominant firm is deemed to pursue an anti-competitive purpose when pricing below AVC. While a price becomes more suspicious the lower it gets, the likelihood of successful recoupment is reduced as the price is reduced. The lower the price, the greater the loss, everything else equal; thus, a greater profit is required to successfully recoup the loss. In other words, the lower the price, the more suspicious is the price despite the increased difficulty of successful recoupment. This creates a paradoxical result as the prices which are usually most suspicious may end up being treated the most leniently due to the difficulty of proving recoupment and vice versa.[907] This also stands as a strong argument for not having recoupment as an absolute requirement; i.e., the *Akzo-test* takes precedence over proof of recoupment.

---

905. Competitors or potential entrant must, of course, observe the adverse effects of the dominant firm's predatory conduct to build a reputation. However, this does not require full information of the foreclosure as even when the cause is not known, foreclosure can discourage entry of a potential competitor by indicating low market profitability.
906. *See* Leslie (2013), at 1741 & 1744. *See also* Hovenkamp, Erik & Hovenkamp, Herbert, *Exclusionary Bundled Discounts and the Antitrust Modernization Commission*, 53 Antitrust Bulletin (2008) 517, at 539.
907. *See* Padilla & O'Donoghue (2013), at 313.

3.1.2.2 Quantitative Versus Qualitative

Proving successful recoupment is a complex process. It requires the plaintiff (or the Commission) to obtain and evaluate data which is inherently complex and can be exceedingly difficult and costly if it requires detailed quantitative evidence that the dominant firm has, in fact, recouped its losses or is likely to do so.[908] In other words, predictions on future profits are inherently difficult –[909] even for firms themselves. Therefore, future profits cannot be measured with precision. They will be estimates. These future profits would also need to be discounted to a value that can be compared to the losses incurred during the period of Predation if they have yet to be earned. A decision on the period of time for which future profits can be earned must then be made and a discount rate must be determined. Measuring cost also involves uncertainties. Under a measure of losses tied to the dominant firm's cost, the size of the losses is sensitive to the measure of cost applied.[910] Consequently, the choice of cost may be chosen on the grounds of speculations. This creates uncertainties of the losses that has actual been incurred. Such inaccuracy of both losses and profit increases error costs in the form of both false negatives and false positives.

A quantitative approach requires in this way an additional degree of complication that is not present in any other antitrust cause of action.[911] Despite all of this, this should not be the reason for dismissing a requirement of recoupment – even if it requires a quantitative analysis. A complex and correct assessment should not be dismissed for a simple and wrong assessment. On the other hand, an argument can always be made that the assessment is too complex in terms of required enforcement cost that may even surpass the benefits from the enforcement action. However, the benefits and the potential losses from false negatives and positives[912] may be impossible to estimate. Moreover, enforcement actions do not only influence a specific case but will likely involve preventive effects as well.

Assessing recoupment is not reserved for a forecast of future profits, though. It can also be done by assessing whether the dominant firm, through its conduct and the market conditions, achieves a position that enables it to raise its prices;[913] i.e., whether the firm is able to benefit from the low pricing-period.[914] In other words, the assessment may rely on a qualitative analysis, as the aim is to show a reasonable prospect of recoupment. Proving a reasonable prospect of recoupment will generally require proof of sustainable market power; i.e., the ability to raise prices (or otherwise exploit consumers) over some significant but not necessarily unlimited period of

---

908. *See* Bolton, et al. (2000), at 2512.
909. *See* Hemphill, Scott, *The Role of Recoupment in Predatory Pricing Analyses*, 53 Stanford Law Review (2001) 1581, at 1597.
910. *See id.* at 1596–7.
911. *See* Leslie (2013), at 1763–4.
912. Wrong conclusions may either chill competition or allow/incentives anti-competitive conduct which all is to the detriment of consumers.
913. *See* Padilla & O'Donoghue (2013), at page 312. *See also* Hemphill (2001), at 1581.
914. *See* for that effect *the Article 102 Guidance Paper*, at 70.

time.[915] Sufficient market power seems likely when a dominant firm has high market share and when there are both entry and re-entry barriers.[916]

The assessment may, therefore, take the form of either a quantitative or qualitative analysis. Nevertheless, recoupment is generally perceived as a qualitative analysis.[917] This also includes the Commission who applied such analysis in its assessment of whether recoupment was likely in *Wanadoo*.[918] This is also true for its *Article 102 Guidance Paper*.[919] In consequence, the assessment will rely on an inquiry of whether different factors (such a market conditions (e.g., entry barriers), the dominant firm's conduct etc.) facilitate a prospect of recoupment. This is also the most sensible approach as requiring the Commission to calculate losses and profits would be subject to many estimates and assumptions that can give many different results. Nonetheless, evidence that the dominant firm has been able, or unable, to raise its price can assist in proving an ability to recoup.

3.1.2.3   Ex-ante Versus Ex-post

Demonstrating recoupment does not require proof of *actual* recoupment as *likely* recoupment suffices.[920] Moreover, depending on when enforcement actions are taken, proof of likely recoupment may be the only way to demonstrate recoupment; thus, proof of actual recoupment ought not to be a prerequisite as the probability of recoupment is as important. Accordingly, the assessment may take either an *ex-ante* or an *ex-post* approach –[921] or potentially a mix of both.[922]

In principle, assessing recoupment *ex-post* is easier than *ex-ante*. After foreclosure, it is possible to observe how the dominant firm acts; i.e., whether it has started recouping its losses and whether recoupment has been successful or is likely to be. In contrast to that approach, the prospect of recoupment *ex-ante* relies on estimates regarding future events and market conditions. While it may be near impossible to

---

915. *See* Hemphill (2001), at 1587; Bolton, et al. (2000), at 2264; Joskow & Klevorick (1979), at 225–34.
916. *See* Ordover & Willig (1981). *See also* Case COMP/38.233, *Wanadoo Interactive*, at 332–9.
917. *See* e.g., Padilla & O'Donoghue (2013), at 312 ("Recoupment requires proof that the loss-making prices would increse the predator's market power and allow it to recover the initial losses through supra-competitive prices in future").
918. *See* Case COMP/38.233, *Wanadoo Interactive*, at 338.(the Commission examined the entry barriers and entry costs which characterised the relevant market and which rendered plausible a recoupment of the losses by the dominant firm in the long run).
919. *See the Article 102 Guidance Paper*, at 70.
920. As concluded in Chapter 3 a likely anti-competitive foreclosure effect is sufficient. *See also* Case COMP/38.233, *Wanadoo Interactive*, at 332–367 (the Commission examined the probability of a recoupment). This also the view taken in literature, *see* e.g., Baumol, William, *Principles Relevant to Predatory Pricing, in The Pros and Cons of Low Prices, in* The Pros and Cons of Low Prices (Konkurrensverket ed., 2003, at 25 (he states that "that there must be a reasonable prospect of recoupment of at least whatever initial costs to the firm were entailed in the firm's adoption of the price in question").
921. *See* Hemphill (2001).
922. *See* for that effect Case COMP/38.233, *Wanadoo Interactive*, at 365–367 (The Commission found that Wanadoo' margin began to show an upward trend over time).

predict the profits a firm will earn in the future it is not a matter of how much the dominant firm will earn but rather whether it has a reasonable prospect of recouping its losses (see above).[923]

While it could be argued that the *ex-post* approach should be preferred over the *ex-ante* approach since it adds an additional layer to *ex-ante* approach, the assessment of recoupment must be done from an *ex-ante* vantage point. The question is not whether the dominant firm has, in fact, recouped its losses, or whether it is underway, but rather whether there is the ability to do so in long run and, as a result, an *ex-ante* approach must be relied on.[924] If an *ex-ante* approach were not applied, it would contradict the conclusion that the assessment will rely on a qualitative analysis. Moreover, the dominant firm should not benefit from, for example, miscalculations of profits in the Recoupment-period.[925]

The assessment of a reasonable prospect of recoupment, obviously, must then follow a forward-looking assessment.[926] This is also implied in the prospect of recoupment; the aim is to assess the ability to take advantage of the foreclosure effect.

3.1.2.4 Static Versus Dynamic View

Another important step in creating an understanding of how recoupment can be proved is what may be termed as static versus dynamic views. The former view follows the simple explanation in the introduction to section 2; i.e., the dominant firm lowers its price and then raises it again. But, it may not necessarily be that simple that the dominant firm tries to recoup in the market which it predates. In addition, it may even be a product which is priced low and when foreclosure is successful that product is withdrawn again [allowing recoupment on another product].

In both examples, the dominant firm has not recouped its loss when viewed statically. However, if a more dynamic view is taken it may be the case. The purpose may be the protection of a connected market or an established product. If that understanding of recoupment is not incorporated, it may create false negatives (by not concluding likely recouping). Such false negative is evaded by how recoupment is examined. Although the dominant firm is not recovering the losses incurred in that market or for that product, the purpose is still likely to be recoupment. In consequence, recoupment cannot only be viewed in a static sense but must be viewed in a dynamic sense as well.[927] This type of recoupment is especially important in regards of Signalling Predation and reputation building predation.

---

923. *See* Baumol (2003), at 25.
924. A similar conclusion is reached by Motta, *see* Motta (2004), at 450. *See also* Rousseva (2010).
925. *See* Motta (2004), at 405 (who also mentions enforcement actions which ends the Recoupment-period).
926. *See* Mano, Miguel de la & Durand, Benoît, *Three-Step Structured Rule of Reason to Assess Predation under Article 82*, 2005, Office of the Chief Economist Discussion Paper, available at http://ec.europa.eu/dgs/competition/economist/pred_art82.pdf, at 25.
927. *See* Bolton, et al. (2000), at 2242–50 (who criticizes the static approach (which formed the recoupment requirement in US antitrust law) since modern economics does not support a static approach).

3.1.2.5 Entry Barriers

When applying recoupment to the assessment of anti-competitive foreclosure effects, it must be done with care as this element may be quite complex. This also has an impact on the elements which are included in the assessment of recoupment. Take for example entry barriers. They are extremely important, but the problem is that entry barriers can be perceived differently. Some rely on the view that re-entry by excluded competitors (or entry by potential competitors) are easy; thus, recoupment is generally unlikely since the dominant firm will not be able to price excessively after the Predation-period.[928] This view, obviously, goes back to the Chicago School in which entry barriers were viewed very narrowly. Entry barriers were limited to, for example, intellectual property rights and governmental rights; thus, economic of scales, advertising, building a factory, customer loyalty and so on could not constitute entry barriers.[929]

However, this may not necessarily be true,[930] and it will depend on the specific market.[931] In addition, if the dominant firm succeeds in creating a predatory reputation it may succeed in creating an entry barrier by its reputation. In that sense, entry would not occur even when the dominant firm charges monopoly profits in a market without entry barriers since potential competitors would calculate that its entry into the market would depress the price and its actual rate of return would be insufficient to recover its entry costs in a timely manner.[932]

Finally, even if [re-]entry is observed one cannot conclude that recoupment is prevented. The observed entry may be too weak to compel the dominant firm to reduce its price.[933] This relates to the aspect of whether competitors have the incentive and ability to compete. It may be that competitors lack the incentive, and hence, follow the dominant firm's "orders". It may reduce the dominant firm's revenue, but not

---

928. *See* e.g., Easterbrook, Frank, *The Limits of Antitrust*, 63 Texas Law Review (1984) 1, at 27 (who discussed the likelihood of competition from 'resurgent firms'); Bork (1978), at 151–2. (who discussed the possibility of competitors avoiding losses by closing operations until re-entry is feasible); McGee (1958), at 140 (who asserted the possibility of re-entry).
929. *See* Hovenkamp, Herbert, *Antitrust Policy after Chicago*, 84 Michigan Law Review (1985), at 226–29; Posner (1979), at 929–32.
930. *See* e.g., Baumol, William & Willig, Robert, *Fixed Costs, Sunk Costs, Entry Barriers, and Sustainability of Monopoly*, 96 The Quarterly Journal of Economics (1981) 405, at 418–9 (Who show that the need for an entrant to incur sunk costs can be an entry barrier); Ordover & Willig (1981), at 11–2 (who argues costs of e.g., salvaged equipment, dispersed labour force and management, discontinued advertising, and unmaintained reputation constitute [re-]entry barriers).
931. *See* e.g., Craswell, Richard & Fratrik, Mark, *Predatory Pricing Theory Applied: The Case of Supermarkets v. Warehouse Stores*, 36 Case Western Reserve Law Review (1985) 1, at 33 (who argued the cost of rehiring employees or rebuilding the loyalty of angry customers are significant); Wagle (1988), at 96 (Who refers to Baumol and Willing); Dempsey, Paul Stephen, *Predatory Practices & Monopolization in the Airline Industry: A Case Study of Minneapolis/St. Paul*, 29 Transportation Law Journal (2002) 129, at 159–60 (who discussed Northwest Airline's predation conduct in the Minneapolis/St. Paul market with an absence of re-entry by airlines chased out of market).
932. *See* Leslie (2013), at 1716.
933. *See* Tor, Avishalom, *The Fable of Entry: Bounded Rationality, Market Discipline, and Legal Policy*, 101 Michigan Law Review (2002) 482, at 559.

necessarily in a devastating manner and, possibly, not enough to prevent recoupment. In consequence, it is important when assessing recoupment that entry barriers are not viewed too narrowly.

It should be noted that proof of [market power and] entry barriers may not always be a needed in showing that market conditions facilitate recoupment. This can also be proved directly by showing such anti-competitive effects. If the dominant firm has been able to raise its price (significantly) after successful Predation without inducing [re-]entry, then the market conditions have been in such a condition as to facilitate recoupment. Obviously, this can only be used after foreclosure has been successful and forms, therefore, a potential addition to the *ex-ante* assessment.

In consequence, the conditions on the relevant market are an essential element. Without entry barriers that prevent or hinders [re-]entry, it is difficult to see a dominant firm having a reasonable prospect of recoupment. The foreclosed competitors would simply re-enter or new competitors would enter. However, since it is a forward-looking assessment it also should consider whether entry barriers are likely to be strengthened and created. It may be that there are no significant entry barriers before engaging in Predation but that the dominant firm's conduct is likely to create such. For example, that conduct may in itself create a reputation which keeps firms from entering, lowering their price or the like. The impact on market shares can, in the same way, increase the ability to recoup as it indicates the market power, which the dominant firm has.[934] In addition, an increased market power, everything else equal, increases the probability of recoupment.[935]

3.1.2.6 Dominance as Proof of Recoupment?

Proving a reasonable prospect of recoupment will generally require proof of sustainable market power.[936] Accordingly, similarities between the criteria for recoupment and dominance exist. It has even been argued that since a dominant position implies the possession of a high market share, great entry barriers and a certain degree of "immunity" due to the position that position assures that the dominant firm will be able to its losses.[937]

However, they do not overlap completely.[938] Most importantly there is a time difference. Proof of a reasonable prospect of recoupment means that the dominant firm's market power persists in the future, while the finding of a dominant position refers to the time of its exclusionary conduct.[939] The fact that the firm was dominant at

---

934. *See* Padilla & O'Donoghue (2013), at page 312.
935. *See the Article 102 Guidance Paper*, at 70.
936. *See* Hemphill (2001), at 1587; Bolton, et al. (2000), at 2264; Joskow & Klevorick (1979), at 225–34. *See also* Funk, Michael & Jaag, Christian, The More Economic Approach to Predatory Pricing, 2016, Swiss Economics Working Paper 0057 available at https://www.swiss-economics.ch/docs/Predatory_Pricing_Jaag_v2.pdf.
937. *See* Lang & O'Donoghue (2002), at 145–6.
938. *See* Rousseva (2010), at 166.
939. *See* Opinion of Advocate General Mazák of 25 September 2008 in Case C-202/07 P, *France Télécom SA v. Commission of the European Communities*, at 76. ("In my concluding remarks on

the time it engages in Predation does not mean that it will have a reasonable prospect of recoupment. In other words, proof of the possibility of recoupment is inherently forward-looking, assessing the market structure as it will be. Additionally, the threshold for dominance has a reputation of being low and simply relying on market shares.

According to these findings, the Commission was, therefore, correct not to rely solely on the dominant position when it assessed the ability to recoup in *Wanadoo* but to look at a wide range of barriers to entry. This allowed the Commission to establish whether Wanadoo would have a reasonable prospect of recoupment in the long run. While it can be debated whether these were great enough to make recoupment possible,[940] it stands as an indication that the Commission does not support the view that recoupment is simply implied by dominance.[941]

While recoupment and dominance are not two sides of the same coin, the majority of the relevant considerations taken into account in determining recoupment are likely to be identical with the considerations relevant to the finding of dominance.[942] Therefore, factors such as the market position of the dominant firm and its competitor, entry barriers and countervailing buyer power will be relevant factors to include in the assessment of recoupment.[943] But, as pointed out, the importance lies in how these factors are applied.

3.1.2.7 *Creating a Profit That Allows Recoupment*

Another aspect worth addressing is how a dominant firm creates a profit [margin] that allows recoupment. This is most logical done by raising the price in such a way that maximizes profits. That is, in the Recoupment-period, the dominant firm will set its price so as it maximizes its profits. Some understand this as prices being set at the monopoly price.[944] However, a dominant firm can apply "limited pricing" referring to prices set at a level just below that which a potential entrant would need to charge to sustain a successful entry.[945] This means that the supra-competitive price can be set at a level that allows recoupment to occur at a reasonable pace without provoking entry,

---

the question of proof of the possibility of recoupment I would like to point out that I am not convinced by the Commission's line of argument that in Europe and under Article 82 EC recoupment is implied by the dominance, not least because the determination of dominance is often based on historical market conditions, whilst as I explained above proof of the possibility of recoupment is inherently ex-ante and forward-looking, assessing the market structure as it will be in the future."). *See also* Padilla & O'Donoghue (2013), at 317–8.

940. *See* Ritter, Cyril, *Does the Law of Predatory Pricing and Cross-Subsidisation Need a Radical Rethink?*, 27 World Competition (2004) 613, at 647.
941. This is quite ironic as the Commission argued before the ECJ that the existence of dominance presupposes recoupment, *See* Opinion of Advocate General Mazák in Case C-202/07 P, *France Télécom*, at 67.
942. *See* Rousseva (2010), at 167.
943. These factors are listed by the Commission as relevant factors for the assessment of dominance in it *Article 102 Guidance Paper*.
944. *See* Hovenkamp (1985), at 231.
945. *See* Leslie (2013), at 1716.

which would have driven the price down.[946] Accordingly, the question of whether a dominant firm is able to recoup cannot only rely on monopoly pricing as a more "modest" mark-up during the Recoupment-period may make new entry far less attractive given the significant short-run costs that any new competitor would have to incur. This aspect may be important in markets requiring great start-up costs.

In addition, a dominant firm may aim at recoupment, either fully or partially, by lowering its costs. Successful foreclosure may allow a dominant firm to reduce its investments in, for example, innovation or maintenance not only allowing it to recoup its losses but also to harm consumers' interest. Alternatively, the low price-period was perhaps achieved through an increase in costs, which is then lowered afterwards. Lastly, recoupment may be achieved by means other than its operating results.[947] By strengthening its dominant position, it may increase the firm's market value (e.g., by enlarging its customer base). This can be a relevant strategy for a firm if it plans to sell the firm off or in the event of a capital increase. In consequence, recoupment may be achieved by other means than simply raising the price. Accordingly, there are other methods to achieve recoupment than raising the price.

3.1.2.8   The Importance of a Correct Counterfactual Scenario

Before the dominant firm launches the Predation-period, a higher price has previously been set.[948] That price may be termed as the "pre-predation price". In other words, a reduction in price is needed to engage in Predation. This may, for example, be achieved through a period of pricing low or a discount on a list price (i.e., a rebate). In the textbook event where the dominant firm is a monopoly, the pre-predation price will equal the monopoly price. What is also important is that in that event the price in the Recoupment-period will also equal the monopoly price. Accordingly, consumers do not experience a higher price compared to the one existing before Predation. In fact, consumers experience a [temporary] reduction in price instead.

As a result, one could argue that consumers' interest is not harmed since there is no increase in price but rather a reduction in price. However, one would be wrong to reach such conclusion. Consumers are in fact harmed since a longer period with a lower price level has been prevented given foreclosure had not been allowed.[949] Consumers may also see an adverse effect in the form of, for instance, innovation and quality. By preventing increased competition – either by hindering access to the market or discourages price competition among current competitors – the dominant firm

---

946. *See* Carstensen, Peter, *Predatory Pricing in the Courts: Reflection on Two Decisions*, 61 Notre Dame Law Review (1986) 928, at 938.
947. *See* Case COMP/38.233, *Wanadoo Interactive*, at 334 fotenote 408.
948. As concluded in section 2.2, Predation may take place by introducing a product that is withdrawn following successful foreclosure. The price for that product will (most likely) remain unchanged from its introduction until its withdrawal. In that event, the pre-predation price will be the price for the product (or products) that is sought protected. Alternatively, costs have been increased.
949. Of course, this must be proven. But with a price going from monopoly price to below costs to monopoly price again that seems very likely.

succeeds in returning to its pre-predation price. While this has been illustrated by a monopoly price, it does not preclude the same event from occurring with prices below the monopoly price.

Accordingly, it is important to have the correct counterfactual scenario. Comparing the price set in the Recoupment-period with the pre-predation price would be incorrect. Instead, the correct counterfactual scenario is the price that would have reigned without foreclosure. In other words, the detrimental effect to consumers' effect in regards to a higher price is the difference between the price that would have reign without foreclosure and the price that the dominant firm sets (is like to set) in the Recoupment-period.

3.1.2.9   Who is the Consumer?

A related aspect when discussing how recoupment is understood is how consumers are viewed. They are often, indirectly, assumed to be the same in both the Predation-period and the Recoupment-period (this issue may not even be considered). However, they are not necessarily the same meaning that some consumers will benefit while others are put worse off even if recoupment is not successful. While it is not clear cut when Predation takes place within one market, the issue is especially clear where a firm price low in one (geographic) market while pricing "excessively" in another (geographic) market. It has been argued that it is problematic when some consumers benefit from such conduct while others do not – even when recoupment is unlikely (or unsuccessful).[950]

However, this raises the question: why would a dominant firm behave in such a manner if recoupment is unlikely? One answer could be that the dominant firm was simply competing. In other words, it lowered its prices to compete with its competitors. On the other hand, it may still have behaved in an anti-competitive manner since, for example, recoupment is taken place somewhere else, or that recoupment simply failed even though it was the purpose. If recoupment is understood as presented in these sections most of this issue is clarified.

The reason why it is referred to as "most of this issue" is two folded. First, the anti-competitive element may relate to a reduced level in, for example, innovation or quality (innovating firms or firms willing to provide a better product has been foreclosed). Second, the scenario of some consumers benefiting while others do not is happening all the time. Just take the example of promotional offers or individual bargaining power. In effect, therefore, the issue raised is a matter of discrimination (or even exploitative behaviour). The dominant firm is charging its customers different prices and such behaviour – given that recoupment, reduced innovation or the like is unlikely – cannot suggest the existence of an exclusionary abuse.[951]

---

950. *See* Leslie (2013), at 1742.
951. *See* Case C-209/10, *Post Danmark I*, at 30.

3.1.2.10   Attempted Recoupment

In criminal law, a case may deal with the situation where attempted murder has been unsuccessful. The attempted murder, despite being unsuccessful, will still be regarded unlawful.[952] That this should not be true for competition law as well (i.e., attempt to recoup) seems inappropriate. On the other hand, the main rule is that conduct cannot be classified as abuse in the absence of anti-competitive effects.[953] However, where a dominant firm implements conduct with the purpose of harming effective competition the fact that the desired result is not ultimately achieved does not alter its categorization as abuse within the meaning of Article 102 TFEU.[954] Using that analogy, proof of actual recoupment, even concerning historical conduct, would be unfit if attempted recoupment is proven. An attempt to distort effective competition cannot be tolerated. On the other hand, it may reduce the fine imposed and the claims for damages due to the infringement being less grave.

That attempted recoupment is sufficient can even be held as (indirectly) supported by economic literature. For instance, when explaining the Areeda/Turner-test, the authors stated that it would make little economic sense for a firm to engage in Predation unless there is a *substantial prospect* of recoupment.[955] In other words, without an expectation of recoupment low pricing conduct makes little economic sense. The real issue was therefore not the specific prices set but that prospect of recoupment. This, at least indirectly, recognizes that attempted recoupment can suffice.

Lastly, one must be aware that predictions may not hold up or even change. New products may render the dominant firm's product superfluous, consumers may not be willing to pay the price in the Recoupment-period and so on. As a result, a dominant firm may abandon the idea of recouping all of its losses and instead concentrate instead on balancing its future costs and revenues.[956] In consequence, attempted recoupment can be sufficient even if recoupment shows to be unsuccessful or unlikely.

3.1.3   *A Note on Predatory Rebates*

Rebates, both single- and multi-product, can cause anti-competitive effects through either Predation or Exclusion. Whether it is the former or the latter depends on the mechanisms behind the particular rebate [scheme]. If a rebate falls within Predation (i.e., a predatory rebate), then focus is that of a low price. Note that while predatory rebates embrace a great number of different types of rebates, "rebates" in the form of selective pricing are part of "traditional predatory pricing". As concluded in Chapter 5, predatory rebates are those that represent a true rebate. The stand-alone price (i.e., the

---

952. Given the specific conditions in the respectively jurisdiction is fulfilled; e.g., the offender took some action towards killing another person and the offender's act was intended to kill a person.
953. *See* for that effect Case C-52/09, *TeliaSonera*, at 66.
954. *See id.* at 65.
955. *See* Areeda & Turner (1975), at 698.
956. *See* Bolton, Patrick, et al., *Predatory Pricing: Response to Critique and Further Elaboration*, 89 Georgetown Law Journal (2001) 2495, at 2512–3.

price without the rebate) is the price that would have been set absent the rebate. When a rebate is offered in that event, it represents a reduction in the price and not an increase in [the stand-alone] price.

Predatory rebates are very similar to predatory pricing with some differences. As with predatory pricing, the first step is to assess actual or likely foreclosure. In addition to a price below costs,[957] a Theory of Predation is also important. One theory that would be relevant is Financial Predation (section 3.1.1.1). When a conditional rebate is applied, the dominant firm may incur losses or sacrifice of profits on the incremental share of the sale but not necessarily on average. Accordingly, the dominant can finance the Predation-period. This aspect makes it more likely for a dominant firm to succeed in Financial Predation. This does not preclude the relevance of other theories of Predation, but Financial Predation is certainly a credible one.

However, a foreclosure effect is not sufficient in itself. Accordingly, a reasonable prospect of recoupment is required. Maybe the biggest difference lies in how the anti-competitive element in regards of recoupment is achieved. When dealing with predatory pricing, the scenario is more or less that the dominant firm is reducing its price and that loss/sacrifice of profits should be recouped. For predatory rebates, recoupment may occur to a lesser degree. As noted above, the dominant firm does not necessarily have to make losses on average, but only on the incremental share. Nonetheless, the same aspect as analysed above will be relevant for the assessment of predatory rebates.

3.1.4 Summarizing

In the preceding subsections, the foreclosure and anti-competitive element, respectively, have been analysed for the purpose of providing a framework for the assessment of when predatory pricing is abusive according to the effect-based approach. This included a note on predatory rebates. These findings answer the uncertainty of how to deal with prices between LRAIC and AAC without a predatory intent. First, a price below LRAIC is insufficient to establish a foreclosure effect. An explanation is required. This may be done by Financial Predation, Signalling Predation or Reputation Predation.

If a foreclosure effect is demonstrated, proof of recoupment is required. This does not entail a quantitative analysis, as the issue is whether the dominant firm has a reasonable prospect of recoupment. The means that a forward-looking assessment is applied as the issue is not whether the dominant firm *ex-post* recouped but was *ex-ante* in a position that would allow recoupment. A dominant firm should not benefit from having made wrong predictions or the like.

Note that while the above, indirectly, presupposes that the *Akzo-test* will be continued in future cases (i.e., prices below AAC constitutes a by object restriction), the findings can be applied to the event where it does not. That may be the case where

---

957. Note that a price below AAC will most likely constitute a by object restriction according to the *Akzo-test*. Therefore, the relevant cost benchmark is likely to be LRAIC.

such prices do not presume an anti-competitive effect or the event where it does not presume either a foreclosure or anti-competitive effect.

3.2 Margin Squeeze

Margin squeeze, also known as price squeeze, has clear similarities and contrasts to predatory pricing and rebates. In contrast to the two other types of exclusionary conduct, margin squeeze occurs where a vertically integrated firm sells a product or service to competitors on an upstream market and competes with these competitors on a downstream market for which the product or service is used as an input. Such conduct may also take place in the opposite event; i.e., where the dominant firm and its competitors compete on the upstream market. However, to simplify the analysis below – and since the first scenario must be seen as more likely – this section is based on competition for [customers in] the downstream market.

More importantly, margin squeeze differs from "classical" predatory pricing in the way that it does not require below-cost pricing in the classical sense.[958] Since the potential competition law issue relates to a vertically integrated firm the exclusionary concern is not whether the downstream price is predatory [or whether the wholesale is excessive].[959] The concern is that the margin is unlawful. I.e., the spread between the upstream price and the downstream price is either negative or insufficient to cover the specific costs that the dominant firm must incur to supply its own products/services on the downstream market. In this way, unlawful margin squeeze may be found without the dominant firm pricing below its cost, since what matters is not the actual costs it incurs in regards to its upstream input but the price which downstream competitors are charged – this will also be referred to as a matter of opportunity costs in the following. Despite this, it still takes a starting point in the AEC-test as it is asked whether an as efficient competitor, who buys the dominant firms' upstream input, can compete with the downstream prices set by the dominant firm.[960] In other words, the competition law issue concerns whether the dominant firm is able to operate on the downstream market only at a loss, or alternatively at artificially reduced levels of profitability if itself had to pay the upstream price. Therefore, while margin squeeze differs from predatory pricing and rebates, it is still within the Predation framework as laid out in section 2.[961]

3.2.1 Foreclosure

As concluded in Chapter 5, margin squeeze can be assessed within Predation when the dominant firm is in one or another way restricted from raising its upstream price. Finding unlawful margin squeeze will then require that the method presented in section 2 is applied. To do so, margin squeeze can be seen as a form of "above cost-predatory pricing" since the inquiry of whether the dominant firm has been

---

958. *See* Gaudin & Mantzari (2016), at 15–6.
959. *See* Case C-52/09, *TeliaSonera*, at 34; Case C-280/08 P, *Deutsche Telekom*, at 176 & 183.
960. *See* Case C-52/09, *TeliaSonera*, at 41; Case C-280/08 P, *Deutsche Telekom*, at 198.
961. For the assessment under Exclusion, *see* Chapter 7 section 3.3.

pricing below costs (i.e., the below cost-period) will include opportunity cost that is not included in a "classical" predatory pricing case.[962] In short, this means that the upstream price, which competitors are charged for access to the upstream input, is used instead of the true cost incurred. This approach mimics the situation where the dominant firm is paying the same price for the access to its upstream input as its competitors. While this may be seen as a way of creating fairness,[963] it is a way including the opportunity costs of not supplying its competitors the costs,[964] and thereby, examining whether the dominant firm is pricing below costs.[965] If such opportunity costs are not included in the calculation of the relevant costs false negatives are risked.[966] All in all, to demonstrate a foreclosure effect a below-cost period must first be proved and that requires the inclusion of opportunity costs which in practice is done by substituting the true cost of the upstream input for the price charged. This is, accordingly, one of the important contrasts to "classical" predatory pricing.

In examining whether foreclosure is likely, it follows clearly from case law that an "at least potentially exclusionary [effect] is probable" where the level of margin squeeze is negative (i.e., the upstream price is *higher* than the downstream price).[967] In other words, the foreclosure element is proven where the margin is negative. In such an event, as efficient competitors would be compelled to sell at a loss. If the margin remains positive (i.e., the upstream price is *lower* than the downstream price), it must be demonstrated that the application of such conduct "was, by reason, for example, of reduced profitability, likely to have the consequence of making it at least more difficult for [as efficient competitors] to trade on the market concerned."[968] Summarized, a negative margin equals a probable foreclosure effect while a positive margin may be able to result in such effect. The question of when a positive margin is able to result in foreclosure effects then arises.

Answering this question may be done in two steps. First, it must be asked whether a positive margin which does not cover AAC falls into the same category as under "classical" predatory pricing; i.e., the foreclosure effect is presumed since such prices indicate a sacrifice of profits that is the only ration due to a reasonable prospect recoupment.[969] That seems to be the best approach. It creates coherence between the approach taken towards margin squeeze and other types of Predation. In addition,

---

962. *See* Gaudin & Mantzari (2016), at 15–7.
963. *See* for that effect e.g., Hay & McMahon (2012), at 271.
    Case C-52/09, *TeliaSonera*, at 34 ("It must moreover be made clear that since the unfairness, within the meaning of Article 102 TFEU, of such a pricing practice is linked to the very existence of the margin squeeze and not to its precise spread [...]".)
964. The importance of including opportunity costs relates further to the anti-competitive element (i.e., recoupment), *see* section 3.2.2.
965. *See* Chapter 5. *See also* Gaudin & Mantzari (2016); Petzold (2015); Jullien, et al. (2014).
966. *See* Gaudin & Mantzari (2016).
967. *See* Case C-52/09, *TeliaSonera*, at 73.
968. *See id.* at 74.
969. Note that while a such prices constitutes a by object restriction under predatory pricing this is not the case here. While an as efficient competitor under predatory pricing will be pricing below AAC this may not be the case with margin squeeze as it depends on the competitors' reliance on the dominant firm's upstream input, *see* section 3.2.2.

since they are advocated to fit the same theory of harm coherence is essential. Additionally, the approach to margin squeeze asks what the impact would be if the dominant firm had paid the upstream price itself; hence, it asks the same question as under predatory pricing (i.e., would it in effect be able to compete with itself). The rationality that such a margin causes a foreclosure effect is, therefore, valid. In consequence, the [presumed] foreclosure effect can be extended from negative margins to include positive margins that do not cover the dominant firm's AAC.

This would leave a "grey area" to include prices between AAC and LRAIC – just as it is the case with "classical" predatory pricing. Accordingly, the second step is to ask when prices below LRAIC (but above AAC) can cause foreclosure effects. This includes whether the presumed foreclosure effect must be extended from prices below to AAC to price below LRAIC or whether a Theory of Predation must apply. Initially, it is clear from case law that it must be assessed whether margin squeeze makes it [more] difficult for as efficient competitors to compete on the downstream market. In other words, such foreclosure effect can be demonstrated by showing that the dominant firm's own downstream arm could not operate profitably based on the upstream price charged to its downstream competitors and the downstream price which customers are charged.[970]

For that purpose, the Commission has relied on LRAIC as the relevant cost measure to assess whether it is made at least more difficult for competitors to compete on the market concerned.[971] This means that the Commission has substituted AAC for LRAIC when it comes to margin squeeze. I.e., when prices are set below LRAIC (including the upstream price) a probable foreclosure effect exists. This is grounded in the fact that it is more sensible to look at the medium-long run costs than the short-run costs. The idea is that, if the revenues associated with the downstream activity fall below LRAIC, a rational and profit-maximizing firm, at least as efficient as the dominant firm "has no economic interest in offering downstream services in the medium term. It could increase its overall result by either raising downstream prices to cover the additional costs of providing the service or – where there is no demand for this service at a higher price, to discontinue providing the service while holding its output of all other products fixed."[972]

It might be argued that such conclusions should be made cautiously.[973] For instance, the cases, which have dealt with margin squeeze, have primarily concerned former monopolies in the telecommunications/broadband sector. These markets, and other network industries, tend to be quite different from most other industries because the former have much larger fixed costs.[974] A price that equates to the variable cost of a service may be substantially lower than the price the firm needs to cover the cost of

---

970. *See* Case AT.39523, *Slovak Telekom*, at 828.
971. *See id.* at 860 *See also* Case COMP/38.784, *Wanadoo España v. Telefónica*; Case COMP/C-1/ 37.451, 37.578, 37.579, *Deutsche Telekom AG*.
972. *See* Case COMP/38.784, *Wanadoo España v. Telefónica*, at 321. *See also* Commission Decision of 20 March 2001 in Case COMP/35.141, *Deutsche Post AG*, at 36.
973. *See* e.g., Padilla & O'Donoghue (2013), at 383 (who argue that there are no reasons why other incremental cost benchmarks could not be used).
974. *See* Case COMP/38.784, *Wanadoo España v. Telefónica*, at 317.

providing the service in the long term.[975] Accordingly, to assess the profitability of prices which are to be applied over time by a firm, and which will form the basis of that firm's decisions to invest, the costs considered must include the total costs that are incremental to the provision of the service. On that basis, it may be reasonable to apply, for instance, AAC in markets that are not categorized in the same way.[976] That may be the case where the upstream price is regulated so as the price equals the costs of the upstream input (i.e., LRAIC). Both the dominant firm's downstream arm and its competitors will then have the same cost related to the upstream input. A standard predatory pricing analysis of foreclosure may then be more sensible. The result would then be, as it has been argued in literature,[977] that a Theory of Predation, as covered in section 3.1.1, should be applied for margin squeeze as well. This must, however, be done with care since the ECJ has established that even where the upstream price is set by a national regulator that fact does not justify a margin squeeze.[978]

Nevertheless, it seems to be most sensible to rely on LRAIC as the vertical integrated dominant firm is often competing against non-vertical integrated firms. Moreover, the use of LRAIC is further supported by the *Article 102 Guidance Paper*,[979] which means that the Commission will most likely rely on LRAIC in future margin squeeze cases.[980] It must be stressed that this does not have the result that a single price below LRAIC equals a foreclosure effect. The assessment will be based on the same considerations made in section 2.2 including whether to apply aggregated versus detailed approach and a period-by-period versus multi-period analysis. Accordingly, what matters is whether the prices, in given period, were below or above LRAIC and not whether an individual price was.

3.2.2 Anti-competitive

As explained in Chapter 4, if a foreclosure effect is established an at least potential anti-competitive effect of a margin squeeze is probable when the upstream input is indispensable. In that situation, a likely anti-competitive effect is not required. Instead, such effect is presumed.[981] On the other hand, when the upstream input is *not* indispensable, the anti-competitive effect is not probable. Case law has not been specific on how to assess an anti-competitive effect in that case, though. The ECJ has merely stated that one must, among other things, consider the dominant position of the firm concerned in the upstream market to assess whether the margin squeeze may be

---

975. *See* Communication of the Commission of 22 August 1998 OJ 98/C 265/02, *Notice on the application of the competition rules to access agreements in the tele-communications sector* ("*Telecommunication Sector Access Notice*"), at 113–5.
976. *See* Padilla & O'Donoghue (2013), at 383.
977. *See* Gaudin & Mantzari (2016), at 17–20.
978. *See* Case C-280/08 P, *Deutsche Telekom*, at 44.
979. *See* the *Article 102 Guidance Paper*, at 80.
980. *See* Case AT.39523, *Slovak Telekom*.
981. *See* Case C-52/09, *TeliaSonera*, at 71.

capable of having anti-competitive effects.[982] The question, therefore, is what the anti-competitive effect refers to when the ECJ refers to the dominant position, among other things.

As the point of departure, that effect will, with reference to section 2, be recoupment (i.e., the ability to recoup).[983] This might be seen as contradicting case law. Besides stating that recoupment under predatory pricing in not a prerequisite,[984] the ECJ has held a similar point of view in *TeliaSonera*.[985] It concluded that margin squeeze might be the result not only of an abnormally low price in the downstream market but also of an abnormally high price in the upstream market. In consequence, a firm, which engages in conduct that results in margin squeeze, does not necessarily suffer losses. However, this is a clear indication that the ECJ are aware that margin squeeze can be problematic due to either Predation or Exclusion. Accordingly, if the issue is *not* the downstream price but instead the upstream price, then it is a matter of Exclusion since the dominant firm is raising its competitors' costs. However, since the issue here is the downstream price, recoupment is the concern. As a reminder (see Chapter 5), this is the case if the dominant firm is unable to adjust the upstream price.

To understand why recoupment is the concern [when it falls within Predation] it will help to take a different look at the adjusted costs when applying the AEC-test (adjusting the input cost to match that of the competitors). Instead of seeing the increase in costs as a way to provide equal costs between the dominant firm and its competitors in terms of the upstream service it can be seen as an opportunity cost.[986] If the dominant firm, for example, offers its upstream service at EUR 10 and that is EUR 5 more than its true costs (EUR 5), the margin squeeze calculation basically includes an increase of EUR 5 in the true costs by setting the dominant firms' upstream costs to EUR 10 (EUR 5 + EUR 5). If this is seen as an opportunity cost rather than a method to create fairness, this means that a profit of EUR 5 is foregone by not selling to its competitor. Furthermore, if the total costs relating to the downstream activity (excluding the upstream input), for instance, are EUR 10[987] and since the true cost of the upstream input is EUR 5, the dominant firm will be profitable if it sets a downstream price at EUR 15 or above. In contrast, an as efficient competitor would have to set a price at least EUR 20 to be profitable. As a result, by setting a downstream price between EUR 15 and EUR 19 the dominant can foreclose its [as efficient] competitors since the as efficient competitor cannot set a price lower than EUR 20 to operate profitably. While the dominant firm is not pricing below its true cost (EUR 15) it is only earning a profit between EUR 0 and EUR 4 which is less than the EUR 5 it would have earned by supplying its competitor. Accordingly, if margin squeeze were successful a rational profit maximizing firm would raise its downstream price to recoup its sacrificed profit.

---

982. *See id.* at 34.
983. For a more defensive purpose – e.g., protecting its upstream position – *see* Chapter 7.
984. *See* Case C-202/07 P, *France Télécom*, at 110.
985. *See* Case C-52/09, *TeliaSonera*, at 96–103.
986. *See* Gaudin & Mantzari (2016), at 166.
987. To simplify the illustration, the downstream costs are the same in both periods.

In consequence, when margin squeeze is assessed as Predation the anti-competitive concern is that of a reasonable prospect of recoupment. The same considerations from section 3.1.2 will be therefore relevant here in the inquiry of whether there is a reasonable prospect of recoupment. Therefore, when the ECJ in *TeliaSonera* held that "it is again for the referring court to satisfy itself that, even where the [upstream] product is not indispensable, the practice may be capable of having anti-competitive effects on the markets concerned" it left it open for interpretation of how anti-competitive effect may be determined; thereby, allowing recoupment to be one method. In effect, a similar assessment as the one in section 3.1.2 will be required to show unlawful margin squeeze within Predation.

At the same, there is an important difference between margin squeeze and predatory pricing. This notable difference is the fact that the dominant firm is a vertically integrated firm who offers its upstream input to its competitors at a price it cannot determine freely (e.g., due to an imposed a duty to deal). As a result, its downstream competitors [and itself] must rely on an upstream input to enter and operate in the downstream market. In that respect, it is essential whether the dominant firm's input enables it to benefit from the foreclosure effect; hence why indispensability proof a potential anti-competitive effect. Following case law, that assessment will rely on different things including the dominant firm's position.[988] While it was concluded in section 3.1.2.6 that the dominant position merely hints at whether the dominant firm is able to take advantages of that position (i.e., it does not suffice alone), it has a more prominent role under margin squeeze. The greater market power, the more likely it is that the upstream input is important for the dominant firm's competitors.

This certainly has been the case in the EU Courts' case law. In *Telefónica*, the GC concluded that the Commission had not errored in law by not finding an indispensable upstream input since "competitors on the retail market did not have a viable alternative input."[989] In other words, while the "Bronner condition" may not have been satisfied in the specific case (i.e., there are alternatives, or it is at least possible to "duplicate" the input)[990] competitors had no other viable alternative due to the position of the dominant firm. However, an important aspect was the fact that Telefónica's position in the upstream market originated from a state monopoly, which had led to the existence of regulatory obligations imposing a duty to deal.[991] In effect, that had structured the market in an irreversible manner; i.e., competitors had incurred considerable investments in order to use Telefónica's upstream input creating a relationship of reliance on Telefónica's upstream input.[992] The Commission (and afterwards the EU Courts) were, therefore, able to rely on the dominant position due to the [special] circumstance of a former state monopoly being regulated. That this enabled the finding of an

---

988. *See* Case C-52/09, *TeliaSonera*, at 72.
989. *See* e.g., Case T-336/07, *Telefónica*, at 275. Upheld in Case C-295/12 P, *Telefónica*, at 119.
990. *See* for that effect *the Article 102 Guidance Paper*, at 83.
991. *See* Case COMP/38.784, *Wanadoo España v. Telefónica*, at 109–119.
992. *See id.* at 548.

anti-competitive effect without relying on the "Bronner condition" was repeated in by the Commission in its decision in *Slovak Telekom*.[993]

Concluding, when margin squeeze is assessed as a form of "above-cost predatory pricing" the anti-competitive element is recoupment. The rationality for engaging in margin squeeze is to earn a higher profit following successful foreclosure.[994] However, if the upstream input is indispensable or the dominant firm is imposed a duty to deal, and competitors do not have a viable alternative upstream input, then an anti-competitive effect is probable. In such an event, the outcome of the foreclosure effect will be a monopoly (since competitors have no viable alternative that can enable them to stay in the market). Lastly, note that the elements in section 3.1.2 also applies here; for instance, the issue is a reasonable prospect of recoupment.

3.2.3 *Summarized*

In this subsection, the foreclosure and anti-competitive element, respectively, have been analysed for the purpose of providing a framework for the assessment of when margin squeeze (when subject to Predation) is abusive according to the effect-based approach. This built on the framework laid out in respect of predatory pricing. Margin squeeze, in this event, can be seen as an above-cost predatory pricing assessment. Therefore, the first step is to examine whether the downstream price is below costs. These costs include the dominant firms LRAIC, as the main rule, plus the difference between the access fees charged to its competitors and the true cost incurred for the upstream input. In practice, this will be the costs incurred in downstream market plus the access fee. This measures whether the dominant firm is foregoing profits. The anti-competitive element is demonstrated if the dominant firm has a reasonable prospect of recoupment. It is forgoing profit; thus, without such a prospect that conduct is not rational. Due to the differences between margin squeeze and predatory pricing the dominant position may play a greater role in the assessment of recoupment.

---

993. *See* Case AT.39523, *Slovak Telekom*, at 363 ("the circumstances of the present case, and in particular the existence of a regulatory framework for the access to ULL market and the existence of ST's obligation to give access to its local loop are different from the circumstances in [Bronner]").
994. Margin squeeze is not reserved exclusively for such assessment, though. *See* Chapter 7.

CHAPTER 7

Exclusion

1 INTRODUCTION

This chapter will focus on Exclusion. These types of conduct are those where the exclusionary tool is not a low price. Effective competition can be foreclosed by, for instance, customers being tied up; thereby, preventing competitors from achieving economies of scales, their minimum viable scale, access to low costs input or the like. As a result, this chapter will analyse how a theory of harm can be applied to these types of conduct. This chapter is divided into two main parts. First, the theory of Raising Rivals' Costs ("RRC") is discussed and how it can be applied to Article 102 TFEU. Next, different types of exclusionary conduct are addressed involving how to assess anti-competitive foreclosure effects in these cases.

2 THE THEORY OF HARM

While the theory of harm concerning conduct within Predation is fairly uncontroversial, it is rather the opposite for the types of conduct relevant for this chapter. Predation occurs when a seller prices its goods below cost with the aim of foreclosing competitor(s) and, after that, recouping its "investment". Exclusion, by contrast, occurs when a dominant firm "raises its competitors" costs' and takes advantage of hereof by, for instance, raising its price; i.e., no low pricing-period or recoupment-period is necessary. "Raising competitors" costs' entails that the dominant firm, for example, forecloses access to channels of distribution (customers) or input (suppliers) to prevent competitors from achieving minimum efficient scale ("MES") or minimum viable scale ("MVS").[995] While Exclusion often builds on MES and MVS by looking at, for instance, economies of scale, it is not always a prerequisite.[996] A dominant firm can raise costs

---

995. *See* Moore & Wright (2015), at 1206.
996. *See* e.g., Elhauge (2009).

through other methods than preventing MES or MVS; for example, by preventing its competitors' access to a low-cost supplier. To be clear, when this book refers to Exclusion, it refers to a myriad of methods that a dominant firm might use to raise costs; thereby, harming effective competition. The mechanism of Exclusion refers to a set of strategies that a dominant firm employs to deprive a competitor of competing for MES or MVS, and thus, raising its costs and reducing the competitive constraint that was imposed upon the dominant firm.[997] Ultimately, the issue is that this harms consumers through higher prices, lower innovation, worse quality, etc.[998]

As it was noticed earlier, the Chicago School is well known for its strong criticism of the possibility of anti-competitive effects from various types of conduct by dominant firms.[999] Doing so, it challenged the view of the Harvard School that had led to an intensive US antitrust regulation in the 1940s and 1950s'.[1000] Especially in the 1970s the Chicago school rose to fame.[1001] Two important arguments of this school were: (i) that Predation is unlikely to be profitable,[1002] and (ii) that exclusionary practices (e.g., exclusivity agreements and tying/bundling) are much more likely to be evidence of efficiencies (i.e., pro-competitive effects) than anti-competitive effects. Therefore, the Chicago School saw little need for intervention.

As a response to the Chicago School's criticism regarding the possibility of anti-competitive exclusive dealing, the Post-Chicago School developed the concept of RRC.[1003] The RRC theory recognized that an effective anti-competitive strategy could be used by one (or a group of) firm(s) against competitors to engage in conduct that raises those competitors' costs. A manufacturer could employ exclusivity agreements to tie up a market's most efficient distribution channels, thereby raising its competitors' costs of distribution.[1004] RRC showed thereby that it was possible for, among other things, exclusivity agreements to be anti-competitive. All of this makes RRC a distinct paradigm to Predation,[1005] even though they may share some resemblances;[1006] in particular, a high price as the primary consumer harm.

It is important to note that RRC is within the effect-based approach (or rule of reason as it is termed in the US); thus, it was created for analysing whether exclusionary conduct produces an actual or likely anti-competitive effect, not an anti-

---

997. *See* Salop (2006), at 311.
998. *See* Klein, Benjamin, *Exclusive Dealing as Competition For Distribution "On the Merits"*, 12 George Mason Law Review (2003) 119, at 223–4; Krattenmaker, Thomas & Salop, Steven, *Anticompetitive Exclusion: Raising Rivals' Costs to Achieve Power over Price*, 96 The Yale Law Journal (1986) 209.
999. *See* e.g., Hovenkamp (1985).
1000. *See* Rousseva (2010), at 26. *See* also e.g., Jacobs, Michael, *An Essay on the Normative Foundations of Antitrust Economics*, 74 North Carolina Law Review (1995); Easterbrook, Frank, *Workable Antitrust Policy*, 84 Michigan Law Review (1986) 1696.
1001. *See* generally Bork (1978). Of relevance is also Easterbrook (1986).
1002. *See* Chapter 6. *See* also e.g., Posner (1979).
1003. The seminal "RRC papers" are Krattenmaker & Salop (1986); Salop, Steven & David Scheffman, *Raising Rivals' Costs*, 73 The American Economic Review (1983).
1004. *See* Krattenmaker & Salop (1986), at 223–7.
1005. *See* e.g., Salop (2006), at 317.
1006. *See* Scheffman, David, *The Application of Raising Rivals' Costs Theory to Antitrust*, 37 Antitrust Bulletin (1992) 187.

competitive object. This follows from the fact that merely raising competitors' costs has not necessarily harmed competition (see below). Nevertheless, it may be that experience shows us that this is likely or a brief analysis in a concrete case shows harm to competition making a comprehensive analysis redundant. That is, in the same way that a price below AVC/AAC is viewed irrational without a reasonable prospect of recoupment (hence, a by object restriction), RRC can also assist in explaining why some types of conduct constitute a by object restriction.

Additionally, an argument could potentially be made that since RRC is more harmful than Predation, see below, conduct under Exclusion should be subject to a stricter analysis.[1007] Even so, the assessment should at least be based on showing actual or likely foreclosure in the specific case rather than presuming it on a general level. Finding abusive RRC conduct, in other words, should include at a minimum some sort of analysis in the context of the specific case. This would be the case if it were analysed whether a competitor would be able to achieve its MVS or its MES. In consequence, a naïve foreclosure analysis (e.g., measuring simply the percentage of the market foreclosed) does not fit within this approach.[1008]

While Exclusion may be bit unknown for Article 102 TFEU, it is a theory of harm applied in the EU Merger Regulations in respect of vertical mergers.[1009] The theory of harm is applied to assess whether a vertical merger results in likely foreclosure by hampering or eliminating actual or potential competitors' access to supplies or markets thereby reducing their ability and incentive to compete. This foreclosure will be regarded as anti-competitive where the merging companies will be able to increase the price charged to consumers profitably.[1010] Therefore, RRC is not an unknown theory within EU competition law; hence, that cannot be a reason why it should be troublesome for the Commission to implement it in its enforcement.

2.1   The Standard: Raising Rivals' Costs

As mentioned, the theory of RRC was a response to the Chicago School's view on, among other things, exclusive agreements and tying. The basic idea behind RRC, however, can be traced back to before the seminal RRC Papers[1011]. In an article from 1956, the two Chicago scholars Director and Levi seemingly predicted RRC by referring to a special case where a firm with market power "can decide to impose additional costs upon itself for the sake of [an exclusionary] restriction. Such a restriction might be valuable if the effect of it would be to impose greater costs on possible competitors."[1012] The theory, nonetheless, was not formalized until the mid-1980. Here, RRC was illustrated as a dominant firm's strategy to raise the market price by raising the price of one or more input(s) used by its competitors (and in some events itself) to the

---

1007. *See* in that context Salop (2006), at 317.
1008. *See* Wright (2012).
1009. *See* the *Non-Horizontal Merger Guidelines*.
1010. *See id.* at 29.
1011. *See* footnote 1003.
1012. *See* Director, Aaron & Levi, Edward, *Law and the Future: Trade Regulation*, 51 Northwestern University Law Review (1956) 281.

detriment of consumers. This simplicity of the theory also helped the understanding as it was presented as a logical theory.[1013] This goes for both economists and lawyers. It was easy to understand that if a firm was able to foreclose competitors from access to low-cost suppliers, the input price would increase with the possible effect of raising the output price.

The underlying idea of RRC is that some types of conduct, such as in particular exclusive dealing, tying and bundling and refusal to deal/supply, is better explained as a cost-raising (input/customer foreclosure) strategy rather than Predation. The reasoning is further intuitive. In contrast to Predation, RRC does not require a low pricing-period followed by a recoupment-period. Instead, by applying RRC an increase in price incurs from the start since prices above the competitive level are achieved by raising costs.[1014] RRC is in this way presented as less risky strategy compared to Predation; hence, also likely to be more profitable.[1015] For those reasons, it may even be a more common strategy. Lastly, this also means that the effect on effective competition, and thereby consumers, in theory, is less ambiguous as it is not necessary to weigh two periods for a net effect.[1016]

At the same time, however, anti-competitive foreclosure effects stemming from RRC conduct cannot be assumed. For these types of conduct to constitute abuse of dominance, two[1017] conditions must be true.[1018] First, the dominant firm's conduct must increase the costs of its competitors. Second, that increase in costs must enable the dominant to benefit from its cost-raising conduct by, for instance, raising its (output) price above the competitive level. These aspects are discussed in sections 2.2 and 2.3, respectively. In practice, they may be examined together since they can be closely intertwined.

Note that a dominant firm may achieve foreclosure by one of two ways. The first is where the downstream competitors are restricted in their access to an important input[1019] ("input foreclosure"). The second is where upstream competitors are restricted in their access to a sufficient customer base ("customer foreclosure"). It is worth mentioning that both can be illustrated as input. Distributors can act as input for firms as they supply retailing services to the firms.[1020] As a result, input will be applied as a reference to both types of foreclosure.

As shown, the RRC framework has a number of qualities. The analysis is straightforward, and one does not need to be an economic theorist to grasp the basic

---

1013. *See* e.g., Scheffman (1992). This article presents the logic of the theory with both texts and graphs.
1014. *See* Salop (2016), at 9.
1015. *See* for that effect Salop (2006), at 315ff.
1016. *See*, however, below in which it is noticed that the effect on consumers is ambiguous.
1017. Other commentators have extended the RRC theory to compromise four conditions to condemn conduct, thereby, including whether competitors have any effective counterstrategies and whether the dominant firm have any economic justifications for its conduct. *See* e.g., Monti, Giorgio, *EC Competition Law*, 2007, at 165 & 173–7.
1018. *See* Krattenmaker & Salop (1986), at 214.
1019. This is not only strictly input as it may also be, for instance, services, access to infrastructure, license to IPR's and so on.
1020. *See* Krattenmaker & Salop (1986), at 226.

logic. In some senses, the results are theoretically powerful.[1021] A cost-raising strategy is further likely to be profitable from its beginning, and as a result, it is argued that such conduct is generally, if not always, going to be superior to Predation that requires recoupment.[1022] Some commentators, therefore, argues that these types of conduct should be the predominant concern compared to Predation.[1023,1024] Another strength, at least for some of the RRC literature,[1025] is that empirically testable conditions are derived.[1026] Despite these strong points, it is also open to criticism.[1027]

The effects of RRC conduct are in itself ambiguous.[1028] As it will be stressed below, the fact that a dominant firm engages in such conduct does not prove, by itself, that it is anti-competitive.[1029] In consequence, and which has been pointed out in some of the first RRC papers, cost-raising conduct by a dominant firm, as a matter of theory, may raise or lower price, raise or lower total welfare, and even raise or lower the profits of its rivals.[1030] This ambiguity in the effects of RRC conduct arises from a number of sources. The most straightforward reason is that, in the theoretical models, the dominant firm prices according to the elasticity of demand that it faces.[1031] RRC conduct shifts out the demand faced by the dominant firm, but it is possible that it also makes the demand more elastic – potentially, meaning that the profit maximising price falls since an increase in price leads to a greater change in demand. It potentially becomes unprofitable for the dominant firm, as it is not able to charge the expected price. Nevertheless, RRC theory lays out, in principle, testable conditions under which, in a specific situation, cost-raising strategies are likely to be anti-competitive.[1032] Such types of conduct may also be the result of efficiencies that must be balanced (in regards of efficiency defences).

1021. *See* Scheffman, David & Higgins, Richard, *Twenty Years of Raising Rivals' Costs: History, Assessment, and Future*, 12 George Mason Law Review (2003) 371.
1022. *See* Salop (2006), at 315–6.
1023. *See* e.g., *Id.*
1024. Note that this author does not share the view that Exclusion (and RRC) is superior to Predation, but rather that Exclusion and Predation complements each other. Where Predation fails, Exclusion may succeed (in showing the true effect) and vice versa.
1025. *See*, in particular, Ordover, Janusz & Saloner, Garth, *Predation, Monopolization, and Antitrust, in* Handbook of Industrial Organization (Richard Schmalensee & Robert Willig eds.), 2000, at 537–96; Salop, Steven & Scheffman, David, *Cost-Raising Strategies*, 36 The Journal of Industrial Economics (1987) 19; Salop, Steven, et al., A Bidding Analysis of Special Interest Regulation: Raising Rivals' Costs in a Rent Seeking Society, 1984, FTC Working Paper No. 114 available at.
1026. *See* Scheffman & Higgins (2003), at 377.
1027. *See* e.g., Brennan, Timothy, *Understanding "Raising Rivals' Costs"*, 33 Antitrust Bulletin (1988) 95.
1028. *See* Krattenmaker & Salop (1986). *See* also Kovacic, William, *The Intellectual DNA of Modern U.S. Competition Law for Dominant Firm Conduct: The Chicago/Harvard Double Helix*, 2007 Columbia Business Law Review (2007) 1.
1029. In addition, the theory has focused largely on dominant firms and not monopolies; thus, although it appears simple these models are actually quite complex in generating general results – like all general models that involve market power short of monopoly.
1030. *See* e.g., Salop & Scheffman (1987).
1031. *See* Scheffman & Higgins (2003), at 378.
1032. *See id.*

A more serious limitation of RRC is that it is said not to provide guidance on how to distinguish anti-competitive from pro-competitive conduct.[1033] It has then been held that, in principle, models could tackle this by having cost-raising conduct also to impact market demand or the production costs of the dominant firm to incorporate the possibility of the strategy, which increases competitors' costs, makes the dominant firm more efficient.[1034] Such changes would increase the already ambiguity of the competitive effects of RRC conduct. Nonetheless, inspiration may be found in the EU Merger Regulation where efficiencies (cost savings) can act as a factor counteracting the harmful effects on effective competition.[1035] However, that is a matter of efficiency defences.

Accordingly, RRC theory has both strengths and weaknesses as all theories do. It has further some advantages/complementary effects on Predation. First, RRC is more likely to cause harm than Predation due to the lack of a low pricing-period, second, RRC may be less costly than Predation, and third, no short-term consumer benefit is achieved with RRC.[1036] In consequence, RRC may prevail where Predation fails to show anti-competitive effects (and vice versa): hence, it is an important theory despite its weaknesses/limitations as it supports Predation under the effect-based approach.

2.1.1   The Input Cost

Before analysing how the foreclosure and anti-competitive element can be demonstrated under this theory of harm, it is worth first to address the input costs. The traditional theoretical literature has focused on raising variable (or marginal) costs.[1037] When a (dominant) firm seeks to foreclose competition, it does so by raising the cost curve of competitors; thus, altering their optimal price setting. This adds to the general simplicity of the theory of harm as a (significant) increase in, for instance, a raw material will clearly affect a firm optimal price setting. This was illustrated, generally, by either foreclosing an essential input or using regulation tactics – for instance, lobbying for regulation to disadvantage generic medication.[1038] However, such strategies may also affect fixed costs [besides variable costs].[1039] Accordingly, some of the ways in which exclusionary conduct can be applied to raise competitors' fixed costs or even their fixed entry cost, is addressed below.[1040]

1033. *See* Holt, Charles & Scheffman, David, *Strategic Business Behavior and Antitrust, in Economics and Antitrust Policy* (Robert Larner & James Meehan Jr. eds.), 1989.
1034. *See* Scheffman & Higgins (2003), at 378.
1035. *See the Non-Horizontal Merger Guidelines*, at 76–88.
1036. *See* generally Salop (2006), at 315–6.
1037. This focus on variable/marginal costs is also held in section 2.2. However, this does not mean fixed costs are unimportant.
1038. *See* e.g., Oster, Sharon, *The Strategic use of Regulatory Investements by Industry Sub-Groups*, 20 Economic Inquiry (1982) 604.(Who was the first to formalise the idea that a firm might be able to use regulation strategically to raise variable costs).
1039. *See* Hviid, Morten & Olczak, Matthew, *Raising Rivals' Fixed Costs*, 23 International Journal of the Economics of Business (2016) 19, at 22.(who argue such strategies will often predominantly affect fixed costs).
1040. Note that this list is no way an exhaustive list.

2.1.1.1   Regulation

This type of raising fixed costs relates to lobbying for regulation. While typically seen as a means of raising variable costs through increased tariffs, some costs related to trade policy can be fixed.[1041] Studies show that competitors can face a trade-off between: (i) incurring high fixed application costs to obtain a tariff and a marginal cost reduction, or (ii) accepting the high tariff and consequently having high marginal but low fixed costs.[1042] Clearly, exiting the market is also an option. Accordingly, in a market where firms cannot compete viable without a tariff reduction, a dominant firm may successful foreclose competition, in particular, potential competition, by lobbying for an increase in the fixed application costs.

Another example is increasing compliance costs. Such costs are typically independent of output levels and hence represent a genuine increase in fixed costs.[1043] Many different forms of regulation impose significant compliance costs on firms competing within, or considering entering, an industry.[1044] Studies have shown for example, how both the Occupational Safety and Health Administration and the Environmental Protection Agency in the US have been used as means to foreclose effective competition by RRC.[1045]

2.1.1.2   Vexatious Litigation

Vexatious litigation[1046] is legal action that is brought, regardless of its merits, solely to harass or subdue an adversary. This offers an alternative way of raising a competitor's fixed costs. Although competitors can bring such conduct to court, establishing that the litigation is truly vexatious is clearly very demanding.[1047] In consequence, vexatious litigation is a plausible strategy to raise a competitor's fixed costs. Of course, in jurisdictions where legal costs are borne by the losing firm RRC may seem less likely; however, it may be a relatively small part of the full opportunity cost of defending a case. Additional costs such as court fees, expert advice and the opportunity costs of the officers and other staff of the company tied up in the court proceedings are typically not recoverable and are almost invariably fixed.[1048]

1041. *See* Hviid & Olczak (2016), at 33.
1042. *See* e.g., Depken, Craig & Ford, Jon, *NAFTA as a Means of Raising Rivals' Costs*, 15 Review of Industrial Organization (1999) 103. *See* as a comment Sawyer, Charles, *NAFTA as a Means of Raising Rivals' Costs: A Comment*, 18 Review of Industrial Organization (*2001*) 127.
1043. *See* Hviid & Olczak (2016), at 33.
1044. *See* Hillman, Amy, et al., *Corporate Political Activity: A Review and Research Agenda*, 30 Journal of Management (2004) 837; Shaffer, Brian, *Firm-level Responses to Government Regulation: Theoretical and Research Approaches*, 21 Journal of Management (1995) 495.
1045. *See* Bartel, Ann & Thomas, Lacy Glenn, *Predation Through Regulation: The Wage and Profit Effects of the Occupational Safety and Health Administration and the Environmental Protection Agency*, 30 Journal of Law and Economics (1987) 239.(While the title refers to predation, the mechanism is clearly RRC).
1046. This may also be referred to as spurious litigation, nuisance suits or sham suits.
1047. *See* Hviid & Olczak (2016), at 33.
1048. *See id.*

This type of RRC is more likely to be a problem in industries in which intellectual property rights are particularly important. In recent times, a great number of litigations, or threats of action, has been observed in technology markets. Studies have also shown that firms in their patenting decisions may plan both offensively and defensively for vexatious litigation;[1049] hence, work on patent thickets suggests that a firm's patenting behaviour may be influenced by future litigation possibilities aimed at RRC.[1050]

A similar effect may be achieved by advertising. This is done by "drowning out" competitors' advertising.[1051] If advertising reduces the effectiveness of competitors' message, a dominant firm can raise the cost either of advertisement that forces competitors to do the same or to exit. This example perfectly illustrates the fine line between Predation and Exclusion. Advertising conduct can just as well be assessed within Predation as a tool to reduce profits short term with the purpose of raising that profit following successful foreclosure (i.e., increased advertising cost → reduced profits (i.e., pricing below costs) and vice versa).

2.1.1.3 Specialized Inputs

Specialized input depends on the specific market, and the same goes for its relevance. In some markets, such input constitutes an important element in the entry costs. Accordingly, by reducing or increasing the cost of specialized input, the fixed cost, and potentially the sunk cost, is increased. While this will also affect the cost raising-firm (i.e., the dominant firm), it may be profitable if it deters entry in a market. Accordingly, this does not affect the variable cost but rather the fixed cost.

This has been illustrated by paying inflated wages where it is argued that, despite long-term labour contracts are unusual, long-term relationships through implicit contracts may be less so, especially with key personnel, which can raise the fixed cost of such input (i.e., the key personal/workers).[1052] For example, many incentive schemes for managers include fixed elements achieved over time. However, the extent to which a dominant firm can hurt a competitor through such conduct is an unresolved empirical matter.[1053] Nonetheless, where it would be possible, at least part of the cost increase will relate to fixed rather than variable costs.

1049. *See* Lerner, Josh, *Patenting in the Shadow of Competitors*, 38 Journal of Law and Economics (1995) 463.(Who shows that firms with high litigation costs try to avoid patenting in areas where there are rivals and in particular where rivals with low-litigation costs have previously patented).

1050. *See* Rubinfeld, Daniel & Mannes, Robert, *The Strategic Use of Patents: Implications for Antitrust*, 2005.(Who shows work on patent thickets suggests that a firm's patenting behaviour may be influenced by future litigation possibilities aimed at RRC).

1051. *See* Hilke, John & Nelson, Philip, *Noisy Advertising and the Predation Rule in Antitrust Analysis*, 74 The American Economic Review (1984) 367. (Who provided evidence of a dominant firm, Maxwell House, used such a strategy when facing entry by a competitor. A particularly interesting aspect of their strategy was that they chose their advertising to be as close to the entrant's campaign as possible, thereby hoping to create confusion between the two brands, something which was likely to harm the incumbent the least).

1052. *See* Hviid & Olczak (2016), at 34.

1053. *See id.*

A better example may be competition for scarce input. Many different types of scarce input which is essential for entering competition can be used to restrict effective competition to the detriment of consumers by raising the price thereof or by preventing the access to it.[1054] This could shelf-space, locations, advertisements blocks etc. Concerning shelf-space, it is well recognized in the literature that such competition may lead to anti-competitive foreclosure effects.[1055] A study found that such conduct raises competitors' costs because they are the means by which the dominant firm bids up the price of an essential input.[1056] In some markets, advertising is essential to compete in or to enter the market. In such markets, consequently, advertising can be used strategically to raise rivals' costs. This may be achieved by blocking the message space – similar to preventing access to essential input – through, for instance, securing exclusivity for the customers' advertising during specified periods.[1057] This may also serve as an increase in marginal costs.

2.2 The Foreclosure Effect

The first step to demonstrate anti-competitive exclusionary conduct is to show a foreclosure effect. As hinted in Chapter 3, this first step may be straightforward for conduct falling within Exclusion. If a dominant firm, for example, enters an exclusivity agreement with a customer it is quite simple to see how that creates a foreclosure effect. That customer's demand is removed from the competitive situation between the dominant firm and its competitors; thus, competitors are foreclosed from that particular demand. It further prevents the customer from making additional purchases from a competitor to the dominant firm.[1058] The same goes for the event where a competitor is hinder or prevented access to the market, for instance, by being denied access to an input or infrastructure. Moreover, a plaintiff may bring an allegation due to, for instance, the dominant firm refusing to deal with it or has been unable to sell to a customer due to an exclusivity agreement; thus, indicating foreclosure.

1054. For instance, this is the case for the recent cases relating to broadband services where access to an essential input which a former legal monopoly possesses has been in focus. While most of these cases has concerned margin squeeze, refusal to deal with the effect of preventing or hindering access has also been dealt with, *see* e.g., Case AT.39523, *Slovak Telekom.*
1055. *See* generally Bloom, Paul, et al., *Slotting Allowances and Fees: Schools of Thought and the Views of Practicing Managers*, 64 Journal of Marketing (2000) 92. *See* also e.g., Foros, Øystein, et al., *Slotting Allowances and Manufacturers' Retail Sales Effort*, 76 Southern Economic Journal (2009) 266; Kuksov, Dmitri & Pazgal, Amit, *The Effects of Costs and Competition on Slotting Allowances*, 26 Marketing Science (2007) 259; Wright, Joshua, *Slotting Contracts and Consumer Welfare*, 74 Antitrust Law Journal (2007) 439.
1056. *See* Shaffer, Greg, *Slotting Allowances and Optimal Product Variety*, 5 Advances in Economic Analysis & Policy (2005) 1, at 3.
1057. *See* Tharp, John, *Raising Eivals' Costs: Of Bottlenecks, Bottled Wine, and Bottled Soda*, 84 Northwestern University Law Review (1989) 321, at (Who shows that the "Calendar Marketing Agreements" (CMA), used by, for example, Pepsi and Coca-cola in the US, to secure exclusive promotional services can RRC).
1058. *See* Bernheim & Heeb (2015), at 20.

2.2.1 Raising Costs

While it is clear that some degree of foreclosure occurs when customers are tied up, or competitors are hindered or prevented access to the market, it does not suffice to fulfil the foreclosure element. A standard must be set; it would otherwise capture too many types of conduct as being exclusionary. In the same way as the AEC-test (combined with a Theory of Predation) sets a standard for pricing conduct, even though any price can potentially produce a foreclosure effects,[1059] a story must be provided for these types of exclusionary conduct as well. The AEC-test tells the story that only foreclosure of competitors as efficient as the dominant firm matters due to a price below costs. In contrast, the story here is that competitor's competitiveness is harmed by increasing their costs. Accordingly, this is whether costs are increased, or likely to do so, due to the dominant firm's exclusionary conduct. It should be noted that the same effect (i.e., foreclosure) can also be achieved by preventing competitors from achieving lower costs. Here the counterfactual scenario is what costs could have been rather than what there were. All in all, how costs can be increased (or how lower costs is prevented) is the required explanation.

Foreclosure can occur either directly or indirectly. Direct foreclosure involves conduct where the dominant directly affects its competitors' costs by, for instance, foreclosing the low-cost supplier or a sufficient number of customers preventing, for example, MES.[1060] Alternatively, lobbying for regulation would also directly affect competitors. Indirect foreclosure, on the other hand, involves conduct where the dominant raises its competitors' costs by affecting the input market (i.e., the market where the suppliers/customers operate); for example, facilitating collusion among suppliers. Four examples can be provided in that respect.[1061] These are: (i) the "bottleneck"; (ii) the "real foreclosure"; (iii) the "cartel ringmaster"; and (iv) the "Frankenstein Monster". All four situations have the effect of raising costs by foreclosure; i.e., by restricting the supply available to rivals of a key input without similarly restricting the amount available to satisfy its own demand.

These examples demonstrate conditions under which the input price may be increased due to non-pricing conduct by a dominant firm. These are of course not exhaustive but merely examples. In other words, it does not matter, in the end, whether a story matches one of the above. The important matter is whether a [likely] rise in costs (i.e., a reduction in the competitiveness level) can be demonstrated. Accordingly, it is not important how costs are in fact increased but rather that they have been increased and, as will be discussed below, by how much. Note that both types of foreclosure are very similar.

1059. *See* Chapter 6. Even a price above costs can have a foreclosure effect on inefficient competitors, but that effect those not matter unless special circumstances are present.
1060. *See* Moore & Wright (2015), at 1206.
1061. *See* Krattenmaker & Salop (1986), at 234–42.

2.2.1.1 Direct Foreclosure

The first two – "bottleneck" and "real foreclosure" – are based on foreclosing supply of input (also called direct foreclosure of input), thereby increasing competitors' input cost. By foreclosing supply using, for instance, an exclusivity agreement or refusal to supply, the dominant firm forces its rivals to pay more for the input; hence, raising their costs.

In the "Bottleneck", a purchaser obtains exclusionary rights from all[1062] of the lowest cost suppliers (or the lowest cost supplier).[1063] Thus, competitors must purchase their goods from less efficient suppliers who charge a higher price. Alternatively, the suppliers could supply their input to the dominant firm's rivals under disadvantaged terms; either, for example, due to a promise to the dominant firm or due to the situation that the suppliers have a limited number of low-cost input products which is reserved for the dominant firm.

Similarly, in "Real Foreclosure" a purchaser acquires an exclusionary right over a large enough portion of the supply to drive up the market price for the rest of the supply of the input.[1064] Accordingly, the focus here is on the degree of foreclosure, or put simple, the amount of input foreclosed. This may occur either where the dominant firm forecloses the inputs without using it[1065] or overbuys supply[1066]. The "Bottleneck" is, therefore, also a version of "Real Foreclosure" were all input is foreclosed instead of a "large enough portion".[1067]

The "Bottleneck" and "Real Foreclosure" can be illustrated with the example of an existing railroad bridge that is the least costly alternative to cross a river – alternatives are building another bridge, using ferries or the like. If a competitor cannot use the bridge to cross the river, it will incur greater costs. In the example, the existing bridge has limited capacity[1068] but, at the same time, there is enough capacity to satisfy the current demand; i.e., the input price can be the same for both the dominant firm and its competitors. However, if one firm succeeds in getting an exclusivity right to use the bridge[1069] with the result that, for instance, only that firm can use the bridge or other firms can use the bridge on disadvantaged terms, then competitors' costs are

---

1062. Alternatively, a number of the low-cost suppliers might be sufficient but that event is categorized under the "Real Foreclosure".
1063. *See* Krattenmaker & Salop (1986), at 234.
1064. *See id.* at 236.
1065. An example could be the naked restrictions applied by *Intel* in Case T-286/09, *Intel*, at 198–220.
1066. In that event, the dominant firm obtains more supply than it demands, shifting both the supply and the demand curve (in the former only the supply curve is shifted), but since the supply curve "shift more" than the demand curve, the input price increases for its rivals.
1067. "Real Foreclosure" may, however, be more likely to be successful than "Bottleneck". It is more uncertain whether the dominant firm gains anything for its conduct since it also will pay the higher price for the input. However, circumstance of a relevant case may explain why it is profitable. For example, the price which the dominant firm pays may be protected by a contract or it has certain bargain power. *See* for that effect Krattenmaker & Salop (1986), at 238.
1068. Expanding the bridge or building a new one could increase capacity.
1069. An alternative could be vertical integration and acquire the bridge owner (or already be vertical integrated).

increased either because they have to use, for example, ferries or the bridge on disadvantaged terms. Accordingly, by gaining control over the bridge trough exclusionary conduct, the dominant firm is able to directly foreclose it competitors by raising its costs. Competitors are thereby disadvanged in the competition with the dominant firm and they may even have to exit the market depending on the increse in costs. Note that besides an increase in input price, a reduction in the quantity of the input likely occurs.

2.2.1.2   Indirect Foreclosure

The last two examples – the "Cartel Ringmaster" and the "Frankenstein Monster" – involve raising competitors' costs by inducing collusive conduct among suppliers (also called indirect foreclosure of input).[1070] Accordingly, the input cost is raised by having an influence on the input market. This is achieved by leaving a small number of firms to supply its competitors. The biggest difference is, therefore, the power, which the suppliers (or alternative only one supplier) left to supply the dominant firm's competitors, achieves – which may enable them to set monopoly prices. Instead of input prices being set where the supply curve intersects the demand curve, the price is then, potentially, set where marginal revenue equals marginal cost (which is greater than the former).

In the "Cartel Ringmaster", the dominant firm may enter agreements with suppliers to charge higher prices to the dominant firm's competitors (i.e., discrimination) by, for example, charging monopoly prices. The dominant firm, thereby, orchestrates cartel behaviour between the suppliers.[1071] Alternatively, the dominant firm may orchestrate some suppliers to refuse to supply the dominant firm's competitors, thereby, potentially creating a market sharing agreement between suppliers. If successful, it may even be that the suppliers compensate the firm for facilitating the cartel behaviour.

In the "Frankenstein Monster", the dominant firm does not directly orchestrate collusion among the suppliers. Instead, it may, for instance, agree on exclusivity with multiple suppliers thereby removing their supply as well as its own demand from the market. This causes a reduction in both the supply and demand leaving its competitors with one or a few suppliers. But this does not in itself change the input price since demand and supply may still intersect at the price which it would have without the dominant firm's exclusionary conduct; i.e., both the demand and supply curve shifts due to the exclusivity agreement between the dominant firm and the affected suppliers that enters exclusivity (and there is no overbuying or the like) which means that the input price remains the same (although quantity changes). However, since the number of suppliers has been reduced this may enable the remaining suppliers to collude either tacitly or expressly.[1072] The extreme case is, accordingly, where only one supplier is left to supply the dominant firm's competitors and that a monopoly has been created.

1070. *See* Krattenmaker & Salop (1986), at 238.
1071. *See id.*
1072. *See id.* at 240-1.

The difference between the "Frankenstein Monster" and the "Cartel Ringmaster" is, therefore, that in the "Frankenstein Monster" the increase in input price is inflicted by suppliers who are not directly part of the dominant firm's conduct. But is important to note that in both examples, the dominant firm achieve foreclosure indirectly through its exclusionary conduct as it depends on the suppliers to either fulfil the agreement to discriminate against its competitors or to collude.

2.3 The Anti-competitive Effect

As repeated heavily throughout this book, foreclosure effects do not suffice to establish abuse under the effect-based approach. It only constitutes a screening tool in regards to whether that particular conduct is exclusionary. For instance, tying up customers/suppliers or, in others words, removing their demand/supply from competition is not abusive in itself. That is only the case if, subsequently, [likely] harm to effective competition can be demonstrated.

2.3.1 Gaining Power over Price

The logic of RRC goes as a [dominant] firm who succeeds in raising its competitors' costs is then enable to increase the price charged for the outputs that it and its competitors sell. The firm, in other words, has gained power over price. However, the firm may not have gained anything by succeeding in raising costs and, more importantly, consumers may not be harmed.[1073] To be anti-competitive, its conduct must be detrimental to competition, not just to (some) competitors. This also fits within the framework of Article 102 TFEU.[1074] Competition is harmed only if the dominant firm can, owing to its exclusionary conduct, raise price above the competitive level or in some other way harm consumers. In general, under two conditions is such power over price *not* gained. That is the case if: (i) only an insignificant impact on costs is suffered and/or (ii) competitors still have the ability and incentive to compete effectively with the dominant firm.

It should be noted that gaining power over price does not only refer the situation where the price is increased from the previous price. Exclusionary conduct within this category may serve a defence strategy. By means of these types of exclusionary conduct, the dominant firm may prevent the price from falling to the competitive level that would otherwise have prevailed. It could also slow down the entrance/expansion by competitors, the innovative process in the market or the like. Such strategy is especially relevant when the dominant position is sought protected.

1073. *See id.* at 242.
1074. *See* e.g., Case C-209/10, *Post Danmark I*, at 21 & 22; Case C-52/09, *TeliaSonera*, at 43.

2.3.1.1   Significant Impact

The first condition is the effect on competitors' costs.[1075] If the competitor only suffers an insignificant increase in costs, an effect on prices is unlikely. This either occurs (i) if the increase in input price is small (e.g., from EUR 10,000 to EUR 10.001) or (ii) if the input (which for example goes from EUR 1 to EUR 2) is only one of many inputs and that input represent an insignificant amount of the total costs (e.g., if the costs are EUR 1,000). Such increase in competitors' costs is unlikely to enable power over price. This could be viewed as contradicting the EU Courts' case law. While the anti-competitive effect of conduct must be, at least, probable, there is no need to show it is of a serious or appreciable nature.[1076] Exclusionary conduct may give rise to an abuse due to the structure of competition on the market is already weakened.[1077] Accordingly, while this theory of harm requires a significant effect, case law has the opposite view. On the other hand, it could be argued that the anti-competitive effect is not probable if the [likely] foreclosure effect is insignificant. The anti-competitive effect may in that event be more hypothetical than probable. The ECJ has established that an anti-competitive effect must be demonstrated and that a potential effect is sufficient.[1078] However, it suffices not establish an effect of purely hypothetical character.[1079] The impact must, therefore, be significant to be anti-competitive.[1080]

2.3.1.2   Ability and Incentive to Compete

Given the increase in costs is significant, power over price is not necessarily achieved. Anti-competitive effects may be prevented by the existence of and continued competition from a sufficient number of non-foreclosed competitors. These other competitors might prevent the dominant firm from gaining power over price. This outcome can occur if: (i) non-foreclosed competitors have the ability to match the dominant firm's exclusionary conduct, and (ii) that these remaining non-foreclosed competitors do not coordinate price [with the dominant firm].[1081]

When the dominant firm's exclusionary conduct raises the costs of all or most its competitors, that conduct will likely give the dominant firm power over price and cause harm to effective competition. Not every competitor is necessarily affected by exclusionary conduct of a dominant firm, though. Competitors may, for example, enter exclusivity agreements themselves or be able to duplicate the product/infrastructure

---

1075. *See* Krattenmaker & Salop (1986), at 243.
1076. *See* Case C-23/14, *Post Danmark II*, at 74.
1077. *See* for that effect Case C-202/07 P, *France Télécom*, at 107.
1078. *See* Case C-52/09, *TeliaSonera*, at 64. *See* also Case C-23/14, *Post Danmark II*, at 66.
1079. *See* Case C-23/14, *Post Danmark II*, at 65.
1080. *See* for that effect e.g., Case C-209/10, *Post Danmark I*. A price offered to one customer was found to be below costs; hence, a (potential) foreclosure effect was present. However, that foreclosure effect was insignificant which meant it was unable to create an anti-competitive effect; thus, no abuse could be established.
1081. *See* Krattenmaker & Salop (1986), at 243–5.

from which they are being refused.[1082] That one competitor is foreclosed from the market does not necessarily entail power over price is gained. Therefore, the specific case and its circumstance must be taken into consideration. If not, an event may occur where competitors are able to compete but chose to freeride on the dominant firm's investments.[1083]

Even if there are non-foreclosed competitors left in the market, they may not have the incentive to compete with the dominant firm.[1084] This may be the case where the remaining rivals are so few that restraints on their pricing (and output) decisions are removed. In other words, a few firms left in the market may facilitate either explicit or tacit collusion. There cannot be a rule for when explicit or tacit collusion is likely and unlikely to occur, as this will depend on the specific case. For example, it may be relevant to examine whether firms are competing on output or price; i.e., Cournot competition versus Bertrand competition.

Lastly, it should be noted that even if competitors lack the ability or the incentive to compete, power over price might not be gained if there is sufficient potential competition.[1085] Consequently, either having existing entry barriers or creating some through the cost raising strategy is important for any anti-competitive effect to arise trough RRC.

3 FRAMEWORK FOR ASSESSING DIFFERENT TYPES OF EXCLUSION

In the preceding subsection, it has been analysed how exclusionary conduct falling with Exclusion can be assessed according to an effect-based approach. This revealed, among other things, that the foreclosure effect is demonstrated by showing an increase in competitors' costs which provides the dominant firm with either a cost advantage or prevent competitors from gaining access to the market (alternatively induce their exit). This means that the standard for foreclosure is raised compared to the one established in Chapter 3. It further revealed that the anti-competitive element is demonstrated if the dominant firm is likely to gain power over price (or has gained power price). All in all, the dominant firm succeeds in raising its price through the means of an increase in its competitors' costs. The findings from the analysis are therefore in accordance with how Exclusion was presented in Chapter 5; i.e., as a mechanism to increase the price over the competitive level from the beginning.

In this section, it will be analysed how this framework of an effect-based approach can be applied to different types of exclusionary conducts. This include: (i) exclusivity agreements and rebates, (ii) tying and bundling, and (iii) refusal to deal/supply. Note that this is not an exhaustive list.

1082. Note that this element is addressed under foreclosure in section 3; for instance, the requirement of an indispensable input is part of establishing foreclosure for refusal to deal.
1083. *See* for that effect e.g., Case C-7/97, *Bronner.*
1084. In terms of a "softening" of competition, *see* e.g., O'Brien, Daniel & Shaffer, Greg, *On the Dampening-of-Competition Effect of Exclusive Dealing*, 41 The Journal of Industrial Economics (1993) 215.
1085. *See* Krattenmaker & Salop (1986), at 246–7.

3.1 Exclusivity Agreements and Rebates

Exclusivity agreements and rebates (hereafter generally referred to as exclusivity agreements) are the classic examples of Exclusion. A dominant firm may raise its competitors' costs by either preventing them from accessing particular inputs or distributions channels (e.g., it ties up the low-cost supplier) or denying its competitors a sufficient share of distribution needed to achieve MES (or MVS). As a matter of definition exclusivity agreements, in general, involve a supplier conditioning its sales on the buyer's commitment not to purchase from that supplier's competitors and *vice versa*.[1086] While this technical definition requires the buyer to forego all purchases from the rival supplier, one can imagine agreements involving partial exclusivity.[1087] Such conduct is common in many markets and is often viewed as being pro-competitive [rather than anti-competitive].[1088] According to the findings in Chapter 4, however, exclusivity agreements are generally viewed as anti-competitive when applied by a dominant firm (i.e., by object restriction); they are "by their very nature capable of restricting competition."[1089]

Although exclusivity agreements have historical been viewed strictly, there are indications that this view has been relaxed. In *Van den Bergh Foods,* an effect-based approach where indirectly applied, as the assessment of abuse relied on the assessment made according to Article 101 TFEU.[1090] The Commission has further signalled a policy shift [towards the effect-based approach] in its *Article 102 Discussion Paper*[1091] and afterwards in its *Article 102 Guidance Paper.*[1092] Despite these positive signals, the Commission still relied on historical case law in *Intel* to find an unlawful exclusivity rebate.[1093] The GC shared that view. Although the ECJ is still to decide whether it agrees with the Commission and the GC one may consider it unlikely for the ECJ to annul the decision/judgment.[1094] This suggests a continuous strict approach.

One may argue in favour of a shift away from that strict view since the Commission's decision in *Intel* was initiated before the *Article 102 Guidance Paper* (and decided only months after the publication of the *Article 102 Guidance Paper*). It is also safe to say that among most commentators (primarily economists) there exists a widespread agreement that exclusivity agreements can only restrict competition by

---

1086. *See* Kaplow, Louis & Sharpio, Carl, *Antitrust, in* Handbook of Law and Economics (A. M. Polinsky & Shavell Steven eds.), 2007.
1087. 70%–80% exclusivity has sufficed in case law, *see* Chapter 5.
1088. *See* Bishop & Walker (2010), at 249.
1089. *See* Case T-286/09, *Intel*, at 85. *See* also Case 85/76, *Hoffman La Roche*, at 90 ("they are not based on an economic transaction which justifies this burden or benefit but are designed to deprive the purchaser of or restrict his possible choices of sources of supply and to deny other producers access to the market").
1090. *See* Commission Decision of 11 March 1998 in Case Case Nos IV/34.073, IV/34.395 and IV/35.436, *Van den Bergh Foods Limited.* Upheld in Case C-552/03 P, *Van den Bergh Foods*; Case T-65/98, *Van den Bergh Foods.*
1091. *See Article 102 Discussion Paper*, at 134-76.
1092. *See the Article 102 Guidance Paper*, at 32-6.
1093. *See* Case COMP/37.990, *Intel*, at 920-5.
1094. *See* Chapter 4, section 5.1.2 in which this aspect was discussed.

effect and not by object.[1095] Since the Commission does not refrain itself from implementing developments and findings from legal and economic literature in its enforcement (see e.g., Article 101 TFEU and the EU Merger Regulation) one may expect future cases to be more in keeping with the *Article 102 Guidance Paper*. And even if the ECJ upholds *Intel*, it would not preclude the Commission from finding abuse by assessing the likely effects rather than assuming them.[1096] This will still require a greater reliance on the *Article 102 Guidance Paper* on the Commissions part, though. All in all, it is still relevant to analysis how exclusivity agreements and rebates can be found to restrict competition by effect.[1097]

3.1.1 Foreclosure Effect

Although exclusivity agreements are common practice in most markets, these analyses have their focus on the anti-competitive foreclosure effect of such exclusionary conduct in the settings of a dominant firm [as opposed to the event of assessment under Article 101 TFEU].[1098] This latter part has played a pivotal role in the strict view on exclusivity agreements in case law. For example, the ECJ suggested in *Hoffman La Roche* that "the concept of an abuse [...] in principle includes any obligation to obtain supplies exclusively from an undertaking in a dominant position which benefits that undertaking."[1099] In addition, exclusivity rebates granted by a dominant firm were found to be capable of foreclosing competitors due to their very nature in *Intel*.[1100] Constructing an analytical framework for the assessment of foreclosure effects under an effect-based approach against such a backdrop is challenging. The prospect of seeing a greater reliance on the *Article 102 Guidance Paper* from the Commission's part is, therefore, essential. Without it, this section would be pointless as foreclosure would otherwise be presumed. This also means that the following subsections will assist in showing that exclusivity agreements by dominant firms cannot always be viewed as by object restrictions.

1095. *See* Tirole (1988), at 186. A view maintained today as well, *see* Padilla & O'Donoghue (2013), at 424.
1096. Whether the ECJ will accept a rejection of abuse on the grounds that the Commission did not find a likely effect (while historic case law could have been applied) is less certain.
1097. *See* for that effect Padilla & O'Donoghue (2013), at 433 (Who shares a similar positive view: "It is also assumed that the EU Courts would boadly look to the Commission for policy and intellectual leadership in this area, which, again, is not an unfair reading of the case law since 2006.").
1098. For the importance of dominance *see* e.g., Zenger, Hans, *When does Exclusive Dealing Intensify Competition for Distribution?Comment on Klein and Murphy*, 77 Antitrust Law Journal (2010) 205.
1099. *See* Case 85/76, *Hoffman La Roche*, at 121.
1100. *See* Case T-286/09, *Intel*, at 87. *See* also paragraph 89: "Although exclusivity conditions may, in principle, have beneficial effects for competition, so that in a normal situation on a competitive market, it is necessary to assess their effects on the market in their specific context [...], those considerations cannot be accepted in the case of a market where, precisely because of the dominant position of one of the economic operators, competition is already restricted."

3.1.1.1 The Rationality of Exclusivity Agreements

If attention is then turned to legal and economic literature an opposing point of view is found. As noted in section 2, the likelihood of exclusivity agreements being anti-competitive has been heavily criticized. The critique essential asked: if the agreement harms the buyer/supplier, why does he agree to it?[1101] According to that view, exclusivity agreements are more likely to be evidence of efficiencies benefiting the buyer/supplier and in the end consumers. This was illustrated by the scenario where a supplier, S, enters exclusivity agreements with retailers, R, who in turn sell the product to final consumers.[1102] The potentially anti-competitive motivation associated with these contracts is related to the limitation they place upon R's ability to sell rival products to final consumers. The anti-competitive foreclosure effect deriving from these types of agreements, generally, emerges only if S is able to foreclose competitors from a large enough fraction of the market to deprive S's rivals of the opportunity to achieve MES or MVS.[1103] The (well-known) critique then argued that R will have no incentive to enter into contracts which facilitate monopolization because they will then suffer the consequences of facing a monopolist in their chain of distribution.[1104] One can think of this criticism as drawing the analogy to a conspiracy among retailers, R, organized by the dominant firm, S, to exclude S's competitors from access to distribution.[1105] Like any other conspiracy, it is generally the case that each retailer has the incentive to deviate and remain outside the agreement by contracting with S's rivals and expanding its own output at the expense of rival retailers.[1106] Retailers have, in other words, the incentive to avoid entering agreements that will ultimately harm them, and S will not be able to compensate retailers enough to alter this incentive and persuade them to enter into the anti-competitive exclusive contract. The critique goes on to argue that if exclusivity agreements are observed, they must be motivated by efficiencies rather than by anti-competitive effects.

This view has since been challenged.[1107] Economic literature has grown to include a series of theoretical models contemplating scenarios in which S can sufficiently compensate R to join and remain within the conspiracy, and therefore to accomplish anti-competitive conduct.[1108] These anti-competitive theories of exclusive dealing generally assume that S supplies a product that is essential (or is an unavoidable trading partner in the EU Courts' language) to R and that there are substantial

---

1101. See Farrell, Joseph, *Deconstructing Chicago on Exclusive Dealing*, 50 The Antitrust Bulletin (2005) 465, at 466.
1102. The critique also applied for conduct such as bundling/tying and refusal to deal.
1103. *See* e.g., Moore & Wright (2015), at 1215.
1104. *See* Abbott, Alden & Wright, Joshua, *Antitrust Analysis of Tying Arrangements and Exclusive Dealing*, in Antitrust Law and Economics (Keith N. Hylton ed., 2010, at 206.
1105. *See* e.g., Klein (2003). (Where this analogy is explored and used to derive the economic conditions necessary for exclusive contracts to cause anti-competitive effects.)
1106. *See* Granitz & Klein (1996).
1107. *See* Farrell (2005).
1108. *See* Abbott & Wright (2010), at 207.

economies of scale in manufacturing.[1109] This development in economic literature has increased the knowledge surrounding the potential anti-competitive foreclosure effects of exclusivity agreements. The models generating anti-competitive foreclosure effects often rely on strict assumptions concerning the existence of significant economies of scale, barriers to entry, and absence of efficiency justifications.[1110] Where the necessary conditions of those models are satisfied, they demonstrate that exclusivity agreements may harm effective competition; thus, are an appropriate subject for antitrust scrutiny and further analysis.[1111]

Since adverse effects are not unthinkable, the question is how such effects can occur. The first step in that enquiry is foreclosure [effects]. As noted in Chapter 3, conduct such as exclusivity agreements will always be exclusionary (i.e., have a foreclosure effect) since they prevent customers from making additional purchases from a competitor to the dominant firm.[1112] But as explained in section 2.2 such standard would be too strict. A story of how the exclusivity agreement produces a foreclosure effect is needed; more specifically, how it succeeds (or is likely to succeed) in raising the competitors' costs. This will follow the outcomes of section 2.2 although foreclosure effects are not exclusively reserved for these examples. The *Article 102 Guidance Paper* will likewise feature a prominent role. As explained above, the positive view regarding a change in policy (i.e., away from a strict view) is owing to/relies on the *Article 102 Guidance Paper*.

3.1.1.2   Unavoidable Trading Partner Status

According to the *Article 102 Guidance Paper,* an important aspect is whether competitors are able to compete for an individual customer's entire demand. If they are [able to compete for the entire demand], exclusivity agreements are viewed as "generally unlikely to hamper effective competition."[1113] This is in accordance with the models above that shows how exclusivity agreements can be rational. A market may be characterized in a way where customers can only be satisfied by one supplier or where customers conduct bidding competition (tenders) for their requirements.[1114] In such

---

1109. *See*, among others, Fumagalli, Chiara & Motta, Massimo, *Exclusive Dealing and Entry, when Buyers Compete*, 96 The American Economic Review (2006) 785; Farrell (2005); Carlton, Dennis & Waldman, Michael, *The Strategic Use of Tying to Preserve and Create Market Power in Evolving Industries*, 33 The RAND Journal of Economics (2002) 194–220; Segal, Ilya & Whinston, Michael, *Naked Exclusion: Comment*, 90 The American Economic Review (2000) 296; Rasmusen, Eric, et al., *Naked Exclusion*, 81 The American Economic Review (1991) 1137.
1110. Note that the last part is not relevant in finding anti-competitive foreclosure effects, *see* Chapter 3.
1111. This has meant that RRC has been applied in antitrust cases in the US to demonstrate that exclusivity agreements (by dominant firms) had anti-competitive effects, *see* Wright (2012); Scheffman & Higgins (2003), at 383–7.
1112. *See* for that effect also Case T-286/09, *Intel*, at 87 ("It should moreover be noted that exclusivity rebates granted by an undertaking in a dominant position are by their very nature capable of foreclosing competitors").
1113. *See the Article 102 Guidance Paper*, at 36.
1114. *See* e.g., Commission Decision of 22 June 2005 in Case COMP/A.39.116/B2, *Coca-Cola*, at 24.

markets, competition is for the customer (alternatively the market) and not for a part of the demand; thus, exclusivity is an integrated part of the competition making it unwise to condemn it.

Competitors may not be able to compete for an individual customer's entire demand, though. This will be the case when the dominant firm is an unavoidable trading partner.[1115] This essentially means that part of the customers' demand is a non-contestable share, which only the dominant firm can satisfy. The customer has in that event no effective choice but to deal with the dominant firm for that proportion of its requirements. This may allow the dominant firm to take advantages hereof by imposing exclusivity. If the customer does not accept exclusivity it loses the essential product/service from the dominant firm; for example, declining exclusivity may entail missed sales by not stocking the dominant firm's product (leading to a decline in profits, bad PR or the like). By having such a position on the market, the dominant firm may effectively force customers into accepting exclusivity. This presupposes that the adverse effect from not being supplied by the dominant firm is greater than the adverse effect from only being supplied by the dominant.

Such a status may be concluded when the dominant firm's product is a must stock product or when competitors are unable to meet the expectations and demand requirements of customers effectively.[1116] In the event of the latter (i.e., capacity constraints among competitors) one must be careful, though. A dominant firm should not be penalized for the limitations of its competitors unless it can be attributed to the dominant firm. That may be the case if, for instance, the dominant position originates in a former state monopoly or it has been built through exclusive rights (e.g., a patent).[1117] The dominant firm may them have succeeded in altering the market structure.

However, if the dominant firm is not an unavoidable trading partner, then it is difficult to see how an exclusivity agreement may restrict competition. Competitors are able to compete on the same merits (i.e., able to offer the same exclusivity agreement) meaning that the firm who wins the contract is the one who performs better; for example, offers the best price, the best product and so.[1118] In consequence, if a dominant firm succeeds in entering exclusivity agreements in such an event it is owing to better performance – given the price is not predatory.

1115. *See the Article 102 Guidance Paper*, at 36.
1116. *See* for that effect *id. See* also Case Case Nos IV/34.073, IV/34.395 and IV/35.436, *Van den Bergh Foods Limited*, at 259. Upheld in Case T-65/98, *Van den Bergh Foods*, at 156.
1117. This can be supported by the ECJ's view on the applicability of AEC-test in *Post Danmark II*, *see* Case C-23/14, *Post Danmark II*, at 59. The ECJ held: "[I]n a situation such as that in the main proceedings, characterised by the holding by the dominant undertaking of a very large market share and by structural advantages conferred, *inter alia*, by that undertaking's statutory monopoly, which applied to 70% of mail on the relevant market, applying the as-efficient-competitor test is of no relevance inasmuch as the structure of the market makes the emergence of an as-efficient competitor practically impossible.
1118. *See* for that effect e.g., Klein, Benjamin & Murphy, Kevin, *Exclusive Dealing Intensify Competition for Distribution*, 75 Antitrust Law Journal (2008) 433.

Although only held indirectly (see the criticism made in Chapter 4), this has also been an important element in case law.[1119] The method for finding an unavoidable trading partner status is, however, up to debate. The EU Courts have repeatedly indicated that dominant firms by virtue of their dominant position are an unavoidable trading partner.[1120] Such approach obviously goes too far.[1121] With the somewhat vague definition of dominance (and the possibility of finding dominance with 40% market shares),[1122] a status of an unavoidable trading partner cannot just be presumed. On the other hand, the Commission seems to understand this point. In *Intel*, the Commission did carefully examine whether Intel's products had a must-stock status.[1123]

The first step of finding a foreclosure effect is, therefore, whether the dominant firm is an unavoidable trading partner. Without such a status, the dominant firm will be unable to impose exclusivity agreement. That does not say that exclusivity agreements cannot occur, though. As noted above they are common practice in many markets. The point, however, is that dominant firms cannot force their trading partner into entering such agreement unless he sees a benefit as well. In that event, Article 101 TEFU would be a better fit since the agreement is not imposed unilaterally but in agreement with the supplier or buyer. While Article 102 TFEU applies even when the supplier or buyer request the contract,[1124] common sense dictates that Article 101 TFEU is a better fit where customers actively seek exclusivity.[1125]

3.1.1.3   The Extent of the Contracts

If the dominant firm holds an unavoidable trading partner status, the next step is whether the exclusivity agreement(s) raises competitor's costs (or is likely to do so). This may be achieved either directly or indirectly as concluded above in section 2. It is sometimes argued that a distinction between input and customer foreclosure is required.[1126] It may be true that alternative distribution methods are more accessible/easier to seek than alternatives for input; for instance, self-distribution versus self-supply. In both events, however, careful considerations must be made to whether competitors have alternatives. For example, the possibility of backwards and forward integration, respectively, in the supply chain will be important information. In the same sense, foreclosure may occur in both events were a low-cost input, or distribution channel is tied up, or a sufficient amount/number is tied up.

1119. *See e.g.*, Case T-286/09, *Intel*, at 92 & 103.
1120. *See id.* at 91; Case T-155/06, *Tomra*, at 269; Case C-95/04 P, *British Airways*, at 75; Case 85/76, *Hoffman La Roche*, at 41.
1121. *See* Padilla & O'Donoghue (2013), at 438.
1122. *See* Case C-95/04 P, *British Airways*.
1123. *See* Case COMP/37.990, *Intel*, at 867–74.
1124. *See* Case 85/76, *Hoffman La Roche*, at 89.
1125. A somewhat similar conclusion is reached by Padilla & O'donoghue, *see* Padilla & O'Donoghue (2013), at 435–6.
1126. *See e.g., Id.* at 438.

If the concern relates to the number of tied up suppliers or distributors, it must be assessed to what extent to which the exclusivity agreements are prevalent on the market. This will provide a number illustrating how much foreclosure there is. Some may argue in favour of a 30% safe harbour rule in that respect (i.e., any foreclosure below 30% cannot be anti-competitive).[1127] Such argument would have some support in the *Vertical Restraints Guidelines*. According to this communication, Article 101 TFEU does not apply if the parties' market shares each are 30% or less.[1128] While it may serve as a good starting point, there cannot be a magic number for when foreclosure can or cannot occur. It will depend on the specific case. This is also the understanding of the ECJ.[1129] Also, such rule risks overlooking the important aspect that a particular input or customer may create a foreclosure effect. A customer may serve as the cheapest distribution channel or be important for a competitor's expansion or entry.

When assessing whether the extent of the exclusivity agreement(s) causes a foreclosure effect it is, therefore, important not to rely on "naive foreclosure"-theory (see also section 3.1.6 regarding the counterfactual scenario).[1130] The concern according to that view is that an exclusivity agreement between a supplier and a customer prevents competitors from access to that supplier or customer.[1131] The fact that a supplier or customer is no longer available to competitors does not imply that competitors are foreclosed, though.[1132] Instead, a link between the exclusivity agreements and the required MES (or MVS) is needed.[1133] The extent of the exclusivity agreements must prevent competitors from reaching efficiency. Alternatively, the extent of the agreements may limit remaining supply available to a competitor so that it will lead the remaining suppliers to bid up the price of that supply thereby increasing their costs to the point that the purchaser obtains power over price (see section 2.2.1.2).[1134] Either way, it must be demonstrated that the exclusivity agreements either directly or indirectly raises competitors' costs.

3.1.1.4 *The Importance of the Supplier/Customer*

A dominant firm may not only raise its competitors' costs by the extent of its exclusivity agreements. It may also succeed through the selective nature of the exclusivity agreement(s) (see Chapter 5, section 3.4). A certain supplier may produce an input at a lower cost compared to other suppliers, a customer may be a distribution channel that is required to enter the market and so on. By tying up such a supplier or customer,

---

1127. A 40% safe harbour in the US has (indirectly) been proposed, *see* Wright (2012), at 1182; Wright, Joshua, *Antitrust Law and Competition for Distribution*, 23 Yale Journal on Regulation (2006) 169, at 197; Klein (2003), at 126.
1128. *See the Vertical Restraints Guidelines*, at 23.
1129. *See* Case C-549/10 P, *Tomra*, at 43 ("It would, however, be artificial to establish without prior analysis the portion of the tied market beyond which the practices of a dominant undertaking may have an exclusionary effect on competitors").
1130. *See* Wright (2012).
1131. *See* Krattenmaker & Salop (1986), at 231-2.
1132. *See* Bork (1978), at 304-9; Krattenmaker & Salop (1986), at 232-4.
1133. *See* Wright (2012), at 1168; Klein (2003), at 126. *See* also Crane & Miralles (2011).
1134. *See* Krattenmaker & Salop (1986), at 259.

the dominant firm gets a cost advantage over its competitors. The method to achieve this type of foreclosure was also illustrated by the "Bottleneck" in section 2.2.1.1.

Achieving foreclosure is dependent on the fact that one or more suppliers produce a low-cost input compared to remaining suppliers. Alternatively, a supplier may not produce a low-cost input but a high-quality input.[1135] If the market is not characterized in such a way, foreclosure by means of selectivity is not possible. Competitors would be able to seek out comparable input not incurring any harm – unless the extent of the agreements raises the costs. Therefore, this type of foreclosure necessitates the possibility to identify important suppliers or customers.

3.1.1.5 The Duration of the Contract

It is generally acknowledged that the shorter the duration of an exclusivity agreement is the less serious that conduct is. In other words, short durations (alternatively the ability to terminate with short notice) mitigate an exclusivity agreement's anti-competitive foreclosure effect.[1136] The argument is straightforward. The more often competitors can rebid, the less likely they are to be foreclosed (either due to the extent or the selective nature of the exclusivity agreements).

However, this assumes an ability on the competitors' part to compete effectively with the dominant firm. If the dominant firm's position as an unavoidable trading partner does not change over time, it will still be able to force its suppliers or customer into exclusivity in the same manner as before the exclusivity agreement.[1137] In effect, this means that while the supply or demand comes up for bidding regularly, it does not alter the fact that the dominant firm can abuse its dominant position. On the other hand, it will be important if the assessment follows that under Article 101 TFEU.[1138]

This may explain the limited attention to this element by the EU Courts. For instance, in *Van der Bergh* the GC considered "the fact that retailers have the option of terminating their distribution agreements with HB at any time [...] in no way precludes the effective enforcement of the agreements in question."[1139] While this may seem as contradicting the *Article 102 Guidance Paper*, it is actually in line with it. It is true that it is first stated that: "In general, the longer the duration of the obligation, the greater the likely foreclosure effect."[1140] But it goes on to say: "However, if the dominant

---

1135. If the supplier possesses such competitive advantage, then it may have such a strong buyer power that the dominant firm (i.e., the buyer) is actually not dominant (or cannot abuse it). While this would be a matter for of assessing dominance, under normal circumstances, it may be relevant factor if the assessment of dominance has relied more on market shares.
1136. See Padilla & O'Donoghue (2013), at 443.
1137. Padilla & O'donoghue, at least indirectly, assumes the dominant firm is not an unavoidable trading partner when discussing the mitigating factor of duration, *see id.* at 443. ("Thus, for example, where the product concerned is relatively homogeneous and competitors are not capacity constrained, early termination should allow rivals to compete to supply customers' requirments on an equaly footing with the dominant firm.")
1138. See e.g., *the Vertical Restraints Guidelines*, at 83, 108, 113 & 133.
1139. See Case T-65/98, *Van den Bergh Foods*, at 105.
1140. See *the Article 102 Guidance Paper*, at 36.

undertaking is an unavoidable trading partner for all or most customers, even an exclusive purchasing obligation of short duration can lead to anti-competitive foreclosure."[1141]

This means that the duration of the individual exclusivity agreements is of minor importance. The important element is the duration of the dominant firm's conduct. Even if the exclusivity agreements are of a "short" period that period can become a "long" period if they are renewed.[1142] Additionally, depending on the characteristics of the market short exclusivity agreement without renewals may still result in foreclosure. In Tomra, the sales were "lumpy" due to the characteristics of the market. A customer would buy in big volume orders at a time meaning that the demand was satisfied until the machines needed to be replaced (effectively for the next 7–10 years).[1143] In consequence, although the agreements only lasted for six months the actual duration was 7–10 years. In this way, Tomra was able to foreclose competitors' access to specific suppliers or customers or a larger amount enabling it to raise these competitors' costs. Therefore, if the duration is given importance, it lies in the agreements' actual duration (including renewals, whether the option to terminate is used or likely to be used, the market characteristics etc.).[1144]

3.1.1.6   The Counterfactual Scenario

An important finding of the analyses above is the need for a counterfactual scenario; i.e., what would the result have been absent the exclusivity agreement(s). This can also be termed as a "net foreclosure rate".[1145] It is the [percentage of the] suppliers' or customers' capacity that was available to competitors before the exclusivity agreement(s) was adopted, but that is no longer available because of the agreement(s). In the extreme event, there may be zero foreclosure. This has even lead to the concept of "zero foreclosure".[1146] The most obvious advantage of such counterfactual assessment is the isolation of the foreclosure effects stemming from the exclusivity agreement(s) from other factors.

Such approach provides a better result compared to merely measuring the number/percentage of suppliers (customers) that have been tied up. But this requires that a reliable assessment of the counterfactual scenario can be made. In its most simple form it would be the difference in the dominant firm's market share before and after the exclusivity agreement(s);[1147] for example, if the market shares of the dominant firm increase from 50% to 60% the foreclosure rate is 10%. If such data is not

---

1141. See id.
1142. See for that effect Distrigaz in which some contracts had tacit renewal clauses, see Case Case COMP/B-1/37966, Distrigaz, at 22. Note that the Commission also found that customers were only tied under their contracts until the first opportunity they had to terminate the contract and that the Distrigaz was not found to be an unavoidable trading partner.
1143. See Commission Decision of 29 March 2006 in Case Case COMP/E-1/38.113, Prokent-Tomra, at 122.
1144. See for that effect Case T-65/98, Van den Bergh Foods, at 105.
1145. See Krattenmaker & Salop (1986), at 259.
1146. Note that it refers to tying and bundling, see Areeda & Hovenkamp (2015).
1147. See Wright (2012), at 1187.

available, the non-contestable share may serve as [a starting point for] an estimate. However, one must be careful when applying such assessment as exclusivity agreements may not only be used as a mechanism to win market shares but also to protect the dominant position. Accordingly, "zero" foreclosure or even a decrease in market shares cannot prove legitimate conduct. A strong argument can, therefore, be made that the counterfactual scenario should be based on the non-contestable share.

While it is an important element in the assessment of foreclosure, it does not, in itself, tell anything about whether there is a foreclosure effect (according to the RRC standard referred to above). The elements analysed above does. It serves instead as a screening tool for whether the potential foreclosure effect steaming for the exclusivity agreement(s) can be attributed to the dominant firm.

3.1.2 Anti-competitive Effect

If foreclosure is successful (or likely to be), the next step is whether the increase in competitors' costs enables the dominant firm to gain power over price; i.e., whether anti-competitive effects are likely. Gaining power over price does not only refer to the situation where an increased in price occurs, though. Exclusivity agreements and rebates may serve a defensive strategy. By means of exclusivity agreements, the dominant firm can prevent the price from falling to the competitive level due to entrance or expansion of competitors. It may also prevent innovative competitors from entering the market, or gain a foothold, which would otherwise have resulted in the dominant firm's product being replaced. Therefore, this requires an assessment of whether the [likely] foreclosure effect is likely to harm effective competition to the detriment of consumers' interest.

The first matter of importance is whether the impact on competitors' costs is significant (see section 2.3.1.1). If it is not the case, then the dominant firm will not be able to harm competition. This may be the case if the increase in costs is small or if the input is only one of many inputs (alternatively one of two inputs where the second has much higher cost). Then the increase will not influence competitors' behaviour. As with foreclosure, there cannot be a magic number or percentage of when an increase in costs is significant. And since the ECJ has also established that a probable anti-competitive effect is sufficient without there being a need to show that it is of a serious or appreciable nature,[1148] this aspect is a matter of showing the effect is not of purely hypothetical character.[1149]

The fact that one or more competitors are foreclosed does not necessarily mean that power over price is achieved, and effective competition is harmed. This may be prevented by the existence of and continued competition from a sufficient number of non-excluded competitors. These other competitors might prevent the dominant firm or firms from raising its price.[1150] For example, when the dominant firm is a monopolist, and its exclusivity agreement raises the costs of all of its entrants into the market,

---

1148. *See* Case C-23/14, *Post Danmark II*, at 74.
1149. *See id.* at 65.
1150. *See* Krattenmaker & Salop (1986), at 242–3.

that conduct will likely give the monopolist power over price and cause harm to effective competition. Because monopolists charge prices that exceed their costs, successful entry into a monopoly market generally leads to lower prices, even if the viable entrants are less efficient than the monopolist is.[1151] Since the dominant firm holds a monopoly in that event, all potential entrants are deterred access to the market entailing that there are no non-excluded competitors to provide a downward pricing pressure on the dominant firm's pricing. In most events, however, the dominant firm will not be a monopolist but face competition in the market. While one or more competitors may be affected by the exclusivity agreements, it is therefore not certain that it goes for all competitors. It is, therefore, necessary to examine whether competitors can enter exclusivity agreement with other buyers or suppliers or, for instance, engage in self-distribution.

Even if the remaining competitors have the ability to compete with the dominant firm, preventing power over price also requires the remaining competitors not to coordinate prices.[1152] They have an incentive to compete. For example, that will not be the case if the exclusivity agreement facilitates collusion (i.e., a cartel). This may occur either directly or indirectly. In assessing whether collusion may be facilitated through exclusivity agreements, inspiration from Article 101 TFEU as well as legal and economic literature could be applied. For instance, whether the cartel has sufficient stability or if there is an incentive for non-foreclosed competitors to "cheat".

The principle that foreclosure of one or more competitors is not necessarily problematic might be difficult to reconcile with case law. According to case law, customers should have the opportunity to benefit from whatever degree of competition is possible in the market. In addition, it is not the role of the dominant firm to dictate how many viable competitors will be allowed to compete for the remaining contestable portion of demand.[1153] This could be interpreted as all foreclosure, even if it does not allow the dominant firm to gain power price, is contrary to Article 102 TFEU. Such a stance cannot be applied to the effect-based approach; thus, it must be circumvented if an effect-based approach is to be applied to exclusivity agreements (and for that matter every other types of exclusionary conduct). For example, this could be achieved if this aspect refers to consumers' interest in general. I.e., the reference to "should have the opportunity to benefit from whatever degree of competition is possible on the market" refers to an increase in innovation, variety and quality.

Therefore, an aspect that may be important in the assessment of the anti-competitive element regarding exclusivity agreements (and all other types of exclusionary conduct) is the reduction in consumer choice.[1154] If competitors are foreclosed, the variety is reduced. Although this does not result in harm to consumers' interest as a general fact, it will be harmful if it results in consumer demand not being satisfied. For example, consumer demand may be greater than before, if an entrant is allowed to

---

1151. *See* Salop (2016), at 26.
1152. *See* Hemphill, Scott & Wu, Tim, *Parallel exclusion*, 122 Yale Law Journal (2013) 1182.
1153. *See* Case C-549/10 P, *Tomra*, at 42.
1154. For a review of consumer choice and its role within competition law, *see* e.g., Nihoul, et al. (2016).

enter since some consumers would like to buy that entrant's product, but not the products already available on the market. That this aspect is important is illustrated by the weight it was giving in the Commission's assessment of the anti-competitive effects stemming from Intel's use of exclusivity rebates (and naked restrictions).[1155] This aspect may also help to understand why the Commission and the EU Courts have historically held a very strict view on exclusivity agreements when made by dominant firms.

3.1.3 A Note on Loyalty-Inducing Rebates

The analysis in Chapter 5, section 2.2.1 revealed that conditional rebates could be assessed as exclusivity agreements when they are loyalty-inducing. According to case law, this is the case when the rebate is retroactive and applied over a one-year reference period. However, this does not necessarily tell us whether the price is the exclusionary mechanism or not. While neither the EU Courts nor the Commission has directly stated so, it is likely that the complexity and uncertainties, which occurs when applying a price/cost-test, has been a contributory factor in dismissing such test.[1156]

Besides these drawbacks relating to a price/cost-test for the assessment of conditional rebates, that test will fail to show the true effects if the rebate represents a penalty [for disloyal customers] rather than a true discount; i.e., the rebate is applied to an artificial high stand-alone price (the price customers is charged for the non-contestable share). For the reasons, many customers will choose to buy the contestable share at the dominant firm instead seeking out an alternative supplier, since they incur a penalty for not choosing the dominant firm. This is especially the case if the stand-alone price exceeds the price that (most) customers are willing to pay; for example, if the stand-alone price minus the rebate equals the monopoly profit. Under such circumstances, the same assessment as the one above can be applied for loyalty-inducing rebates.

3.1.4 Summarizing

In the preceding subsections, the foreclosure and anti-competitive element, respectively, have been analysed for the purpose of providing a framework for the assessment of when exclusivity agreements produce an anti-competitive foreclosure effect according to the effect-based approach. It faces a big challenge, though. Case law has, so far, viewed exclusivity agreements as a by object restriction when applied by a dominant firm. An effect-based approach to exclusivity agreement is, therefore, subject to reservations. On the other hand, positive indications can be found, as pointed out above, and a more optimistic may, therefore, be held. Given that an effect-based approach is applied in future cases, the findings in the subsections are in line with existing case law meaning that the framework can be implemented under Article 102

1155. *See* Case COMP/37.990, *Intel*, at 1598–1611.
1156. *See* Chapter 5, section 2.2.1.3.

TFEU. The difference lies mainly in the anti-competitive effect (which has been presumed) and the greater attention to whether the dominant firm is an unavoidable trading partner.

3.2 Tying and Bundling

Tying and bundling (referred to as tying in the following) refer to a combination of two or more products in a sale. Three overall variants of tying are available to a firm.[1157] First, "tying" – which can take place on a technical or contractual basis –[1158] refers to the situation where customers who purchase a product from the primary market(s) (i.e., the tying product) are also required to purchase another product from the secondary market(s) (i.e., the tied product). "Bundling" refers to the way products are offered and priced. Bundling may be either "pure bundling" or "mixed bundling". Regarding pure bundling, two or more products are sold only jointly in fixed proportions – resembling tying. In the case of mixed bundling (also known as a multi-product rebate), the products are made available separately, but a rebate is received if bought together.

This type of exclusionary conduct is ubiquitous.[1159] Many examples of tying can be found and this type of exclusionary conduct, at least from the economic point of view, is argued as tending to involve efficiencies (for instance, lower production costs, reduced transaction and information costs and increased convenience and variety) rather than anti-competitive effect.[1160] This led some commentators to suggest a (modified) per se legality rule for tying on the basis that the efficiency effects are often ubiquitous, while the anti-competitive effects are highly non-robust.[1161] This is not surprising, as one rationale of tying is to price discriminate by metering demand. This part of tying is not within the scope of this book, though.

On the other hand, tying can also cause harm to effective competition through Exclusion, and thereby harm consumers' interest.[1162] The core objective of tying in that

---

1157. See e.g., the Article 102 Guidance Paper, at 49.
1158. Technical tying occurs when the tying product is designed in such a way that it only works properly with the tied product (and not with the alternatives offered by competitors). Contractual tying occurs when the customer who purchases the tying product agrees also to purchase the tied product (and not the alternatives offered by competitors).
1159. See Padilla & O'Donoghue (2013), at 597; Bishop & Walker (2010).
1160. See e.g., Evans, David & Salinger, Michael, Why Do Firms Bundle and Tie? Evidence from Competitive Markets and Implications for Tying Law, 22 Yale Journal on Regulation (2005) 37; Kobayashi, Bruce, Does Economics Provide a Reliable Guide to Regulating Commodity Bundling by Firms? A Survey of the Economic Litterature, 1 Journal of Competition Law and Economics (2005) 707. The Commission also acknowledges this, see the Article 102 Guidance Paper, at 49.
1161. See e.g., Evans, David, et al., Tying in Platform Software: Reasons for a Rule-of-Reason Standard in European Competition Law, 25 World Competition (2002) 509; Ahlborn, Christian, et al., The Antitrust Economics of Tying: A Farewell to per Se Illegality, 49 The Antitrust Bulletin (2004) 287.
1162. See Kuhn, Kai-Uwe, et al., Economic Theories of Bundling and their Policy Implications in Abuse Cases: An Assessment in Light of the Microsoft Case, 2004, Working Paper #04-019, available at http://papers.ssrn.com/sol3/papers.cfm?abstract_id=618589. (who argue a "laissez faire" approach cannot be based on the current state of the economic literature).

sense is that tying removes or restricts customers' freedom to choose supplier.[1163] That may hamper the so-called competition on the merits.[1164] Unlawful tying can occur where a firm holds a dominant position in one or more market (i.e., the "primary market(s)") while it faces effective competition in (an)other market(s) (i.e., the "secondary market(s)"). Such firm may try to foreclose effective competition on the secondary market(s) by use of tying or bundling (and indirectly the primary market).[1165] How tying may succeed in foreclosing competition, and what can be achieved by applying such conduct, is analysed below.

3.2.1   Foreclosure Effect

While there are many pro-competitive explanations for tying,[1166] these analyses have their focus on the anti-competitive effect of exclusionary conduct; in particular, how such effects may occur. Additionally, it is viewed in the settings of a dominant firm, which, as with exclusivity agreements, is an important aspect. An assessment of anti-competitive effects requires, first, the demonstration of foreclosure. When a dominant firm applies tying it is generally liable to foreclose competitors.[1167] It restricts a customer's freedom to choose his supplier for the secondary product freely with the effect of removing that customer's demand from the competitive situation between the dominant firm and its competitors. However, any tying conduct does not automatically produce a foreclosure effect; i.e., such effect cannot be presumed. This is illustrated by the analysis below.

3.2.1.1   Distinct Products

As to why tying does not automatically produce a foreclosure effect one must look at the products. Unlawful tying requires, first, distinct products. By its definition tying involves two or more distinct products that are sold together. Therefore, if the products cannot be held as being distinct, it falls out of scope of tying. The dominant firm's

---

1163. Alternatively, it may restrict suppliers' freedom to choose distributor. The following will refer to customers but the same comments also apply for suppliers.
1164. *See* Padilla & O'Donoghue (2013), at 598.
1165. The possible incentives to do so are discussed in section 4.2.
1166. It may, among other things, (i) create economies of scale (*see* e.g., MacCrisken, Jack & Murphy, Kevin, *Economic Perspectives on Software Design: PC Operating Systems and Platforms, in* Microsoft, Antitrust and the New Economy: Selected Essays (David S. ed., 2002.), (ii) reduce searching costs (*see* e.g., Evans, et al. (2002).), (iii) improve product and services (*see* e.g., Petrin, Amil, *Quantifying the Benefits of New Products: The Case of the Minivan*, 110 Journal of Political Economy (2002) 705.), (iv) ensure quality (*see* e.g., Posner (2001).), and (v) avoid double marginalisation (*see* e.g., Tirole (1988).). For a general overview *see* also Nalebuff, Barry, *Bundling, Tying, and Portfolio Effects - Part 1: Conceptual Issues*, 2003, DTI Economics Paper, available at. http://faculty.som.yale.edu/barrynalebuff/BundlingTyingPortfolio_Conceptual_DTI2003.pdf
1167. The following discussions presuppose an asymmetric product line; that is, the dominant firm has wider product line. If this is not the case, competition will be for the bundle.

conduct may instead be assessed as another type of exclusionary conduct; for instance, as an exclusivity agreement or predatory pricing.

Testing for distinct products can rely on customer demand and supply-side considerations. However, the test must rely on consideration concerning customer demand. That said, supply-side considerations may be helpful,[1168] but in the end, it is the customers who decide whether two products are distinct.[1169] If customers do not see two products as distinct (or only an insignificant part do), then the fact that there exist independent sources of supply should not entail distinct products. For example, if a firm is able to bundle two historically distinct products in a new way that benefits consumers, it should not be punished for doing so.[1170] It is not for competition law to hinder innovation but to support effective competition. This includes encouraging innovation and product development as effective competition must necessarily involve the departure of product or services that are less attractive to consumers from the point of view of, among other things, price, choice, quality or innovation.[1171]

Such events may leave one to find third-party suppliers despite there not being sufficient customer demand. That may be due to, for example, bad business plans or market developments. For instance, in the early days of satellite navigation systems (or radios) tying or bundling such systems with the sale of a car might have been viewed as distinct products as a substantial number of customers would purchase the tying product (a car) while, possibly, buying the tied product (a satellite system) from another supplier if given the choice. However, today's customers are likely, at least in regards to some car manufacturers, to expect the two being sold jointly, and hence, would not have bought the tied product elsewhere. The product once distinct becomes part of the existing bundle (the chassis, tires, doors, engine and so on). In consequence, customers' demand must be decisive element.[1172]

3.2.1.2   Coercion

Concluding distinct products is not sufficient to establish foreclosure. It must be established whether costs are likely to be raised due to the tying. Prior to *Microsoft,* such foreclosure effects were usually presumed if two distinct products were tied or

---

1168. It may, for instance, provide indirect evidence of customer demand, *see* Case COMP/C-3/37.792, *Microsoft,* at 804.
1169. Supply-side considerations seem to be part mainly of the older, more formalistic case law. Compare e.g., Case IV/30.787 and 31.488, *Eurofix-Bauco v. Hilti,* at 55 with Case COMP/C-3/37.792, *Microsoft,* at 803.
1170. Some commentators have argued that due to similar considerations, a software-specific test should exist. That is, if a new software product bundles two historic distinct products there should be no problem. However, stating it is a software-specific test would be unwarranted. It is a general issue that can, as illustrated, be handled by the requirement of two distinct products. *See* for that effect Langer, Jurian, *A Four-step Test to Assess the Exclusionary Effects of Bundling under Article 82 EC,* 2007, at 322-3.
1171. *See* for that effect Case C-209/10, *Post Danmark I,* at 22.
1172. *See* for a similar conclusion Padilla & O'Donoghue (2013), at 622 (Who notice that a test depending on whether there are third-party suppliers for the tied product is questionable as matter of economics).

bundled.[1173] Such formalistic approach seems to be history, though.[1174] In *Microsoft*, for instance, one can identify the use of RRC concerning the Commission's finding of foreclosure effect. Tying the Windows Operating System with Windows Media Player had, first of all, the result of ensuring Windows Media Player a ubiquitous position. This meant that competitors on the secondary market were left with less efficient channels of distribution.[1175] As it follows, the intuition was that such disadvantage raised or was likely to raise (distribution) costs. Such a shift is further in line with the economic view of tying.[1176]

However, to get to the point where competitors' costs are increased, the dominant must prevent or limit access to the secondary market(s). It is in this regard that coercion is important. If the secondary product is not forced upon customers in the secondary market, there can be no harmful effect.[1177] In other words, if customers choose to buy the product together at their own request, common sense dictates that it is owing to a better performance by the dominant firm.[1178] While coercion is often associated with contract clauses, de facto refusal to supply the primary product, technical commingling and so,[1179] coercion is not just a test of whether two products (or more) are sold together as this is implied in the definition of tying. Instead, it is a matter of whether the dominant firm can force the tying on its customers, which also follows from the definition of coercion in *Microsoft*: "Coercion exists when a dominant undertaking deprives its customers of the realistic choice of buying the tying product without the tied product."[1180]

This is very similar to the point made under exclusivity agreements concerning the status of an unavoidable trading partner. In fact, tying has many similarities with exclusivity agreements as well as refusal to deal.[1181] When dealing with exclusivity agreements the non-contestable share and the contestable share can be seen as a primary and secondary market, respectively, in the same manner as under tying. In addition, tying can be seen as the de facto refusal to supply/give access to the primary product. Some commentators have been puzzled by *Microsoft* (the WMP part) not being a refusal to deal case.[1182] The difference lies however in the fact that tying deals with complementary products and refusal to deal with an input used in the secondary market. It would be difficult to imagine Microsoft's competitors in the market for media

---

1173. *See* e.g., Case C-53/92 P, *Hilti*; Case C-333/94 P, *Tetra Pak II*.
1174. *See* Case AT.39230, *Rio Tinto Alcan*.
1175. *See* Case COMP/C-3/37.792, *Microsoft*, at 858–76.
1176. *See* Abbott & Wright (2010).
1177. *See* Dolmans, Maurits & Graf, Thomas, *Analysis of Tying under Article 82 EC: the European Commission's Microsoft Decision in Perspective*, 27 World Competition (2004) 225, at 230.
1178. *See* Padilla & O'Donoghue (2013), at 237 (who finds that coercions is way to screen out cases where customers happens to buy two products together).
1179. *See* e.g., Dolmans & Graf (2004), at 230. *See* also Padilla & O'Donoghue (2013), at 627; Rousseva (2010), at 251–2. *See* in contrast Bishop & Walker (2010), at 289 (who indirectly acknowledges that coercion embraces more than just two products being sold together).
1180. *See* Case T-201/04, *Microsoft*, at 955.
1181. *See* e.g., Rousseva (2010), at 228–30 (who address the similarities between tying and refusal to deal).
1182. *See* Petit, Nicolas & Neyrinck, Norman, *Back to Microsoft I and II: Tying and the Art of Secret Magic*, 2 Journal of European Competition Law & Practice (2011) 117.

players asking for access to its operating system.[1183] Nevertheless, if unlawful refusal to deal presupposes an essential [primary] product it is difficult to see why unlawful tying should not presuppose a somewhat similar standard. Therefore, to achieve foreclosure it is important that the dominant firm is able to force the secondary product on the sale of the primary product.

Coercion has beencriticized despite it being an element in the finding of an anti-competitive foreclosure effect.[1184] This is owing to the fact that the Commission, in any case, must prove a dominant position. It should be noted that in *Hilti*, *Tetra Pak II* and *Microsoft* the dominant firms had a very strong position on the primary markets. For example, Microsoft had around 90% in market shares, and Tetra Pak had a position that was referred to as quasi-monopolistic.[1185] Accordingly, this aspect was indirectly addressed.[1186] However, as pointed out in section 3.1.1.2 a dominant position does not necessarily mean that that firm can force sales on a customer.

Therefore, a similar assessment as the one made in regards to an unavoidable trading partner is needed.[1187] One could argue that an essential (i.e., indispensable) primary product should be demonstrated as under refusal to deal. However, the consequence of tying is not a duty to deal with competitors but rather to end the combination of the relevant products. The outcome resembles, therefore, more the one from exclusivity dealing.[1188] This assessment will show whether the dominant firm is capable of forcing its secondary product onto the sale of its primary product.

3.2.1.3   Extent or Selectivity

Besides the similarity regarding the power of the dominant position, tying shares similarities with exclusivity agreement in regards of how competitors' costs may be increased. As with exclusivity agreements, it may occur due to either the extent or the selectivity. Therefore, the findings in section 3.1.1 apply also here including the findings relating to the duration and the counterfactual scenario. In *Microsoft*, for example, the pure extent of its conduct meant that the tying of the Windows Operating System with Windows Media Player had the result of ensuring Windows Media Player a ubiquitous position on the secondary market. This meant that competitors on the secondary market were left with less efficient channels of distribution. In that way,

---

1183. This is even noticed by the same commentators, *see id.* at 120 note 27.
1184. *See* Rousseva (2010), at 237 ("On the assumption that coercion is made an element of the abuse test, it would add little to the exiting requirement to prove dominance under Article 82."). *See* also Padilla & O'Donoghue (2013), at 627–8.
1185. *See* Commission Decision of 24 July 1991 in Case IV/31043, *Tetra Pak II*, at 12. Similarly noted by the ECJ, *see* Case C-333/94 P, *Tetra Pak II*, at 28.
1186. *See* for example Case COMP/C-3/37.792, *Microsoft*, at 844 (Windows constituted a key platform for the distribution of software to customers: "No other distribution mechanism or combination of distribution mechanisms attains this universal distribution").
1187. Tying has been analysed where the tying market is duopoly which could indicate that a requirement of an unavoidable trading partner is unfit, but in this analysis it is noted that it is a matter of (tacit) coordination and not exclusionary conduct. *See* Chen, Yongmin, *Equilibrium Product Bundling*, 70 The Journal of Business (1997) 85.
1188. On the other hand, it may be wise to impose a greater threshold if the outcome would be that the primary product must be altered, redesign or the like.

Microsoft prevented access to the most efficient distribution channel (i.e., itself). As it follows, the intuition was that such disadvantage raised or was likely to raise distribution costs.[1189]

It must be noticed that for such foreclosure to be at least likely, it presupposes that the secondary market is imperfectly competitive;[1190] i.e., it is characterized with entry barriers (e.g., research costs), economies of scale, network or learning effect or the like.[1191] Without such market characteristics, costs will not be affected by the amount of output meaning the dominant firm cannot raise the costs of its competitors. For instance, if the competitiveness in the secondary market is imperfect tying can, if there are costs to entering the tied market, deter entry by an [as efficient] competitor by foreclosing enough of the secondary market to make entry profits lower than entry costs; i.e., preventing the competitor from achieving MES.[1192] In the same manner, fixed costs can cause market exit.[1193]

Such foreclosure analysis can be found in *Microsoft*. A few remarks are relevant. First, it was noticed in the case that due to the tying the OEMs face negative incentive to include an additional media player (that would use up hard-drive capacity and offers essentially similar functionality) since it would increase OEMs' costs and users, in turn, are unlikely to pay a higher price for such a bundle;[1194] hence, raise competitors' costs as they would have to compensate OEMs. The increase in costs for OEMs also related to customer confusion and increased support and testing costs.[1195] Second, downloading (the alternative to be included by the OEMs) was considered less efficient.[1196] This alternative raised competitors' costs as they had to spend resources to overcome end-users inertia and persuade them to ignore the pre-installation of Microsoft's media player.[1197] Third, the secondary market was characterized by network effects meaning that applications would likely to be primarily developed for Microsoft's media player creating entry barriers to the market.[1198]

3.2.2 Anti-competitive Effect

This leaves the question of how the anti-competitive element is demonstrated; i.e., in which circumstances are a dominant firm likely to gain power over price by foreclosing

---

1189. One might benefit from recalling the bridge example, *see* section 2.2.1.1.
1190. *See* Whinston, Michael, *Tying, Foreclosure, and Exclusion*, 80 The American Economic Review (1990) 837. *See* also the discussion of the anti-competitive element below.
1191. In *Microsoft* the findings were based on the fact that the market for media players was characterised by significant indirect network effects, *see* Case T-201/04, *Microsoft*, at 1061–2.
1192. *See* Nalebuff, Barry, *Bundling as an Entry Barrier*, 2004, Quarterly Journal Of Economics, Vol. 119 Nalebuff, Barry, *Bundling as an Entry Barrier*, 119 The Quarterly Journal of Economics (2004) 159.
1193. *See* Whinston (1990).
1194. *See* Case COMP/C-3/37.792, *Microsoft*, at 851.
1195. *See id.* at 852.
1196. *See id.* at 858ff.
1197. *See id.* at 870.
1198. *Id.* at 861–3.

competition by means of tying.[1199] While tying has historically been viewed as a by object restriction, a shift towards an effect-based approach has been indicated with *Microsoft*.[1200] This means that the first part of the assessment (i.e., foreclosure) has a pedigree in case law while the second element represents a greater novelty to case law. This also follows from the disagreement that surrounds *Microsoft* including whether it followed an effect-based approach.[1201]

The aim of this subsection is to analyse how a dominant firm can achieve power over price through tying. The first matter that must be analysed is whether the impact on competitors' costs is significant (see section 2.3.1.1). If it is not the case, then the dominant firm will not be able to harm competition. In *Microsoft*, for example, it was implicitly stated that the increase in [distribution] costs were significant.[1202] As with exclusivity agreements this element is primarily a matter of showing the effect is not of purely hypothetical character. If the assessment of foreclosure reveals that competitors are unable to attain MES, then it is unlikely that the effect is purely hypothetical.

When turning to the anti-competitive element, the competitive concern is fairly straightforward. In general, the competitive concern relating to tying is that the dominant firm leverages its dominant position (market power) from the primary to the secondary market; thereby, harming effective competition on the secondary and/or the primary market. It should be noticed that tying can also constitute (price) discrimination conduct (it enables the dominant firm to extract consumer surplus by means of discrimination). However, it falls out of scope to discuss such price discrimination including whether it is in the interest of consumers.[1203] The analysis is broken up into two subsections dealing with the impact on the secondary and the primary market, respectively.

3.2.2.1 Impact on the Secondary Market

The classical concern of tying is that the dominant firm leverages its dominant position from the primary market into the secondary market, and thereby, restricts effective competition in this secondary market. By doing so, it allows the dominant firm to

---

1199. As the analysis in Chapter 4 showed, such effect has generally been presumed in historic case law. But just assuming a dominant firm will gain power over price by foreclosing competition on the secondary market would be naïve answer to why it is a concern for competition law as economic theory does not support such view, *see* for that effect Nalebuff (2003). It is therefore (implicitly) assumed that the Commission will continue its approach from *Microsoft*.

1200. *See* also Case AT.39230, *Rio Tinto Alcan*.

1201. Contrast Ahlborn & Evans (2009). (Who criticize it for rejecting an effect-based approach) with Rousseva (2010); Këllezi (2009), at (who has more positive view). *See* also Chapter 4.

1202. *See* Case COMP/C-3/37.792, *Microsoft*, at 871 ("For the above reasons, downloading is not an adequate alternative to pre-installation, that is to say, it is not an alternative which would off-set the negative impact that tying WMP has on competition.").

1203. For a review of the effects of such price discrimination *see* Elhauge, Einer & Nalebuff, Barry, *The Welfare Effects of Metering Ties*, 2016, Harvard Public Law Working Paper No. 16-20, available at http://papers.ssrn.com/sol3/papers.cfm?abstract_id = 2591577. *See* also Hovenkamp, Erik & Hovenkamp, Herbert, *Tying Arrangements and Antitrust Harm*, 52 Arizona Law Review (2010) 926. (Who argue consumers are unlikely to be harmed); Elhauge (2009). (Who argues consumers are likely to be harmed).

extend its market power (i.e., dominant position) into that market. This classical leverage theory of harm (also known as offensive leverage) has been criticized by economists using the "one monopoly profit" theorem.[1204] It also resulted in commentators advocating a per se legality towards tying. According to this theorem, profits cannot be increased by leveraging market power into another market in which it faces competition given the same consumers are buying both products in fixed proportions. There is only one monopoly profit to be earned which it already earns in the primary market; i.e., the only monopoly rent the dominant firm can extract from its conduct would be on its own primary product.[1205] In that case, it is the total price of the bundle that determines sales and thereby the dominant firm's pricing decisions.[1206] As a result, the dominant firm will have to lower its price on the primary product to keep the total price unchanged at the profit maximising level.[1207] Any market power, which that firm has, is, according to this theorem, already fully exploited in the absence of tying and do not gain any extra profits.[1208] In effect, there can be no anti-competitive effect, since the dominant firm cannot gain power over price. This means that a dominant from that perspective will not have an incentive to engage in tying unless it is due to cost-savings or other pro-competitive reason; thus, tying can only benefit consumers' interest.

While the theorem is powerful and simple, it is limited to only static considerations. This was observed as early as in 1958 by Kaplow.[1209] While the benefits of leveraging market power may be limited in a static framework, a dominant firm can gain power over price when dynamic considerations are considered. In other words, for the "one monopoly profit" theorem to hold two strict assumptions must hold.[1210] First, the secondary market must not be competitive; i.e., the competitiveness of the secondary market is fixed.[1211] This relates not only to entry barriers[1212] but also to, for example, economies of scale/scope, learning effects and so on.[1213] Second, it is

---

1204. Bork has denoted this theorem as the fallacy of double counting, *see* Bork (1978), at 140.
1205. In the context of a case, *see* e.g., Stigler, George, *United States v. Loew's Inc.: A Note on Block-Booking*, 1963 The Supreme Court Review (1963) 152.
1206. If the price for the tied product becomes higher than customers would have had to pay on the "open market", customers will experience an increase in price. If that increase is not outweighed in the price for the tying product, customers will demand less of that product, and thus, buy less.
1207. *See* Posner (2001), at 199.
1208. *See* Bishop & Walker (2010), at 282-3 (who show that the profit is the same with and without tying and bundling).
1209. *See* Kaplow, Louis, *Extension of Monopoly Power through Leverage*, 85 Columbia Law Review (1985) 515, at 530 (He stated, among other things, that it was hard to understand why so much of the criticism operates primarily in a static framework).
1210. For an extensive review of these assumptions and the critique which can be applied to the theorem *see* e.g., Elhauge (2009). *See also* Bishop & Walker (2010), at 227-8 (who notes the assumptions are arguably often unrealistic).
1211. *See* for critique of this assumption Elhauge (2003).(who shows that by foreclosing through tying a market can create anti-competitive effects by depriving rivals of network effects or economies of scale, scope, distribution, supply, research, or learning). *See also* Rasmusen, et al. (1991); Krattenmaker & Salop (1986).
1212. As will be recalled, the Chicago School is rather infamous for viewing entry barriers very narrowly.
1213. In *Microsoft* the secondary market was characterized by network effects, *see* Case COMP/C-3/37.792, *Microsoft*, at 448–64.

assumed that the products are used in fixed proportions.[1214] While this may be the case in some event, it is not necessarily so.[1215] Besides these two assumptions it is also, indirectly, assumed that customers are perfectly informed; i.e., they are able to calculate the price of the bundle contra the standalone price.[1216] Otherwise, the dominant firm is able to charge a higher (effective) price on the tied product; i.e., customers are exploited.[1217] When these assumptions are relaxed tying may be a tool to gain power over price.

This is achieved by altering the market structure of the secondary market as discussed in section 3.2.1.[1218] In effect, this means that competitors are foreclosed from the market due to a decrease in efficiencies.[1219] However, the dominant firm may not extract profits from customers, since there is still only one monopoly profit that the dominant firm can extract from its customers. On the other hand, if the secondary product can be used for other purposes than with the primary product, or by other customers, it can allow the dominant firm to gain power over price for that proportion.[1220] This illustrates perfectly the difference between the static view of the "one monopoly profit" theorem and a more dynamic view. If foreclosure decreases competitors' efficiency, it will worsen the market options available to customers and lessen the constraint on the dominant firm's market power in the tied market; thus, enabling it to raise prices in the tied market.[1221]

Tying may also harm competitors' competitiveness by decreasing rival aggressiveness or expandability.[1222] This may happen in at least two scenarios. First, if firms in the tied market engage in "Cournot competition", where each firm sets output in response to the output choices of others, then tying can encourage competitors in the secondary market to reduce output and charge higher prices.[1223] Second, if the secondary market is concentrated, but (absent tying) would be undifferentiated and result in "Bertrand competition" that drives prices down to cost, tying can effectively differentiate the secondary market and induce the competitor to charge higher prices for the secondary product.[1224] Tying in both scenarios will increase profits for the dominant firm if, absent tying, the revenue from the primary product would exceed the one from the secondary product, which is typical, the case in tying cases.[1225]

1214. This is an important, restrictive assumption which needs to hold for the theorem to hold, *see* e.g., Whinston (1990), at 837–8.
1215. *See* for that effect Case IV/31043, *Tetra Pak II*.
1216. *See* Langer (2007), at 301.
1217. This may seem to indicate that it is an issue for exploitive abuse. However, it explains why a dominant firm can have an incentive to foreclose effective competition on the secondary market.
1218. *See* Padilla & O'Donoghue (2013), at 603.
1219. Note that in the model it means that competitors exit the secondary market or are denied access to it (i.e., fully excluded), *see* e.g., Nalebuff (2004).
1220. *See* Carlton, Dennis & Heyer, Ken, *Appropriate Antitrust Policy Towards Single-Firm Conduct: Extraction v. Extension*, 22 Antitrust (2008).
1221. *See* Elhauge (2009), at 413.
1222. *See id.* at 414.
1223. *See* Carbajo, José, et al., *A Strategic Motivation for Commodity Bundling*, 38 The Journal of Industrial Economics (1990) 283, at 283, 285–6 & 290–2.
1224. *See id.* at 285 & 287–9.
1225. *See id.* at 292.

Even if profits are not increased, customers may still suffer a loss as a result of the limitation of the choices available to them.[1226] According to case law that would be abusive. One could question the dominant firm's incentive, though. One answer may lie in the fact that real markets differ from the theoretical world. For instance, customers may not think of the subsequent costs relating to the tied product when buying the tying product; thereby, creating an aftermarket.[1227] In that event, the customer's choice of product in the primary market depends solely on the tying products price and not the combined price. As a result, there are now two monopoly profits.[1228] Moreover, the dominant firm may simply not have known that there was only one monopoly profit, but nevertheless intended to increase profits. The result of the tying has been mistakenly thought to result in obtaining larger profits.[1229] A second answer may lie in the reduced level of innovation. If innovation is reduced, fewer costs are allactoed to R&D. Consequently, (long-term) profits are secured. This could further aggravate the effect relating to the first answer as it may increase the lifetime of the tying product and thereby the time profits can be earned.

3.2.2.2   Impact on the Primary Market

Besides affecting the primary market in a negative way, tying can also have a negative impact on the primary market. By foreclosing the secondary market, it can benefit in the primary market. Tying may allow the dominant firm to gain power over price by protecting its dominant position in the primary market.[1230] This is also a respond to the "one monopoly profit" theorem. The dominant firm may not be able to increase its monopoly profit, but it may be able to preserve that profit (or at least some of it). The importance is not whether profits are sought increased, but whether tying is likely to hinder competition on the primary market to the detriment of consumers' interest. That would result in power of price as the dominant firm keeps the price above an otherwise competitive price or limit innovation (and thereby reduces costs). This type of conduct is therefore also known as defensive leverage.[1231]

In general, tying can have negative impact on the primary market as it preserves, alternatively increases, the market power in the primary market (i.e., the dominant position) by either: (i) foreclosing enough of the tied market to deter or delay later entry into the tying market, (ii) raising the costs of a partial substitute that constraints tying market power, or (iii) transferring market power from a waning technology to the next-generation technology.[1232] In all three scenarios, tying enhances the dominant position [by protecting it] compared to what it would have been in the "but-for world" without tying.

1226. *See* Case AT.39230, *Rio Tinto Alcan*, at 79; Case COMP/C-3/37.792, *Microsoft*, at 981.
1227. *See* Monti (2007), at 188–9.
1228. *See id.* at 189.
1229. *See* Rousseva (2010), at 246.
1230. *See* Carlton & Waldman (2002).
1231. *See* Feldman, Robin, *Defensive Leveraging in Antitrust*, 87 Georgetown Law Journal (1999) 2079.
1232. *See* Elhauge (2009), at 417.

This first scenario builds on the event where competitors in the secondary market pose a threat to the primary market; i.e., being able to enter the primary market (if successful in the secondary market). Literature shows that successful firms in a secondary market are likely to evolve into the primary market in future periods, in which case a dominant firm has incentives to foreclose competitors in the secondary market to prevent or reduce the erosion of its tying market power over time.[1233] Alternatively, the dominant firm's position in the primary market might be vulnerable to future entry by a single-market competitor. By foreclosing competitors in the secondary market, it prevents an entrant in the primary market which does not produce the secondary product as well.[1234]

The second scenario builds on the event where the secondary product is a partial substitute for the tying product. That the products are partial substitutes essentially means that they failed the SSNIP-test[1235] but the secondary product still restricts or can potentially restrict the pricing on the primary product.[1236] In other words, the dominant firm is unable to extract the full monopoly profit in the primary market due to the secondary product. Foreclosing the market for such a secondary product can immediately protect or enhance the dominant firm's position in the primary market.[1237]

The third scenario builds on the event where there is a technological trend from the primary market (where the dominant firm has its market power) to a secondary market. In such a case, a firm can use foreclosure not just to delay the erosion of its current dominant position in a waning technology, but to develop a new dominant position over the technology of the future.[1238] The dominant firm is thereby able to guard itself against innovation that would otherwise have threatened its existence.

Defensive leverage is generally seen as more harmful than offensive leverage.[1239] As the analysis of offensive leverage showed, it is subject to certain conditions if tying is to be anti-competitive. This does not mean that offensive leverage is impossible, but it should entail a more careful examination. The same is, of course, true for defensive leverage, but it still provides a possible theory of how a dominant firm can gain power of price – see for that effect also the analysis relating to refusal to deal (section 3.4).

1233. *See* e.g., Areeda & Hovenkamp (2015); Carlton & Waldman (2002); Carlton, Dennis, *A general analysis of exclusionary conduct and refusal to deal – why Aspen and Kodak are misguided*, 68 Antitrust Law Journal (2001) 659; Feldman (1999).
1234. *See* Elhauge (2009), at 417.
1235. The SSNIP test is used to assess substitution among products. It asks whether customers will change to the other product in the event of a small but significant and non-transitory increase in price. *See* Communication of the Commission of 9 December 1997 97/C 372 /03, *on the definition of relevant market for the purposes of Community competition law* ("*Relevant Market Guidelines*"), at 15–9.
1236. *See* Elhauge (2009), at 418.
1237. *See* Whinston (1990), at 852–4. *See* also Elhauge (2009), at 418.
1238. *See* Carlton & Waldman (2002), at 196–7; Carlton (2001), at 670–1.
1239. *See* Elhauge (2009), at 417–8.

3.2.3 *A Note on Mixed Bundling*

The analysis in Chapter 5, section 2.2.1 revealed that mixed bundling could be assessed as tying. This is the case when the rebate granted when the distinct products are both together represents a penalty [for disloyal customers] rather than a true discount. I.e., the rebate is applied to an artificial high stand-alone price that is only able due to the dominant position in the primary market(s). For example, absent mixed bundling, the dominant firm would have set a stand-alone price for the primary product at EUR 100 but with mixed bundling that stand-alone price is EUR 120 with a rebate of EUR 20.

This means that the same framework applies for the assessment of mixed bundling in these circumstances. To establish a foreclosure effect, it must be proved that: (i) the products are distinct, (ii) there are coercion, and (iii) the extent and/ selective use of mixed bundling leads to higher costs by, for example, hindering the competitor from reaching MVS. And in regards to anti-competitive effect, it must be proven that: (i) the impact is significant enough to harm competitors' ability to compete with the dominant firm (not just individual competitors), and (ii) market power is enhanced or protected in the primary and/or secondary market.

However, this begs the question of how coercion is fulfilled if customers are provided with a choice to buy the products together (i.e., the bundle) or separately. They are not forced to buy the both products due to contractual or technical coercion as with tying (including pure bundling). Nevertheless, for the reasons above, many customers will choose to buy the bundle instead of buying the secondary product at an alternative supplier since they incur a penalty for not choosing the bundle. This especially the case if the stand-alone price exceeds the price that (most) customers are willing to pay; for example, if the stand-alone price minus the rebate equals the monopoly profit.

3.2.4 *Summarizing*

In the preceding subsections, the foreclosure and anti-competitive element, respectively, have been analysed with the purpose of providing a framework for the assessment of unlawful tying under the effect-based approach. These findings are also in line with case law. According to case law four conditions are required to demonstrate unlawful tying: (i) the primary and secondary products are two separate products, (ii) the firm is dominant in the primary market, (iii) the dominant firm does not give customers a choice to obtain the primary product without the secondary product, and (iv) the dominant firm's tying forecloses competition in the primary and/or the secondary market.[1240] The first two aspects are part of the foreclosure element analysed in section 3.2.1, the third aspect is indirectly also part of section 3.2.1, and the fourth aspect is part of the anti-competitive element analysed in section 3.2.2.

1240. *See* Case T-201/04, *Microsoft*, at 794.

3.3 Refusal to Deal/Supply

Refusal to deal or supply (referred to as refusal to deal in the following) is a special type of exclusionary conduct. First, the dominant firm is directly harming competition. This is due to the fact that the dominant firm is a vertically integrated firm who controls an upstream (alternatively downstream) service or product ("upstream input") which its downstream competitors request.[1241] Second, while the remedies relating to other types of exclusionary abuse involves the dominant firm must end that unlawful behaviour, the remedies relating to refusal to supply includes a duty to give access to the input. This infers with the freedom to contract and basic property rights. As the clear starting point, a dominant firm is therefore allowed to choose their own business partners and a duty to give access requires special circumstances.[1242] The existence of such obligation may undermine a firm's incentives to invest. Knowledge or expectations of such obligation against one's own free will may lead dominant firms (or firms anticipating to become dominant) not to invest, or alternatively, invest less. The obligation may further tempt competitors to free ride on the dominant firm's investments instead of investing themselves; thus, reducing competition in the relevant market. None of these possible consequences are, as a minimum in the long run, in the interest of consumers. While a refusal to deal is subject to negative effects, an obligation is in some events required to ensure or protect effective competition in the interest of consumers. That is when the benefits of a duty to deal must outweigh the negative effects.

3.3.1 Competitors Versus Customers

It is, first, necessary to distinguish between a refusal to deal with a competitor and one with a customer. The former arises when the dominant firm is vertically integrated and refuses to deal with one or more of its downstream competitors.[1243] The other event may occur where a firm, dominant in the upstream market, controls an upstream input that is requested by firms in the downstream market, but the dominant firm is not active in the downstream market (i.e., it is not vertical integrated). Such refusal rarely causes concern in terms of exclusionary abuse. It is instead an issue of secondary-line discrimination. This does not preclude any adverse effects in the downstream market, but if it does, it is most likely an issue for discriminatory abuse.

On the other hand, it may have secondary effects on upstream competitors in certain circumstances. It can be a tool to foreclose, for example, distribution opportunities to the downstream market with the effect of preventing or hinder access to the

---

1241. An exclusionary refusal to supply or deal necessarily presupposes two markets; an upstream and a downstream market, see e.g., Lang, John Temple, *Essential Facilities in The European Union: Bronner and Beyond*, 10 Columbia Journal of European Law (2004) 1; Lang & O'Donoghue (2002). See also Opinion of Advocate General Jacobs of 28 May 1998 in Case C-7/97, *Oscar Bronner GmbH & Co. KG v. Mediaprint Zeitungs- und Zeitschriftenverlag GmbH & Co. KG*, at 61.

1242. *See* for that effect *the Article 102 Guidance Paper*, at 75.

1243. *See* for that effect *id.* at 76.

relevant upstream market. When a refusal to deal induces such effects, it then shifts to an issue of primary line discrimination. The (potential) adverse effect goes from being vertical to being horizontal (i.e., harming upstream competitors rather than down-stream customers). The question is then whether upstream competition is distorted. This may be the case where the refusal serves as a punishment for not entering a [quasi] exclusivity or tying agreement. For instance, a customer shifts sales to a [new] competitor and in an effort to prevent that competitor from being successful in the upstream market the dominant firm refuses to deal with that customer – or threatens to do so. This may further send a signal to other customers that they will experience the same consequence if they build a relationship with that competitor. A dominant firm may then be able to tie up customers with the effect of distorting competition.

The ECJ has dealt with a somewhat comparable case in *United Brands*. A long-standing customer had chosen to become the exclusive importer (and distribu-tor)[1244] of a competitor to United Brands and, as a result, United Brands refused to deal with that customer. The ECJ found that conduct unlawful since a dominant firm "cannot stop supplying a long-standing customer who abides by regular commercial practice if the orders placed by that customer are in no way out of the ordinary."[1245] At first glance, this greatly restricts dominant firms from acting freely. However, the ECJ justified this on the grounds that the refusal "would limit markets to the prejudice of consumers and would amount to discrimination which might, in the end, eliminate a trading party from the relevant market."[1246] Accordingly, the ECJ seems, indirectly, to require harm to the competition in the upstream market.[1247] This is further supported by the statement that "the adoption of such a course of conduct is designed to have a serious adverse effect on competition on the relevant banana market by only allowing firms dependent upon the dominant undertaking to stay in business."[1248] In other words, that conduct prevented competitors in the upstream market from achieving the needed economies of scale to compete effectively with United Brands. This, of course, presupposes that a customer would be significantly hurt for such adverse effect to occur in the event of a refusal. In other words, the product in question must be sufficiently important for the customer. The customer must have the incentive to react on the refusal.

In a decision of interim measures by the Commission, refusal to deal with a customer was also found exclusionary.[1249] The Commission found the fact that "a customer of a dominant producer becomes associated with a competitor or a potential competitor of that manufacturer does not normally entitle the dominant producer to withdraw all supplies immediately or to take reprisals against that customer."[1250]

1244. Note that this does not mean it entered an exclusivity agreement with the United Brands competitor as it was still depending on the United Brands' product.
1245. *See* Case 27/76, *United Brands*, at 182.
1246. *See id.* at 183.
1247. *See* also Padilla & O'Donoghue (2013), at 587 (who directly infers this by citing the line as "eliminate a [competitor] for the relevant market." *See* also page 586).
1248. *See* Case 27/76, *United Brands*, at 194.
1249. *See* Commission Decision of 29 July 1987 in Case IV/32.279, *BBI/Boosey & Hawkes: Interim measures*.
1250. *See id.* at 19.

However, this case involves some special circumstances. First, the Commission found a purpose of foreclosing upstream competition and the refusal to deal was part of this plan.[1251] Second, there was a substantial likelihood that the two customers would go out of business as a result of the refusal.[1252] This had a serious effect on the competitor as the refusal then worked as an indirect attack on its financial viability, since the two customers in question founded it (and its distribution channel). Therefore, the Commission found abuse due to the upstream competition being distorted. The Commission recognized that where "a customer transfers its central activity to the promotion of a competing brand it may be that even a dominant producer is entitled to review its commercial relations with that customer and on giving adequate notice terminate any special relationship."[1253] Consequently, the instant refusal and the plan to foreclose were two cornerstones in finding abuse. Without those, upstream competition may not have experienced an adverse effect; thus, a refusal would have been lawful.

As can be noticed from the analysis of refusal to deal with a customer, the anti-competitive foreclosure effect resembles that of exclusivity agreement or tying (alternatively loyalty and bundle rebates). The refusal represents a punishment for either not agreeing to deal [quasi-]exclusive or enter a tying agreement. *United Brands* can even be seen as defensive leveraging as it sought to protect its dominant position. As a result, the assessment of whether a refusal to deal with customer constitutes exclusionary abuse will follow the method presented in the subsections above. The following discussion will focus only on the event where the dominant upstream firm is also active in the downstream market (i.e., vertical integrated).

3.3.2 *Foreclosure Effect*

When a vertically integrated firm, who holds a dominant position in an upstream market, refuses to supply its upstream input to its downstream competitors it is clear that there is some sort of foreclosure effect. Access to the downstream market is made more difficult. Despite the fact that a refusal to deal is generally exclusionary,[1254] a standard for demonstrating a foreclosure element is warranted. A foreclosure effect is not necessarily demonstrated since, according to section 2.2, it must be shown that it raises competitors' costs. This ensures that a dominant firm does not fall under suspicion every time it refuses to deal with a competitor. In addition, care should be taken to the negative effects of imposing a duty to deal.

1251. A customer and a repair shop holding contracts with Boosey and Hawkey ("B&H"), the dominant firm, created a competitor to B&H. B&H the attempted to prevent that competitor from establishing itself on the market to protect its own position on the upstream market.
1252. B&H refusal to deal harmed the profitability of the customers. This had a serious effect on establishing the new competitor as the refusal worked as an indirect attack on its financial viability (cutting the creators funds), *see* Case IV/32.279, *BBI/Boosey & Hawkes: Interim measures*, at 13.
1253. *See id.* at 19.
1254. *See* Chapter 3, section 3.1.

3.3.2.1   Indispensable Input

For refusal to deal the standard of foreclosure is higher compared to other types of conduct within Exclusion. As already explained, there are powerful remedies related to an unlawful refusal and, owing to this, a high standard of foreclosure is justified. A lenient approach risks discouraging innovations and encourages free riding. Refusal to deal is for those reasons often analysed under the "essential facility" doctrine. This doctrine originates in commentary on US antitrust law for the situation where an owner of an "essential" or "bottleneck" upstream input is required to provide access.[1255] The doctrine set out that refusal to deal can cause competitive concern only when the facility (i.e., the upstream input) is essential. EU competition law has incorporated this doctrine in the analytical framework of refusal to deal.[1256] As a result, the upstream input must be essential ("indispensable")[1257] to allow a finding of unlawful refusal to deal.[1258]

The test for indispensability has been clearly articulated in a series of judgments (and decisions).[1259] It is therefore not necessary to analyse the test in vast.[1260] As laid out in case law, it requires the upstream input to be essential for the exercise of the activity in question.[1261] I.e., there are no actual or potential viable alternatives to the dominant firms upstream input or there are technical, legal or economic obstacles[1262] capable of making it impossible or at least unreasonably difficult for any firm seeking to operate in the downstream market to create, possibly in cooperation with other operators, the alternative products or services.[1263] If it is possible, and economically sound, to replicate the input, then the requesting party should carry out its own investment. Firms would otherwise not invest since competitors would be able to simply free ride on those investments. That would have adverse effects on effective competition.[1264]

1255. *See* Bishop & Walker (2010), at 322–3.
1256. Besides case law relating to Article 102 TFEU *see*, for instance, *Telecommunication Sector Access Notice*.
1257. This requirement may also be termed as the input being objectively necessary, *see the Article 102 Guidance Paper*, at 83–4.
1258. *See id.* at 81 *See* also Case C-7/97, *Bronner*, at 41.
1259. *See* e.g., Case T-201/04, *Microsoft*; Judgment of 29 April 2004 in Case C-418/01, *IMS Health GmbH & Co. OHG v. NDC Health GmbH & Co. KG* ("*IMS Health*"); Case C-7/97, *Bronner*. For a more extensive review of the test *see* e.g., Lang (2004).
1260. For an extensive criticism of the indispensability requirement developed in case law *see* e.g., Rousseva (2010).
1261. *See* Case C-418/01, *IMS Health*, at 28; Case C-7/97, *Bronner*, at 43–4.
1262. In terms of economic obstacles, it must be assessed whether, at the very least, that the creation of such upstream input is economically viable for production on a scale comparable to that of the dominant firm. *See* Case C-418/01, *IMS Health*, at 28; Case C-7/97, *Bronner*, at 46.
1263. *See* Commission Decision of 2 June 2004 in Case COMP/38.096, *Clearstream (Clearing and Settlement)*, at 227.
1264. *See* for that effect Opinion of Advocate General Jacobs in Case C-7/97, *Oscar Bronner*, at 58. (Who stated that "if access to a production, purchasing or distribution facility were allowed too easily there would be no incentive for a competitor to develop competing facilities. Thus, while competition was increased in the short term it would be reduced in the long term. Moreover, the incentive for a dominant undertaking to invest in efficient facilities would be reduced if its competitors were, upon request, able to share the benefits. Thus, the mere fact

From an economic point of view, one could also add a third requirement in that there must be excess capacity.[1265] Without an extra capacity an unlawful refusal, and thereby a duty to deal, would result in a restriction of the output which the dominant firm can produce itself. While it is an important aspect in terms of whether a duty to deal would harm the dominant firm, it does not say whether the upstream input is indispensable. It may be an issue of whether the refusal can be justified.

A requirement of indispensability may seem to contradict the findings in section 2.2 since competitors' costs can be raised even if the upstream input is not indispensable (there a potential alternatively although at a higher cost). But it must be remembered that imposing an obligation to deal infers with the freedom to contract and basic property rights. These are essential to the free market economy on which the EU is based.[1266] Accordingly, imposing an obligation to supply or deal should only be done in *limited* circumstances,[1267] and even then with care.[1268] It is crucial that the assessment not only relies on the upstream market power but also focuses more on the importance that that upstream input has in ensuring effective competition on the downstream.[1269] It is on these grounds that it is justified to set a stricter requirement for the anti-competitive effects related to a refusal compared to other types within this chapter.

On the other hand, it may be reasonable to ease on the requirement when an imposed duty does not directly interfere with the incentive to invest.[1270] This would be the case where the firm has obtained its upstream input without having born the risk and costs of the investment. The prime example here is former state monopolies. These firms have obtained their upstream input in the absence of competition and, in most cases, with financial support from the state. In such cases, the issue of protecting the firm's investment not as important since it will not have an influence on cases where the input is obtained under competition.[1271] It will, of course, be preferred that this

---

that by retaining a facility for its own use a dominant undertaking retains an advantage over a competitor cannot justify requiring access to it.")

1265. *See* Bishop & Walker (2010), at 330; Motta (2004), at 67.

1266. *See* Article 119 and 120 of the TFEU. *See* also Opinion of Advocate General Jacobs in Case C-7/97, *Oscar Bronner*, at 56. (Who held that "[...] it is apparent that the right to choose one's trading partners and freely to dispose of one's property are generally recognised principles in the laws of the Member States, in some cases with constitutional status. Incursions on those rights require careful justification.").

1267. *See* Case T-201/04, *Microsoft*, at 691. *See* for that effect also e.g., Padilla & O'Donoghue (2013), at 509; Bishop & Walker (2010), at 322.

1268. *See* Case COMP/39.525, *Telekomunikacja Polska*, at 700.

1269. *See* for that effect e.g., Opinion of Advocate General Jacobs in Case C-7/97, *Oscar Bronner*, at 58. (Who stated that it will "be unsatisfactory, in a case in which a competitor demands access to a raw material in order to be able to compete with the dominant undertaking on a downstream market in a final product, to focus solely on the latter's market power on the upstream market and conclude that its conduct in reserving to itself the downstream market is automatically an abuse. Such conduct will not have an adverse impact on consumers unless the dominant undertaking's final product is sufficiently insulated from competition to give it market power.")

1270. *See* Motta (2004), at 68.

1271. *See id.*

mentioned when applied in the case.[1272] This view is also supported by the Commission in its *Article 102 Guidance Paper*.[1273] As a result, arguments of easing the requirement in circumstances of former state monopoly or the like are reasonable.[1274] It would also be in line with case law to ease the requirement of foreclosure when the structure of competition is distorted due to a former state monopoly.[1275]

If the dominant firm's upstream input is indispensable for downstream competitors' competitive behaviour, then a foreclosure effect is inherent in any refusal.[1276] A somewhat similar view is held by the Commission who "considers that a dominant undertaking's refusal to supply is generally liable to eliminate, immediately or over time, effective competition in the downstream market."[1277] While the Commission refers to effective competition (the matter of issue in section 3.4.3), it indirectly refers to foreclosure effects.[1278] When compared to the framework in section 2.2, it is seen that refusal to deal represents a version of the "Bottleneck". Accordingly, there should be no doubt that a refusal to deal an indispensable upstream input raises competitors' costs.

A truly indispensable input will further cause "fully foreclosure" (i.e., the exit of a competitor or deter its entry) as it will have no viable alternative due to the refusal. However, it does not necessarily have to be so.[1279] While there may be no viable alternative so that the competitor is unable to compete effectively with the dominant firm *in the long run*, it may be able to seek out a less efficient or more expensive input and to settle for a niche of the market [in the short run]. While not all competition in the downstream market is foreclosed, this still clearly raises competitors' costs; i.e., exits may not necessarily be observed over the course of an investigation, as it may occur in the long run.[1280] In consequence, a refusal to supply an indispensable input will result in foreclosure. In terms of the anti-competitive effect that is not necessarily the case as the analysis below illustrates.

3.3.2.2 A Note on Cases Involving Constructive Refusal and Margin Squeeze

Even if indispensability is concluded there still, obviously, need to be a refusal. There is no doubt of refusal if the dominant firm outright refuses to supply its upstream input.

1272. *See* for that effect the critique below in relations to the event where the dominant firm was already imposed a duty to deal. The requirement of an indispensable input has been rejected, rightly so, but they reason has not been followed clearly.
1273. *See the Article 102 Guidance Paper*, at 82.
1274. *See* further Chapter 5, section 2.2.2. *See* also Motta (2004), at 68 (who extends this argumenation to cases such as Magill as the obligation would have negative effects on the input owner's centives to invest and innovate upstream, whether *ex ante* or *ex post*).
1275. *See* for that effect Case C-209/10, *Post Danmark I*, at 23.
1276. That foreclosure is inherent in a refusal has been criticized. However, that criticism relates to the anti-competitive effect; i.e., whether effective competition is harmed (*see* below).
1277. *See the Article 102 Guidance Paper*, at 85.
1278. There can be no anti-competitive harm without a foreclosure effect, *see* Chapter 3.
1279. Case T-201/04, *Microsoft*, at 428 & 560–3.
1280. *See* for that effect *id.* at 561.

But the concept embraces more than an outright refusal.[1281] Constructive refusal or margin squeeze can be sufficient. Such refusal could, for example, take the form of unduly delaying or otherwise degrading the supply of the input or involve the imposition of unreasonable conditions in return for the supply. Constructive refusal has further been the issue of matter in recent decisional practice by the Commission.[1282]

What is more important (and potentially controversial) is that the ECJ has allowed constructive refusal to be found abusive without the need to establish indispensability. It has even had a direct effect on the Commission's decisional practice.[1283] In *TeliaSonera*, the ECJ found that the requirements relating to abusive refusal to deal (namely that of indispensability) not necessarily also applies to the assessment of "conduct which consists of supplying services or selling goods on conditions which are disadvantageous or on which there might be no purchaser."[1284] Such statement can be seen as highly controversial. Outright and constructive refusal should be based on the same considerations. If an obligation to deal cannot be imposed then, for the same reason, no obligation to deal on reasonable terms can be imposed. Anything else is illogical.

While it may seem highly controversial from the outset, it is not necessarily so. First, the principle works for refusals that are assessed as other types of conduct; for example, exclusivity agreements, tying, predatory pricing[1285] or discrimination. As the analysis in section 3.3.1 showed, refusal may be a matter of exclusivity agreements. That seems further to be the point of the ECJ.[1286] Second, it is only common sense that the requirement of an indispensable upstream input is redundant when the firm is already bound by an obligation to deal.[1287] The analysis in Chapter 5, section 2.2.2 also addressed this aspect. In such an event, the firm is breaching an existing obligation. It is not a matter of whether a duty to deal should be imposed but whether that obligation to deal is abused. In other words, it is in that event not necessary to consider the negative effect relating to a duty deal since such duty is already imposed. This explains why the Commission found a requirement of indispensability (within the meaning of *Bronner*) as irrelevant in, for example, *Slovak Telekom* and *Telekomunikacja Polska* (cases in which both dominant positions were under regulation).[1288]

1281. *See* Judgment of 9 September 2009 in Case T-301/04, *Clearstream Banking AG v. Commission of the European Communities ("Clearstream")*. *See* also Commission Decision of 20 September 2016 in Case CASE AT.39759, *ARA Foreclosure*, at 101ff (Access was only given to individual regions and not the whole of Austria).
1282. *See* Case AT.39523, *Slovak Telekom*; Case COMP/39.525, *Telekomunikacja Polska*.
1283. *See* Case AT.39523, *Slovak Telekom*, at 355–71 (The Commission concluded in paragraph 370 that "there is no reason to extend the case law on abusive refusal to supply essential facilities developed in Bronner, to all types of refusal to supply.").
1284. *See* Case C-52/09, *TeliaSonera*, at 55.
1285. *See* Chapter 6, section 3.3.
1286. *See* Case C-52/09, *TeliaSonera*, at 57–8 (The ECJ stated, among other things, that the ECJ in Bronner did not make comments on other types of abuse "such as tied sales.").
1287. It would be reasonable to presuppose that the necessary balancing of incentives (for instance, to innovate *ex ante* and *ex post*) has already been made by the public authority when imposing such an obligation to supply. *See* for that effect *the Article 102 Guidance Paper*, at 82.
1288. *See* e.g., Case AT.39523, *Slovak Telekom*, at 370.

3.3.3 Anti-competitive Effect

If foreclosure is demonstrated, in accordance with the above, then an anti-competitive effect is in most events likely. Refusal to deal a truly indispensable upstream input to its downstream competition is liable to eliminate, immediately or over time, effective competition in the downstream market.[1289] It is likely that the dominant firm gains power over price due such refusal since, owing to the indispensable nature of the input: (i) the increase in competitors' costs is significant and (ii) the ability (and likely also their incentive) for competitors to compete is either hampered or eliminated. However, and as will be seen in the below, anti-competitive effects cannot be presumed on the grounds of an indispensable product under the effect-based approach.

3.3.3.1 A Regulated Upstream Price and Leverage

First of all, the same issue that occurs with tying occurs here as well; i.e., the "one monopoly profit" theorem. The dominant firm will not be able to extract more profits by foreclosing competition in the downstream market.[1290] Therefore, it has no incentive to engage in refusal to deal unless it is due to pro-competitive reasons. As it was the case with tying, however, the "one monopoly profit" theorem does not always apply meaning that refusal can serve as means to achieve anti-competitive effects. The analysis of the anti-competitive effect focuses on why a refusal is engaged if it does not have a negative impact on profits.

The first scenario is in the case of a regulated upstream price.[1291] A regulated upstream price prevents the dominant firm from extract the monopoly profit in the upstream market. This event will enable the dominant firm to extract more profits than it would otherwise do absent the refusal by foreclosing the [unregulated] downstream market.[1292] Accordingly, the "one monopoly profit" theorem cannot hold. While this is a possible strategy, it is only really an issue where regulation already exists. It would be unlikely that a dominant is unable to raise its upstream price absent regulation. Moreover, in the event of regulation, the dominant firm is imposed a duty to deal meaning that an outright refusal is not possible. Margins squeeze may by a method, but that will require a reduction in downstream price followed by an increase after successful foreclosure; hence, it will be a matter of Predation and not Exclusion.[1293] Despite the "one monopoly profit" theorem does not hold, refusal is more likely to be viewed as Predation in this event.

An alternative, as noted in Chapter 5, section 2.2.2, would be where the dominant firm is refrained from raising the price due to a likelihood of intervention by a competition authority due to excessive pricing. This might be a rational strategy in a market characterized with network effect where the price charged to extract monopoly

---

1289. *See* Case T-201/04, *Microsoft*, at 563. *See* also *the Article 102 Guidance Paper*, at 85.
1290. *See* section 3.2.2.
1291. *See* Bishop & Walker (2010), at 326–7.
1292. *See the Article 102 Guidance Paper*, at 88.
1293. *See* Chapter 5, section 2.2.2.

profit will appear to very high; thus, refusal to deal can allow the dominant firm to extract the monopoly profit in a less visible fashion.[1294] While it serves as an alternative, it is rather theoretical and therefore unlikely to occur in the real world. All in all, this event is more likely to be caught by regulation or Predation.

Another possible reason for engaging in refusal to deal is defensive and offensive leverage as analysed under tying. The same analysis as in section 3.2.2 would, therefore, be relevant here. The dominant firm may seek to protect its position in the downstream market in fear of technological developments.[1295] Regarding offensive leverage, the dominant firm could seek to monopolies the downstream market if the products in the two markets are not sold in fixed portions. This argument was used by the Commission in *Microsoft* to reject the argument by Microsoft that it had no interest in refusal [due to the "one monopoly" theorem].[1296]

3.3.3.2   New Product

Finding an abusive refusal, and thereby imposing a duty to deal, requires a balancing of the *ex ante* and *ex post* effects stemming from such intervention. Besides the "essential facility" doctrine, a requirement of "new product" has been advocated to ensure that this balancing is done.[1297] Such requirement will further ensure a benefit to consumers' interest.[1298] When the requesting competitor merely seeks to duplicate the downstream product the benefits for consumers' interest are ambiguous compared to the event where a new product is introduced. In the event of duplication, the principal benefit would be increased price competition in the downstream market. However, a fee for access to the input must be settled and, owing to the balancing of *ex ante* and *ex post* effects, the scope for increasing price competition may be limited (to encourage innovation a fee above costs will most likely be required and the dominant may be able to extract its monopoly profit though that access fee).[1299] The requirement of a new product serves in that sense as a method to ensure a concrete benefit to consumers' interest (and to protect effective competition rather than individual competitors).

This requirement has also been implemented under the EU Court's law referred to as "the emergences of a new product."[1300] However, it has, so far, only been applied when the refusal concerned an Intellectual Property Right ("IP") and not physical assets.[1301] The reason could be based on the fact that a physical asset does not restrict

---

1294. *See* Carlton, Dennis & Klamer, Mark, *The Need for Coordination Among Firms, with Special Reference to Network Industries*, 50 The University of Chicago Law Review (1983) 446.
1295. *See* for that effect Case COMP/C-3/37.792, *Microsoft*, at 764–78.
1296. *See id.* at 538.
1297. *See* Padilla & O'Donoghue (2013), at 524.
1298. It also satisfies Article 102 TFEU(b) in terms of "prejudice to consumers".
1299. For an analysis of the available terms and their application in case law, *see* Padilla & O'Donoghue (2013), at 933–42.
1300. This element was first introduced in Judgment of 6 April 1995 in Joined Cases C-241/91 P and C-242/91 P, *Radio Telefis Eireann (RTE) and others v. Commission of the European Communities ("Magill")*. *See* also *the Article 102 Guidance Paper*, at 87.
1301. It was not included in the famous *Bronner* case even though it was delivered after *Magill*.

the right to duplicate a product like IPs does. The requirement of a new product could, in that regard, be viewed a compromise to protect the essence of IPs.[1302] On the other hand, the general economic equivalence of physical assets[1303] and IPs might suggest that the requirement of a new product is required for the physical asset as well.[1304] If consumers are able to obtain a new product, then they obviously benefit in the same way. It can be argued that investments in IPs are inherently costly, and not always successful;[1305] thus, mandating a requirement of a new product. Nevertheless, that also goes for physical assets. Creating an infrastructure is not inexpensive. In addition, while this requirement is not explicitly referred to in case law it should be noticed that when access to a physical asset has been requested, the requesting party has generally sought to bring a new product to the market.[1306] As a result, the requirement of a new product is fitting for physical assets as well.

While the requirement has been incorporated in case law, it is subject to criticism.[1307] This concerns what a "new product" entails; especially following *Microsoft*. For instance, the requirement has been held as "not only problematic to apply [...], but also leads to undesirable consequences"[1308] and without "solid economic foundation."[1309] In *Microsoft*, the GC found that the requirement is not precluded from a new product but also includes the event "where there is a limitation not only of production or markets but also of technical development."[1310] The GC noted at the same time that this related to the meaning of "causing prejudice to consumers within the meaning of Article 82(b) EC"[1311] and that competitors did not seek "reproducing [the downstream product]."[1312] That interpretation of a "new product" has been

---

1302. *See* Padilla & O'Donoghue (2013), at 563.
1303. *See id.* at 55–7; Rousseva (2010), at 128–9.
1304. *See* Padilla & O'Donoghue (2013), at 563.
1305. The literature shows that investments include many failures, *see* e.g., Grabowski, Henry, *Patents, Innovation and Access to New Pharmaceuticals*, 5 Journal of International Economic Law (2002) 849.(Who shows that approx. 1 out of 435 drugs that are considered are ever marketed).
1306. *See* e.g., Commission Decision of 21 December 1993 in Case IV/34.689, *Sea Containers v. Stena Sealink – Interim measures*. (The requesting party wished to offer a new high speed ferry service which the dominant firm did not offer at the time). But contrast e.g., Case AT.39523, *Slovak Telekom*; Case COMP/39.525, *Telekomunikacja Polska*. (The requesting parties generally limited themselves to offer the same service. The cases differ, however, substantially from the first due to the former monopolies. It should also be noticed that it was still possible to differentiate the services – e.g., connection speed). *See* section 4.3.2.3.
1307. *See* for that effect e.g., Rousseva (2010), at 122–8.
1308. *See* Geradin, Damien, *Limiting the Scope of Article 82 EC: What Can the EU Learn from the U.S. Supreme Court's Judgment in Trinko in the Wake of Microsoft, IMS, and Deutsche Telekom?*, 41 Common Market Law Review (2004) 1519, at 1538.
1309. *See* Ridyard, Derek, *Compulsory Access Under EC Competition Law - A New Doctrine of "Convenient Facilities" and the Case for Price Regulation*, 25 European Competition Law Review (2004) 669, at 670.
1310. *See* Case T-201/04, *Microsoft*, at 647.
1311. *See id.*
1312. *See id.* at 658 & 665.

criticized,[1313] but it is difficult to criticize the GC for relying on the wording of Article 102 TFEU.[1314] This is reinforced by the fact, as pointed out above, that competitors sought to develop new products.

Therefore, the criticism seems to be a discussion of the exact degree of novelty required. Instead, assessing a "new product", including technical developments, ought to be qualitatively in the sense that the competing product is clearly not duplicating the dominant firm's product.[1315] This means that improvements will not satisfy the criterion. Instead, the product should, in economic terms, satisfy potential demand by meeting the needs of consumers in a way that existing product does not. One method to test for such qualities would be whether the new product increases demand;[1316] i.e., whether demand with the new product are larger than without it. The strength of this test is that it directly shows if the new product merely seeks to replace the existing product (i.e., steals market shares rather than expanding the market).

3.3.3.3 A Note on Refusal in the Settings of Regulation

In two recent decisions by the Commission – *Slovak Telekom* and *Telekomunikacja Polska* – the criterion of a "new product" was not included in the assessment.[1317] Albeit it concerned constructive refusal (including margin squeeze in *Slovak Telekom*) and not outright refusal the cause is to be found in the background for the enforcement actions brought against them. Both firms had a dominant position originating in a former legal monopoly that had led to regulation; i.e., a duty to provide access to their upstream input. As noted in section 3.4.2.2, this had an effect on the requirement of proving an indispensable upstream input as a duty to deal had already been imposed. That a duty deal has already been imposed [through regulation] is also the reason why a "new product" was not required in these cases. The point of requiring a new product was that consumers benefit in that event, and hence, a duty to deal would be justified. If there are no need to justify a duty to deal, since that has also already been imposed on the dominant firm, it is not relevant to demonstrate a new product for the same reasons it is not necessary to demonstrate an indispensable product. As a result, if refusal to deal (typically in the form of constructive refusal or margin squeeze) is treated in the settings of regulation (i.e., a duty is already imposed) the criteria of an "indispensable input" and a "new product" are unnecessary.[1318]

1313. *See* Ahlborn & Evans (2009); Andreangeli, Arianna, *Case T-201/04, Microsoft v. Commission, Judgment of the Grand Chamber of the Court of First Instance of 17 September 2007*, 45 Common Market Law Review (2008) 863.
1314. *See* Padilla & O'Donoghue (2013), at 556.
1315. *See* Vesterdorf, Bo, *Article 82 EC: Where Do We Stand after the Microsoft Judgement?*, Global Antitrust Review (2008).
1316. *See* Chapter 2, section 3.3. *See* also Padilla & O'Donoghue (2013), at 560–1.
1317. *See* e.g., Case AT.39523, *Slovak Telekom*; Case COMP/39.525, *Telekomunikacja Polska*. (The requesting parties generally limited themselves to offer the same service).
1318. It then becomes a matter of whether that duty to deal has been breached due to constructive refusal or margin squeeze which further explains why such conduct can constitute by object restrictions, *see* in more detail Chapter 4.

3.3.4   Summarizing

In the preceding subsections, the foreclosure and anti-competitive element, respectively, have been analysed for the purpose of providing a framework for the assessment of unlawful refusal to deal under the effect-based approach. These findings are also in line with case law. The framework differs to a great extent from the previously discussed types of abuse, though. As noted above, a dominant firm will likely gain power over price by refusing to supply an indispensable input as the increase in costs are significant, and competitors ability to compete effectively are hampered. Despite these facts, an additional condition is required; i.e., the emergence of a new product.

PART IV Conclusions and Discussions

CHAPTER 8

Final Remarks

1 OVERVIEW

The aim of this book has been to shed light on the effect-based approach by answering the research question, which is:

> [...] this book seeks to analyse and discuss exclusionary abuse within the meaning of Article 102 subsequent *Post Danmark I* and other recent case law. The aim of the book is two folded as it seeks to analyse (i) when the effect-based approach applies to exclusionary conduct and (ii) how anti-competitive foreclosure effects contrary to Article 102 TFEU can be demonstrated according to the effect-based approach.[1319]

In that light, it has been examined when exclusionary conduct within Article 102 TFEU is subject to an assessment following the effect-based approach and, in the event where such assessment is applied, how anti-competitive foreclosure effects can be demonstrated. To reach that aim, the book has included a multidimensional approach; i.e., it has combined methods (and theories) from both the legal and economic framework. Nonetheless, the legal framework has constituted the main methodology, since the problem statement is set in the settings of Article 102 TFEU. This has been done to ensure that the provided answers are in agreement with the legal principles and concepts of that provision. Since the primary aim of the research question has been to provide clarifications on how dominant firms can and cannot behave according to these legal principles and concepts, rather than just how Article 102 TFEU ought to be framed in general, the legal framework is important. Nonetheless, it has also been necessary to "fill in the blanks", which is especially true for the inquiry of how to apply the effect-based approach. Accordingly, the book included analyses made *de lege lata* to support the suggestions made *de sententia ferenda*.[1320]

1319. *See* Chapter 1, section 2.
1320. One could also refer to it as a positive analysis rather than a normative analysis.

Different commentators have provided proposals on how exclusionary conduct can and should be handled.[1321] This book may be interpreted along the same lines. Commentators have questioned whether anti-competitive foreclosure effects are required under Article 102 TFEU.[1322] It proposes that the assessment must rely on anti-competitive foreclosure effects being demonstrated. This finding is tied to the conclusion that such effects can be demonstrated either due to the object of alleged conduct or due to its effect. The consequence of the former is that the anti-competitive foreclosure effect is more or less presumed since a potential effect suffices. In contrast, an actual or likely effect must be demonstrated for the latter. In that respect, the assessment of exclusionary conduct's effects must respect the difference between Predation and Exclusion. Regarding Predation, the issue is a low price which competitors are unable to compete with. In contrast, the issue of Exclusion is that of raising competitors' costs by preventing them access to suppliers or customers. In effect, this means that effects detriment of consumers' interest can occur in two different ways.

2 MAIN CONCLUSIONS

Based on the analyses and discussions throughout the book, different conclusions have been reached in respect of the effect-based approach's role subsequent *Post Danmark I*. Before the two research questions could be answered, the framework of Article 102 TFEU had to be analysed, though. This included, first, the purpose of Article 102 TFEU, and second, what is understood by an anti-competitive foreclosure effect. That inquiry was important for the two research questions, as they are based on these two aspects (i.e., they are important for the legal framework). For example, answering the research question of how anti-competitive foreclosure effects can be demonstrated will depend on the purpose of the provision (i.e., what is sought protected), and how such effects are defined.

It was concluded that the purpose of Article 102 TFEU is that of protecting effective competition. By protecting effective competition, consumers' interest is safeguarded. This does not purely refer to safeguarding consumers from higher prices, but also other ways that exclusionary conduct can be to the detriment of consumers. This includes a lower level of innovation, reduced quality or less variety. The last part also refers to consumer choice; an aspect that has been important in recent case law in regards to showing that consumers can suffer negative effects besides a higher price. Due to this purpose, the anti-competitive foreclosure effect refers to effective competition.

One of the reasons why uncertainties surround exclusionary conduct is that there a debate of whether anti-competitive foreclosure effects are a novelty within the assessment of exclusionary abuse. While considerations [by the EU Courts] to these

---

1321. *See*, among others, Rousseva (2010). (Who proposes, among other things, that all types of vertical conduct are assessed under Article 101 TFEU); Crane & Miralles (2011). (Who proposes one unified test for all types of exclusionary conduct involving a requirement of substantial foreclosure).
1322. *See*, among others, Gormsen (2013).

effects may seem limited, it was concluded that such effects have always been required to establish exclusionary abuse. This goes all the way back to the first Article 102 TFEU case, namely *Continental Can*. In addition, the requirement of an anti-competitive effect in *TeliaSonera* was based on the definition of abuse established in *Hoffman La Roche* – a definition that has been recurring in case law since that judgment. Therefore, a requirement of anti-competitive foreclosure represents no novelty within the provision. The term is new, though.

Based on this, the book was able to define anti-competitive foreclosure effects. This involved the foreclosure and the anti-competitive element, respectively, as screening tools. The first screens whether conduct is exclusionary conduct (or e.g., excessive conduct) and the second whether that foreclosure is harmful to effective competition. In addition, it is not required to show an actual anti-competitive foreclosure effect, since a likely or potential effect is sufficient. If a likely effect can be demonstrated, it would be pointless to require proof of actual effects, as competition might suffer irreversible injuries if the Commission should wait for the actual effect. In that context, historical evidence may assist either if it can confirm that the likely effect did, in fact, occur, or if there was no effect. Two points must be noticed, though. First, anti-competitive foreclosure effects do not only cover the event where the dominant firm gains market power, but also where it preserves it or slows a decline in that market power. Accordingly, a decline in market shares, for instance, cannot disprove an anti-competitive foreclosure effect. Second, if a dominant firm applies exclusionary conduct with the purpose of foreclosing effective competition, the fact that the desired result is not ultimately achieved does not alter its categorization as abuse. Furthermore, a De Minimis threshold for the purposes of determining whether there is an abuse of a dominant position is not justified within Article 102 TFEU. As the provision only applies to dominant firms, a threshold is already applied. On the other hand, it may be relevant whether the effect is appreciable. When alleged conduct affects the market in which the dominant firm holds its dominant position the effect is, by its very nature, liable to be appreciable. However, if it affects a distinct market, in which that firm is not dominant, then the effect must be appreciable.

2.1   Research Question No. 1

The first research question asked:

When is exclusionary conduct subject to the effect-based approach?

The analysis in this part had its focus on the approach that can be taken to the assessment of Article 102 TFEU. This resulted in an analysis of the form-based and effect-based approaches in terms of what extent they apply to the assessment of exclusionary conduct. In that respect, it was first concluded that the form-based approach represents an approach where anti-competitive foreclosure effects are tied to the nature of that particular exclusionary conduct. In contrast, the effect-based approach represents an approach where anti-competitive foreclosure effects are tied to the outcomes of that conduct. These two approaches were termed as by object restrictions and by effect restrictions, respectively.

Next step was when the effect-based approach is required. The book has answered this question by analysing when exclusionary conduct is *not* subject to the effect-based approach; i.e., by elimination. In effect, this part has analysed whether different types of exclusionary conduct can constitute a by object restriction. Such restrictions involve a prima facia abuse (not per se abuse) meaning that that particular exclusionary conduct is abusive if the dominant firm cannot justify it. It was concluded that by object restrictions are present within case law. In particular, exclusivity agreements and rebates, loyalty-inducing rebates, predatory pricing, and margin squeeze are all examples of exclusionary conduct that may constitute a by object restriction. For example, exclusionary conduct that is caught by the famous *Akzo*-test constitutes a by object restriction. This led to the conclusion that the assessment of exclusionary abuse under Article 102 TFEU cannot only rely on by effect restrictions but also on by object restrictions.

This part further analysed and discussed how by object restrictions can be defined. This led to a definition involving two conditions. First, exclusionary conduct must show a capability to restrict competition. This may occur if exclusionary conduct restricts consumers' freedom to choose supplies or if it bars competitors from access to the market. Second, exclusionary conduct must reveal a sufficient degree of harm. This involves whether there are relevant circumstances that either confirms or disconfirms this general capability; i.e., whether it restricts competition in the case at hand. For example, a price below AAC is generally capable of restricting competition, but if the market is characterized as a two-sided market, then that market may necessitate a price below costs (even that the product is given away for free). In that event, a sufficient degree of harm is not present.

2.2 Research Question No. 2

The second research question asked:

How are anti-competitive foreclosure effects demonstrated under the effect-based approach?

The analysis in this part had its focus on how the effect-based approach is applied when it is required. This entailed an analysis of whether one theory of harm fits all types of exclusionary conduct. It was concluded that this is not the case since anti-competitive foreclosure effects can occur, generally, in one of two ways; i.e., either by means of Predation and Exclusion. The former harms effective competition through a low pricing-period, while the later harms effective competition by raising its competitors' costs.

As a result, exclusionary conduct can fall within either of these categories. While it depends on the specific case, conclusions were made on how to classify different types of exclusionary conduct into these categories. This meant that exclusionary conduct such as conditional rebates and margin squeeze could fall into both categories depending on the specific case. A rebate may be assessed as a form of predatory pricing, exclusivity agreement or tying/bundling. It was concluded that exclusivity rebates and loyalty-inducing rebates fall within Exclusion due to, in particular, the fact that they do not represent a true rebate (but rather a penalty for disloyal customers). In contrast, predatory rebates fall within Predation.

Concerning the assessment of exclusionary conduct within Predation, that assessment will rely on the AEC-test. This involves a comparison of relevant prices and costs with the purpose of examining whether a competitor as efficient as the dominant firm can compete effectively with the dominant firm. Or, in other words, whether the dominant firm can compete with its own prices. Due to the conclusions reached above (research question no. 1), the relevant cost benchmark is LRAIC. Prices below AAC constitute a by object restrictions. However, since such pricing is not abnormal behaviour even by dominant firms, it was concluded that a theory of Predation is required. This involves an explanation for why the "as efficient competitor" cannot compete with these prices; for instance, due to the competitor's relationship with its investor(s) being hampered (unable to earn enough to pay back its investor in the time-period). If a low-pricing period coupled with a theory of Predation is established the foreclosure element is demonstrated. The anti-competitive element is demonstrated by showing a reasonable prospect of recoupment. Without such a prospect, effective competition is not harmed. This conclusion has support in case law. While recoupment has been rejected as an absolute requirement, it is the rationale behind the *Akzo*-test. However, this does not result in lawful conduct if recoupment turns out to be unsuccessful. The point is whether the dominant firm had a prospect of recoupment because of its exclusionary conduct. A dominant firm should not benefit from, for instance, miscalculations or wrong market forecasts. In addition, effects to the detriment of consumers' interest can also incur by reducing the choices available or the quality of the products available.

Concerning the assessment of exclusionary conduct within Exclusion, that assessment will rely on an examination of whether competitors' costs are raised due to that conduct, and whether this enables the dominant firm to gain power over price. While the types of conduct within this category (e.g., exclusivity agreements, tying/ bundling and refusal to deal/supply) are generally exclusionary, they do not necessarily produce a foreclosure effect. For instance, an exclusivity agreement will prevent competitors from accessing that customer's demand (or that suppliers' supply), but competitors are not necessarily affected by it. Therefore, an increase in costs is a prerequisite for a foreclosure effect. Cost may be raised by, among other things, preventing competitors getting access to a low-cost input or obtaining economies of scale. This provides an explanation for why competitors are foreclosed. That foreclosure is then anti-competitive if the dominant firm gains power over price. This means that the dominant firm is able to raise the price (alternatively prevent a decline in price) because of the increase in its competitors' costs. As a result, the increase in costs must be significant enough to have an impact on competitors. More importantly, it must remove their ability and incentive to compete effectively with the dominant firm.

3   GUIDELINES FOR FUTURE ASSESSMENTS

Based on these conclusions, guidelines can be provided for future assessments of exclusionary within Article 102 TFEU. It must be stressed that these are subject to some degree of uncertainty, as it remains to be seen how the Commission and the EU Courts will tackle exclusionary abuse subsequent recent case law; for instance, how the ECJ will rule in *Intel*. Nonetheless, since the findings have their basis in Article 102 TFEU and its case law, they should accord with that case law.

The first aspect is by object restrictions. When exclusionary conduct by dominant firms is assessed, it will be relevant to assess whether that conduct restricts effective competition by object before it is assessed whether it has such an effect. Based on the findings within this book, examples of exclusionary conduct, which may be categorized as a by object restriction, can be given (see Table 8.1). Having a list of exclusionary conduct that restricts competition by object has different advantages (but also disadvantages – see Chapter 4). This may limit the required resources that would otherwise have been needed for assessing the actual or likely effect. Additionally, dominant firms experience legal certainty as they know that certain types of conduct, will generally, be regarded as abuse given they cannot justify it.

Table 8.1   Examples of by Object Restrictions

Type of Conduct	
Predatory Pricing	*– Prices below average variable costs – Price between average variable and total costs with a predatory intent*
Exclusivity agreements/rebates	*– Obliging a customer to purchase all or most its demand from the dominant firm*
Loyalty-inducing rebates	*– Rebates that have a similar effect of that of an exclusivity rebates*
Margin Squeeze	*– A margin below LRAIC for an indispensable upstream input*

Note: These types of exclusionary conduct are merely examples and do not always classify a by object restriction. Neither is this an exhaustive list.

The types of exclusionary conduct listed above are not an exhaustive list but merely examples. Other types of conduct can also constitute by object restrictions if the assessment shows that that conduct restricts competition by object. That assessment will rely on two conditions that must be met. First, that conduct must be capable of restricting competition (not just competitors). Second, it must reveal a sufficient degree of harm. If these conditions are fulfilled, then proof of an actual or likely anti-competitive foreclosure effect is not needed. In that regard, it must be stressed that the types of exclusionary conduct listed above are not necessarily always a by object restriction. They may not reveal sufficient degree of harm. For example, competition may be for the customer meaning exclusivity is inherent in the market. Then the dominant firm is competing on the merits.

The second aspect is the effect-based approach and how anti-competitive effects can be demonstrated under this approach. For example, the findings of the book could have been applied in *Post Danmark I*. While the ECJ concluded that an anti-competitive foreclosure was needed if abuse was to be established, it was not specified how such an effect could be demonstrated. An answer to this issue has been provided in the book. Since the type of conduct within that case was classified as [selective] low pricing conduct (that did not qualify as by object restriction), demonstrating a reasonable prospect of recoupment would have been required.

The findings within this book further provide guidelines for the assessment of rebates that have initiated a wide-ranging discussion over the last decades with especially cases like *British Airways*, *Tomra*, *Intel* and *Post Danmark II*. One of the aspects of this discussion has been the relevance of the AEC-test. This test has been advocated as the tool to assess whether a rebate is unlawful. Not only did the book conclude that rebates may fall within either Predation or Exclusion depending on the specific case, but also provided guidelines for when Predation or Exclusion is the better fit for a rebate. In short, when a rebate constitutes a true rebate, then Predation is the relevant framework, while it is Exclusion when the rebate constitutes a penalty. In the latter event, the issue is not a low price that competitors are unable to compete with [thereby allowing the dominant firm to recoup its loss], but rather whether the rebate ties up customers thereby raising competitors' cost in a way that allows the dominant firm to gain power over price. In other words, the issue may be the same as the one relating to exclusivity agreements or tying rather than predatory pricing.

The guidelines are not limited to only rebates. The findings provide guidelines for all types of exclusionary conduct by dominant firms. This involves an assessment of whether that particular conduct falls within Predation or Exclusion, and how the foreclosure and anti-competitive element can be demonstrated. Regarding the latter, Table 8.2 provides a quick overview of the requirements for demonstrating an anti-competitive foreclosure effect. While the book has only gone in details with some of the possible types of exclusionary conduct, which a dominant firm can apply, the two theories of harm can be applied to other types. For example, misleading representations to patent offices, the issue in *AstraZeneca*[1323], could be assessed according to Exclusion. This type of conduct prevented competitors from entering the market; hence [indirectly] raising their costs enabling AstraZeneca to gain power over price. In effect, AstraZeneca sought to protect its dominant position. It should be noted that this type of conduct is not necessarily reserved to the effect-based approach. It could just as well be assessed as a by object restriction. It would not be difficult to frame an argument that

---

1323. *See* Commission Decision of 15 June 2005 in Case Case COMP/A. 37.507/F3, *AstraZeneca*. Upheld in Judgment of 1 July 2010 in Case T-321/05, *AstraZeneca AB v. European Commission* (*"AstraZeneca"*); Judgment of 6 December 2012 in Case C-457/10 P, *AstraZeneca AB v. European Commission* (*"AstraZeneca"*).

misleading representations to patent offices are generally capable of restricting competition. Whether it reveals a sufficient degree of harm will depend on the specific case.[1324]

Table 8.2   Conditions for an Anti-competitive Foreclosure Effect

	Foreclosure	Anti-competitive
Predation	Low pricing period & a Theory of Predation	Reasonable prospect of recoupment
Exclusion	Competitors' costs are raised	'Power over price' is achieved

In consequence, this book has not only provided answers to questions that are of theoretical importance but also of practical importance. Owing to the fact that this book is grounded in an industrial PhD project, it has been important that the answers provide guidance for future cases (and compliance). While there are still questions within Article 102 TFEU which need to be analysed (e.g., how to demonstrate justifications and efficiency defence) and the assessment of the anti-competitive effect will depend on the specific circumstances of the case, guidelines have been provided. Since these guidelines improve the understanding of exclusionary abuse within Article 102 TFEU, they have also provided greater legal certainty for dominant firms (and their competitors).

4   IMPLICATIONS

According to the findings, a full shift from a formalistic approach to an effect-based approach has and will not happen. Instead, some types of exclusionary conduct can constitute a by object restriction depending on the specific case. In these cases, an effect-based approach will not be required. This conclusion is based on the faith that the EU Courts will not deviate from preceding case law – which cases such as *Post Danmark II*, *Intel* and *Téléfonica* hint at. This has the implication that the effect-based approach cannot be imposed on case law (only when it is applicable) and that such debate will be incapable of producing any result. Time (i.e., academic debate) ought, therefore, to be spent on how case law is optimized within that setting. While examples of by object restrictions have been outlined, including a definition, these are subject to further research and elaboration.

This also has an impact on the value of the *Article 102 Guidance Paper*. For example, the *Article 102 Guidance Paper* indicates that prices below AAC only prove the foreclosure element, while such prices constitute by object restrictions according to case law. If case law continues to take precedence over the *Article 102 Guidance Paper*

1324.   It seems as though it did reveal a sufficient degree of harm as the ECJ held that AstraZeneca's "misleading representations actually enabled it to obtain SPCs either to which it was not entitled, as was the case in Germany, in Finland and in Norway, or to which it was entitled only for a shorter period, as was the case in Belgium, in Luxembourg, in the Netherlands and in Austria", *see* Case C-457/10 P, *AstraZeneca*, at 107.

(i.e., the EU Courts do not deviate from that case law), the relevance of the *Article 102 Guidance Paper* is reduced. In consequence, the findings within this book have the consequence that different viewpoints in the *Article 102 Guidance Paper* do not hold. This includes, among others things, the point of view that the AEC-test is the applicable tool for assessing conditional rebates (it is only one option), that prices below AAC does not entail a potential anti-competitive effect, and that exclusivity agreements are subject to the effect-based approach (both constitute by object restrictions). That said, the *Article 102 Guidance Paper* still provides guidance where it is in agreement with case law.

It is worth repeating that this book has not articulated a complete framework for the assessment of abuse dominance within Article 102 TFEU. Instead, the focus has been on how exclusionary conduct can produce anti-competitive foreclosure effects. As a result, justifications and efficiency defences have not been addressed. Acknowledging the possibility of justifying anti-competitive conduct is important as it is generally acknowledged that anti-competitive conduct, even by dominant firms, can benefit consumers due to lower costs or the like. Should the Commission (or a national competition agency) succeed in demonstrating an anti-competitive effect from a dominant firm's conduct, it is open for that firm to provide justification for its conduct. For that purpose, that firm may demonstrate either that its conduct is objectively necessary, or that the exclusionary effect produced may be counterbalanced, outweighed even, by advantages in terms of efficiency that also benefit consumers. Considering that by object restrictions exist within Article 102 TFEU, how to justify anti-competitive exclusionary conduct is important. Accordingly, it will be relevant for future research to address this aspect.

Additionally, the focus was not on the dominant position, but it was rather assumed that such a position was present. This aspect is highly important, though. Without a dominant position, Article 102 TFEU does not apply. Additionally, the assessment of dominant positions raises different questions relating to anti-competitive foreclosure effects. For example, conduct by dominant firms, compared to non-dominant firms, are generally viewed as more likely to cause harm to consumers (e.g., exclusivity agreements only assessed under Article 101 TFEU), since competition is already hampered. Accordingly, it is relevant for future research to examine whether that is true when a dominant position is established under the current method.

Besides these two aspects, which were not covered by the book, different questions still surround exclusionary abuse within the meaning of Article 102 TFEU. Therefore, the book has not unravelled all the uncertainties relating to exclusionary abuse. A few are worth mentioning. The concept of consumer choice as a way in which consumers' interest is harmed is open for future research; for example, if it can trump the lack of reasonable prospect of recoupment and how that assessment is done. In the same sense, the concept of a conditional rebate constituting a penalty rather than a true rebate is open for further elaboration and research. Accordingly, the findings also set up possibilities for future research.

Bibliography

Abbott, Alden & Wright, Joshua, *Antitrust Analysis of Tying Arrangements and Exclusive Dealing, in* Antitrust Law and Economics (Keith N. Hylton ed.), 2010.

Ahlborn, Christian & Evans, David, *The Microsoft Judgment and Its Implications for Competition Policy towards Dominant Firms in Europe*, 75 Antitrust Law Journal (2009).

Ahlborn, Christian, et al., *The Antitrust Economics of Tying: A Farewell to per Se Illegality*, 49 The Antitrust Bulletin (2004) 287.

Ahlborn, Christian & Padilla, Jorge, *From Fairness to Welfare: Implications for the Assessment of Unilateral Conduct under EC Competition Law, in* European Competition Law Annual 2007 (Claus-Dieter Ehlermann & Mel Marquis eds.), 2008.

Akman, Pinar, *The Concept of Abuse in EU Competition Law: Law and Economic Approaches*, 2012.

Akman, Pinar, *The Reform of the Application of Article 102 TFEU: Mission Accomplished?*, Forthcomming Antitrust Law Journal (2016).

Albaek, Svend & Claici, Adina, *The Velux Case – An In-Depth Look at Rebates and More*, 2 Competition Policy Newsletter (2009) 44.

Albors-Llorens, Albertina, *The European Court of Justice, More Than a Teleological Court, in* Cambridge Yearbook of European Legal Studies, Vol 2 (Alan Dashwood & Angela Ward eds.), 1999.

Albæk, Svend, *Consumer Welfare in EU Competition Policy, in* Aims and Values in Competition law (Caroline Heide-Jørgensen, et al. eds.), 2013.

Allan, Bill, *Rule-Making in the Context of Article 102 TFEU*, 13 Competition Law Journal (2014).

Anchustegui, Ignacio Herrera, *Competition Law through an Ordoliberal Lens*, 2 Oslo Law Review (2015) 139.

Andreangeli, Arianna, *Case T-201/04, Microsoft v. Commission, Judgment of the Grand Chamber of the Court of First Instance of 17 September 2007*, 45 Common Market Law Review (2008) 863.

Areeda, Phillip & Hovenkamp, Herbert, *Antitrust Law: An Analysis of Antitrust Principles and Their Application*, 2015.

Areeda, Phillip & Turner, Donald, *Predatory Pricing and Related Practices under Section 2 of the Sherman Act*, 88 Harvard Law Review (1975) 697.

241

Arezzo, Emanuela, *Is there a Role for Market Definition and Dominance in an effects-based Approach?*, in Abuse of Dominant Position: New Interpretation, New Enforcement Mechanisms? (Mark-Oliver Mackenrodt, et al. eds.), 2008.

Arnull, Anthony, *The European Union and its Court of Justice*, 2006.

Averitt, Neil & Lande, Robert, *Using the "Consumer Choice" Approach to Antitrust Law*, in Choice – A New Standard for Competition Law Analysis? (Paul Nihoul, et al. eds.), 2016.

Bailey, David, *Restrictions of Competition By Object under Article 101 TFEU*, 49 Common Market Law Review (2012) 559.

Bain, Joe, *Barriers to New Competition: Their Character and Consequences in Manufacturing Industries*, 1956.

Baker, Jonathan, *Predatory Pricing After Brooke Group: An Economic Perspective*, 62 Antitrust Law Journal (1994) 585.

Barazza, Stefano, *Post Danmark: The CJEU Calls for an Effect-Based Assessment of Pricing Policies*, Journal of European Competition Law & Practice (2012).

Barnett, Randy, *Foreword: Post-Chicago Law and Economics*, in Symposium on Post-Chicago Law and Economics (Randy E. Barnett & Jules L. Coleman eds.), 1989.

Bartel, Ann & Thomas, Lacy Glenn, *Predation Through Regulation: The Wage and Profit Effects of the Occupational Safety and Health Administration and the Environmental Protection Agency*, 30 Journal of Law and Economics (1987) 239.

Batchelor, Bill & Jebelli, Kayvan Hazemi, *Rebates in a State of Velux: Filling in the Gaps in the Article 102 TFEU Enforcement Guidelines*, 32 European Competition Law Review (2011) 545.

Baumol, William, *Predation and the Logic of the Average Variable Cost Test*, 39 The Journal of Law & Economics (1996) 49.

Baumol, William, *Principles relevant to predatory pricing*, in The Pros and Cons of Low Prices, in The Pros and Cons of Low Prices (Konkurrensverket ed.), 2003.

Baumol, William, *Quasi-Permanence of Price Reductions: A Policy for Prevention of Predatory Pricing*, 89 The Yale Law Journal (1979) 1.

Baumol, William & Willig, Robert, *Fixed Costs, Sunk Costs, Entry Barriers, and Sustainability of Monopoly*, 96 The Quarterly Journal of Economics (1981) 405.

Bender, Christian, et al., *Effective Competition: Its Importance and Relevance for Network Industries*, 46 "Effective competition" in telecommunications, rail and energy markets (2011) 4.

Bengoetxea, Joxerramon, *The Legal Reasoning of the European Court of Justice: Towards a European Jurisprudence*, 1993.

Bergqvist, Christian, *Final curtain or another around on Post Danmark?*, 34 European Competition Law Review (2013) 287.

Bernheim, Douglas & Heeb, Randal, *A Framework for the Economic Analysis of Exclusionary Conduct*, in The Oxford Handbook of International Antitrust Economics (Roger D. Blair & D. Daniel Sokol eds.), 2015.

Bien, Florian & Krah, Matthias, *The Ruling of the CJEU in Post Danmark: Putting an End to Selective Price Cuts as an Abuse Under TFEU Article 102 and Turning Towards a More Economic Approach*, 33 European Competition Law Review (2012) 482.

242

Bishop, Simon & Walker, Mike, *The Economics of EC Competition Law: Concepts, Application and Measurement*, 2010.

Blanco, Luis Ortiz & Colomo, Pablo Ibáñez, *Evolving Priorities and Rising Standards: Spanish Law on Abuses of Market Power in the Light of the 2008 Guidance Paper on Article 82 EC, in* European Competition Law: The Impact of the Commission's Guidance on Article 102 (Lorenzo Federico Pace ed.), 2011.

Bloom, Paul, et al., *Slotting Allowances and Fees: Schools of Thought and the Views of Practicing Managers*, 64 Journal of Marketing (2000) 92.

Bolton, Patrick, et al., *Predatory Pricing: Response to Critique and Further Elaboration*, 89 Georgetown Law Journal (2001) 2495.

Bolton, Patrick, et al., *Predatory Pricing: Strategic Theory and Legal Policy*, 88 Georgetown Law Journal (2000) 2239.

Bolton, Patrick & Scharfstein, David, *A Theory of Predation Based on Agency Problems in Financial Contracting*, 80 The American Economic Review (1990) 93.

Bork, Robert, *The Antitrust Paradox: A Policy at War With Itself*, 1978.

Brennan, Timothy, *Understanding "Raising Rivals' Costs"*, 33 Antitrust Bulletin (1988) 95.

Brodley, Joseph & Hay, George, *Predatory Pricing: Competing Economic Theories and the Evolution of Legal Standards*, 66 Cornell Law Review (1981) 738.

Buttigieg, Eugène, *Competition Law: Safeguarding the Consumer Internet. A Comparative Analysis of Uk Antitrust Law and EC Competition Law*, 2009.

Calzado, Javier Ruiz & Scordamaglia-Tousis, Andreas, *Groupement des Cartes Bancaires v. Commission: Shedding Light on What is Not a 'by Object' Restriction of Competition*, 6 Journal of European Competition Law & Practice (2015) 495.

Carbajo, José, et al., *A Strategic Motivation for Commodity Bundling*, 38 The Journal of Industrial Economics (1990) 283.

Carlton, Dennis, *A General Analysis of Exclusionary Conduct and Refusal to Deal – Why Aspen and Kodak are Misguided*, 68 Antitrust Law Journal (2001) 659.

Carlton, Dennis, *Should "Price Squeeze" be a Recognised Form of Anticompetitive Conduct?*, 4 Journal of Competition Law and Economics (2008) 271.

Carlton, Dennis & Heyer, Ken, *Appropriate Antitrust Policy Towards Single-Firm Conduct: Extraction vs. Extension*, 22 Antitrust (2008).

Carlton, Dennis & Klamer, Mark, *The Need for Coordination Among Firms, with Special Reference to Network Industries*, 50 The University of Chicago Law Review (1983) 446.

Carlton, Dennis & Perloff, Jeffrey, *Modern Industrial Organization*, 2004.

Carlton, Dennis & Waldman, Michael, *The Strategic Use of Tying to Preserve and Create Market Power in Evolving Industries*, 33 The RAND Journal of Economics (2002) 194–220.

Carstensen, Peter, *Predatory Pricing in the Courts: Reflection on Two Decisions*, 61 Notre Dame Law Review (1986) 928.

Chan, Sunny, *Post Danmark II: Per Se Unlawfulness of Retroactive Rebates Granted by Dominant Undertakings*, 37 European Competition Law Review (2016) 43.

Chen, Yongmin, *Equilibrium Product Bundling*, 70 The Journal of Business (1997) 85.

Clark, John, *Competition as a Dynamic Process*, 1961.

Clark, John, *Toward a Concept of Workable Competition*, 30 The American Economic Review (1940) 241.

Colino, Sandra Marco, *All Eyes on Intel: A Stepping Stone to a Fresh Legal Framework for the Analysis of Rebates Under EU Competition Law*, Forthcomming Concurrences (2017).

Colomo, Pablo Ibáñez, *Appreciability and De Minimis in Article 102 TFEU*, 7 Journal of European Competition Law & Practice (2016) 651.

Colomo, Pablo Ibáñez, *Beyond the 'More Economics-Based Approach': A Legal Perspective on Article 102 TFEU Case Law*, 53 Common Market Law Review (2016) 709.

Colomo, Pablo Ibáñez, *Post Danmark II: The Emergence of a Distinct 'Effects-Based Approach to Article 102 TFEU*, 7 (2016) 113.

Cooter, Robert & Ulen, Thomas, *Law and Economics*, 2011.

Coscellia, Andrea & Edwards, Geoff, *Dominance and Market Power in EU Competition Law, in* Handbook on European Competition Law: Substantive Aspects (Ioannis Lianos & Damien Geradin eds.), 2013.

Crane, Daniel, *Mixed Bundling, Profit Sacrifice, and Consumer Welfare*, 55 Emory Law Journal (2006) 423.

Crane, Daniel, *The Paradox of Predatory Pricing*, 91 Cornell Law Review (2005) 1.

Crane, Daniel & Miralles, Graciela, *Toward a Unified Theory of Exclusionary Vertical Restraints*, 84 Southern California Law Review (2011) 605.

Craswell, Richard & Fratrik, Mark, *Predatory Pricing Theory Applied: The Case of Supermarkets v. Warehouse Stores*, 36 Case Western Reserve Law Review (1985) 1.

Creane, Anthony, *An Informational Externality in A Competitive Market*, 14 International Journal of Industrial Organization (1996) 331.

Davie, Yann, *EU and US Antitrust: Converging Approaches to Monopolies?*, 2014.

Dempsey, Paul Stephen, *Predatory Practices & Monopolization in the Airline Industry: A Case Study of Minneapolis/St. Paul*, 29 Transportation Law Journal (2002) 129.

Depken, Craig & Ford, Jon, *NAFTA as a Means of Raising Rivals' Costs*, 15 Review of Industrial Organization (1999) 103.

Director, Aaron & Levi, Edward, *Law and the Future: Trade Regulation*, 51 Northwestern University Law Review (1956) 281.

Dolmans, Maurits & Graf, Thomas, *Analysis of Tying under Article 82 EC: the European Commission's Microsoft Decision in Perspective*, 27 World Competition (2004) 225.

Easterbrook, Frank, *The Limits of Antitrust*, 63 Texas Law Review (1984) 1.

Easterbrook, Frank, *Predatory Strategies and Counterstrategies*, 48 The University of Chicago Law Review (1981) 263.

Easterbrook, Frank, *Workable Antitrust Policy*, 84 Michigan Law Review (1986) 1696.

Economides, Nicholas, Loyalty/Requirement Rebates and the Antitrust Modernization Commission: What is the Appropriate Liability Standard?, 2009, NET Institute Working Paper No. #09-02 available at http://papers.ssrn.com/sol3/papers.cfm?abstract_id=1370699.

Economides, Nicholas, *Tying, Bundling, and Loyalty/Requirement Rebates, in* Research Handbook on the Economics of Antitrust Law (Einer R. Elhauge ed., 2013.

Edlin, Aaron, *Stopping Above-Cost Predatory Pricing*, 111 The Yale Law Journal (2002) 941.

Edlin, Aaron & Farrell, Joseph, *The American Airlines Case: A Chance to Clarify Predation Policy*, in The Antitrust Revolution: Economics, Competition, and Policy (John E. Kwoka & Lawrence J. White eds.), 2004.

Ehlermann, Claus-Dieter, *The Contribution of EC Competition Policy to the Single Market*, 29 Common Market Law Review (1992) 257.

Eilmansberger, Thomas, *Dominance—The Lost Child? How Effects-Based Rules Could and Should Change Dominance Analysis*, 2 European Competition Journal (2006) 15.

Elhauge, Einer, *Defining Better Monopolization Standards*, 56 Stanford Law Review (2003) 253.

Elhauge, Einer, *How Loyalty Discounts Can Perversely Discourage Discounting*, 5 Journal of Competition Law and Economics (2009) 189.

Elhauge, Einer, *Tying, Bundled Discounts, and the Death of the Single Monopoly Profit Theory*, 123 Harvard Law Review (2009) 397.

Elhauge, Einer, *Why Above-Cost Price Cuts to Drive out Entrants Are Not Predatory: And the Implications for Defining Costs and Market Power*, 112 The Yale Law Journal (2003) 681.

Elhauge, Einer & Nalebuff, Barry, *The Welfare Effects of Metering Ties*, 2016, Harvard Public Law Working Paper No. 16-20, available at http://papers.ssrn.com/sol3/papers.cfm?abstract_id=2591577.

Evans, David, *The Online Advertising Industry: Economics, Evolution, and Privacy*, 23 The Journal of Economic Perspectives (2009) 37.

Evans, David, et al., *Tying in Platform Software: Reasons for a Rule-of-Reason Standard in European Competition Law*, 25 World Competition (2002) 509.

Evans, David & Salinger, Michael, *Why Do Firms Bundle and Tie? Evidence from Competitive Markets and Implications for Tying Law*, 22 Yale Journal on Regulation (2005) 37.

Farrell, Joseph, *Deconstructing Chicago on Exclusive Dealing*, 50 The Antitrust Bulletin (2005) 465.

Federico, Giulio, *The Antitrust Treatment of Loyalty Discounts in Europe: Towards a more Economic Approach*, 2 Journal of European Competition Law & Practice (2011) 277.

Federico, Giulio, *Tomra v. Commission Communities: Reversing Progress for Rebates?*, 32 European Competition Law Review (2011) 139.

Feldman, Robin, *Defensive Leveraging in Antitrust*, 87 Georgetown Law Journal (1999) 2079.

Fogt, Howard, *US and EU Converging on Dominant-Firm-Abuse Theory*, 2013.

Foros, Øystein, et al., *Slotting Allowances and Manufacturers' Retail Sales Effort*, 76 Southern Economic Journal (2009) 266.

Fox, Eleanor & Sullivan, Lawrence, *Antitrust – Retrospective and Prospective: Where Are We Coming From? Where Are We Going?*, 62 New York University Law Review (1987) 936.

Fudenberg, Drew & Tirole, Jean, *A "Signal-Jamming" Theory of Predation*, 17 The RAND Journal of Economics (1986) 366.

Fumagalli, Chiara & Motta, Massimo, *Exclusive Dealing and Entry, when Buyers Compete*, 96 The American Economic Review (2006) 785.

Fumagalli, Chiara & Motta, Massimo, *On the Use of Price-Cost Tests in Loyalty Discount: Which Implications From Economic Theory*, 2015, CEPR Discussion Paper No. DP10550 available at http://papers.ssrn.com/sol3/papers.cfm?abstract_id = 2596630.

Fumagalli, Chiara & Motta, Massimo, *A Simple Theory of Predation*, 56 The Journal of Law & Economics (2013) 595.

Funk, Michael & Jaag, Christian, The More Economic Approach to Predatory Pricing, 2016, Swiss Economics Working Paper 0057 available at https://www.swiss-economics.ch/docs/Predatory_Pricing_Jaag_v2.pdf.

Gates, Sean, *Antitrust by Analogy: Developing Rules for Loyalty Rebates and Bundled Discounts*, 79 Antitrust Law Journal (2013) 99.

Gaudin, Germain & Mantzari, Despoina, *Margin Squeeze: An Above-Cost Predaotry Pricing Approach*, 12 Journal of Competition Law and Economics (2016) 1.

Geradin, Damien, *Is the Guidance Paper on the Commission's Enforcement Priorities in Applying Article 102 TFEU to Abusive Exclusionary Conduct Useful?*, in Competition Law and the Enforcement of Article 102 (Ioannis Kokkoris ed., 2010.

Geradin, Damien, *Limiting the Scope of Article 82 EC: What Can the EU Learn from the U.S. Supreme Court's Judgment in Trinko in the Wake of Microsoft, IMS, and Deutsche Telekom?*, 41 Common Market Law Review (2004) 1519.

Geradin, Damien, *Loyalty Rebates After Intel: Time for the European Court of Justice to Overrule Hoffman-La Roche*, 11 Journal of Competition Law and Economics (2015) 579.

Geradin, Damien, et al., DG Comp's Discussion Paper on Article 82: Implications of the Proposed Framework and Antitrust Rules for Dynamically Competitive Industries 2006, available at http://papers.ssrn.com/sol3/papers.cfm?abstract_id = 894466.

Geradin, Damien, et al., The Concept of Dominance in EC Competition Law, 2005, Research Paper on the Modernization of Article 82 EC, available at http://papers.ssrn.com/sol3/papers.cfm?abstract_id = 770144.

Geradin, Damien, et al., *EC Competition Law and Economics*, 2012.

Gerber, David, *Constitutionalizing the Economy: German Neo-Liberalism, Competition Law and the "New" Europe*, 42 The American Journal of Comparative Law (1994) 25.

Gerber, David, *Law and Competition in Twentieth Century Europe: Protecting Prometheus*, 2001.

Gormsen, Liza, *Are Anti-Competitive Effects Necessary for an Analysis under Article 102 TFEU?*, 36 World Competition (2013) 223.

Gormsen, Liza, *The Parallels between the Harvard Structural School and Article 82 EC and the Divergences between the Chicago and Post-Chicago Schools and Article 82 EC*, 4 European Competition Journal (2008) 221.

Gormsen, Liza, *Why the European Commission's Enforcement Priorities on Article 82 EC Should Be Withdrawn*, 31 European Competition Law Review (2010) 45.

Goyder, Joanna, *Cet Obscur Objet: Object Restrictions in Vertical Agreements*, 2 Journal of European Competition Law & Practice (2011) 327.

Goyder, Joanna & Albors-Llorens, Albertina, *Goyders's EC Competition Law*, 2009.

Grabowski, Henry, *Patents, Innovation and Access to New Pharmaceuticals*, 5 Journal of International Economic Law (2002) 849.

Granitz, Elizabeth & Klein, Benjamin, *Monopolization by "Raising Rivals' Costs": The Standard Oil Case*, 39 The Journal of Law & Economics (1996) 1.

Graupner, Frances, *The Battle over the Role of the European Competition Policy: Now You See it, Now You Don't*, 6 Competition Law Journal (2007) 89.

Greenlee, Patrick, et al., *An Antitrust Analysis of Bundled Loyalty Discounts*, 26 International Journal of Industrial Organization (2008) 1132.

Hawk, Barry, *Article 82 and Section 2: Abuse and Monopolizing Conduct*, 2008, Fordham Law Legal Studies Research Paper No. 1301690, available at http://papers.ssrn.com/sol3/papers.cfm?abstract_id=1301690.

Hawk, Barry, *System Failure: Vertical Restraints and EC competition law*, 32 Common Market Law Review (1995) 973.

Hay, George & Kelley, Daniel, *An Empirical Survey of Price Fixing Conspiracies*, 17 Journal of Law and Economics (1974) 13.

Hay, George & McMahon, Kathryn, *The Diverging Approach to Price Squeezes in the United States and Europe*, 8 Journal of Competition Law & Economics (2012) 259.

Heide-Jørgensen, Caroline, et al., *Aims and Values in Competition Law*, 2013.

Heimler, Alberto, *Below-Cost Pricing and Loyalty-Inducing Discounts: Are They Restrictive and If So, When?*, 1 CPI Journal (2005).

Heimler, Alberto, *Is a Margin Squeeze an Antitrust or a Regulatory Violation?*, 6 Journal of Competition Law & Economics (2010) 879.

Hemphill, Scott, *The Role of Recoupment in Predatory Pricing Analyses*, 53 Stanford Law Review (2001) 1581.

Hemphill, Scott & Wu, Tim, *Parallel Exclusion*, 122 Yale Law Journal (2013) 1182.

Hilke, John & Nelson, Philip, *Noisy Advertising and the Predation Rule in Antitrust Analysis*, 74 The American Economic Review (1984) 367.

Hillman, Amy, et al., *Corporate Political Activity: A Review and Research Agenda*, 30 Journal of Management (2004) 837.

Holt, Charles & Scheffman, David, *Strategic Business Behavior and Antitrust, in Economics and Antitrust Policy* (Robert Larner & James Meehan Jr. eds.), 1989.

Hovenkamp, Erik & Hovenkamp, Herbert, *Exclusionary Bundled Discounts and the Antitrust Modernization Commission*, 53 Antitrust Bulletin (2008) 517.

Hovenkamp, Erik & Hovenkamp, Herbert, *Tying Arrangements and Antitrust Harm*, 52 Arizona Law Review (2010) 926.

Hovenkamp, Herbert, *Antitrust Policy after Chicago*, 84 Michigan Law Review (1985).

Hovenkamp, Herbert, *Federal Antitrust Policy: The Law of Competition and Its Practice*, 2016.

Hovenkamp, Herbert, *Post-Chicago Antitrust: A Review and Critique*, 2001 Columbia Business Law Review (2001).

Hovenkamp, Herbert & Hovenkamp, Erik, *Complex Bundled Discounts and Antitrust Policy*, 57 Buffalo Law Review (2009) 1227.

Hviid, Morten & Olczak, Matthew, *Raising Rivals' Fixed Costs*, 23 International Journal of the Economics of Business (2016) 19.

Jacobs, Michael, *An Essay on the Normative Foundations of Antitrust Economics*, 74 North Carolina Law Review (1995).

Jacobson, Jonathan, *Another Take on the Relevant Welfare Standard for Antitrust*, The Antitrust Source (2015) 1.

Jacobson, Jonathan, *Exclusive Dealing, "Foreclosure", and Consumer Harm*, 70 Antitrust Law Journal (2002) 311.

Jones, Alison, *Identifying an Unlawful Margin Squeeze: The Recent Judgments of the Court of Justice in Deutsche Telekom and TeliaSonera, in Cambridge Yearbook of European Legal Studies* (Alan Dashwood & Angela Ward eds.), 2010.

Jones, Alison, *The Journey toward an Effects-Based Approach under Article 101 TFEU—The Case of Hardcore Restraints*, 55 The Antitrust Bulletin (2010) 783.

Jones, Alison & Sufrin, Brenda, *EU Competition Law: Text, Cases, and Materials*, 2014.

Joskow, Paul & Klevorick, Alvin, *A Framework for Analyzing Predatory Pricing Policy*, 89 The Yale Law Journal (1979) 213.

Jullien, Bruno, et al., The Economics of Margin Squeeze, 2014, CEPR Discussion Paper No. DP9905 available at http://papers.ssrn.com/sol3/papers.cfm?abstract_id= 2444927.

Kallaugher, John & Sher, Brian, *Rebates Revisited: Anti-Competitive Effects and Exclusionary Abuse Under Article 82*, 21 European Competition Law Review (2004) 263.

Kaplow, Louis, *Extension of Monopoly Power through Leverage*, 85 Columbia Law Review (1985) 515.

Kaplow, Louis & Sharpio, Carl, *Antitrust, in* Handbook of Law and Economics (A. M. Polinsky & Shavell Steven eds.), 2007.

Këllezi, Pranvera, *Rhetoric or Reform: Does the Law of Tying and Bundling Reflect the Economic Theory?, in Article 82 EC: Reflections on its Recent Evolution* (Ariel Ezrachi ed., 2009.

Klein, Benjamin, *Exclusive Dealing as Competition For Distribution "On the Merits"*, 12 George Mason Law Review (2003) 119.

Klein, Benjamin & Lerner, Andres, *Price-Cost Tests in Antitrust Analysis of Single Product Loaylty Contracts*, 80 Antitrust Law Journal (2016) 631.

Klein, Benjamin & Murphy, Kevin, *Exclusive Dealing Intensify Competition for Distribution*, 75 Antitrust Law Journal (2008) 433.

Kobayashi, Bruce, *Does Economics Provide a Reliable Guide to Regulating Commodity Bundling by Firms? A Survey of the Economic Litterature*, 1 Journal of Competition Law and Economics (2005) 707.

Kolstad, Olav, *Object Contra Effect in Swedish and European Competition Law*, 2009, Report on behalf of the Swedish Competition Authority.

Korah, Valentine, *EEC Competition Policy—Legal Form or Economic Efficiency*, 39 Current Legal Problems (1986) 85.

Kovacic, William, *The Intellectual DNA of Modern U.S. Competition Law for Dominant Firm Conduct: The Chicago/Harvard Double Helix*, 2007 Columbia Business Law Review (2007) 1.

Krattenmaker, Thomas & Salop, Steven, *Anticompetitive Exclusion: Raising Rivals' Costs to Achieve Power over Price*, 96 The Yale Law Journal (1986) 209.

Kreps, David & Wilson, Robert, *Reputation and Imperfect Information*, 27 Journal of Economic Theory (1982) 253.

Kuhn, Kai-Uwe, et al., *Economic Theories of Bundling and their Policy Implications in Abuse Cases: An Assessment in Light of the Microsoft Case*, 2004, Working Paper #04-019, available at http://papers.ssrn.com/sol3/papers.cfm?abstract_id = 618589.

Kuksov, Dmitri & Pazgal, Amit, *The Effects of Costs and Competition on Slotting Allowances*, 26 Marketing Science (2007) 259.

Künzler, Adrian, *Economic Content of Competition Law: The Point of Regulating Preferences, in* The Goals of Competition Law (Daniel Zimmer ed., 2012.

Lambert, Thomas, *Evaluating Bundled Discounts*, 89 Minnesota Law Review (2005) 1688.

Lande, Robert, *Consumer Choice as the Ultimate Goal of Antitrust*, 62 University of Pittsburgh Law Review (2001).

Lande, Robert, *The Rise and (Coming) Fall of Efficiency as the Rule of Antitrust*, 33 Antitrust Bulletin (1988) 429.

Lande, Robert & Connor, John, *How High Do Cartels Raise Prices? Implications for Reform of the Antitrust Sentencing Guidelines*, 80 Tulane Law Review (2005) 513.

Lang, John Temple, *Article 82 EC - The Problems and the Solution*, 2009, FEEM Working Paper No. 65, available at SSRN: http://ssrn.com/abstract = 1467747.

Lang, John Temple, *Essential Facilities in The European Union: Bronner and Beyond*, 10 Columbia Journal of European Law (2004) 1.

Lang, John Temple & O'Donoghue, Robert, *Defining Legitimate Competition: How to Clarify Pricing Abuses Under Article 82 EC*, 26 Fordham International Law Journal (2002) 83.

Langer, Jurian, *A Four-step Test to Assess the Exclusionary Effects of Bundling under Article 82 EC*, 2007.

Lerner, Josh, *Patenting in the Shadow of Competitors*, 38 Journal of Law and Economics (1995) 463.

Leslie, Christopher, *Predatory Pricing and Recoupment*, 113 Columbia Law Review (2013) 1695.

Levenstein, Margaret & Suslow, Valerie, *What Determines Cartel Success?*, 44 Journal of Economic Literature (2006) 43.

Lianos, Ioannis, *Some Reflections on the Question of the Goals of EU Competition Law*, 2013, CLES Working Paper Series 3/2013 available at http://dx.doi.org/10.2139/ssrn.2235875.

Loewenthal, Paul-John, *The Defence of "Objective Justification" in the Application of Article 82 EC*, 28 World Competition (2005) 455.

Lundqvist, Björn & Ølykke, Grith Skovgaard, *Post Danmark, now concluded by the Danish Supreme Court: clarification of the selective low pricing abuse and perhaps the embryo of a new test under article 102 TFEU?*, 34 European Competition Law Review (2013) 484.

MacCrisken, Jack & Murphy, Kevin, *Economic Perspectives on Software Design: PC Operating Systems and Platforms*, in Microsoft, Antitrust and the New Economy: Selected Essays (David S. ed., 2002.

Maduro, Miguel Poiares, *Interpreting European Law: Judicial Adjudication in a Context of Constitutional Pluralism*, 1 European Journal of Legal Studies (2007) 137.

Maier-Rigaud, Frank & Schwalbe, Ulrich, *Do Retroactive Rebates Imply Lower Prices for Consumers?*, 2013, LEM 2013-11, available at http://papers.ssrn.com/sol3/papers.cfm?abstract_id = 2276396.

Mandorff, Martin & Sahl, Johan, *The Role of the 'Equally Efficient Competitor' in the Assessment of Abuse of Dominance*, 2013, Konkurrensverket Working Paper Series in Law and Economics, available at http://www.konkurrensverket.se/globalassets/english/publications-and-decisions/the-role-of-the-equally-efficient-competitor-in-the-assessment-of-abuse-of-dominance.pdf.

Mano, Miguel de la & Durand, Benoît, *Three-Step Structured Rule of Reason to Assess Predation under Article 82*, 2005, Office of the Chief Economist Discussion Paper, available at http://ec.europa.eu/dgs/competition/economist/pred_art82.pdf.

Marty, Frederic, *As-Efficient Competitor Test in Exclusionary Pricing Strategies: Does Post-Danmark Really Pave the Way Towards a More Economic Apporach?*, 2014, GREDEG Working Paper, available at http://www.gredeg.cnrs.fr/working-papers/GREDEG-WP-2013-26.pdf.

McGee, John, *Predatory Price Cutting: The Standard Oil (N. J.) Case*, 1 The Journal of Law & Economics (1958) 137.

McGee, John, *Predatory Pricing Revisited*, 23 Journal of Law and Economics (1980) 289.

Meisel, John, *The Law and Economics of Margin Squeezes in the US Versus the EU*, 8 European Competition Journal (2012).

Melamed, Douglas, *Exclusionary Conduct under the Antitrust Laws: Balancing, Sacrifice, and Refusals to Deal*, 20 Berkeley Technology Law Journal (2005) 1247.

Milgrom, Paul & Roberts, John, *New Theories of Predatory Pricing*, in Industrial Structure in the New Industrial Economics (Giacomo Bonanno & Dario Brandolini eds.), 1990.

Miralles, Graciela, *Tomra: Exclusive Dealing and Rebates in the Light (and Shadows) of Dominance*, 2 European Journal of Risk Regulation (2011) 129.

Monti, Giorgio, *Article 82 EC: What Future for the Effects-Based Approach?*, 1 Journal of European Competition Law & Practice (2010) 2.

Monti, Giorgio, *EC Competition Law*, 2007.

Monti, Giorgio, *EU Competition Law from Rome to Lisbon – Social Market Economy*, in Aim and Values in Competition Law (Caroline Heide-Jørgensen, et al. eds.), 2013.

Monti, Mario, *A New Strategy For The Single Market*, 2010, Report to the President of the European Commission José Manuel Barroso.

Moore, Derek & Wright, Joshua, *Conditional Discounts and the Law of Exclusive Dealing*, 22 George Mason Law Review (2015) 1205.

Mosso, Carles, *The More Economic Approach Paradigm: An Effects-based Approach to EU Competition Policy*, in Structure and Effects in EU Competition Law: Studies on Exclusionary Conduct and State Aid (Wolfgang Wurmnest & Jürgen Basedow eds.), 2011.

Motta, Massimo, *Competition Policy: Theory and Practice*, 2004.

Murray, Grant, *In Search of the Obvious: Groupement des cartes bancaires and "by Object" Infringements under EU Competition Law*, 36 European Competition Law Review (2015) 47.

Nalebuff, Barry, *Bundling as an Entry Barrier*, 119 The Quarterly Journal of Economics (2004) 159.

Nalebuff, Barry, *Bundling, Tying, and Portfolio Effects – Part 1: Conceptual Issues*, 2003, DTI Economics Paper, available at.

Nazzini, Renato, *The Foundation of European Union Competition Law*, 2012.

Niels, Gunnar & Jenkins, Helen, *Reform of Article 82 EC: Where the Link Between Dominance and Effects Breaks Down*, 11 European Competition Law Review (2005) 605.

Nihoul, Paul, *The Ruling of the General Court in Intel: Towards the End of an Effect-based Approach in European Competition Law?*, 5 (2014) 521.

Nihoul, Paul, et al., *Choice – A New Standard for Competition Law Analysis?*, 2016.

O'Brien, Daniel & Shaffer, Greg, *On the Dampening-of-Competition Effect of Exclusive Dealing*, 41 The Journal of Industrial Economics (1993) 215.

Orbach, Barak, *The Durability of Formalism in Antitrust*, 100 Iowa Law Review (2015) 2197.

Ordover, Janusz & Saloner, Garth, *Predation, Monopolization, and Antitrust*, in Handbook of Industrial Organization (Richard Schmalensee & Robert Willig eds.), 2000.

Ordover, Janusz & Willig, Robert, *An Economic Definition of Predatory Product Innovation*, 91 The Yale Law Journal (1981) 8.

Oster, Sharon, *The Strategic Use of Regulatory Investements by Industry Sub-Groups*, 20 Economic Inquiry (1982) 604.

Pablo, Alfonso Lamadrid de, *The Double Duality of Two-sided Markets*, 64 Competition Law Journal (2015) 5.

Padilla, Jorge & O'Donoghue, Robert, *Law and Economics of Article 102 TFEU*, 2013.

Peeperkorn, Luc, *Conditional Pricing: Why the General Court is Wrong in Intel and What the Court of Justice Can Do to Rebalance the Assessment of Rebates*, 12 Concurrences (2015) 43.

Petit, Nicolas, *The Advocate General's Opinion in Intel v. Commission: Eight Points of Common Sense for Consideration by the CJEU*, Forthcoming Concurrences (2017).

Petit, Nicolas, *From Formalism to Effects? The Commission's Communication on Enforcement Priorities in Applying Article 82 EC*, 32 World Competition (2009) 485.

Petit, Nicolas, *The Future of the Court of Justice in EU Competition Law*, in The Court of Justice and the Construction of Europe: Analyses and Perspectives on Sixty Years of Case-law (The European Court of Justice ed., 2013.

Petit, Nicolas, *Intel, Leveraging Rebates and the Goals of Article 102 TFEU*, 11 European Competition Journal (2015) 26.

Petit, Nicolas & Neyrinck, Norman, *Back to Microsoft I and II: Tying and the Art of Secret Magic*, 2 Journal of European Competition Law & Practice (2011) 117.

Petrin, Amil, *Quantifying the Benefits of New Products: The Case of the Minivan*, 110 Journal of Political Economy (2002) 705.

Petzold, Daniel, *It Is All Predatory Pricing: Margin Squeeze Abuse and the Concept of Opportunity Costs in EU Competition Law*, 6 Journal of European Competition Law & Practice (2015) 346.

Pitofsky, Robert, *How the Chicago School Overshot the Mark: The Effect of Conservative Economic Analysis on U.S. Antitrust*, 2008.

Plender, Richard, *The Interpretation of Community Acts by Reference to the Intentions of the Authors*, 2 Yearbook of European Law (1982) 57.

Porter, Michael, *The Competitive Advantage: Creating and Sustaining Superior Performance*, 1998.

Posner, Richard, *Antitrust Law*, 2001.

Posner, Richard, *The Chicago School of Antitrust Analysis*, 127 University of Pennsylvania Law Review (1979) 925.

Posner, Richard, *Economic Analysis of Law*, 2007.

Posner, Richard, *Exclusionary Practices and the Antitrust Laws*, 41 The University of Chicago Law Review (1974) 506.

Rasmusen, Eric, et al., *Naked Exclusion*, 81 The American Economic Review (1991) 1137.

Rey, Patrick & Venit, James, *An Effect-Based Approach to Article 102: A Response to Wouter Wils*, 38 World Competition (2015) 3.

Ridyard, Derek, *Compulsory Access Under EC Competition Law – A New Doctrine of "Convenient Facilities" and the Case for Price Regulation*, 25 European Competition Law Review (2004) 669.

Riley, Alan, *The EU Reform Treaty and the Competition Protocol: Undermining EC Competition Law*, 2007, CEPS Policy Brief No. 142, available at http://aei.pitt.edu/7535/.

Ritter, Cyril, *Does the Law of Predatory Pricing and Cross-Subsidisation Need a Radical Rethink?*, 27 World Competition (2004) 613.

Roeller, Lars-Hendrik & Stehmann, Oliver, *The Year 2005 at DG Competition: The Trend towards a More Effects-Based Approach*, 29 Review of Industrial Organization (2006) 281.

Rohlfs, Jeffrey, *A Theory of Interdependent Demand for a Communications Service*, 5 The Bell Journal of Economics and Management Science (1974) 16.

Rompuy, Ben Van, *The Impact of the Lisbon Treaty on EU Competition Law: A Review of Recent Case Law of the EU Courts*, 1 CPI Antitrust Chronicle (2011) 1.

Rousseva, Ekaterina, *Rethinking Exclusionary Abuses in EU Competition Law*, 2010.

Rousseva, Ekaterina & Marquis, Mel, *Hell Freezes Over: A Climate Change for Assessing Exclusionary Conduct under Article 102 TFEU*, 4 Journal of European Competition Law & Practice (2013) 32.

Rubinfeld, Daniel, *3M's Bundled Rebates: An Economic Perspective*, 72 The University of Chicago Law Review (2005) 243.

Rubinfeld, Daniel & Mannes, Robert, *The Strategic Use of Patents: Implications for Antitrust*, 2005.

Rule, Charles, *Statement for the Hearing of the Antitrust Modernization Commission: "Treatment of Efficiencies in Merger Enforcement"*, 2005, available at http://govinfo.library.unt.edu/amc/commission_hearings/pdf/Statement-Rule.pdf.

Rummel, Per, *Rebate Schemes under Article 102 TFEU: Post Danmark II*, 53 Common Market Law Review (2016) 1121.

Salop, Steven, *Exclusionary Conduct, Effect on Consumers, and the Flawed Profit-Sacrifice Standard*, 73 Antitrust Law Journal (2006) 311.

Salop, Steven, *The Raising Rivals' Cost Foreclosure Paradigm, Conditional Pricing Practices and the Flawed Incremental Price-Cost Test*, 2016, Georgetown Law Faculty Publications and Other Works, available at http://scholarship.law.georgetown.edu/facpub/1620.

Salop, Steven & David Scheffman, *Raising Rivals' Costs*, 73 The American Economic Review (1983).

Salop, Steven & Scheffman, David, *Cost-Raising Strategies*, 36 The Journal of Industrial Economics (1987) 19.

Salop, Steven, et al., A Bidding Analysis of Special Interest Regulation: Raising Rivals' Costs in a Rent Seeking Society, 1984, FTC Working Paper No. 114 available at.

Sawyer, Charles, *NAFTA as a Means of Raising Rivals' Costs: A Comment*, 18 Review of Industrial Organization (*2001*) 127.

Scheffman, David, *The Application of Raising Rivals' Costs Theory to Antitrust*, 37 Antitrust Bulletin (1992) 187.

Scheffman, David & Higgins, Richard, *Twenty Years of Raising Rivals' Costs: History, Assessment, and Future*, 12 George Mason Law Review (2003) 371.

Scherer, Frederic, *Predatory Pricing and the Sherman Act: A Comment*, 89 Harvard Law Review (1976) 869.

Scherer, Frederic, *Some Last Words on Predatory Pricing*, 89 Harvard Law Review (1976) 901.

Scherer, Frederic & Ross, David, *Industrial Market Structure and Economic Performance* 1990.

Schmalensee, Richard, *On the Use of Economic Models in Antitrust: The ReaLemon Case*, 127 University of Pennsylvania Law Review (1979) 994.

Schwartz, Barry, *The Paradox of Choice: Why More Is Less*, 2004.

Segal, Ilya & Whinston, Michael, *Naked Exclusion: Comment*, 90 The American Economic Review (2000) 296.

Shaffer, Brian, *Firm-level Responses to Government Regulation: Theoretical and Research Approaches*, 21 Journal of Management (1995) 495.

Shaffer, Greg, *Slotting Allowances and Optimal Product Variety*, 5 Advances in Economic Analysis & Policy (2005) 1.

Shapiro, Carl, *Exclusivity in Network Industries*, 7 George Mason Law Review (1999) 673.

Sinclair, Duncan, *Abuse of Dominance at a Crossroads – Potential Effect, Object and Appreciability under Article 82 EC*, 25 European Competition Law Review (2004) 491.

Sng, Yi Heng Alvin, *The Distinction Between "Object" and "Effects" in EU Competition Law and Concerns after Groupement des Cartes Bancairs (C-67/13 P)*, 37 European Competition Law Review (2016) 179.

Stewart, Charles, *Economic Concentration and the Monopoly Problem*, 80 Monthly Labor Review (pre-1986) (1957).

Stigler, George, *United States v. Loew's Inc.: A Note on Block-Booking*, 1963 The Supreme Court Review (1963) 152.

Szyszczak, Erika, *Controlling Dominance in European Markets*, 33 Fordham International Law Journal (2011) 1738.

Tharp, John, *Raising Eivals' Costs: Of Bottlenecks, Bottled Wine, and Bottled Soda*, 84 Northwestern University Law Review (1989) 321.

Tirole, Jean, *The Theory of Industrial Organization*, 1988.

Tom, Willard, et al., *Anticompetitive Aspects of Market-Share Discounts and Other Incentives to Exclusive Dealing*, 67 Antitrust Law Journal (2000) 615.

Tor, Avishalom, *The Fable of Entry: Bounded Rationality, Market Discipline, and Legal Policy*, 101 Michigan Law Review (2002) 482.

Tvarnø, Christina & Nielsen, Ruth, *Retskilder og retsteorier*, 2014.

Ulmer, Peter, *Schranken zulässigen Wettbewerbs marketbeherrschender Unternehmen*, 1977.

Vanberg, Viktor, *The Freiburg School: Walter Eucken and Ordoliberalism*, 2011, Freiburg Discussion Papers on Constitutional Economics 04/11 available at https://www.econstor.eu/bitstream/10419/4343/1/04_11bw.pdf.

Veljanovski, Cento, *Margin Squeeze: An Overview of EU and National Case Law*, e-Competitions: Competition Laws Bulletin (2012) 1.

Venit, James, *Case T-286/09 Intel v. Commission – The Judgment of the General Court: All Steps Backward and No Steps Forward*, 10 European Competition Journal (2014) 203.

Vesterdorf, Bo, *Article 82 EC: Where Do We Stand after the Microsoft Judgement?*, Global Antitrust Review (2008).

Vickers, John, *Abuse of Market Power*, 115 The Economic Journal (2005) F244.

Viscusi, Kip, et al., *Economics of Regulation and Antitrust*, 2005.

Waelbroeck, Denis, *Michelin II: A per se rule against Rebates by Dominant Companies?*, 1 Journal of Competition Law and Economics (2005).

Wagle, Steven, *Predatory Pricing, A Case Study: Matsushita Electric Industries Co. v. Zenith Radio Corporation*, 22 Creighton Law Review (1988) 89.

Weitbrecht, Andreas, *From Freiburg to Chicago and Beyond – The First 50 Years of European Competition Law*, 29 European Competition Law Review (2008) 81.

Werden, Gregory, *The "No Economic Sense" Test for Exclusionary Conduct*, 31 The Journal of Corporation Law (2006) 293.

Wesseling, Rein, *The Modernisation of EC Antitrust Law*, 2000.

Whinston, Michael, *Tying, Foreclosure, and Exclusion*, 80 The American Economic Review (1990) 837.

Whish, Richard, *Intel v. Commission: Keep Calm and Carry on*, 6 Journal of European Competition Law & Practice (2015) 1.

Whish, Richard, *Regulation 2790/99: The Commission's "New Style" Block Exemption for Vertical Agreements*, 37 Common Market Law Review (2000) 887.

Whish, Richard & Bailey, David, *Competition Law*, 2015.

William, Allan, *The Effects-Based Approach Under Article 102 Tfeu: History And State of Play*, in Ten Years of Effects-Based Approach in EU Competition Law: State of Play and Perspectives (Jacques Bourgeois ed.), 2012.

Williamson, Oliver, *Predatory Pricing: A Strategic and Welfare Analysis*, 87 The Yale Law Journal (1977) 284.

Williamson, Oliver, *Williamson on Predatory Pricing II*, 88 Yale Law Journal (1979) 1183.

Wils, Wouter, *The Judgment of the EU General Court in Intel and the So-Called 'More Economic Approach' to Abuse of Dominance*, 37 World Competition (2014) 405.

Wright, Joshua, *Antitrust Law and Competition for Distribution*, 23 Yale Journal on Regulation (2006) 169.

Wright, Joshua, *Moving beyond Naive Foreclosure Analysis*, 19 George Mason Law Review (2012) 1163.

Wright, Joshua, *Slotting Contracts and Consumer Welfare*, 74 Antitrust Law Journal (2007) 439.

Zenger, Hans, *When Does Exclusive Dealing Intensify Competition for Distribution? Comment on Klein and Murphy*, 77 Antitrust Law Journal (2010) 205.

Østerud, Erik, *Identifying Exclusionary Abuses by Dominant Undertakings under EU Competition Law: the Spectrum of Tests*, 2010.

Speeches

Almunia, Joaquín, *Competition and Consumers: The Future of EU Competition Policy*, speech given on 2010 at European Competition Day, Madrid.

Italianer, Alexander, *The Object of Effects*, speech given on 2014 at CRA Annual Brussels Conference, Brussels.

Kroes, Neelie, *Exclusionary Abuses of Dominance – The European Commission's Enforcement Priorities*, speech given on 2008 at Fordham University Symposium, New York.

Lowe, Philip, *Consumer Welfare and Efficiency – New Guiding Principles of Competition Policy?*, speech given on 2007 at 13th International Conference on Competition and 14th European Competition Day, Munich.

Miert, Karel Van, *The Future of European Competition Policy*, speech given on 1998 at the Ludwig Erhard Foundation in Bonn.

Wright, Joshua, *Simple but Wrong or Complex but More Accurate? The Case for an Exclusive Dealing-Based Approach to Evaluating Loyalty Discounts*, speech given on 2013 at the Bates White 10th Annual Antitrust Conference.

Table of Cases

Judgments of the General Court

259

Opinions by Advocate Generals

Non-EU Case Law

Commission Decisions

Table of Legislation

Index

INTERNATIONAL COMPETITION LAW SERIES

1. Ignacio De Leon, *Latin American Competition Law and Policy: A Policy in Search of Identity*, 2001 (ISBN 90-411-1542-0).
2. Wim Dejonghe & Wouter Van de Voorde (eds), *M & A in Belgium*, 2001 (ISBN 90-411-1594-3).
3. Yang-Ching Chao, Gee San, Changfa Lo & Jiming Ho (eds), *International and Comparative Competition Law and Policies*, 2001 (ISBN 90-411-1643-5).
4. Martin Mendelsohn & Stephen Rose, *Guide to the EC Block Exemption for Vertical Agreements*, 2002 (ISBN 90-411-9813-X).
5. Clifford A. Jones & Mitsuo Matsushita (eds), *Competition Policy in the Global Trading System: Perspectives from the EU, Japan and the USA*, 2002 (ISBN 90-411-1758-X).
6. Christian Koenig, Andreas Bartosch, Jens-Daniel Braun & Marion Romes (eds), *EC Competition and Telecommunications Law*. Second Edition, 2009 (ISBN 978-90-411-2564-4).
7. Jürgen Basedow (ed.), *Limits and Control of Competition with a View to International Harmonization*, 2002 (ISBN 90-411-1967-1).
8. Maureen Brunt, Economic Essays on Australian and New Zealand Competition Law, 2003 (ISBN 90-411-1991-4).
9. Ky P. Ewing, Jr., *Competition Rules for the 21st Century: Principles from America's Experience*, Second Edition, 2006 (ISBN 90-411-2477-2).
10. Joseph Wilson, *Globalization and the Limits of National Merger Control Laws*, 2003 (ISBN 90-411-1996-5).
11. Peter Verloop & Valérie Landes (eds), *Merger Control in Europe: EU, Member States and Accession States*, Fourth Edition, 2003 (ISBN 90-411-2056-4).
12. Themistoklis K. Giannakopoulos, *Safeguarding Companies' Rights in Competition and Anti-dumping/Anti-subsidies Proceedings*, Second Edition, 2011 (ISBN 978-90-411-3404-2).
13. Marjorie Holmes & Lesley Davey (eds), *A Practical Guide to National Competition Rules across Europe*, Second Edition, 2007 (ISBN 978-90- 411-2607-8).
14. Sigrid Stroux, *US and EU Oligopoly Control*, 2004 (ISBN 90-411-2296-6).
15. Tzong-Leh Hwang and Chiyuan Chen (eds), *The Future Development of Competition Framework*, 2004 (ISBN 90-411-2305-9).

16. Phedon Nicolaides, Mihalis Kekelekis and Maria Kleis, *State Aid Policy in the European Community: Principles and Practice,* Second Edition, 2008 (ISBN 978-90-411-2754-9).

17. Doris Hildebrand, *Economic Analyses of Vertical Agreements: A Self- Assessment,* 2005 (ISBN 90-411-2328-8).

18. Frauke Henning-Bodewig, *Unfair Competition Law: European Union and Member States,* 2005 (ISBN 90-411-2329-6).

19. Duarte Brito & Margarida Catalão-Lopes, *Mergers and Acquisitions: The Industrial Organization Perspective,* 2006 (ISBN 90-411-2451-9).

20. Nikos Th. Nikolinakos, *EU Competition Law and Regulation in the Converging Telecommunications, Media and IT Sectors,* 2006 (ISBN 90-411- 2469-1).

21. Mihalis Kekelekis, *The EC Merger Control Regulation: Rights of Defence. A Critical Analysis of DG COMP Practice and Community Courts' Jurisprudence,* 2006 (ISBN 90-411-2553-1).

22. Mark R. Joelson, *An International Antitrust Primer: A Guide to the Operation of United States, European Union and Other Key Competition Laws in the Global Economy,* Third Edition, 2006 (ISBN 90-411-2468-3).

23. Themistoklis K. Giannakopoulos, *A Concise Guide to the EU Anti-dumping/ Anti-subsidies Procedures,* 2006 (ISBN 90-411-2464-0).

24. George Cumming, Brad Spitz & Ruth Janal, *Civil Procedure Used for Enforcement of EC Competition Law by the English, French and German Civil Courts,* 2007 (ISBN 978-90-411-2471-5).

25. Jürgen Basedow (ed.), *Private Enforcement of EC Competition Law,* 2007 (ISBN 978-90-411-2613-9).

26. Jung Wook Cho, *Innovation and Competition in the Digital Network Economy: A Legal and Economic Assessment on Multi-tying Practices and Network Effects,* 2007 (ISBN 978-90-411-2574-3).

27. Akira Inoue, *Japanese Antitrust Law Manual: Law, Cases and Interpretation of the Japanese Antimonopoly Act,* 2007 (ISBN 978-90-411-2627-6).

28. René Barents, *Directory of EC Case Law on Competition,* 2007 (ISBN 978-90-411-2656-6).

29. Paul F. Nemitz (ed.), *The Effective Application of EU State Aid Procedures: The Role of National Law and Practice,* 2007 (ISBN 978-90-411-2657-3).

30. Jurian Langer, *Tying and Bundling as a Leveraging Concern under EC Competition Law,* 2007 (ISBN 978-90-411-2575-0).

31. Abel M. Mateus & Teresa Moreira (eds), *Competition Law and Economics – Advances in Competition Policy and Antitrust Enforcement,* 2007 (ISBN 978-90-411-2632-0).

32. Alberto Santa Maria, *Competition and State Aid: An Analysis of the EC Practice,* 2007 (ISBN 978-90-411-2617-7).

33. Barry J. Rodger (ed.), *Article 234 and Competition Law: An Analysis,* 2007 (ISBN 978-90-411-2605-4).

34. Alla Pozdnakova, *Liner Shipping and EU Competition Law,* 2008 (ISBN 978-90-411-2717-4).

35. Milena Stoyanova, *Competition Problems in Liberalized Telecommunications: Regulatory Solutions to Promote Effective Competition*, 2008 (ISBN 978-90-411-2736-5).

36. *EC State Aid Law/Le Droit des Aides d'Etat dans la CE. Liber Amicorum Francisco Santaolalla Gadea*, 2008 (ISBN 978-90-411-2774-7).

37. René Barents, *Directory of EC Case Law on State Aids*, 2008 (ISBN 978-90-411-2732-7).

38. Ignacio De Leon, *An Institutional Assessment of Antitrust Policy: The Latin American Experience*, 2009 (ISBN 978-90-411-2478-4).

39. Doris Hildebrand, *The Role of Economic Analysis in EU Competition Law: TheEuropean School*, Fourth Edition, 2016 (ISBN 978-90-411-6245-8).

40. Eugène Buttigieg, *Competition Law: Safeguarding the Consumer Interest. A Comparative Analysis of US Antitrust Law and EC Competition Law*, 2009 (ISBN 978-90-411-3119-5).

41. Ioannis Lianos & Ioannis Kokkoris (eds), *The Reform of EC Competition Law: New Challenges*, 2010 (ISBN 978-90-411-2692-4).

42. George Cumming & Mirjam Freudenthal, *Civil Procedure in EU Competition Cases before the English and Dutch Courts*, 2010 (ISBN 978-90-411-3192-8).

43. A.E. Rodriguez & Ashok Menon, *The Limits of Competition Policy: The Shortcomings of Antitrust in Developing and Reforming Economies*, 2010 (ISBN 978-90-411-3177-5).

44. Mika Oinonen, *Does EU Merger Control Discriminate against Small Market Companies? Diagnosing the Argument with Conclusions*, 2010 (ISBN 978-90-411-3261-1).

45. Eirik Østerud, *Identifying Exclusionary Abuses by Dominant Undertakings under EU Competition Law: The Spectrum of Tests*, 2010 (ISBN 978-90-411-3271-0).

46. Marco Botta, *Merger Control Regimes in Emerging Economies: A Case Study on Brazil and Argentina*, 2011 (ISBN 978-90-411-3402-8).

47. Jürgen Basedow & Wolfgang Wurmnest (eds), *Structure and Effects in EU Competition Law: Studies on Exclusionary Conduct and State Aid*, 2011 (ISBN 978-90-411-3174-4).

48. George Cumming (ed.), *Merger Decisions and the Rules of Procedure of the European Community Courts*, 2012 (ISBN 978-90-411-3671-8).

49. Eduardo Molan Gaban & Juliana Oliveira Domingues (eds), *Antitrust Law in Brazil: Fighting Cartels*, 2012 (ISBN 978-90-411-3670-1).

50. Giandonato Caggiano, Gabriella Muscolo & Marina Tavassi (eds), *Competition Law and Intellectual Property: A European Perspective*, 2012 (ISBN 978-90-411-3447-9).

51. Ben Van Rompuy, *Economic Efficiency: The Sole Concern of Modern Antitrust Policy? Non-efficiency Considerations under Article 101 TFEU*, 2012 (ISBN 978-90-411-3870-5).

52. Liyang Hou, *Competition Law and Regulation of the EU Electronic Communications Sector: A Comparative Legal Approach*, 2012 (ISBN 978-90-411-4047-0).

53. Barry Rodger, *Landmark Cases in Competition Law: Around the World in Fourteen Stories*, 2012 (ISBN 978-90-411-3843-9).
54. Andreas Scordamaglia-Tousis, *EU Cartel Enforcement: Reconciling Effective Public Enforcement with Fundamental Rights*, 2013 (ISBN 978-90-411-4758-5).
55. Bernardo Cortese (ed.), *EU Competition Law: Between Public and Private Enforcement*, 2014 (ISBN 978-90-411-4677-9).
56. Barry Rodger (ed.), *Competition Law: Comparative Private Enforcement and Collective Redress across the EU*, 2014 (ISBN 978-90-411-4559-8).
57. Nada Ina Pauer, *The Single Economic Entity Doctrine and Corporate Group Responsibility in European Antitrust Law*, 2014 (ISBN 978-90-411-5262-6).
58. Urška Petrovčič, *Competition Law and Standard Essential Patents: A Transatlantic Perspective*, 2014 (ISBN 978-90-411-4960-2).
59. David Telyas, *The Interface between Competition Law, Patents and Technical Standards*, 2014 (ISBN 978-90-411-5418-7).
60. Katerina Maniadaki, *EU Competition Law, Regulation and the Internet: The Case of Net Neutrality*, 2014 (ISBN 978-90-411-4140-8).
61. Horacio Vedia Jerez, *Competition Law Enforcement and Compliance across the World: A Comparative Review*, 2015 (ISBN 978-90-411-5815-4).
62. Kadir Baş, *The Substantive Appraisal of Joint Ventures under the EU Merger Control Regime*, 2015 (ISBN 978-90-411-5816-1).
63. Alberto Santa Maria, *Competition and State Aid: An Analysis of the EU Practice*, Second Edition, 2015 (ISBN 978-90-411-5818-5).
64. Lúcio Tomé Feteira, *The Interplay between European and National Competition Law after Regulation 1/2003: "United (Should) We Stand?"*, 2016 (ISBN 978-90-411-5663-1).
65. Giovanni Pitruzzella & Gabriella Muscolo(eds), *Competition and Patent Law in the Pharmaceutical Sector: An International Perspective*, 2016 (ISBN 978-90-411-5927-4).
66. Małgorzata Cyndecka, *The Market Economy Investor Test in EU State Aid Law: Applicability and Application*, 2016 (ISBN 978-90-411-6102-4).
67. Damiano Canapa, *Trademarks and Brands in Merger Control: An Analysis of the European and Swiss Legal Orders*, 2016 (ISBN 978-90-411-6717-0).
68. Inge Graef, *EU Competition Law, Data Protection and Online Platforms: Data as Essential Facility*, 2016 (ISBN 978-90-411-8324-8).
69. Anders Jessen, *Exclusionary Abuse after the* Post Danmark I *Case: The Role of the Effects-Based Approach under Article 102 TFEU*, 2017 (ISBN 978-90-411-8996-7).